D0801843

LEADING AMERICAN TREATIES

LEADING AMERICAN TREATIES

BY

CHARLES E. HILL

AMS PRESS
NEW YORK

Reprinted from the edition of 1922, New York
First AMS EDITION published 1969
Manufactured in the United States of America

Library of Congress Catalogue Card Number: 72-94316

AMS PRESS, INC.
NEW YORK, N.Y. 10003

TO THE MEMORY

OF

JAMES B. ANGELL

CITIZEN, GENTLEMAN, TEACHER

CONTENTS

FOREWORD

This book is the result of a course taken several years ago with President Angell at the University of Michigan and of my teaching in the George Washington University. The purpose is to give the historical setting and the chief provisions of fifteen of the leading American treaties.

C. E. H.

Takoma Park, D. C.
September 27, 1921.

LEADING AMERICAN TREATIES

CHAPTER I

THE TREATIES WITH FRANCE, 1778

"Men are very apt to run into extremes. Hatred of England may carry some into an excess of confidence in France, especially when motives of gratitude are thrown into the scale. Men of this description would be unwilling to suppose France capable of acting so ungenerous a part. I am heartily disposed to entertain the most favorable sentiments of our new ally and to cherish them in others to a reasonable degree. But it is a maxim founded on the universal experience of mankind that no nation is to be trusted further than it is bound by its own interest; and no prudent statesman or politician will venture to depart from it."—GEORGE WASHINGTON.

Could the Americans have achieved their independence single-handed? Fortunately, Great Britain had aroused the jealousy and the opposition of the three great powers of western Europe: France, Spain, and the Netherlands. France came to the aid of the Americans directly and the other two indirectly. All three assisted, however, not so much because of sympathy for the rebels in the English colonies as because of their united hatred of England.

The English had long been winning competitors with the Dutch for the Baltic and the East India trade. In 1651 the British navigation act declared that foreign vessels could bring to England only such goods as were produced in their own country. The enforcement of this act caused two wars with the Dutch resulting in victory for the English. The Dutch had to give up their promising colony of New Amsterdam and their merchant marine had to assume a definitely second rank. During the Seven Years' War England had extended the contraband list greatly and had refused to recognize the principle that free ships make free goods as provided in the treaty of December 1, 1674.

England had repeatedly humbled the proud position of

Spain and had made indentations upon the Spanish colonial domain, for example Florida in 1763. The rock of Gibraltar had passed to England, and it was more than an emblem of Spain's waning sea power. Then too, Spain had an ambition to acquire Portugal, which Great Britain had often defended. Indeed, the British loaned money to Portugal as freely as they drank the Portuguese wines.

By the peace of Paris, 1763, Great Britain took from France virtually all of her possessions in India, all of Canada except two small islands near Newfoundland on which the French fishermen could dry their codfish, and all of the French rights to the eastern half of the Mississippi Valley. The two contracting parties, France and Great Britain, bound themselves solemnly "to give no succor or protection, directly or indirectly," to the enemies and assailants of the other. And yet the French negotiator of the treaty, the Duc de Choiseul, when he heard of the Stamp Act Congress, sent the Baron de Kalb to America on a secret mission to inquire into the political tendencies and the fighting power of the colonies. As a result de Kalb became better acquainted with American military resources than any other general in the Revolution except George Washington.

Shortly before the American Revolution broke out M. de Vergennes succeeded the Duc de Choiseul in the management of French foreign affairs. A decade had failed to make his convictions any more pliable than those of his predecessor. "The humiliating peace of 1763," said Vergennes, "was bought at the price of our possessions, of our commerce, and of our credit in the Indies; at the price of Canada, Louisiana, Isle Royale, Acadia, and Senegal." [1] At the end of the year, 1775, he reported to Louis XVI. that England was "an enemy at once grasping, ambitious, unjust, and perfidious;" that the Americans were at open war with their mother country; that if the English were foolish enough to destroy their power by their own force, to exhaust their finances, and to engulf themselves in a civil war, why should France interrupt them? At the close of his report he drew three conclusions. "1. As the power of England

[1] Doniol, *Participation de la France*, I.: 2.

diminishes, ours will proportionately increase; 2. As her commerce becomes impoverished and irreparably lost, so much may be counted as our gain; 3. It is highly probable that coming events will enable us to recover a part of the possessions which the English took from us in America, as the fishing grounds, the Gulf of St. Lawrence, Isle Royale, etc., not to mention Canada." [1]

These quotations reveal the two great motives of France in assisting the Americans against their mother country. One, revenge not only for the humiliating Treaty of Paris but for the more than a century of losing rivalry for colonial domain and sea power. France may even have overvalued the importance of America's contributions of timber, hemp, tar, and sailors for the English navy. Two, France had before her the task of reëstablishing the diplomatic leadership of the House of Bourbon in European affairs, a leadership which had been on the wane since the days of Mazarin and Richelieu and Louis XIV. The Duc de Choiseul's greatest contribution had been to arrange the Family Compact between France and Spain in 1761 by which the two branches of the Bourbon family joined in an offensive and defensive alliance. It became Vergennes' task to assist the Americans in throwing off British dominion and thus start the break up of the British Empire. Neither he nor any of his contemporaries could foresee that American independence would mean a reform in British colonial administration. Nor could he believe, although his astute colleague, Turgot, pointed out to him, that French intervention in America would bring on war with England, consequent ruin to France financially, and thus become the precursor of social upheavals within the French state itself.

In the summer of 1775 Vergennes sent Bonvouloir as his secret agent to America. Bonvouloir reported December 28, 1775, that in spite of the rigorous winter the Americans had made good preparations for the campaign in the spring. They had seized several British vessels laden with food and supplies. They had taken Montreal and laid siege to Quebec. They were

[1] Doniol, *Participation de la France*, I.: 244.

well intrenched around Boston and they had even a small navy. They were well commanded and their spirit was excellent. But they lacked three things, a navy, provisions, and money. He advised that France extend to the insurgents secret aid in military stores and money, without seeking any return beyond the political object of the moment. Franklin had asked if it would be prudent to send a plenipotentiary to Paris. Bonvouloir had replied that this would be precipitous, even hazardous, for France could render greater service by furnishing secret aid and by dexterously tranquilizing any apprehensions of the British ministry.[1]

In Paris the American cause had found an able advocate in the eccentric and brilliant Caron de Beaumarchais. In rapid succession he had been a watchmaker, an inventor, and a music master to the daughters of Louis XV. He had acquired considerable property through marriage; and he possessed some literary and dramatic genius, as his *Barber of Seville* and *The Marriage of Figaro* testify. In pleading the American cause as a means of breaking up the British Empire and of enhancing the importance of France he fascinated Louis XVI. and he impressed the cool and expert Vergennes.

Vergennes let Beaumarchais understand that the principles of neutrality would not permit France to give direct aid to the Americans. Thereupon, Beaumarchais organized the fictitious business concern of Roderique Hortalez and Company; and through it Vergennes soon loaned the Americans a million livres and he induced Spain to lend through the same channel another million. Hortalez and Company became surprisingly active, so much so that at one time as many as fourteen ships carried cargoes of arms, munitions, and supplies to the Americans. The British admiralty soon divined the real character of these vessels and by their vigilance made it hazardous for them to leave port. The importance of Beaumarchais' service to the American cause in furnishing the channel for these supplies and in bringing about the active coöperation of the French government can hardly be overestimated. In his latter and

[1] Doniol, I.: 267, 287.

rather bitter days, he fully realized the value of these unrecompensed services. Said he in a letter: "And nevertheless, of all Frenchmen, whoever they may be, I am the one who has done most for the liberty of America, the begetter of our own; for I was the only person who dared to form the plan and commence its execution, in spite of England, Spain, and even of France." [1]

Several months before the Declaration of Independence, November 29, 1775, the Second Continental Congress appointed a "Secret Committee on Foreign Correspondence." Only by March 2, 1776, did this committee commission Silas Deane to go to France. Deane was the son of a Connecticut blacksmith and a graduate of Yale College; he had taught school, practiced law, and had married a widow with six children and a thriving store. He had served in numerous public capacities, notably as a member of the Committee of Correspondence of his colony and as a delegate to the First and Second Continental Congresses. He was a man of courtly appearance and good manners. He knew little French, for Beaumarchais afterwards commented: "He must be the most silent man in France, for I defy him to say six consecutive words in French." Soldiers of fortune did take advantage of his lack of experience in judging Europeans and thus forced themselves with commissions in hand, ranging from lieutenants to major-generals, upon General Washington, whose patience was sorely tried in rendering their presence of as small evil as possible. But Deane was instrumental in securing the services of Kosciuszko and Pulaski, the Polish heroes; of Baron von Steuben, Frederick's veteran, of Baron de Kalb, trained under Marshal Saxe and at one time Choiseul's secret agent in America; and of the Marquis de Lafayette, destined to be remembered the most appreciatively of all.

In France, Deane assumed, at first, the name of Timothy Jones. But the British secret service soon discovered his identity and the British ambassador demanded his expulsion, a request which Vergennes failed to heed. Through the enthusiastic assistance of Beaumarchais he was soon able to send clothing for twenty thousand men, thirty thousand muskets, and large quantities

[1] Lomenie, *Beaumarchais et son temps:* 457.

of cannon, gunpowder, shot, and shells.[1] Even gold to pay the soldiers did he send. But the open and public assistance of the French government he could not secure, although he described in the most roseate colors, as he had been instructed,[2] the brilliant prospects of American trade.

The Continental Congress concluded, therefore, to replace Deane as sole commissioner by a group of agents, who were to act as the representatives of an independent United States, and as such these agents were to seek recognition for their country as a member of the society of nations and to negotiate a treaty of commerce. In September, 1776, Benjamin Franklin, Thomas Jefferson, and Silas Deane were appointed. Jefferson declined to serve because of domestic reasons, so Arthur Lee, then in London, was substituted, much to the later discomfort of Franklin and to the ruin of Deane and considerably so of Beaumarchais.

Franklin had passed his seventieth year and was both wise and famous. His *Poor Richard's Almanac* had run through several editions in French. His investigations in the field of natural philosophy had long before won for him a membership in the French Academy. And his inventions, from which he derived no financial benefit, made his name known in every civilized community throughout the world. Moreover, Franklin was no novice in playing the diplomatic game, for he had spent sixteen years in England as the agent not only of Pennsylvania, but of New Jersey, Georgia, and Massachusetts. During that time he had learned to know the leading Englishmen both in and out of official life as well as the diplomats accredited to the court of St. James. Before he left on his mission to France, Franklin placed his entire earnings in the form of a liberty loan, about £3,000, at the disposal of the Continental Congress, knowing fully that if his cause failed his savings could never be recovered.

Arthur Lee belonged to the famous Virginia family. He was the youngest brother of Richard Henry Lee, a leader in

[1] Wharton, *Diplomatic Correspondence of the American Revolution*, II.: 148.
[2] Ibid., I.: 6, 40.

Congress. Like the sons of many wealthy southerners of that day, Arthur Lee was educated in the United Kingdom, first at Eton, and afterward at Edinburgh. Later he traveled extensively on the continent. At home he turned his attention to politics and decided that he ought to study law at the Temple in London, which he did 1766–70. Thereafter, he practiced law in London, assisted John Wilkes in one of his campaigns for the House of Commons, made the acquaintance of Edmund Burke, and served second to Franklin as the colonial agent for Massachusetts. He ably defended the rights of the colonies in pamphlets and in the London newspapers. But he was ever envious of Franklin's position. By nature Lee was exacting and suspicious, and consequently he detected quickly the faults in his colleagues, and imagined evil where none existed. It can be said of him, however, that he never covered his animosities with a pretense of friendship.

In the letter of credence, dated September 30, 1776, the three were given "full power to communicate, treat, agree and conclude with his most Christian Majesty, the King of France, or with such person or persons, as shall by him be for that purpose authorized, of and upon a true and sincere friendship, and a firm, inviolable, and universal peace for the defence, protection, and safety of the navigation and mutual commerce of the subjects of His Most Christian Majesty, and the people of the United States, and to do all other things which may conduce to those desirable ends." [1] This meant a treaty of commerce, as was apparent from a draft of a treaty which Congress had approved. The same held true of the instructions.[2]

Throughout the Revolution, the Americans emphasized their commercial importance, their ship building resources, and their agricultural products, notably tobacco and rice. With this offer of commercial advantage, they hoped to bargain for aid not only at Paris, but in Madrid, Vienna, St. Petersburg, Berlin, at The Hague, and even in Tuscany and Naples.

[1] Lyman, Theodore, *Diplomacy of the United States*, I.: 26.
[2] Force, *American Archives*, fifth series, II.: 1343, 1359.

In December of 1776, Franklin landed at Nantes. Lord Rockingham declared that his arrival more than counterbalanced the British victory on Long Island and the capture of New York City. Lord Stormont, the British ambassador in Paris, wrote to Vergennes that he would leave if the "chief of the American rebels" should be permitted to come to the city. Vergennes replied that he had sent word by a courier to Franklin not to come; but that if the message should miscarry and Franklin should come to Paris, it would be a violation of the principles of hospitality to expel him. The message did miscarry. Franklin came to Paris. And the French government assigned to him the commodious house and the garden of M. Ray de Chaumont in Passy, then a half mile from Paris. There he lived, though his colleagues knew it not, rent free.[1] He was probably the only American diplomatic representative ever sent to Europe who did not have to hunt his own quarters and pay for them.

In a few days Franklin and his two colleagues were granted a private audience with Vergennes; a private audience because France was not yet ready to recognize American independence. They laid before Vergennes their letter of credence, the draft of a proposed treaty of commerce, and a request for eight war vessels to convoy the well laden ships of Hortalez and Company.[2]

Vergennes replied that he could not furnish the convoy, for such action would mean that France openly espoused the cause of the Americans and would undoubtedly mean war with Great Britain. So Hortalez and Company was left to be slowly strangled by the British navy. But Vergennes did offer a secret loan to be repaid without interest; this offer Franklin gladly accepted. The draft of the treaty of commerce Vergennes promised to take under advisement.[3] There was small hope of negotiating the treaty quickly, for such negotiation implied the recognition of the independence of the United States. Fur-

[1] John Adams later wrote about Franklin in this house: "At what rent I never could discover; but, from the magnificence of the place, it was universally suspected to be enormously high."

[2] Wharton, *Diplomatic Correspondence*, I.: 184.

[3] Ibid., I.: 198.

thermore, the only advantage the Americans offered to France in this draft was free trade with their country which lay beyond three thousand miles of ocean with the greatest maritime power for an enemy. The military situation warranted only dark forebodings. The British had taken New York City; they were going to take Philadelphia; and the plans were well laid for Burgoyne to start south from Canada by way of Lake Champlain and the Hudson, thus cutting off New England, and making ready to crush the Americans by piecemeal.

In a very real sense, Franklin made his house in Passy one of the centers of the American Revolution. The tales of the British ambassador that the Americans were in the severest straits and about to yield, Franklin dubbed facetiously as "Stormonts," which became in French society a polite word for a lie. And when the British took Philadelphia, Franklin asserted with confidence that Philadelphia had taken General Howe. Franklin was the embodiment of the American cause. He alone could secure favorable action from statesmen. Although the matters of finance and supplies had been assigned to Deane, it was with Franklin that the financiers wanted to negotiate the loans, which from France alone mounted up to twenty-six million francs. Later, when France had joined in the war, Franklin issued the letters of marque and reprisal to privateersmen. He saw to it that the prizes could be sold in the ports of France and Spain. It was in Paris rather than in America that the validity of the captures was passed upon. Noteworthy it is that throughout, Franklin had no staff of clerks at his command, no devoted subordinates to collect information, and no one to take charge of the mass of trifling but necessary correspondence. Nine-tenths of the correspondence addressed to the American commissioners went to Franklin, so his colleagues admitted. He had no one to save his energy or his time from the impudence of soldiers of fortune or of sham philosophers. His only assistant was his elder grandson who could "write from dictation and copy letters in good round hand."

Socially Franklin captured Paris. Entertainments and receptions were considered complete only when he graced them with his presence. From every jeweler's counter the image of his face shone out from snuff boxes, rings, bracelets, and watches. He grew weary of sitting for portraits, busts, and medals. The guiding principle of his conduct was simple. "It is my intention while I stay here, to procure what advantages I can for our country by endeavoring to please the court."

Four months elapsed after Franklin's departure from Philadelphia before he received any despatches from Congress. In April, 1777, supplementary instructions arrived, dated December 30, 1776. Congress had become convinced that in order to obtain French aid more than mere freedom of trade must be conceded. The American commissioners were therefore empowered to offer, first, that if Newfoundland and Nova Scotia were captured France should have one-half of Newfoundland and an equal share in the fisheries. Secondly, they were empowered to offer provisions to the value of $2,000,000 and six frigates of twenty-four guns each to coöperate with French forces against the British West Indies; and all the islands thus captured were to belong wholly to France. Thirdly, His Most Christian Majesty and the United States could agree "to render any other assistance which may be in their power, as becomes good allies." [1] Clearly, the United States, in the danger of failing to make good its independence, had overcome its fear of a compromising alliance. Clearly, too, these supplementary instructions gave the American commissioners additional bargaining power, the most significant being that relating to an alliance.

Why should France want to join the Americans openly against Great Britain? According to Vergennes the primary question was whether France and Spain could afford to see the colonies return either directly or indirectly to British control. If the colonies did return Britain would again be the mistress of North America. Britain's place as a world power would be preëminent, and she could threaten the position of the Bourbons whether it be in Europe, in South America, in the West Indies, or in any corner of the globe. It was infinitely cheaper for France to continue with secret loans and subventions of war material for

[1] *Secret Journals of Congress*, II.: 39–40.

the Americans than to carry on open war with England. But Vergennes' estimate of the situation was that the Americans and the English would make mutual concessions, and thereupon the two would unite in war against France and Spain. And Franklin had suggested that if France delayed too long such might be the inevitable result.[1]

On July 23, 1777, Vergennes submitted to the King a memoir which stated that the situation called for an offensive and defensive alliance between the Bourbons and the Americans in which all parties should bind themselves not to abandon the war without the consent of the others. Louis XVI. approved the memoir[2] the same day, and shortly it was on its way to be presented at the court of Madrid, where it encountered the scrutiny of Florida Blanca.

Blanca recognized that Spain had larger colonial holdings in the Americas than had France and he admitted that British sea-power was a menace; but he could not believe that the independence of the Americans would remove the danger; indeed, with almost prophetic vision, he pointed out that the danger to the Spanish colonies would be increased. Blanca felt satisfied with the policy of letting the English and the Americans destroy each other; and with that end in view, he was willing to lend the Americans money on "the express condition of an inviolable secrecy."[3]

On November 30, 1777, the news reached France that the Americans had won a victory over Burgoyne at Saratoga. Vergennes quickly interpreted the victory as of decisive importance, but he had the task of securing the approval of the Bourbons both in Paris and Madrid before he could act.

The American commissioners sent him a memoir on December 8, in which they reviewed the various proposals they had made to him and to which he had given no definite reply, and they asked him to set a day for an audience. Vergennes met them on December 12. He answered all questions with the reservation

[1] See Corwin, *French Policy and the American Alliance*, Chapters 5 and 6; also Van Tyne in *American Hist. Rev.*, 21: 528–41.
[2] Doniol, II.: 460–69.
[3] Ibid.,II.: 695.

that the consent of Spain was necessary. The Americans presented a statement that it would be of importance to Congress to know explicitly what might be expected from France and Spain; otherwise Congress might be obliged to consider overtures from Great Britain. Vergennes promised to give it consideration. And in a few days, one of the secretaries, Gerard, went to Passy by order of the King to say that His Majesty had decided to acknowledge the independence of the United States and to make a treaty of amity and commerce. The terms of the treaty would be such as France would make with a state long established and in the fullness of power. Gerard intimated that in consequence France might soon be engaged in war with England; that the King would expect no compensation from the Americans on that account; nor would he pretend that he acted wholly out of good will to the American cause, for "it was manifestly the interest of France that the power of England should be diminished." Gerard said that the King would not insist that the Americans should bind themselves not to make a separate peace; the only condition that he would require was that the United States should never give up its independence. Just as soon as the courier returned from Spain the negotiations would begin.[1] No treaty of alliance was mentioned.

The adroit thrust of Franklin had gone home. Vergennes feared above all the reconciliation of the Americans with the English. He promised an additional three million livres and also convoys for the supply ships. England and France were preparing to recall their ambassadors. Stocks fell in both London and Paris. War was imminent.

The courier from Madrid failed to arrive until the last day of the year; and the word that he carried indicated that Spain would not join. Vergennes had to secure action from France alone. On January 7, 1778, the royal council convened at Versailles and declared unanimously for a treaty of commerce with the United States and a treaty of alliance as well. This is the first definite mention of a treaty of alliance which the correspondence shows. The royal council indicated that this

[1] Wharton, *Diplomatic Correspondence*, I.: 259.

treaty should embody five provisions. First, it should become operative on the outbreak of war between France and England. Second, it should secure the absolute independence of the United States. Third, the two powers should reciprocally guarantee their possessions in North America and the West Indies. Fourth, neither party would sign a treaty of peace without the consent of the other. And fifth, Spain should be given the privilege of joining later.[1]

Thereupon, Gerard made another visit to Passy. He pledged the American commissioners to secrecy. Then he asked them upon what terms they would agree to reject all propositions from the English which failed to concede complete independence in matters of trade and government. The Americans replied that a treaty of commerce and alliance with France would be sufficient. Gerard announced that the King was agreeable to such an arrangement, provided it took the form of two treaties, a commercial treaty and a treaty of alliance. But Gerard indicated that he could speak for France alone; with Spain the Americans would have to reach a separate agreement, which was a disappointment to Franklin. A few days later the American commissioners through Deane handed Gerard a memoir showing what they would ask in order to give up the privilege of considering British proposals to return within the empire. They asked for "an immediate engagement on the part of France and Spain or either of them to guarantee the present possessions of the Congress in America, with such others as they may acquire on the Continent during the War, and either to enter into a War against England or furnish the Congress with the Money" until "all the English now possess on the Continent shall be conquered" and the English fisheries be secured "to the United States and their allies." [2]

On January 18, 1778, Gerard, who had been appointed the negotiator for Louis XVI., submitted to Franklin, Lee, and Deane tentative drafts of the two treaties. Two weeks were spent in agreeing on the details. One of the most troublesome

[1] Doniol, II.: 729.
[2] *The Deane Papers*, II.: 313.

discussions related to a proposal by Gerard that France would agree to impose no export duty on molasses purchased by Americans in the French West Indies in return for which the United States should agree to place no export duty upon any American commodity purchased by Frenchmen. At first Arthur Lee approved this project, but later he changed his mind, with the result that Franklin and Deane yielded to his contention. And Gerard had to secure the promise of Vergennes that after the treaty should be signed, the two articles concerned would be mutually rescinded, which they were.[1] The treaties were signed February 6, 1778.

Although the two treaties were signed coördinately, the treaty of commerce was considered as standing first. It was the treaty that the American commissioners had been instructed specifically to secure.

Article II granted mutually most favored nation treatment "in respect of commerce and navigation" . . . "freely, if the concession was freely made, or on allowing the same compensation, if the concession was conditional." This clause furnishes the keynote to the differences which the United States has had with other powers concerning the interpretation of the most favored nation clause. Various countries have at different times claimed that reciprocity treaties were not limited to the contracting parties, but by operation of this clause the privileges conceded by such a treaty became immediately extended to the nationals of states on the most favored nation basis. The United States has consistently withstood such interpretation by showing that "if the concession was conditional" the same compensation would have to be allowed. Moreover, the United States has always reserved the right to pass upon the question whether the compensation offered was the same.[2] Articles III, IV, and V, delimited and made specific the most favored nation clause.

Article VI provided for the protection by France in her waters and ports of American vessels and their cargoes and also for a

[1] Wharton, *Diplomatic Correspondence of the American Revolution*, II.: 477, 481.

[2] See report by U. S. Tariff Commission, *Reciprocity and Commercial Treaties:* 417 ff. (Washington, 1919).

convoy by French ships of war of American vessels on the high seas. This provision was of importance because the Americans had almost no navy with which to protect their merchantmen. By Article VII the United States promised to furnish similar protection for the vessels and cargoes of French subjects, and to "use all their endeavours to recover and cause to be restored the said vessels and effects that shall have been taken within the jurisdiction of the said United States, or any of them." This clause has become unnecessary in present-day treaties, for the principle contained therein has by international law become a part of the neutrality obligation of a state.

By Article VIII Louis XVI. agreed to use his good offices with the Barbary states to provide for the safety of American merchantmen. Indeed, it was estimated before the Revolution that one-sixth of the wheat, one-fourth of the dried and pickled fish, and a large amount of the rice exported from the United States, found their best market in the Mediterranean ports. But the good offices of Louis XVI. turned out to be of no value.

By Article IX Frenchmen and Americans could not fish within the territorial waters of the other. To-day it is unnecessary to make such a statement in a treaty; in 1778 the rights of fishermen were not so clear. Article X reserved to the French their fishing rights off Newfoundland as specified in the Treaty of Utrecht, 1713.

Article XI abolished between the United States and France the *droit d'aubaine* and the *droit detraction.* This provision is found in the earliest treaties between the Hanseatic League and the princes of that time; and it was for the purpose of protecting the Hanse merchants residing in foreign lands from paying a heavy tax on their property when they removed therefrom (*droit detraction*) or from forfeiting to the local sovereign either part or all of their property when they died within his jurisdiction (*droit d'aubaine*). This practice of the princes has fallen into disuse and the exemption has crystallized into a principle of international law and is, therefore, omitted from present-day treaties.

Articles XII, XIII, XIV, XV, XXVII, and XXVIII provided for visit and search when either party should be at war; and the principle was laid down that enemy ships made enemy goods two months after war had begun. Article XVI provided for the mutual restoration of goods and merchandise rescued from pirates. Article XVII permitted the ships of war and privateers of either party to take prizes into the ports of the other; but this privilege was not to be accorded to the enemies of either party. Jay paid no attention to this article when he made the treaty with Great Britain, 1794, Article XXV.

By Article XVIII assistance and relief was to be given to the shipwrecked. This provision is to-day a relic; but during the thirteenth and fourteenth centuries, and even later, kings would confiscate the wrecks of foreigners that had foundered upon their shores. Article XIX contained the provision that public and private ships of either nationality might take refuge in the ports of either party because of stress of weather or pursuit by pirates. Refuge was also provided for in case of pursuit by enemies; and the ships were to have permission to depart whenever and whither they pleased. This latter provision allowed the use of the ports of the other party as a military base, which modern principles of neutrality would not sanction.

If war should occur between France and the United States, Article XX allowed six months after the declaration of war to the merchants for selling out and transporting their goods to their home country. Articles XXI and XXII stated that no subjects of the French King and no nationals of the United States could take out letters of marque and reprisal from their home government against the other. And if they did take out letters of marque and reprisal from any other state they were to forfeit their rights under the treaty.

Article XXIII declared that free ships made free goods, except such goods as were contraband of war. This principle was a concession to the views of Franklin. He would like to have had neutral goods on enemy's ships free as well, but Article XIV shows that he did not succeed.

Article XXIV defined contraband. The term comprehended "arms, great guns, bombs with fuses, and other things belonging to them, cannonball, gunpowder, match, pikes, swords, lances, spears, halberds, mortars, petards, grenades, saltpetre, muskets, musket ball, bucklers, helmets, breastplates, coats of mail, and the like kinds of arms proper for arming soldiers, musket rests, belts, horses with their furniture, and all other warlike instruments whatever." But a long list of articles which should never be included under contraband was inserted, such as wool, flax, silk, cotton, tin, iron, copper, wheat, barley, salted flesh and fish, cheese, butter, sugar, tar, ropes, sail-cloths. All of which shows that the two powers united in opposition to British sea power.

Article XXV specified that if either party were engaged in war the vessels belonging to the people of the other party should carry passports, in accordance with a form agreed upon, manifests, and certificates showing port of departure and destination.

Article XXIX provided for the mutual right of having consuls in the ports of the other party, and their functions were to be described by a special agreement. This agreement was not reached until 1788.

Article XXX was drafted so as to have unilateral effect. France granted the Americans one or more free ports subject to the regulations which related to them. These regulations France could change at any time. Consequently the grant was worth only so much as France chose to make it.[1]

Copies of the treaty were drawn both in the French and the English languages; but the French was stated to be the official copy. The treaty was to be ratified within six months. As a matter of fact Congress ratified it within three months on May 4, 1778.

The Treaty of Alliance provided for a defensive alliance,[2] which should become operative when war broke out between France and Great Britain. The object of the alliance was to "maintain effectually the liberty, sovereignty, and independence, absolute and unlimited" of the United States. Each party

[1] Malloy, *Treaties, Conventions, etc.*, I.: 468.
[2] Ibid., I.: 479.

reserved to itself the right to judge of the manner in which it might coöperate most effectively with the other. If the British possessions in the northern parts of America and the Bermudas were captured, they were to pass to the United States; France renounced all claim. But France was to have such British islands in the Gulf of Mexico as might be captured.

Neither party should conclude a peace or truce with Great Britain without securing first the formal consent of the other. There was to be no after claim of compensation, whatever might be the result of the war. Article X was intended as an invitation to Spain to join the alliance. This invitation was made more specific in a secret article added to the treaty.

By Article XI the United States guaranteed "to his Most Christian Majesty, the present possessions of the Crown of France in America" and "His Most Christian Majesty" guaranteed to the United States its sovereignty and independence and all its possessions "from any of the dominions now, or heretofore possessed by Great Britain in North America." When France appealed to the United States for aid, 1793, in accordance with the terms of the treaty, Great Britain warned the Americans that any material aid given France would mean war. Hamilton and Jefferson chose opposite sides of the question. Hamilton contended that France was conducting an aggressive and not a defensive war, and that the government with whom the Treaty of Alliance had been made had been overthrown, consequently the United States was not bound. The first argument was valid, although Jefferson did not so recognize it; but the second argument had no merit except to show that Hamilton did not realize that the treaty had been made with France and not essentially with the Bourbon government. President Washington solved the difficulty by issuing the neutrality proclamation.[1] Congress enacted the principles of the proclamation into law in 1794.[2] Washington justified

[1] See copy in Moore, *Principles of American Diplomacy:* 41.

[2] The main features of the law of June 5, 1794, were:

1. Persons may not enlist or accept a commission on American soil to serve against a country at peace with the United States.

his action on the right of a state to preserve its own existence. The Americans had not recovered from the stress of the Revolution; and with a population only of about three million there was danger that the United States might lose its independence if it joined France. As it was the United States had a troublesome time getting rid of the treaties of 1778 even after their abrogation by an act of Congress, July 7, 1798.

The Treaty of Alliance has great significance in American history. The armed support of France was of great assistance. At Yorktown the Americans shared the honors of victory with the French. Moreover, Great Britain was to be attacked in her plans for controlling seagoing trade in which her colonies were but one factor. France in her American alliance made the United States a party in determining the balance of power in Europe, for thereby she hoped to weaken England and to enhance her own position. Insignificant in its beginning the American question had become one of European and of world-wide importance.

Franklin, Lee, and Deane were officially received by the King,[1] March 20, 1778.[2] Gerard, the French negotiator of the treaties, was commissioned minister plenipotentiary to the United States and enjoyed the distinction of being the first from any state.

On February 17, 1778, in the House of Commons, Charles James Fox asked Lord North whether a treaty had not al-

2. No belligerent may use any part of the United States as a military base against a state at peace with the United States.

3. Americans could not fit out or aid in fitting out vessels that were to cruise against a power at peace with the United States.

4. The shipment by Americans of arms and warlike supplies to a belligerent was permitted, but at the risk of capture and condemnation as contraband. 1 Statutes at Large, 381.

[1] Journal of Arthur Lee in R. H. Lee, *Life of Arthur Lee*, I.: 403.

[2] On February 13, 1778, Captain John Paul Jones of the "Ranger" off Quiberon Bay, asked Admiral Picquet if a salute would be returned. Admiral Picquet replied that he would return the salute in the same manner as the French returned it to the Dutch or any other republic; namely four guns less. Jones replied that the haughty English returned gun for gun to flag officers of equal rank and only two less for a captain and requested an equal number for the honor of the United States. On February 14 he decided to fire the salute of thirteen guns and the French answered with a return of nine. *John Paul Jones Papers*, II., and *Letters of John Paul Jones in Papers of Continental Congress*, I.: 27, 31.

ready been made ten days before between the French and the Americans and whether it was not too late to press measures looking toward reconciliation with the former colonies. Lord North admitted that he had heard rumors of such an event, but the measures were passed nevertheless. The French ambassador in London, the Marquis de Noailles, announced to the British government on March 13, 1778, that France had made a treaty of friendship and commerce with the United States. The English and French ambassadors were thereupon recalled; and the respective fleets of the two powers sailed for American waters.

Charges made by Arthur Lee that Silas Deane and Beaumarchais were levying exorbitant profits upon the goods furnished by France bore fruit. Congress recalled Deane and later Lee as well. This left Franklin as the sole American minister to France, and he served until 1785 when he was relieved by Thomas Jefferson. Lee served afterwards as a delegate to Congress under the Articles of Confederation and as a member of the Virginia Assembly, but the only diplomatic assignment he again held was that of a negotiator with the Indians. Deane returned and attempted to secure an appropriation from Congress for his services and for his expenditure of private funds. But he was unable to refute Lee's rather baseless charges. He retired from the doors of Congress in a sullen mood, went to England, and accepted service with the British government. Not until fifty-eight years after his death, August 11, 1842, did Congress appropriate $36,998 for Deane's heirs, a tardy recognition of work that had great influence upon American history.

In 1781 Deane presented Beaumarchais' claims to Congress, but that body would not act. Six years later Beaumarchais wrote an appeal to Congress, which was referred to Arthur Lee, who, consistent with his earlier suspicions, declared that the goods furnished Roderique Hortalez and Company were gifts from the French government and that Beaumarchais owed the United States 2,000,000 livres. In 1793 Hamilton examined the claims and reported that the United States owed Beaumarchais 2,280,000 livres and possible more, but Congress failed to act. Beaumarchais died in poverty. In 1822 his daughter went to

Washington and presented her claims in person. But not until eleven years later did Congress appropriate a sum which amounted to one-fourth of that which Hamilton had said was Beaumarchais' rightful due.

BIBLIOGRAPHY

CHANNING, EDWARD.—*History of the United States*, Vol. III. 1761–1789. New York, 1916.

CLARK, GEORGE L.—*Silas Deane.* New York, 1913.

CORWIN, EDWARD S.—*French Policy and the American Alliance of 1778.* Princeton, 1916.

DEANE, SILAS.—*The Deane Papers*, 1774–1790. (New York Historical Society.) 5 volumes. New York, 1887–1890.

DONIOL, HENRI.—*Histoire de la Participation de la France a l'Établissement des États-Unis d'Amerique.* Paris, 1886–1892. 5 volumes.

HAZARD, BLANCE E.—*Beaumarchais and the American Revolution.* Boston, 1910.

Harper's Atlas of American History, edited by D. R. Fox, New York, 1920.

Journal of the Continental Congress, 23 volumes. Edited by Gaillard Hunt. Washington, 1904–1914.

LEE, ARTHUR, Journal in RICHARD HENRY LEE, *Life of Arthur Lee*, 2 volumes. Boston, 1829.

LOMENIE, LOUIS DE.—*Beaumarchais et son Temps.* The essay won for the author membership in the Academy. Paris, 1857.

LYMAN, THEODORE.—*The Diplomacy of the United States.* 2 volumes. Boston, 1828. This work covers the period from 1778 to 1825.

Secret Journals of Congress. 4 volumes. Boston, 1821.

TRESCOT, WILLIAM H.—*The Diplomacy of the Revolution.* New York, 1852.

TREVELYAN, GEORGE OTTO.—*The American Revolution.* Vol. IV. New York, 1912.

VAN TYNE, C. H.—*The American Revolution.* New York, 1905.

WHARTON, FRANCIS.—*Diplomatic Correspondence of the American Revolution.* 6 volumes. Washington, 1889.

WINSOR, JUSTIN.—*Narrative and Critical History of America.* Vol. VII. Boston, 1888.

CHAPTER II

THE TREATY OF INDEPENDENCE. PARIS, 1783

"We hazard nothing in saying that not only the most important event of the past two hundred years, but one of the most important events of all time, was the advent of the United States into the family of nations. Its profound significance was not then unfelt, but in the nature of things its far reaching effects could not be foreseen. Even now as we survey the momentous changes of the last few years, we seem to stand only on the threshold of American history, as if its domain were the future rather than the past."—JOHN BASSETT MOORE.

The ultimate object of all American diplomatic efforts in Europe was to secure a treaty of peace with England and thereby to complete the recognition of independence. In the estimation of the Continental Congress the alliance with France was a great step and the next one to be made was to obtain the accession of Spain, for which the treaty had left an opening. Spain held a position of first rank among the nations, and everyone knew of her dislike for the British Empire.

Franklin had early cultivated the friendship of the Spanish ambassador in Paris, the Count d'Aranda. But d'Aranda was rather a politician in exile than the confidential diplomatic agent of the Escurial. Hence, Arthur Lee was sent to Madrid; but the chief minister of Charles III., the Marquis de Grimaldi, would not allow Lee even to approach the capital. The two met at Burgos; and with pledges of monetary aid through the hands of the French, Grimaldi induced Lee to return.[1] The Spanish ministry and the royal council feared the influence which the action might have upon their own colonies if Spain should openly assist the English rebels. However, Grimaldi's attitude was marked by impartiality and disinterestedness, determined somewhat by the fact that he was born a Genoese. In 1777 he fell from power and was succeeded by an intensely Spanish character, the Count de Florida Blanca.

[1] Wharton, *Diplomatic Correspondence*, I.: 403, 408.

Florida Blanca revealed considerable chagrin when he heard of the Franco-American alliance; he had hoped that this treaty would depend upon his own leisurely decision. He conceived that the United States was destined to become a greater enemy to the Spanish colonial possessions than Great Britain herself; especially anxious was he to keep the Americans away from the Mississippi River.[1] The rôle of mediator between France and Great Britain appealed both to Charles III. and Blanca. France accepted their proposal on the basis of the Treaty of Alliance, but the British laid down the impossible requirements that the French fleet should be recalled from American waters and that the French should stop giving aid to the Americans. Such requirements would ordinarily have killed any mediation project, but not so. Florida Blanca saw an advantage in delaying Spain's entry into the war. He proposed that France be willing to approve the entry by the English into a long truce with the Americans, as Spain had done with the Netherlands;[2] the purpose was to make the Americans feel that their eventual independence rested upon the good will of the Bourbon crowns. At the same time Florida Blanca asked, if the mediation should fail, what advantages might Spain obtain if she joined arms with France.[3]

Vergennes replied to the query about the long truce that France would approve one which should run from twenty to fifty years, provided the English would treat the Americans as independent and would withdraw all of their armed forces from the United States. Vergennes consulted Franklin, and according to Vergennes' statement, Franklin acknowledged that independence, whether recognized as a matter of right or only as one of fact, would be a very good thing for the United States; that with the advantages of peace or of a truce the Americans could perfect their political arrangements and internal order. An Englishman, David Hartley, had written a letter to Franklin in which he had broached this same idea of

[1] Doniol, II.: 748, 750, 753.
[2] Ibid., III.: 622.
[3] Ibid., III.: 619, 641, 681.

a long truce.[1] To the second proposition about the advantages France might promise Spain to secure her as an ally, Vergennes replied that Louis XVI. had so much confidence in the virtues of the King, his uncle, that he would approve in advance all that the King of Spain might deem pertinent to Spanish interests.[2]

But Florida Blanca wanted exact stipulations. The negotiations for these culminated in the secret convention signed at Aranjuez, April 12, 1779. By Article I Spain promised that if His Britannic Majesty rejected the offer of Spain's friendly offices, which had been made on April 3, Spain would then join France against Great Britain. The other leading provisions were: neither party would make peace with England without the other; France should regain the right to fortify Dunkirk, lost by the Treaty of Utrecht; and she was to have Newfoundland, but agreed to share the fisheries with Spain; Spain should have Pensacola, which she had lost in 1763, and also Mobile and Honduras; but the crucial point was that neither party would make peace until Gibraltar had become Spanish again. Article IV stipulated that Spain would not recognize the independence of the United States until Great Britain should do so.[3] During the negotiations Vergennes remarked: "Nothing is to be had gratuitously from Spain. We know that she desires some compensation from the Americans as well as from us, and we shall not oppose her."[4]

France made at Aranjuez a new alliance considerably at the expense of the earlier one with the United States. France had yielded on the point of the recognition of the absolute independence of the United States and had made a tacit allowance for a long truce, instead of engaging "not to lay down their arms until the independence of the United States shall have been formally or tacitly assured by the treaty or treaties that shall terminate the war."—Article VIII, Treaty of Alliance, 1778. She had conceded the possible rights of Spain in the Newfoundland fisheries without as much as consulting the Americans. In

[1] Doniol, III.: 595.
[2] Ibid., III.: 609.
[3] Ibid., III.: 803.
[4] Ibid., III.: 672.

the American treaty the French King had "forever renounced possession of any part of the continent of North America" which had belonged to the British. Pensacola and Mobile were not mentioned; but he had no right to use these as a part of a bargain with Spain, so that Spain might establish her supremacy in the Gulf of Mexico. France would compel her American ally to continue the fight against England and to wait indefinitely for independence until Spain could reconquer Gibraltar, an object wholly foreign to American interests. The lands to the east of the Mississippi received no mention, but it was understood that France would support Spanish rights, whatever these were. Moreover, the negotiations and the Treaty of Aranjuez were to be kept secret, so that France might guide the Americans all the more effectively toward the concealed goal. It needs be said that Vergennes knew nothing of the American claims to the West and that he used his influence to harmonize the two allies of France.[1]

The terms proposed to Great Britain in the offer of mediation on April 3 consisted of a truce of long duration during which Great Britain should hold all the territory in the possession of her military forces, including New York City and Rhode Island. Vergennes did not know of the exact content of the terms till after they had been sent, and then he protested vehemently against the unwarranted concessions of territory. He appealed to the promise of Spain so often made to guard the honor of the crown of France as she would that of her own crown.[2] But George III. saved the honor of the two Bourbon crowns by refusing the mediation. Spain declared war June 16, 1779.

The Continental Congress hoped to secure the complete alliance of Spain, and therefore sent a very able man, John Jay, as minister to Madrid. He knew nothing of the Treaty of Aranjuez, and hence could not understand the failure of his mission. He was never officially received, but he acted with

[1] Phillips, P. C. *The West in the Diplomacy of the American Revolution:* 170.

[2] Doniol, III.: 768.

patience, tact, and dignity throughout the long informal negotiations. Congress went so far as to authorize him to surrender the right of navigating the Mississippi below the thirty first degree parallel as the price for a Spanish alliance.[1] Jay wrote in reply: "The cession of this navigation will, in my opinion, render a future war with Spain unavoidable, and I shall look upon my subscribing to the one as fixing the certainty of the other."[2] Jay acquired in Madrid a suspicion, which, when he later talked it over with John Adams, grew into a conviction, that France was holding Spain back.

It might appear on the surface that Spain and the United States, though not technically allies, were fighting in a common cause against a common enemy. On the contrary the cause had few common characteristics. And Spain succeeded by her dallying with mediation to fritter away the aid which France would otherwise have rendered in 1779. In 1780 Spain did place a small force in Minorca, another along the Mississippi, and she secured with almost no opposition footholds in Florida. She laid siege to Gibraltar, it is true, which was occupied by a small number of British; but that fact was of no assistance to the Americans. Briefly, the alliance of France with Spain may be said to have cost the American cause more than the millions of livres Spain secretly advanced through France and it constituted a potential menace.

Another phase of the diplomatic efforts of the Continental Congress centered in the Netherlands. During the Revolution American trade relations were more intimate with the Dutch than with any other people; chiefly because of the favorable location of the Dutch colony of St. Eustatius in the midst of the rich English, Danish, French, and Spanish West Indies. Under a treaty with England free ships made free goods, therefore Dutch merchantmen carried safely European goods, even English goods, to this depot; and American ships laden with tobacco, rice, and indigo would drop into the assisting trade winds, land at St. Eustatius, make the proper exchange, and return home.

[1] Wharton, *Diplomatic Correspondence*, IV.: 293.
[2] Ibid., IV.: 337.

By this method Amsterdam was able to furnish London with American products and Boston with English products.[1] But the situation exasperated the English. Moreover, John Paul Jones had found refuge in Dutch waters after successful raids upon British merchantmen.

England decided to take high ground in her treatment of neutral carriers, this included the Prussian, Swedish, Danish, and Dutch; but the Dutch had more ships than the others combined and they did most of the carrying trade for Russia. England forbade neutral merchantmen to carry any commodities belonging to nationals of France or Spain; and she proceeded to seize and confiscate those that did.

In the winter of 1779–1780, Spain seized, on much the same pretexts as those of England, two Russian ships laden with wheat and confiscated their cargoes. War almost followed. Frederick the Great persuaded Florida Blanca to offer the fullest reparation to Russia. And he suggested to Count Panin, completely under his domination, that it would be an opportune time for Russia to proclaim to the world that neutral ships and their cargoes, unless contraband, should be exempt from seizure, and that the coastwise trade of belligerents should be open. Count Panin promptly presented the plan to the Empress Catherine, who felt flattered with the opportunity to act as spokesman for the neutral nations. On March 10, 1780, Catherine issued a proclamation, addressed to the courts of London, Versailles, and Madrid, requesting all powers to join her in maintaining the rights of neutral merchantmen.[2] Denmark and Sweden were the first to respond, and they with Russia formed the nucleus for the armed neutrality. France and Spain followed. The Netherlands worried along until they decided to join in 1781. Prussia and Austria followed. Portugal became a party in 1782, and the Two Sicilies in 1783. Even Turkey accepted the principles. Great Britain alone refused, and she well knew that it was against her tactics that the league had been formed; nor did

[1] See Jameson, *St. Eustatius in the American Revolution*, Amer. Hist. Review, VIII.: 683.
[2] James Brown Scott, *The Armed Neutralities:* 273.

she accept any of the principles until the Treaty of Paris, 1856. As for the doctrine of free ships, free goods, contraband excepted, the parties to the armed neutrality observed it only at their convenience. Indeed, Russia was the first to violate it during her war with Turkey in 1788 by seizing Turkish property on Swedish ships.

When the Netherlands joined the armed neutrality, Great Britain claimed immediately that the Dutch had violated the treaties of 1674 and 1715. Another incident did much to ignite the war between the British and the Dutch. While Arthur Lee was at Paris, a brother, William Lee, received instructions to negotiate with Berlin and Vienna. He went only as far as Frankfort; and on the way fell in with a Dutchman, de Neufville. The two amused themselves by drawing up a draft of a treaty between the United States and the Netherlands. In it de Neufville professed to act under instructions from van Berckel, the pensionary of Amsterdam.[1] William Lee sent this draft home to Congress, and when Congress chose its president, Henry Laurens, to negotiate a treaty and a loan at The Hague, this unauthenticated draft of a treaty was enclosed among his papers. The British chased and captured the ship which carried Laurens. He hurriedly threw his papers overboard, but the British sailors fished them up; and Laurens was placed in the Tower of London. The English government demanded peremptorily that the Netherlands disavow the draft of the treaty and punish van Berckel who had apparently authorized it. The Dutch government did disavow the treaty of which it had up to that time known nothing; but van Berckel could not be punished, for under Dutch law he had committed no crime. Great Britain declared war. Britain feared Russia and offered Minorca to Catherine which she did not accept; but neither did she listen to Holland's appeal for assistance under the alliance of the armed neutrality. Catherine consulted Frederick of Prussia, declaring her willingness to join him in a fight for the principles of the league; but the Prussian refused; and thereupon Russia left Holland to her fate.

[1] Wharton, *Diplomatic Correspondence*, I.: 606.

John Adams had been sent to Paris with the express object of being ready to negotiate a treaty of peace with Great Britain. While waiting in Paris he made his presence objectionable to Vergennes, who requested Franklin to urge upon Congress that Adams be recalled. Congress did administer a mild rebuke and soon assigned him to the task of negotiating a treaty with Holland. Due to the fact that each province had a share in treaty making this task became both difficult and tedious. But after two years of unremitting efforts and the news of Cornwallis' defeat at Yorktown he accomplished his purpose, October 8, 1782.

Although this treaty was abrogated by the overthrow of the Dutch government by Napoleon in 1795, the mere negotiation of it had significance. The United States did not beg for help as in the case of the treaties with France in 1778; the United States through John Adams negotiated as the equal of the United Provinces, and most liberal commercial provisions were agreed upon. By this treaty the Dutch recognized that the war had practically closed at Yorktown, and that American independence stood on its own merits, separate and apart from Dutch interests.[1]

By the end of the year 1782 Great Britain found that she had been engaged for seven years in war against her American colonies, four years against France, two years against Spain, and for almost as long against Holland. The armed neutrality of 1780 brought into opposition to Britain and to her policies almost all of the European states. The Americans had one ally in France; one haughty and expensive co-belligerent in Spain; and a friendly co-belligerent in Holland. It had, no doubt, become evident to English statesmen that when George III. refused to receive the petition of the First Continental Congress he projected American affairs into European diplomacy. John Adams aptly said: "It is obvious that all the powers of Europe will be continuously manoeuvering with us to work us into their real or imaginary balances of power." It cannot be said that Britain was whipped; but she had already begun to make peace.

[1] Malloy, *Treaties*, etc., II.: 1233.

Several ineffectual steps toward peace had been taken. As early as 1779, the British premier, Lord North, directed an old friend of Franklin, David Hartley, to open an informal correspondence on the subject of peace with the Americans. Hartley proposed a long truce and the suspension of the objectionable acts of Parliament in return for which the Americans should cancel the treaties with France. Franklin refused. It meant the breaking of faith with France.[1]

In the same year the Empress Maria Theresa wrote Charles III. of Spain to dissuade him from going to war with England. Later Austria offered to mediate between France and England, and likewise failed. By 1781 Joseph II. had succeeded Maria Theresa; and his leading minister, Prince Kaunitz, made preparations to call a peace congress at Vienna. He accepted the advice of Vergennes that the United States be invited not to the congress but to send delegates to Vienna to negotiate peace with England at the same time that the European powers should seek peace among themselves within the formal congress. But the basis for negotiations as insisted upon by Great Britain was the status quo ante bellum and an armistice. John Adams voiced the emphatic refusal of the United States.[2] Austria and Russia refused also. For France, Great Britain added another condition, that France should withdraw from her alliance with the United States. Kaunitz laid upon Great Britain, then, the blame for the failure of his proposed congress.

On Washington's birthday, 1782, Conway's motion against the further continuance of the war passed the House of Commons. In consequence Lord North's ministry resigned, March 20, 1782. Lord Rockingham formed the new ministry with Shelburne as Home Secretary and Fox as Foreign Secretary, both of them old friends of Franklin. Before the Revolution the American colonies belonged in the Home Department; but at this time Shelburne and Fox were not clear as to whose department the Americans belonged. Consequently, two commissioners were sent to Paris. Fox sent Grenville to confer with Vergennes and "with

[1] Wharton, *Diplomatic Correspondence*, II.: 24, 26.
[2] Ibid., III.: 338.

any power or state." This phrase in Grenville's commission applied to the Americans. Franklin scrutinized the words and decided that the commission was unsatisfactory, because England had constantly denied that the Americans constituted an independent state. Grenville was the son of the author of the Stamp Act, an ambitious young man, anxious to establish a reputation as a diplomat. He did succeed in concluding a preliminary agreement with Vergennes of which the principal parts were: 1. England should treat simultaneously with all the belligerents. 2. The independence of the United States should be recognized. 3. The Treaty of Paris, 1763, should be regarded as the starting point.

Shelburne sent Oswald, a wealthy Scot who had acquired considerable property in America through marriage, to confer informally with Vergennes and Franklin. Oswald asked for a statement of what Franklin thought would be essential requirements for the establishment of peace. Franklin advised that Oswald should be designated to treat with the United States alone;[1] and Shelburne afterwards consented. Thereupon, Franklin turned over to Oswald a masterly memorandum, setting out the demands of the United States and laying down the program for the negotiations. These demands were divided into two groups, those which were necessary and those which were advisable. The four necessary requirements were: 1. Independence and the withdrawal of the British troops. 2. The boundaries to be fixed. 3. The intolerable Quebec Act, which gave to the province of Quebec the entire region within the later Northwest Territory, should be disregarded and Quebec be restricted to its old boundaries. 4. The Americans must have the right to fish not only on the Grand Banks but within three miles of the Newfoundland shore. In addition Franklin mentioned four other demands which he deemed advisable for Great Britain to concede in order that the treaty might conform with the interests of the two nations and thus insure a durable peace. These were: 1. Indemnity for the sufferings of the Americans. 2. Parliament should acknowledge its error by repealing the

[1] Wharton, *Diplomatic Correspondence*, II.: 303, 319, 343.

obnoxious acts relating to America. 3. The Americans should be given the right to trade with the British Isles and with British colonies everywhere. This would exempt the Americans from the rigors of the British mercantile system. 4. All of Canada should be surrendered to the United States. For full measure, he inserted that the United States could do nothing for the tory refugees.[1]

Lord Rockingham's death, July 1, 1782, removed the friction between the departments of Fox and Shelburne. Shelburne became Prime Minister and Fox retired from office. Grenville was recalled from Paris and Oswald left in charge. Since the crown had no authority to alienate the territory of the United States without the consent of Parliament a bill was introduced and passed, July 25, 1782, enabling the King to consent to a treaty of independence.

The Continental Congress had authorized a commission of five members to treat with Great Britain: Adams, Franklin, Jay, Laurens, and Jefferson. The illness of his wife detained Jefferson at home. Laurens was still in the Tower of London, but his exchange for Cornwallis had been arranged.

When Franklin saw the turn of events in England and how intensely the British desired peace he wrote Jay to come from Madrid, saying: "Spain has taken four years to consider whether she will treat with us or not, give her forty." Franklin held frequent informal conferences with Oswald which paved the way for an understanding.

Oswald's commission bore the date of August 7, 1782, and a few days later he exhibited it to Franklin and Jay. The commission authorized him "to treat, consult, and conclude with any commissioners named by the said colonies or plantations, or any body or bodies corporate or politic, assembly or assemblies, or description of men, or person or persons whatsoever a peace or truce with the said colonies or plantations or any of them, or any part or parts thereof; any law, act, or acts of Parliament, matter or thing, to the contrary notwithstanding." [2]

[1] Franklin, *Works*, IX.: 354 (Spark's edition).
[2] Wharton, *Diplomatic Correspondence*, V.: 444.

Jay refused flatly to negotiate on such basis; he insisted on the recognition of independence as a prerequisite.

Vergennes thought Oswald's powers sufficient and so did Franklin. But Jay had become disillusioned about French and Spanish philanthropy toward the Americans.[1] He knew that Spain wanted the Appalachian Mountains instead of the Mississippi River as the western boundary of the United States. He knew that Rayneval, the confidential secretary of Vergennes, had submitted a memoir at Madrid which supported the Spanish rather than the American claim.[2] Moreover, the British had intercepted a letter from Marbois, the French chargé d'affaires in America, to Vergennes which urged that the Americans be kept away from the Newfoundland fisheries and that Great Britain be given permanent possession of New York City, Charleston, and the Penobscot.[3] The British placed this letter in Jay's hands, hoping that after reading it he would consent to negotiate on the terms of Oswald's commission. The effect on Jay was exactly the reverse. And when he heard that Vergennes had despatched Rayneval on a secret mission to London his gravest suspicions appeared to him to be well founded.[4]

In his anxiety Jay went beyond good diplomatic usage, and, without consulting Franklin, sent a friend, an Englishman, Benjamin Vaughan, to intercede for the American cause with the members of the British cabinet. Jay instructed Vaughan to argue that it was to the interest of France and not of England to postpone the recognition of independence, that the United States would not make peace without the fisheries, and that the plans for reserving the fisheries for the French and English and for keeping the Americans away from the Mississippi would sow seeds of discord that might lead to future war.[5] Jay sent at the same time a message to Adams to come from The Hague, for Adams was the commissioner most familiar with the fisheries

[1] Wharton, *Diplomatic Correspondence*, IV.: 460; Jay, *Correspondence*, II.: 376.

[2] Jay, *Correspondence*, II.: 398.

[3] W. Jay, *Life of Jay*, I.: 490.

[4] Jay, *Correspondence*, II.: 399.

[5] Ibid., II.: 403.

question; indeed, the fisheries constituted one of the leading industries of Adams' home State, Massachusetts. When Franklin found out about Vaughan's mission he entertained no resentment against Jay, and the two remained good friends to the end.

Jay's suspicion about the object of Rayneval's mission proved to be incorrect, but Vaughan accomplished his purpose. Shelburne asked: "Is a new commission necessary?" Vaughan replied: "It is." So on September 27, 1782, a courier brought a new commission for Oswald to treat with "The Thirteen United States of America,"[1] the identical words used in a draft of a commission submitted by Jay. Jay's victory formed one of the most conspicuous services that he ever rendered to his country, because on it turned the character of the treaty. Independence was conceded beforehand. The treaty recognized the United States and Great Britain as equals.

In the negotiations that followed three points stood out prominently on the American side. First, westward extension to the Mississippi. Second, the free navigation of that river. Third, the right to the Newfoundland fisheries. On the British side Oswald presented two points as essential. First, American independence must be complete and free from France. Second, the debts owed by the Americans to the British must be secured and the rights of the loyalists must be restored.

Four drafts of the treaty were considered before the work was completed. Jay drew up the first one. It embraced boundaries; details of peace, such as the release of prisoners, disposition of archives; the Newfoundland fisheries, both inshore and on the banks; the free navigation of the Mississippi to both parties; and American merchants and merchant vessels should enjoy the same privileges and protection in British ports as the English with the exception of the exclusive use and trade granted to the chartered trading companies. In United States ports British merchants and merchant vessels should enjoy the same protection as the American. With regard to the boundaries Jay proposed to begin with the mouth of the St. Johns River, follow it midstream up to the highlands that formed the watershed

[1] Wharton, *Diplomatic Correspondence*, V.: 446.

between the St. Lawrence and the Atlantic, follow the crest of these highlands southwestward to the Connecticut River, then down that stream to the forty-fifth degree parallel, which to-day bounds Vermont on the north, then along that parallel to the St. Lawrence, thence to the southern point of Lake Nipissing; and from that point by a direct line to the source of the Mississippi River; down that river to the thirty-first degree parallel, which is the present northern boundary of western Florida; thence east to the Chattahoochee River, down it to the junction with the Flint River; then eastward to the head waters of the St. Marys and down the St. Marys to the sea. He included all islands within twenty leagues of the shore.[1]

Throughout these negotiations Oswald exercised no plenipotentiary powers. Each proposal made by the Americans was sent by messenger to the cabinet in London for its action. Franklin and Jay could not communicate with the home government and were therefore obliged to act for themselves. On October 23, 1782, the reply to the first draft came from the cabinet. It carried a tone of exultation instilled by the recent complete defeat of the combined French and Spanish attempt upon Gibraltar. The reply objected to the boundaries and to the omission of a provision for the tories. The reply claimed that Nova Scotia reached to the Kennebec River and that the province of Quebec included all of the subsequent Northwest Territory down to the Ohio River in accordance with the intolerable Quebec Act. The Americans should have no right to dry fish on the shores of Newfoundland and Great Britain refused to modify her navigation laws in favor of American trade. The cabinet thought also that Oswald had more than met his match in Jay and Franklin; so they sent Henry Strachey, Under Secretary for Foreign Affairs, once the secretary of Clive and of Lord Howe's commission, to assist.[2]

Three days later, October 26, John Adams arrived fresh and buoyant from his diplomatic triumph in Holland. He brought with him maps and documents relating to the north-

[1] Wharton, *Diplomatic Correspondence*, V.: 452.
[2] Fitzmaurice, *Life of Shelburne*, III.: 281; Wharton, V.: 472.

eastern boundary and to the fisheries. In the suspicion of France and Spain Adams readily took sides with Jay. Adams wrote: "The doctor heard me patiently but said nothing." A few days later Franklin remarked to Jay: "I am of your opinion and will go on with these gentlemen in the business without consulting this court."[1] This decision on the part of the American commissioners violated the positive instructions from Congress as well as the spirit of Article VIII of the Treaty of Alliance with France. But Jay and Adams reasoned that France was trying to curtail the American claims; and they assumed that their instructions were for the benefit of the United States, and that when circumstances seemed to prove that they were not, then it became the duty of the negotiators to disregard those instructions. "They at once withdrew the interests of their country from the common stock of equivalents, liable to be used like counters to equalize the bargains of the general negotiation. And by saving the pride of the British government, they induced them to offer far easier terms of reconciliation than would have been obtained, had they been passed under the patronage of their most formidable enemy."[2]

Strachey took back to the cabinet the second draft[3] of the treaty on November 5, 1782. The Americans had consented to draw the northeastern boundary back from the St. Johns to the St. Croix River and to project to the westward the northern boundary of Vermont along the forty-fifth parallel until it reached the Mississippi. Fortunately for the Americans the cabinet rejected the forty-fifth parallel west of the St. Lawrence River, for although this line would have given the United States a considerable part of Ontario it would have cut Lake Huron in two and the northern part of Michigan and Wisconsin and of Minnesota north of Minneapolis would have been lost. The third draft[4] on the boundary was substantially the present one, although there have been many conventions and commissions to decide upon its exact location. The boundary followed the

[1] John Adams, *Works*, III.: 336.
[2] Charles Francis Adams in Adams, *Works*, I.: 392.
[3] Wharton, *Diplomatic Correspondence*, V.: 455.
[4] Ibid., V.: 461.

St. Croix to its source; thence to and along the watershed between the rivers that flow into the St. Lawrence River and into the Atlantic Ocean to the northwesternmost head of the Connecticut River; down the middle of that river to the forty-fifth degree north latitude; thence due west to the St. Lawrence; down the middle of that river to Lake Ontario; thence through the middle of this lake, and of the Niagara River, through the middle of Lake Erie, the Detroit River, Lake St. Clair, and the St. Clair River, through the middle of Lake Huron and of the communication with Lake Superior, and through the middle of that lake so as to give Isle Royale and Isle Philipeaux to the United States; thence up the Rainy River to the Lake of the Woods; thence directly across that lake to its northwesternmost corner, and from thence due west to the Mississippi; down the middle of that river to the intersection with the thirty-first degree north latitude; thence east to the Chattahoochee, down the middle thereof to its junction with the Flint River; thence straight to the head of the St. Mary's River and down the middle of that stream to the Atlantic Ocean. Excepting such islands as were a part of Nova Scotia, the United States was to have all the islands within twenty leagues of its coast.[1]

As far as Great Britain and the United States were concerned the free navigation of the Mississippi was assured to the citizens of both countries. Spain held both sides of that river at the mouth. And according to a fairly well-recognized principle of that day the possession of both sides of the mouth of a river gave complete control of the navigation. It was the enforcement of this principle together with Hamilton's excise tax that caused the Whiskey Rebellion in western Pennsylvania.

Three knotty problems remained: The debts incurred before the outbreak of the Revolution, and these were almost wholly owed by the Americans; compensation to the loyalists who had fled either voluntarily or under compulsion and whose property had been confiscated; and the right to the fisheries.

Strachey prided himself greatly on obtaining Article IV: "It is agreed that creditors on either side shall meet with no

[1] Malloy, *Treaties*, etc., I.: 587.

lawful impediment to the recovery of the full value in sterling money, of all bona fide debts heretofore contracted."[1] As a matter of fact, it afterward became very difficult for the British to collect these debts before American juries; and for that reason the British held on to the forts in the northwest longer than dictated by the phrase "all convenient speed," which the treaty provided. These claims were finally paid by the United States under the Convention of 1802, the amount being $2,664,000. But these impediments could not be foreseen.

In regard to the loyalists, Franklin made four points. First: The States alone and not Congress had the power to compensate the loyalists. This was good constitutional law under the Articles of Confederation. Second: It would cost either party less to pay these tories outright than to prolong the war until the States might make payment. Third: France was supporting the claims of the loyalists for the reason that she might prevent an agreement between Great Britain and the United States. And fourth: If the King thought it a bad precedent to make peace without securing payment for the tories he could provide for their payment himself.[2] Franklin drew up an article proposing that England should compensate the Americans for the damages committed by the British forces. No doubt he used this argument as a weapon and threw it away when it no longer served a purpose. The discussion about the tories was prolonged and bitter. Indeed, the negotiations might have been broken off on this account had not the cabinet felt that it was necessary to have the treaty completed by November 25, when Parliament was to convene. The Americans yielded sufficiently to agree that Congress should recommend to the respective State legislatures to make restitution for the rights and properties confiscated from the loyalists. As was generally understood the legislatures were free to refuse to comply with this recommendation, which they did. Parliament made several grants to these unfortunate claimants from 1782 on, but not until 1790 when it became clearly evident what the attitude of the State legisla-

[1] Malloy, *Treities*, etc., I.: 588.
[2] Franklin, *Writings*, VIII.: 527, 621 ff. (Smyth edition).

tures was, did that body make an appropriation of over £3,000,000 for the loyalists.

On the question of the fisheries Adams was at his best, and his colleagues stood loyally by him. He argued that the fisheries furnished a nursery for seamen and that if the Americans did not secure a right to the fishing grounds the French would take possession of them, and consequently the French navy would be strengthened. He argued further that the Americans carried the fish to Portugal and to Spain, then took the money to England, there to buy the manufactured articles needed at home. The English knew well that the Americans were good customers.

He spent the whole day of Friday, November 29, 1782, in arguing this point. Oswald and Strachey had called in Fitzherbert, a brilliant young man of thirty-three, who was conducting the negotiations with France and Spain. Besides Jay and Franklin, Henry Laurens appeared for the first time; he had recently been released from the Tower of London in exchange for Cornwallis. Strachey proposed to substitute "liberty" for the "right" of fishing on such part of the coast of Newfoundland as British fishermen might use and on the coasts, bays, and creeks of other English dominions in America. Adams rose. "Gentlemen, is there or can there be a clearer right? In former treaties,—that of Utrecht and that of Paris,—France and England have claimed the right, and used the word. When God Almighty made the banks of Newfoundland, at three hundred leagues distance from America, and at six hundred leagues distance from those of France and England, did he not give as good a right to the former as to the latter? If Heaven in the creation gave a right, it is ours at least as much as yours. We have been constantly fighting in Canada, Cape Breton, and Nova Scotia, for the defence of this fishery, and have expended beyond all proportion more than you. If, then, the right cannot be denied, why should it not be acknowledged, and put out of dispute? Why should we leave room for illiterate fishermen to wrangle and chicane?" Mr. Fitzherbert replied. "The argument is in your favor. I must confess your reasons appear to be good; but Mr. Oswald's instructions were such that he could not agree. And for my part I have not the honor and felicity to be a man of that weight and authority in my country that you, gentlemen, have in yours. I have the accidental advantage of a little favor with the present minister; but I cannot depend upon the influence of my own opinion to reconcile a measure to my countrymen. We can consider ourselves as little more than pens in the hands of the government at home; and Mr. Oswald's instructions are so particular." [1]

Oswald and Strachey wanted to refer the matter to London. Adams was willing. But Fitzherbert faltered and remarked: "It was going to sea again." He felt, no doubt, that a completed American treaty might hasten his own negotiations with France and Spain. Franklin said that if another messenger had to go to London the article on the debts and on the proposition of compensation for sufferers in America would have to be reconsidered. This was a thrust at Strachey who prided himself on the manner of disposing of the debts owed by Americans to the British when the war broke out. Fitzherbert, Oswald, and Strachey retired for a conference. They returned willing to concede the extent of the inshore fisheries and the privileges of using the harbors and of drying and curing on the uninhabited coasts, but they insisted on the word "liberty" instead of "right" of fishing. Thereupon, the commissioners on both sides agreed to leave the settlement of the fisheries for the definitive treaty. They sat down, read over the whole treaty, made a few corrections, and agreed to meet the next day to sign and seal the preliminary articles which were left for the secretaries to copy.

They did meet the next day, first at Jay's quarters and then at Oswald's. The Americans had inserted in their draft that the loyalists could remain in the United States for twelve months unmolested in order to recover their estates if they could. Strachey had directed that this be left out of the British draft, thus leaving the loyalists unlimited time. The provision was

[1] John Adams, *Works*, III.: 333 (Diary).

inserted. Laurens was a South Carolinian and an owner of slaves. He proposed the insertion of a clause in Article VII providing that the British troops in withdrawing should not carry away "any negroes or other property of the American inhabitants," which was agreed to. A curious secret article was added, providing that if Great Britain should obtain West Florida from Spain, the southern boundary of the United States should be drawn from the mouth of the Yazoo River eastward to the Appalachicola or about one hundred miles north of the boundary established in the treaty. Spain did not cede West Florida to Great Britain and later used this article as proof of title to the strip. The treaties were then signed by Oswald for Great Britain and by Adams, Franklin, Jay, and Laurens for the United States. The seals were affixed and the copies of the treaty exchanged. Whereupon, all of the commissioners drove out to Passy and had dinner with Franklin.[1]

On January 20, 1783, Fitzherbert, Adams, and Franklin signed an armistice. The article on the fisheries was made more specific. Adams had to yield on the word "right" and to accept "liberty to take fish of every kind" on that part of the coast of Newfoundland which British fishermen might use and "on the coasts, bays, and creeks of all other of His Britannic Majesty's dominions in America." The Americans should have the liberty to dry and cure fish in any of the unsettled bays, harbors, and creeks of Nova Scotia, Magdalen Islands, and Labrador; but as soon as these should become settled, agreements would have to be made with the proprietors. Newfoundland was not included in the provision for drying and curing fish.[2]

The secret article was omitted. Otherwise the terms of the provisional treaty, properly documented, were in substance those of the definitive treaty, signed September 3, 1783. The same commissioners signed except that David Hartley had succeeded Richard Oswald.

Only after the signature of the provisional treaty did Franklin

[1] Adams, *Works*, III.: 336.
[2] Malloy, *Treaties*, I.: 588.

communicate to Vergennes the import of the agreement. Vergennes replied: "I am at a loss, sir, to explain your conduct and that of your colleagues on this occasion. You have concluded your preliminary articles without any communication between us, although the instructions from Congress prescribe that nothing shall be done without the participation of the King.—You are wise and discreet, sir; you perfectly understand what is due to propriety; you have all your life performed your duties. I pray you to consider how you propose to fulfill those which are due to the King? I am not desirous of enlarging these reflections; I commit them to your own integrity. When you shall be pleased to relieve my uncertainty I will entreat the King to enable me to answer your demands." [1]

Franklin's reply shows at least an equal mastery of the art of negotiation. "Nothing has been agreed in the preliminaries contrary to the interests of France; and no peace is to take place between us and England till you have concluded yours. Your observation is, however, apparently just, that in not consulting you before they were signed, we have been guilty of neglecting a point of biênseance. But as this was not from want of respect for the King, whom we all love and honor, we hope it will be excused, and that the great work, which has hitherto been so happily conducted, is so nearly brought to perfection, and is so glorious to his reign, will not be ruined by a single indiscretion of ours. And certainly the whole edifice sinks to the ground immediately if you refuse on that account to give us any further assistance."

"It is not possible for any one to be more sensible than I am of what I and every American owe to the King for the many and great benefits and favors he has bestowed upon us. All my letters to America are proofs of this; all tending to make the same impressions on the minds of my countrymen that I felt in my own. And I believe that no prince was ever more beloved and respected by his own subjects than the King is by the people of the United States. The English, I just now learn, flatter themselves they have already divided us. I hope

[1] Wharton, *Diplomatic Correspondence*, II.: 403.

this little misunderstanding will therefore be kept a secret, and that they will find themselves totally mistaken."[1]

Vergennes treasured no ill feeling. But he did write to the French minister in the United States, Luzerne, that he thought the members of Congress ought to know that the commissioners had violated their instructions, but he was not to mention it as a complaint. Robert R. Livingston, the secretary for foreign affairs, wrote a sharp criticism to the commissioners.[2] But their immense services overshadowed small irregularities.

The Americans had carried their main points: independence, boundaries, and the fisheries. The treaty was of incalculable value for both internal and external affairs. The Americans were so exhausted that they needed a period of peace. No one could foresee the great European wars that were to follow from 1793 on; but if the Americans had not been completely free from Great Britain they would have been inevitably pulled into the current, with utter economic exhaustion as a consequence. But the position of the Americans as neutrals enabled them to gain great commercial advantages for they became the great common carriers on the high seas and their products found a ready market in the warring countries of Europe.

The outstanding personal feature of the treaty is the skill, talent, and patience of the American commissioners. It would almost appear fortunate that there existed no wireless, no cables, no speedy means of communication. They were often censured and criticized by their fellow countrymen. They were neglected and slighted by foreign diplomats, or at best intrigued against. At times they were pressed for money to live on, because Congress was irregular in its financial affairs. One cannot escape the conclusion that they bore themselves as the peers of the best diplomats of any or all time.

[1] Wharton, *Diplomatic Correspondence*, II.: 404.
[2] Ibid., V.: 480.

BIBLIOGRAPHY

ADAMS, JOHN.—Ten volumes. Edited by Charles Francis Adams. Boston, 1850–1856.

DONIOL, HENRI.—*Histoire de la participation de la France*, etc. Volumes II and III. Paris, 1886–1888.

FITZMAURICE, EDMOND GEORGE PETTY.—*Life of William, Earl of Shelburne.* Volume III. London, 1875–1876.

FRANKLIN, BENJAMIN.—*Works.* Ten volumes. Edited by Jared Sparks. Boston, 1836–1840.

FRANKLIN, BENJAMIN.—*Writings.* Ten volumes. Edited by Albert Henry Smith. Boston, 1905–1907.

JAMESON, J. F.—*Saint Eustatius*, Am. Hist. Rev. VIII.: 683–708.

JAY, JOHN.—*Correspondence and Public Papers.* Four volumes. Edited by Henry P. Johnston. New York, 1890–1893.

JAY, WILLIAM.—*Life of John Jay.* Two volumes. New York, 1833.

LYMAN, THEODORE.—*The Diplomacy of the United States.* Two volumes. Boston, 1828.

PHILLIPS, PAUL C.—*The West in the Diplomacy of the American Revolution.* Urbana, 1913.

SCOTT, JAMES BROWN.—*The Armed Neutralities of 1780 and 1800.* New York, 1918.

TRESCOTT, WILLIAM H.—*The Diplomacy of the Revolution.* New York, 1852.

WHARTON, FRANCIS.—*Diplomatic Correspondence of the American Revolution.* Six volumes. Washington, 1889.

CHAPTER III

JAY'S TREATY, 1794

"It is as true now as when Washington penned the words, and will always be true, that it is vain to expect nations to act consistently from any motive other than that of interest. . . . It follows from this, directly, that the study of interests, is the one basis of sound and provident policy for statesmen. This involves a wide knowledge of contemporary facts as well as power to appreciate them; but for a nation to exert its full weight in the world such knowledge and appreciation must be wide spread among its plain people also."—A. T. MAHAN.

The treaty granting independence to the United States aroused so much displeasure in England that the adherents of Fox and North in the House of Commons were able to pass a vote of lack of confidence in the cabinet on February 22, 1783. Two days later the Shelburne ministry resigned. Pitt, the younger, secured the ratification of the treaty in George III.'s name on April 19, 1784. Congress had already ratified it on January 14.

The United States wanted a commercial treaty; but leading English business men knew that they had a monopoly on American trade. They knew that wars rarely divert trade routes permanently. Colonial commerce had been and now American commerce was to be carried on largely by the aid of British capital. Lord Sheffield put the idea nicely. "The solid power of supplying the wants of America, of receiving her produce, and of waiting her convenience, belongs almost exclusively to our own merchants." [1] Englishmen understood American conditions better than the French or the Dutch. The common language, common racial characteristics, and a common civilization contributed toward this end. Furthermore, the industrial revolution appeared earlier in Great Britain than on the continent and thus gave the British the lead in the production of manufactures. The English ports established themselves

[1] Lord Sheffield, *Commerce of the American States:* 4.

as entrepôts for the European goods which Americans needed. Great Britain had a stable government; the European countries approached disorder step by step, which left them behind as competitors. Great Britain furnished the best market for the commodities the Americans had to sell and for the articles they wanted to buy. Lord Sheffield gives two incidents from the American Revolution that deserve notice. When France loaned a sum of money to the Continental Congress to obtain clothing for the troops, the American agents went to Holland and bought English cloth and sent it to America. Marbois complained to Congress and received the reply that it was the duty of the American agents to get the best cloth at the least cost. Again, British manufactured goods came via various channels through the American ports in such quantities that the French minister repeatedly protested and had to go to the extent of threatening to withdraw French aid before Congress took action one year before the war closed.[1]

Severe as the restrictions on American commerce had been before the war, the coming of peace found them at the mercy of the English. The Americans were treated as foreigners. The lucrative and necessary trade with the British West Indies was reserved for British vessels exclusively. So was the trade with Canada, Nova Scotia, and Newfoundland, and even the slave trade with the African coasts. British orders in council levied discriminatory tonnage and tariff duties on American vessels and goods as compared with those that were British owned. These measures tended to destroy the merchant marine of New England.

The agents and factors of English merchants established themselves in American ports; and by underselling the American, French, and Dutch business men they rapidly acquired the bulk of the trade in their own hands. They speculated on the wants of the people and had no hesitancy in seizing lands and goods in satisfaction for debts due them. The imports from Great Britain in 1784 amounted to £3,700,000, whereas the exports to Great Britain amounted to only £750,000. The

[1] Lord Sheffield, *Commerce of American States*: 10.

consequence was a drain of specie and an accentuation of the paper money scourge.

No one could prescribe a remedy. Adams advised from Paris that the States give to Congress the power to levy import duties and to regulate commerce and thus permit the United States to present a united front with retaliatory measures.[1] Instead of following Adams' advice, Congress accredited him to the court of St. James in 1785. The King and Queen received him with due dignity; but Pitt failed to reciprocate the courtesy by sending a minister to the United States. The Secretary of State for Foreign Affairs, the Marquis of Carmarthen, and Pitt, too, listened to his tale with interest, but neither made a single promise and both appeared satisfied with the commercial situation. When Adams mentioned the relinquishment of the military posts in the Northwest, they promptly retorted that the English had been unable to collect their debts in America,[2] and that the Americans refused to pay interest for the period of the war. As Adams grew more aggressive the English statesmen grew more civil and more taciturn. Adams reported to Jay: "All parties have committed themselves against us, except Shelburne and Buckingham, and the last of these is against a treaty of commerce with us." [3] Again: "I can obtain no answer from the ministry to any one demand, proposal, or inquiry." [4]

Difficulties connected with the enforcement of the Treaty of Peace continued. The British forces on withdrawing from the seaboard carried away with them a goodly number of slaves, mostly from the Carolinas. Great Britain continued to occupy the posts on the northern and the western frontier, claiming that the Americans had neglected to perform their part of the promise in regard to the loyalists and in regard to the payment of debts legally due Englishmen. Adams' instructions from Congress called on him to request the surrender of the posts, to demand satisfaction for the negroes taken, and to ask for a postponement of the settlement of the debts. The

[1] John Adams, *Works*, VIII.: 241, 280, 311, 313.
[2] Ibid., VIII.: 269, 303.
[3] Ibid., VIII.: 313.
[4] Ibid., VIII.: 321.

reason for the latter was to gain time to recuperate from the devastations of the war. Adams argued that holding the posts had withheld from American merchants a profitable fur trade and that furs to the value of £100,000 would have gone to England in payment of the debts. This was a low estimate, for the list of furs advertised in London in the spring of 1787 contained over 360,000 skins, all from the United States; and they were conservatively valued at £225,000. [1] Adams argued further that the removal of the slaves from the southern States by Sir Guy Carleton meant not merely a removal of their market value but it deprived their masters of their labor with which to produce goods to pay the debts.[2] Nevertheless, Adams could accomplish nothing.

The bitterness among the Americans about the posts increased. Notably was this true of the pioneers who went west to settle on the new lands, for they had to bear the brunt of the attacks from the Indians. Although the savages may not have been aggressively encouraged by the English soldiers, yet the tribes realized fully that the Americans were too weak to take the posts. Moreover, the English officers assumed at times to settle disputes between the English and the Indians on the one hand and the American pioneers on the other. The Americans claimed that such settlements fell short of impartiality and that when they objected they were answered with taunts about the loyalists and the debts.

London merchants continued to enjoy the benefits of free trade in American ports. And the American merchants continued to complain of the restrictions on their shipping. Their fish oil paid eighteen pounds sterling a ton in England and their tobacco paid sixteen pence a pound, five times the original value.[3] Several of the States did levy what was called equalizing tariff laws, that of Pennsylvania in 1785 being noteworthy because it served as a model for the first federal tariff law of July 4, 1789. These tariffs were of a retaliatory nature against

[1] McMaster, *History of the People of the U. S.*, I.: 235.
[2] Adams, *Works*, VIII.: 269.
[3] Ibid., VIII.: 280, 284.

Great Britain and against the other States in the union as well. New Jersey and Delaware levied no duties; neither did the southern States except Virginia, which served as an emphatic invitation to British commerce to come to their ports. British statesmen watched these events and concluded that it was useless to tie their own hands in a treaty with a central government which had no means of compelling the States to observe its provisions. In addition they cherished a remote hope that internal chaos might bring the Americans again within the British Empire. Before the constitution had been adopted Lord Carmarthen remarked to John Adams: "I presume, Mr. Adams, that the States will all immediately adopt the new constitution. I have read it with pleasure; it is very well drawn up." Adams commented to Jay, "All this oracular utterance was to signify to me, what has all along been insinuated, that there is not as yet any national government, but that, as soon as there shall be one, the British Court will vouchsafe to treat with it." [1] Shortly afterward Adams resigned. His patience and forbearance had held out remarkably, equaled perhaps only by those of his grandson at the same court during the trying days of the Civil War.

Washington as President appreciated the danger of friction with England; and he instructed Gouverneur Morris, who was then, 1790, in London on business, to sound the British government on a treaty. Like Adams, Morris accomplished nothing. In 1791 the Senate ratified the appointment of Thomas Pinckney of South Carolina as minister to London. Great Britain decided to reciprocate and sent George Hammond as minister to Philadelphia. Hammond had been secretary to David Hartley who signed the definitive treaty of 1783.

Thomas Jefferson had become Secretary of State, and he discovered that Hammond had no authority to negotiate a treaty of commerce. He decided therefore to consider with the British minister the execution of the Treaty of Peace. In his note of December 15, 1791, Jefferson presented his argument under five headings: First, the British held the north-

[1] Adams, *Works*, VIII.: 475.

western posts, Michillimackinac, Detroit, Fort Erie, Niagara, Oswego, Oswegatchie, etc., contrary to the treaty and these should therefore be immediately delivered. Second, the British officers had attempted to exercise jurisdiction in the vicinity of the posts. They had acted as magistrates for the neighborhood, had issued warrants and conducted trials. These actions constituted a violation of American sovereignty and therefore of the treaty as well. Third, the British had excluded the Americans from navigating their side of the boundary of the Great Lakes and of the streams. This interrupted the American fur trade, which was of consequence. Indeed, one great reason why the English held on to the posts was to monopolize the fur trade. Fourth, American slaves and other property which had been carried away during the withdrawal of the British troops from the coast should be paid for. Fifth, it had been discovered since 1783 that the river St. Croix divided into two branches at the mouth, with a strip of land between that widened as it stretched inland. It had become a matter of importance to know which one of the two branches formed the northeastern boundary of the United States. And he asked for a specification of the acts on the part of the United States which Great Britain considered a non-compliance with the treaty.[1]

Hammond replied at length on March 5, 1792. He justified the retention of the posts because of the vexatious laws of the State legislatures in regard to the loyalists and because of the unjust decisions of the state courts in regard to the debts. He maintained that Congress instead of facilitating the satisfaction of these obligations had thrown obstacles in the way by forbidding the allowance of interest on debts for the period of the war. He said nothing about the other points in Jefferson's despatch.[2]

In response Jefferson reviewed ably the statutes and the decisions of the courts pertaining to the loyalists and the debts. From this review he drew three conclusions. First, under the constitution the treaty was a part of the supreme law of the land

[1] American State Papers, Foreign Relations, I.: 190.
[2] Ibid., I.: 193.

and, therefore, all State laws in contravention of the treaty were null and void. Second, the United States had fulfilled its part of the agreements, which meant that it had recommended to the State legislatures to pay the claims of the loyalists and it had removed all legal obstructions to the collection of the debts. The interest on the debts during the war could not, however, be claimed under the treaty or under international law. Third, the delivery of the posts was a clear and simple duty and could be accomplished on a moment's notice; but the change in legislation in the thirteen States was necessarily difficult and slow.[1] Through Pinckney in London Jefferson could secure no better treatment of his demands. So nothing beyond the joining of the issues had been accomplished when he resigned as Secretary of State in 1792.

On June 8, 1793, war broke out between Great Britain and France. Forthwith, the two belligerents authorized the seizure of provisions in neutral ships destined for an enemy port. The Americans became the great neutral carriers; and their commerce was ground as between two millstones. The number of ships greatly increased but the tonnage decreased. Although the goods and the ships were not always condemned, yet the amount and the time of payment were at the discretion of the captor. In addition Great Britain began the stopping of American vessels upon the high seas, ordering the crew on deck, and pressing into the naval service those whom she chose on the pretext: "Once an Englishman, always an Englishman." To give a few examples. By 1794 St. Eustatia reported one hundred and thirty American vessels condemned; Bermuda, eleven more; Basseterre, thirty-five. The crews and many times the passengers were either imprisoned or impressed. And they did not have a scrap of a treaty right on which to make an appeal. The Americans protested and threatened. "What," said the British, "what can America do with Great Britain, who is determined to have no neutrals in this contest? Six or seven frigates can block your whole coast." [2]

[1] American State Papers, Foreign Relations, I.: 201.
[2] McMaster, II.: 167.

The injury to the commercial interests was so great that Congress discussed a plan of breaking off all relations with Great Britain. But Washington endeavored to make adjustments and to obtain remedies. His first thought was to appoint Hamilton on a special mission to Great Britain. But Monroe convinced the President that it would hardly be a wise choice politically. Thereupon, Jay was selected and Edmund Randolph was made Secretary of State.

Even Jay did not go with unanimous approval. It was pointed out that he held the position of Chief Justice of the Supreme Court and that he ought to give his undivided attention to its duties. He had expressed the opinion that the British could not be expected to return the slaves; although he thought there should be compensation. He had also expressed the opinion that there was some justification for the British retention of the posts. Randolph drew up the instructions. These were grouped around six points: compensation for the slaves, evacuation of the posts, repeal of the orders in council which restricted American trade with France, abolition of the practice of impressment, obtain the right of trading with the British West Indies, and comply with all of America's obligations to France.[1]

In June, 1794, Jay arrived in London. Lord Grenville, son of the author of the Stamp Act, was then minister for foreign affairs, and he received Jay with cordiality. The two carried on their negotiations through informal conversations, so that the chief source of information is in the despatches which Jay sent home.

On the question of the slaves Grenville argued that when these came into English hands their status as property was lost.[2] Jay, as an anti-slavery man, was greatly impressed with Grenville's argument and conceded the point. Grenville argued further that it would be almost impossible to remove immediately the troops from the western posts because of the difficulty in sending orders. Jay accepted that argument as well. But he

[1] Jay, *Correspondence*, IV.: 10.
[2] American State Papers, Foreign Relations, I.: 485.

did oppose the cession of an undefined stretch of territory at the head of the Mississippi River, which Grenville wanted.[1] On the subject of the seizure of American vessels and goods Grenville assured Jay "that it is His Majesty's wish that the most complete and impartial justice should be done to all the citizens of America, who may, in fact, have been injured by any of the proceedings above mentioned." There was no promise of change in the orders in council affecting trade with France. The subject of impressments received just as pleasant and evasive words: "On the subject of the impress, Lord Grenville has only to assure Mr. Jay, that if in any instance, American seamen have been impressed into the King's service, it has been contrary to the King's desire; though such cases may have occasionally risen from the difficulty of discriminating between British and American seamen, especially where there so often exists an interest and intention to deceive."[2] By November 19, 1794, the negotiations were completed, and Grenville and Jay signed the treaty.

Summarized briefly the following were the chief provisions. The British were to have one and one-half years in which to withdraw from the military posts in the northwest. Reciprocal rights of trade across the border between Canadians and Americans were agreed upon. A joint survey should be conducted to find the source of the Mississippi River. A board of commissioners should determine which was the river St. Croix. This commission reported its decision in 1798; but the actual survey was not completed until 1878. Another board was to determine the amount of the debts owed by Americans to British subjects before the war broke out. This board met and remained in session for two years but accomplished nothing because of disagreements. The board revived its sessions after the Treaty of 1802 had provided that the United States should appropriate $2,664,000 for the purpose. A third board was to estimate the losses inflicted on American merchants by the illegal capture of their ships and goods by the British, and, vice versa, similar

[1] American State Papers, Foreign Relations, I.: 491.
[2] Ibid., I.: 481, 482.

losses inflicted on British merchants by the unlawful actions of Americans. The final meeting of this board was held on February 4, 1804; and the total awards in favor of the Americans were $11,656,000 and, in favor of the British, $143,428. British holders of land in the United States were given full right to own and dispose of it as were also American holders of land in the British dominions. In the event of future war between the parties there was to be on either side no sequestration or confiscation of debts owed by the individuals of one to the individuals of the other party. Only the first ten articles are summarized above. They were intended to be permanent and consequently were not abrogated by the War of 1812.[1] The remaining articles, except the twelfth, expired October 28, 1807, as provided in the treaty.

Under Article XII Great Britain consented to allow American vessels to sail for purposes of trade to the British West Indies, but these could not have a carrying capacity of over seventy tons. Moreover, the United States agreed to "prohibit and restrain the carrying of any molasses, sugar, coffee, cocoa or cotton in American vessels, either from His Majesty's islands or from the United States to any part of the world except the United States, reasonable sea stores excepted." The restriction to vessels of seventy tons capacity was irksome; but the provision that no molasses or sugar could be obtained was intolera-able to the rum producing and the rum consuming interests of the country. That Jay should have permitted the restriction on cotton is surprising in the light of the later importance of that product. But in 1793 the cotton yield had been only five million pounds, one-tenth of which was exported. Cotton cloth was unknown. Cotton was used chiefly as the weft or woof with linen warp in velvets, fustians, and jeans. The Senate refused to approve this article; and therefore an additional article was inserted providing for the suspension of Article XII so far as it pertained to trade with the British West Indies.

Americans might trade with the British East Indies, but

[1] See Society for the Propagation of the Gospel *v.* New Haven, 8 Wheaton, 464.

they could not engage in the coasting trade nor carry East India goods to third countries; neither could they take from the East Indies military or naval stores or rice. (Article XIII.) Between Great Britain and Ireland on the one hand and the United States on the other reciprocal freedom of commerce and navigation was provided for. (Articles XIV and XV.) Article XVI permitted each party to appoint consuls. The procedure for the taking of contraband from each other's vessels was prescribed and contraband itself was defined. (Articles XVII and XVIII.) Contraband took on greater scope in this treaty than in that with France, as timber for ship building and all articles that might be used for the equipment of vessels, except unwrought iron and fir planks. Furthermore, articles of food destined for the enemies of either might be declared contraband, but if captured such articles should be paid for. This treaty was one of the first to provide that provisions could be considered contraband. This stipulation stirred up great friction between the United States and France because, in the war then raging, the French wanted to obtain these supplies from the Americans.

The two parties agreed to punish all piracy. Privateering was restricted. They agreed not to resort to reprisals until after satisfaction on a complaint had been either refused or unreasonably delayed. The ships of war of each party were to be hospitably received in the ports of the other. Foreign privateers could not arm or provision their ships in the ports of either party or there sell what they had captured. But the ships of war and privateers of either contracting party could carry wherever they pleased the goods and ships captured from their enemies. On the other hand no shelter could be granted to the prizes taken from the subjects or citizens of either contracting party by a third power. At this provision France not only took umbrage; but she contended that it was in violation of Article XVII of the Treaty of Amity and Commerce, 1778.

Each party was to protect the subjects or citizens of the other and their property within cannon shot of its coast. They agreed on the extradition of fugitives from justice charged with murder or forgery.

The treaty contained no mention of pay for the negroes carried off by Carleton, nor any mention of the abolition of the impressment of American seamen. But the treaty did state that no American merchantman could enter the harbors or rivers of Nova Scotia, New Brunswick, Canada, and of the region subject to the jurisdiction of the Hudson Bay Company.

No American treaty was ever awaited with greater partisan interest. But the President gave out not a single word. He called a special session of the Senate, and that body approved by a vote of twenty to ten, except the twelfth article. Before adjourning, the Senate enjoined its members not to permit a copy of the treaty to be made public. Three days afterward someone gave an inaccurate copy to the newspaper "Aurora." Senator Mason of Virginia, an Anti-Federalist, read it, and thought it would be better to have an accurate copy before the public and gave out the contents of the real treaty.

Immediately the arguments used for and against the treaty in the Senate were presented to mass meetings throughout the country; and a hundred other arguments, most of them quite irrelevant, were added. The Anti-Federalists spent their fury first. When Hamilton attempted to speak in favor of the treaty the New Yorkers pelted him with stones. Jay was burned in effigy in several cities. The squibs, toasts, and jests played with the name of the American negotiator. "A perpetual harvest to America, but clipt wings, lame legs, the pip, and an empty crop to all Jays."

There were six principal points on which the treaty was fiercely attacked by Henry Tazewell, Aaron Burr, Stevens T. Mason, Brockholst Livingstone, and others. First, the evacuation of the posts was deferred too long, one and one-half years. In the meantime the Americans would be almost wholly excluded from the rich fur trade with the Indians. Second, the surrender of the claim for the slaves was unjust. Third, the prohibition on the confiscation or sequestration of debts was a distinct loss to the Americans. In a future war this might be a much needed weapon. Fourth, the right granted to the English to hold lands in America in virtually the same manner as Americans might work mischief. A widespread fear existed that the English might enlarge their already vast tracts of land and through colonization bring America under British influence if not under British jurisdiction again. Fifth, the limitation on trade with the West and the East Indies left the Americans in a worse position than they were before. Sixth, the extension of the contraband list to include food products and naval stores struck a blow at American trade, particularly at a time when France was the best customer.

Jay, himself, furnished the best arguments in defense of his treaty in a famous despatch to Randolph, November 19, 1794. In that despatch he foresaw the leading objections, and he, too, grouped his arguments around six points. First, there was no reason to believe that a better treaty could have been obtained. This point fell short of being a strong defense; but it was thought that without a treaty the Americans would have been forced into the war. Second, the British traders at the military posts had their goods and their credits spread over large areas and over considerable stretches of time. Therefore, eighteen months was a short period in which to evacuate the posts. Third, the liberty of trade and travel across the northern boundary of the United States was a wise concession and would make for future understanding and friendship. Fourth, the payment of the debts was a sine qua non. No treaty could be had without that provision. Fifth, the prohibition on confiscation and sequestration of debts was helpful to the Americans as borrowers. And Jay observed that in all likelihood the Americans would want to borrow foreign captial for a long time. And sixth, the East India provision for trade revealed the good will of the English and the very limited provision for trade with the British West Indies was a considerable concession from the hitherto rigorous mercantile policy. But if this provision were unsatisfactory the whole matter of the West India trade might be reconsidered within two years after Britain's war with France should close.[1]

On March 1, 1796, President Washington issued a proclamation stating that Jay's Treaty was a part of the supreme law of

[1] American State Papers, Foreign Relations, I.: 503.

the land. Not until March 3 did he send the treaty to the House of Representatives for its action on the appropriations involved.

The House spent two months in deliberating whether it should or should not support the treaty. Two great constitutional questions arose. Could the House as a matter of right request the President to furnish the papers pertaining to the treaty? Was it a duty of the House to vote the funds necessary to carry into effect a treaty which the Senate had approved? When the request reached Washington to furnish the papers he promised to give the matter due consideration. He had no reason to fear the result which these papers might have on the House; but he declined to send them. He maintained ably that the House had no right to demand papers which he might think it improper to transmit.[1] Washington's letter settled once for all that whenever the House asks for papers they are to be furnished only at the discretion of the chief executive.

On the second question one of the greatest debates in the House of Representatives occurred. James Madison and Albert Gallatin maintained that the House could refuse the appropriation. Fisher Ames made the notable speech on the subject that the House could not and should not refuse the appropriation. His frame was marked and his spirit was broken by the disease which later caused his death, but Ames took the floor and poured forth his arguments and convictions in words that glowed with the fire of a great cause.[2] He changed a majority of six against the carrying into effect of the treaty to a majority of three in favor of the treaty. Rarely may it be said that a speech in a legislative chamber changes the vote of one of the members. Ever since the victory of Fisher Ames the House has voted the appropriations specified in various treaties.

Jay's treaty is justified on the ground that it was the best that could be had. Speculations deserve to be questioned; but in all likelihood the treaty saved the United States from a war with the British and the Indians at a critical period in America's history. Indirectly, it settled two constitutional questions.

[1] Washington, *Writings*, XI.: 115; XII.: 112. (N. Y., 1848).
[2] Fisher Ames, *Works*, II.: 37 (Boston, 1854).

The treaty did embarrass the United States with France, especially by including articles of food as contraband. But it speaks well for the diplomacy of the period that the United States with no army and no navy was able to carry to a successful conclusion controversies with both Great Britain and France.

BIBLIOGRAPHY

ADAMS, JOHN.—*Works,* Ten volumes. Edited by Charles Francis Adams. Boston, 1850–1856.

American State Papers, Foreign Relations. Volume I. Washington, 1832.

Annals of Congress, 1796.

JAY, JOHN.—*Correspondence and Public Papers.* Four volumes. Edited by Henry P. Johnston. New York, 1890–93.

JAY, WILLIAM.—*Life of John Jay.* Two volumes. New York, 1833.

JOHNSON, E. R. VAN METRE, HEUBNER, AND HANCHETT. *History of Domestic and Foreign Commerce of the United States.* Volume I. Washington, 1915.

MCMASTER, J. B.—*History of the People of the United States.* Volumes I. and II. New York, 1883, 1885.

SHEFFIELD, JOHN LORD.—*Observations on the Commerce of the American States.* London, 1784.

TRESCOTT, W. H.—*The Diplomatic History of the Administration of Washington and Adams,* 1789–1801. Boston, 1857.

CHAPTER IV

THE CONVENTION OF PEACE, COMMERCE, AND NAVIGATION WITH FRANCE, 1800

"Nor shall private property be taken for public use without just compensation."—FIFTH AMENDMENT.

Thomas Jefferson negotiated with France the first treaty to be approved by the United States Senate. This was the Consular Convention of 1788. The certificate of the exchange of ratifications bore the date of January 1, 1790. Jefferson occupied by the latter date the position of Secretary of State. Before the end of that year, December 8, 1790, Washington cautioned Congress about the disturbed situation in Europe. Gouverneur Morris became the American minister in Paris. He grew so charmed with the royal court that he even assisted Louis XVI. in his attempted flight. Upon the execution of the King the revolution assumed a European aspect, France declaring war upon Great Britain, February 9, 1793.

Americans felt an almost universal sentiment of gratitude to France for assistance rendered; and they were decidedly biased in favor of the republican movement. A liberal fulfillment of the treaty obligations to France would have drawn the United States into the war. In the cabinet meetings Jefferson espoused the cause of the French sympathizers and Hamilton led the opposition in favor of American rights. On the question of whether the change in the government of France had terminated the treaties, Washington decided that they were binding and that he would recognize the new republic by receiving its envoy, Citizen Genêt, then on the way. On the question of the eleventh article of the Treaty of Alliance, 1778, by which the United States guaranteed to His Most Christian Majesty against all other powers the French possessions in America, Washington decided that among nations the law of self-preservation is paramount and he issued his famous proclamation, April 22,

1793, which contained not the word "neutrality" but the genuine substance of that word. The conduct of the United States should be "friendly and impartial toward the belligerent powers." [1] Americans engaging in contraband trade would not be protected against the usual forfeitures. And the United States would prosecute all persons who might violate the law of nations.

Genêt landed at Charleston, South Carolina, on April 8, 1793, because of contrary winds; and yet his ship reached Philadelphia before he did. Genêt had brought with him two hundred and fifty blank letters of marque and reprisal; and in Charleston he issued four of these to privateers, which went to sea and soon returned with English prizes, some of them taken within the three mile limit of the United States. The British minister, Hammond, protested. Jefferson wrote a note to the French minister in which he emphasized that the arming and equipping of privateers in American ports, the enlisting of Americans for the French service against a friendly power, and the condemnation of prizes by French consuls constituted acts incompatible with the territorial sovereignty of the United States.[2] Several Americans who had enlisted were punished. The sale of prizes by the French consul in Philadelphia was stopped. A privateersman fitted out in New York was detained.

Genêt and the French consuls protested. They pointed to a decree of the home government which made French consulates complete courts of admiralty. Jefferson replied that the United States could recognize no such exercise of jurisdiction and that there was no basis for it in the treaties between the two countries. Genêt pointed to article twenty-two of the Treaty of Commerce, 1778, as conferring the exclusive right to fit out vessels of war and to sell the prizes taken;[3] but Jefferson retorted that the article expressly denied this right to the enemies of either party.[4] Genêt and the French consuls continued their obnoxious practices. In October, 1793, Genêt reported to his

[1] American State Papers, Foreign Relations, I.: 140.
[2] Ibid., I.: 147.
[3] Ibid., I.: 149, 151, 155.
[4] Ibid., I.: 154, 163.

government that he had commissioned and fitted out fourteen privateers which had taken eighty prizes. Washington had already decided to ask for his recall; and the French government complied with his request. The President revoked also the exequatur of the French vice-consul at Boston. Robespierre is reported to have said: "Genêt has made use of the most unaccountable means to irritate the American government against us." Rather than go back to face the guillotine in Paris, Genêt married a daughter of Governor Clinton and settled in New York.

Citizen Fauchet succeeded Genêt with instructions to ask for the arrest of the latter and to send him back to France. Jefferson declined upon reasons of law and magnanimity. Fauchet carried instructions also to disavow the acts of Genêt and of the French consuls which had infringed upon American neutrality and to open negotiations for a new treaty of commerce. But France was not the only belligerent which had compromised American neutrality; and she pointed to the fact that English privateers had been fitted out in Savannah, Philadelphia, and Boston. Indeed, the very ship on which Fauchet was to embark from Newport after his recall was searched by a British vessel within the three mile limit.[1] The baggage of Fauchet was ransacked, and a part of the papers led to the enforced resignation of Randoph as Secretary of State. Washington asked for reparation from the British.

James Monroe followed Gouverneur Morris as the American minister at Paris. Monroe won the confidence of the French and he dispelled all suspicions about Jay's mission to England. He endeavored to raise the embargo on American ships at Bordeaux, maintained, as the French put the idea, to protect merchantmen from capture by the British. He sought also compensation for the illegal captures of American ships and goods. The news of Jay's Treaty created alarm. The Committee of Public Safety appealed to Monroe for definite information. This he was unable to give. The French discovered quickly that the terms of the treaty granted the English an extension

[1] American State Papers, Foreign Relations, I.: 576.

of the contraband list and forbade the French to take the prizes captured from the English into American ports.[1] Monroe received instructions from home to defend the treaty; but he felt that he could not, and instead he encouraged the French to hope for a change of policy with the approaching presidential election. But the French Directory decreed that the alliance with the United States was at an end and that all goods destined for Great Britain would be treated as contraband. [2] And in November, 1796, the Directory recalled Adet, the minister to the United States.

Monroe was recalled and C. C. Pinckney was commissioned to succeed him. Just before Monroe's departure, December 30, 1796, the members of the Directory notified him that they would not receive another minister from the United States until redress had been made.[3] On his arrival in Paris Pinckney was not officially received and he was so unjustifiably annoyed that he went to Amsterdam. The news of this rebuff reached the United States after the inaugural of John Adams as President. He decided to send three commissioners to Paris to work for a restoration of mutual friendly relations. These were C. C. Pinckney, John Marshall, and Elbridge Gerry. They labored for six months without obtaining official recognition. Talleyrand granted them an informal and meaningless interview; and thereupon three men approached them who claimed to represent the Directory, namely, X, Y, and Z, later revealed to be Bellamy, Hautval, and Hottinguer. These three represented that an apology was due for allusions to the Directory made by President Adams in his address to Congress, that the United States should advance a loan of thirty-two million florins to France, and that the American commissioners should turn over pocket money to the amount of one million, two hundred thousand livres. The Americans protested that they had no authority to consider these requests; and they sought in vain to discuss the real questions at issue. Finally, Mr. X informed them directly that

[1] American State Papers, Foreign Relations, I.: 721, 728, 732; Monroe, *Writings*, II.: 347.

[2] Ibid., I.: 739, 741, 745.

[3] Ibid., I.: 746.

they were expected to offer money. The Americans replied that they had not a sixpence for bribery. Mr. Y replied that if nothing were done French frigates would ravage the coasts of the United States.[1]

The American envoys wrote Talleyrand a long letter reviewing the relations between the two governments.[2] He replied that two of the envoys were persona non grata to the Directory. On April 3, 1798, the Americans asked for their passports and for letters of safe conduct. Pinckney and Marshall, the Federalists, were subjected to discourtesies and left Paris. Gerry, the Republican, would no doubt have done likewise had not the French threatened immediate war if he did so.[3] He remained until August 1, but accomplished nothing for he had no authority to negotiate alone. President Adams declared: "I will never send another minister to France without assurances that he will be received, respected, and honored as the representative of a great, free, powerful, and independent nation."[4]

Relations in the United States with France were at the breaking point. American vessels and cargoes had been appropriated for French use without payment. French merchants and agents of the government refused to pay other obligations of indebtedness. A decree of July 2, 1796, provided that neutrals should be treated by France as they permitted themselves to be treated by Great Britain. This allowed a large amount of arbitrary power to the captains of French war vessels. Another decree of March 2, 1797, provided that enemies' goods on board neutral ships should be seized and that neutral sailors serving on enemies' ships should be deemed pirates. This meant that Americans impressed into the British service might be hanged at the yardarms of the vessel. The French agents in the West Indies issued several decrees directing the seizure of American vessels carrying contraband, or if destined for or coming from British ports. Indeed, it was under these decrees that most of the later spoliation claims arose. A few examples will indicate the char-

[1] American State Papers, Foreign Relations, II.: 158, 161.
[2] Ibid., II.: 169.
[3] Ibid., II.: 214.
[4] Adams, *Works*, IX.: 159.

acter of hundreds of seizures. The schooner "Industry," a duly registered vessel of the United States, sailed from Boston, June 1, 1798, for Surinam with a cargo of merchandise, owned by Marston Watson of Boston, a citizen of the United States. The schooner was lawfully pursuing its voyage when seized and captured on the high seas by the French privateer, "Victoire," was taken into the port of Cayenne, and there libeled, condemned, and sold as a prize. The sole ground for condemnation was that the rôle d'équipage, or list of the ship's crew, which she carried was signed only by one notary public, without the confirmation of witnesses. The total value of the venture was $18,555.[1]

The "Venus" was a duly registered American vessel of Wells, Massachusetts. On September 12, 1796, she was homeward bound from Port au Prince with a cargo of molasses. The French privateer, "La Republique Triomphante" captured her upon the high seas, and took her into Cape François where she was condemned because the captain had not provided himself with a sea-letter and an invoice at Port au Prince; it being therefore presumed that the vessel and cargo were English.[2]

The sloop "Martha" of Fredericksburg, Virginia, sailed from that port on February 15, 1795, with 630 barrels of flour for Fort Dauphin in Hispaniola. Off Port au Paix, the master went in his boat to inquire the state of the market. He was ordered to bring his vessel into port or take the chances of being fired upon. He appealed to General Lavaud, who insisted that the flour should be delivered for the use of the Republic at twelve dollars a barrel and that he should take in return coffee at thirty sols per pound. The master refused and asked permission to leave. This was denied him. At length he yielded and was then compelled to sign an agreement releasing the port authorities from responsibility. The price of the flour was lower than the market value and the price of the coffee was almost triple that of the market.[3]

[1] 22 Court of Claims, 3.
[2] 27 Court of Claims, 117.
[3] Ibid, 218.

The American registered brig, "Juno," left Charleston, November 2, 1797, bound for Santiago de Cuba with a valuable cargo of rice, flour, and beef. On November 11, the brig was illegally captured by the French privateer, "Malounie," taken into Santiago de Cuba, from whence the ship's papers were sent by the French consul to Cape François, where the vessel and cargo were condemned against the protest of the master that the capture and condemnation were contrary to the law of nations and the treaties between the United States and France.[1]

The schooner "Experiment" sailed from Philadelphia for Antigua. She was captured on the high seas August 5, 1798, by the French privateer "Deux Amis." A prize crew was placed on board, which robbed the vessel of a number of articles and carried away the ship's papers. At St. Eustatius the cargo and vessel were sold without any trial or condemnation. Later the tribunal at Basseterre condemned both as good prize on the ground that the rôle d'équipage could not be found among the papers.[2]

The "Commerce" left Newburyport for Jamaica in December, 1796. A French privateer met the vessel, fired a warning gun; the vessel hove to, and forthwith received a broadside which wounded four men. The schooner "Zilpha" left Tobago for Portsmouth, New Hampshire. She was captured by a French privateer, February, 1797, taken into San Juan, Porto Rico, stripped of her sails, rigging, and provisions; and the master and crew received orders to leave her. The ship "Cincinnatus" of Baltimore was taken on the high seas, March 7, 1797. The French tortured the captain with thumbscrews and promised relief if he would declare his cargo to be English property. He refused and was released with his vessel after being robbed of his provisions.

The "Maria" was registered at Portsmouth and was captured on a voyage from Tobago to her home port, taken into Guadeloupe where both vessel and cargo were illegally condemned. The "Statira" was also registered at Portsmouth, valued at

[1] 36 Court of Claims, 240.
[2] 49 Court of Claims, 393.

$9,000. She left Norfolk, Virginia, for London with a cargo of mahogany, logwood, etc., valued at $6,444. On the high seas she was captured by the French vessel "Hazard", taken into Nantes, and after several trials the cargo was unlawfully condemned, and the "Statira" herself was detained for two and one-half years at the end of which time she was sold to pay charges that had been levied upon her. So Thomas Manning, the owner, lost the vessel, the cargo, the freight, the expenses connected with the trials, seamen's wages, and the value of her outfits. The insurance on the vessel was $4,121.40. The net loss was $23,868.80.

On April 27, 1798, Congress passed an appropriation for arming merchantmen. Three days later a Secretary of the Navy was added to the cabinet. Other acts provided for the creation of a marine corps, the purchase of ships, the capture of French vessels, the suspension of intercourse with France, and on July 7, 1798, the abrogation of all treaties with France. President Adams appointed Washington "Lieutenant-General and Commander-in-Chief of all the armies raised or to be raised in the United States." And the President revoked the exequaturs of the various French consuls in the country.

The President proceeded to organize the Navy Department. He appointed Benjamin Stoddert as Secretary. Letters of marque and reprisal were issued to merchantmen, although their opportunity was small, for the French merchant marine had been swept from the seas. Ordinary merchantmen were authorized to "repel by force any assault" while acting on the defensive.[1] By March 1, 1799, three hundred and sixty-five private vessels had been fitted out with arms and acted under orders from the navy. The navy itself grew from almost nothing to forty-five vessels. Congress suspended commercial intercourse with France and her dependencies. There was no declaration of war on either side; but the American vessels captured French armed vessels, recaptured American vessels both public and private; and French merchantmen, their cargoes, and privateers were condemned as prizes in American

[1] Act of June 25, 1798.

courts. The total number of prizes taken was approximately eighty-five. Two of these were afterward given up under the treaty and about a dozen were released as being unlawfully taken. Yet no war existed between the United States and France. Talleyrand and Adet so held for France, as did the French prize tribunals.[1] The United States Court of Claims upheld the same conclusion in numerous cases.[2]

In the summer of 1798 Talleyrand assured William Vans Murray, the American minister at The Hague, that any envoy the United States might send to France "would be undoubtedly received with the respect due to the representative of a free, independent, and a powerful nation." [3] Thereupon, Adams appointed in due time, February, 1799, a commission to go to Paris, composed of Oliver Ellsworth, Chief Justice of the Supreme Court, Vans Murray, and Patrick Henry. The latter declined to serve, so Governor William R. Davie of North Carolina took his place. The three met in Paris early in March, 1800, just as the Directory was overthrown and the Consulate established. They were therefore presented to the First Consul, Napoleon, on March 8; but because of the illness of the chief French commissioner, Joseph Bonaparte, the negotiations did not begin until April 7, 1800, and they lasted nearly six months.

The American commissioners carried instructions to demand an indemnity for spoliations of American commerce. These claims were divided into two classes: first, the claims for spoliations that took place before July 7, 1798, which should be based upon the treaties of 1778; second, the claims for spoliations that took place after July 7, 1798, which should be based upon international law. When the spoliation claims were settled the Americans should then negotiate a treaty of not more than twelve years' duration. This treaty should establish a commission to pass upon claims between the two countries. They

[1] One exception is the "Concord," confiscated by the commercial tribunal on the Isle of France "because the United States and France are in a state of hostilities from July 9, 1798." 35 Court of Claims, 433.

[2] The "Concord," 35 Court of Claims, 432; Gray, Administrator, 21 Court of Claims, 340; Cushing, Administrator, 22 Court of Claims, 1.

[3] American State Papers, Foreign Relations, II.: 242.

should endeavor to exclude French privateers and prizes from American ports; and they should observe Jay's Treaty. They were to omit all mention of an alliance with France, the guaranty of French possessions, any semblance of judicial authority by French consuls, and all promises of aid, financial or otherwise.[1]

On the subject of the spoliations the French commissioners argued that there had been no valid abrogation of the treaties of 1778 by the act of Congress on July 7, 1798, because it required the consent of both parties to sever the compacts. They argued further that the hostilities engaged in did not constitute war in the legal sense; and even if war had existed the treaties were of such a permanent nature that war could not affect them. Hence, the treaties were still in force and would form the basis for the settlement of claims made by either party against the other. But, said the French commissioners, suppose that war had existed and that the war had annulled the treaties, then the war had annulled all claim for indemnity as well.[2] On August 11, 1800, they presented the two horns of the dilemma to the American commissioners: "Either the ancient treaties, carrying with them the privileges resulting from anteriority, together with stipulations for reciprocal indemnity; or a new treaty promising equality, unattended with indemnities." [3] The phrase "the privileges resulting from anteriority" referred to Jay's Treaty. The Americans refused to take either horn and proposed that the validity of the treaties of 1778 and the subject of indemnity for spoliations be left to future negotiations. In the meantime the treaties in dispute should remain inoperative.[4] This became the substance of the second article in the draft.

Other agreements stipulated in the treaty were: Restoration of public ships taken during the hostilities. Return of property captured, except contraband, but not condemned before the exchange of ratifications. Contract debts were revived. Vessels of the two nations, privateers, and prizes were placed on

[1] American State Papers, Foreign Relations, II.: 301.
[2] Ibid., II.: 325, 329.
[3] Ibid., II.: 332.
[4] Ibid., II.: 339.

the most favored nation basis. In substance the droit detraction and the droit d'aubaine were abolished. Debts should not be sequestered or confiscated in time of war. The rights and prerogatives of consuls were placed on the most favored nation basis. Contraband excepted, the ships and merchandise of the citizens of either party could freely go to the ports of an enemy of the other party; and such ships might engage in the coastwise trade of such an enemy country. As compared with that of 1778 the absolute contraband list was revised so as to omit the more antiquated implements of warfare, but there was no mention of a conditional contraband list; and it was specified that the vessel carrying the contraband as well as the residue of the cargo should be free. Free ships made free goods except contraband; but enemy ships conveyed their character to neutral goods on board except such neutral goods as had been placed on board before the declaration of war. The right of visit and search was regulated. Prize courts could sit only in the home country of either party. And the ports of either party should not become a naval base for the enemies of the other.[1]

The crucial article in the treaty was the second. "The Ministers Plenipotentiary of the two parties not being able to agree at present respecting the treaty of alliance of 6th February, 1778, the treaty of amity and commerce of the same date, and the convention of 14th November, 1788, nor upon the indemnities mutually due or claimed, the parties will negotiate further on these subjects at a convenient time, and until they may have agreed upon these points the said treaties and convention shall have no operation, and the relations of the two countries shall be regulated as follows:"

Before approving, the Senate expunged this article and substituted the following: "It is agreed that the present convention shall be in force for the term of eight years from the time of the exchange of the ratifications." The resolution of the Senate bore the date of February 3, 1801.

Napoleon Bonaparte, First Consul, agreed on July 31, 1801, in the name of the French people "to accept, ratify, and confirm

[1] Malloy, *Treaties*, I.: 496.

the above convention, with the addition importing that the convention shall be in force for the space of eight years, and with the retrenchment of the second article: Provided, That by this retrenchment the two States renounce the respective pretensions, which are the object of the said article." [1]

The ratifications were exchanged in Paris, July 31, 1801. In due time President Jefferson submitted the treaty with the additions made by the First Consul of France to the Senate, which body on December 19, 1801, declared the convention ratified and returned it to the President for promulgation. He issued his proclamation on December 21, 1801. "So died the treaties of 1778, with all the obligations which they imposed, and with them passed from the field of international contention the claims of American citizens for French spoliation" said Justice Davis in Gray, Administrator v. the United States, 21 Court of Claims, 387.

But the Convention of 1800 did much to suspend the tension between the two parties. Its success was of a negative character. It put an end to the hostilities, which, if continued, would have made the future acquisition of Louisiana improbable. And the convention relieved the United States of possible entanglements due to the treaties of 1778 and to the Convention of 1788; all three of which had proved troublesome during the previous decade.

The American claims against France up to September 30, 1800, may be divided into two classes. First, those which were the subject of the second article; and these by the action of the United States Senate and of Bonaparte were cancelled. Thereafter, the claimants could look only to the United States for satisfaction. Second, those claims which were the subject of the fourth and fifth articles of the Convention of 1800. These involved debts due for supplies shipped to France or due for preëmption of cargoes; and these involved compensation due for delays to ships and cargoes because of various embargoes and due for property captured but not condemned. This second class of claims was settled by the Treaty of 1803, when the United

[1] Malloy, *Treaties*, I.: 505.

States assumed them to the extent of twenty million livres as part payment of the purchase price for Louisiana.

As was clearly understood the claimants under the spoliations were barred from prosecuting their cases against France. And since the United States had obtained release from irksome treaties by bargaining away their rights, these claimants naturally looked to their own government for reimbursement. The first application to Congress for relief came in 1802. This was referred to a committee, which made a report of the history of the cases; but Congress took no action. Another committee made a favorable report in 1807, but Congress failed to act. In 1822 and 1824 both the Senate and the House committees reported adversely; the only adverse reports that have been submitted. The claimants thereupon increased their activities, which resulted in the publication by Congress of much new material in 1826. In 1835 the Senate passed a bill appropriating five million dollars; but the House did not act. A bill providing for the same amount passed both houses in 1846; but President Polk vetoed it. President Pierce did the same with a similar bill in 1855.* Finally, in 1885, Congress passed a law referring the cases to the Court of Claims.

The statute did not permit the Court of Claims to render a decision in the form of a judgment but in the form of an advisory opinion to Congress based upon the conclusions of fact and law. All petitions had to be filed within two years. These had to show that the claimant was of the next of kin of the original owner who must have been an American citizen at the time of the capture; that the vessel was not bound for a blockaded port; that she had not resisted search; that the owner had no contraband on board, and that the owner or his representative had made a protest before the court which unlawfully condemned the ship or the cargo. The statute made no provision for personal injuries, numerous as these had been; nor did it allow interest on the original claim.[1]

The lapse of nearly a hundred years had destroyed much evidence. In several instances there was no next of kin. Those

[1] 23 Statutes at Large, 283.

claims which could be proved the court reported upon favorably; which meant that Congress might or might not allow the money to satisfy the recommendations of the court. Even then the appropriation ran the risk of a veto, which President Cleveland applied in 1896 to a bill carrying a million dollars. So far Congress has made four appropriations in payment of the awards of the Court of Claims.

March 3, 1891	$1,304,095.37
March 3, 1899	1,055,473.04
May 27, 1902	798,631.27
February 24, 1905	752,660.93
	3,910,860.61

Since 1905 no appropriation has been made to satisfy an award by the Court of Claims in a spoliation claim although awards beyond a million dollars in favor of individual sufferers are awaiting satisfaction. The Court of Claims cleared its docket of all remaining French spoliation cases in 1915. The Attorney General stated in his annual report for 1915 that 6,479 cases relating to 2,309 vessels had been disposed of under the act of January 20, 1885. Out of the total number of cases 4,626 were decided in favor of the United States, leaving 1,853 decided in favor of claimants. It should be stated that the policy of Congress has been to exclude from the appropriations all awards in favor of insurance companies.

The opinion of President Taft on the obligation of Congress to pay the claims deserves to be quoted: "In my last message, I recommended to Congress that it authorize the payment of the findings or judgments of the Court of Claims in the matter of the French spoliation cases. There has been no appropriation to pay these judgments since 1905. The findings and awards were obtained after a very bitter fight, the Government succeeding in about seventy-five per cent of the cases. The amount of the awards ought, as a matter of good faith on the part of the Government, to be paid." (From the message of December 21,

1911.). Many eminent men in public life have favored the payment of these claims. Among them are James Madison, Edward Livingston, DeWitt Clinton, Edward Everett, Daniel Webster, Caleb Cushing, Charles Francis Adams, Rufus Choate, Charles Sumner, and Thomas B. Reed.

The constitutional provision upon which their arguments hung was the clause in the fifth amendment of the Constitution: "Nor shall private property be taken for public use without just compensation."

The other claims of Americans arising out of the international conflicts of that early period in our national history fared better. The claims against Great Britain up to 1796 were settled by a commission in accordance with Jay's Treaty. Henry Wheaton obtained recognition and payment for those against Denmark in 1830. Those against Naples were provided for by the agreement of 1832. Those against Holland for the preemption and condemnation of American goods and ships within her territorial waters during the French occupation were at the suggestion of the Dutch Government presented to France and paid by her under the agreement of 1832. The claims for spoliations under Napoleon after 1801 were presented for payment by the American minister, Joel Barlow, in 1812, during Napoleon's Russian campaign; and Barlow died on the return journey to Paris. Gallatin took up the task in 1816; and William C. Rives completed the negotiations in 1831. France agreed to pay twenty five million francs, or about one fifth of the losses suffered. For several years the Chamber of Deputies refused to appropriate the money. As a protest the United States severed diplomatic relations by recalling the minister, Edward Livingston, from Paris, which was followed by the withdrawal of the French minister, Pageot, from Washington. Great Britain offered her mediation and France took thereupon definite steps to discharge the obligations. The claims against Spain were settled under the Treaty of 1819 by which the United States acquired Florida.

BIBLIOGRAPHY

ALLEN, GARDNER W.—Our Naval War with France, Boston, 1909.

American State Papers, Foreign Relations, Volumes I. and II. Washington, 1832.

Bibliography in Boston Public Library Bulletin, May, 1885.

Court of Claims Reports, Volumes 21 to 50, Washington, 1886–1915.

HILL, FREDERICK TREVOR.—*The affair of X, Y, and Z.* Atlantic Monthly, April, 1914.

KING, GEORGE A.—*The French Spoliation Claims.* Senate Document No. 451, 64th Cong., Ist. Session. Washington, 1916.

SCOTT, J. B.—*The Controversy over Neutral Rights Between the United States and France*, 1797–1800. New York, 1917.

TRESCOT, W. H.—*Diplomatic History*, 1789–1801. Boston, 1857.

CHAPTER V

THE LOUISIANA PURCHASE, 1803

"The instruments which we have just signed will cause no tears to be shed: they prepare ages of happiness for innumerable generations of human creatures. The Mississippi and Missouri will see them succeed one another, and multiply, truly worthy of the regard of Providence, in the bosom of equality, under just laws, freed from the errors of superstition and the scourges of bad government."—ROBERT R. LIVINGSTON.

The welfare of the American settlers west of the Appalachian Mountains depended largely upon the free navigation of the Mississippi. For example, the whiskey insurrection in western Pennsylvania against Hamilton's excise taxes would not have occurred had the Ohio and the Mississippi been open. But the tax made the distillation of whiskey unprofitable; and the cost of transporting the grain to the eastern market consumed the value of the grain. The settlers on the Ohio and the tributaries of the Mississippi fared worse.

In 1790 Spain was on the verge of a rupture with Great Britain. Jefferson thought the time opportune to push the question of the right to navigate the lower Mississippi. Thereupon, President Washington nominated William Carmichæl, then chargé d'affaires at Madrid, and William Short, then chargé d'affaires in Paris, as commissioners plenipotentiary to negotiate and conclude a convention.

These commissioners received instructions to insist upon four main stipulations as a sine qua non of a treaty. First, the southern boundary of the United States should remain at 31 degrees latitude on the Mississippi and should follow the line eastward as described in the treaty of peace with Great Britain, 1783. The western boundary should follow the middle of the channel of the Mississippi, no matter how that channel might vary. Furthermore, Spain should cease to occupy or to exercise jurisdiction within the American boundaries. Second,

Americans should have the right to navigate the Mississippi in its whole breadth and length from its source to the sea, as established by the Treaty of 1763. Third, American vessels, cargoes, and persons on board should not be stopped and should be free from all dues whatsoever. Fourth, such rights should be allowed Americans on the Spanish banks of the river as to make the right of navigation practicable. It was included as desirable that a treaty of commerce be negotiated providing for free intercourse with the ports of Spain and with those of her dominions and for the extradition of fugitives from justice.[1]

The American commissioners met at Madrid early in February, 1793. Diego de Gardoqui had been appointed the Spanish plenipotentiary. He had acted in that capacity before and had repeatedly refused the same requests from the Americans. But the event which turned the tables against the Americans was the execution of Louis XVI. Spain declared war against France. The difficulties between Spain and Great Britain were adjusted and the two entered into a defensive and offensive alliance. Nevertheless, Carmichæl and Short proceeded to argue in accordance with their instructions that Spain had ceded her rights of navigation to Great Britain in 1763; that in 1783 Spain did not recall these rights which had been ceded to Great Britain; that in the same year the United States succeeded to the rights of Great Britain; and that holding the upper waters the Americans had a right to navigate the lower. Gardoqui replied that in accordance with international law the state which held both banks at the mouth controlled the river between them. Great Britain returned to Spain both banks of the Mississippi with no reservation on the right of navigation; hence Great Britain could not cede the right to the United States. And even if the British did have the right to navigate the river after 1783, the Americans could not claim such a right because they had lost their rights as British subjects by declaring their independence.[2] The Americans carried their appeal to Godoy, the chief minister, but accomplished nothing. Neither

[1] American State Papers, Foreign Relations, I.: 252.
[2] Ibid., I.: 260.

could they appeal to Great Britain for assistance because the relations between the United States and Great Britain could hardly be said to promote coöperative efforts in the period preceding Jay's Treaty.

A year later, August, 1794, the Spanish minister to the United States, Jaudenes, intimated to Edmund Randolph that Spain would negotiate with a minister of proper "character, conduct, and splendor." So in November, 1794, Thomas Pinckney was transferred from London to Madrid. He found the first minister, Godoy, anxious for delay, a natural course for Spain held possession of the subjects in controversy. The negotiations were to have begun in June, 1795. Pinckney waited until October 24 without receiving any attention. On that day he asked for his passports. Three days later he affixed his signature to the first treaty between the United States and Spain.[1]

The chief provisions of this treaty were: First, the boundaries to be established in accordance with the Treaty of Paris, 1783, that is, the 31st parallel and the middle of the channel of the Mississippi. Second, the Mississippi was thrown open to American vessels, and New Orleans was made a free port of deposit and transhipment of American goods for three years. The treaty contained provisions for the establishment of a claims commission, for a recognition of the principle of free ships make free goods, and for the exclusion of naval stores and provisions from the contraband list.[2]

On its face this treaty appeared to be satisfactory, but numerous troubles arose. The commissioners could not agree on the boundary line. Spain would not withdraw her troops from American soil until a decision should be reached whether she was to destroy the fortifications or not. And continuous annoyances occurred in connection with New Orleans as a port of deposit.

During the next five years appeared several ominous signs. Spain realized that Louisiana was a constant source of expense. The total receipts of the Spanish government at New Orleans in

[1] American State Papers, Foreign Relations, I.: 545.
[2] Malloy, *Treaties*, II.: 1640.

1801 amounted to 950,000 livres and the expenditures to 2,841,000 livres.[1] After the Treaty of 1795 Spanish commerce from the port of New Orleans decreased while American commerce greatly increased. In 1794 thirty-one vessels from the American seaboard cities entered the custom house and only twenty-three barges from the settlements on the Ohio. In 1799 seventy-eight vessels entered from the American seaboard and one-hundred and eleven river boats from the up river settlements.[2] To this increase Pinckney's treaty and the westward migration contributed their respective shares.

The Convention of 1800 between the United States and France bore the date of September 30. On the very next day, October 1, 1800, France by a secret treaty acquired Louisiana from Spain. The treaty is known as that of St. Ildefonso. According to it France should procure "an aggrandizement" for the Duke of Parma, the son in law of the King of Spain. This aggrandizement might consist of Tuscany or some other well rounded state which would increase his subjects to the number of one million. And the duke was to be given all the rights of royal dignity and the title of king. Six months after these details had been arranged Spain agreed to deliver Louisiana to France "with the same extent that it now has in the hands of Spain, and had while in the possession of France, and such as it ought to be in conformity with the treaties subsequently concluded between Spain and other states."[3]

The untouched resources of the Mississippi and the name of Louisiana appealed to the imagination of the French. Napoleon's ambition included the rebuilding of a colonial empire. In the Treaty of St. Ildefonso he had accomplished the first step. The signing of the preliminary articles of peace at London October 1, 1801, constituted the second step. The third step consisted in subjugating San Domingo. That island held the key to the rebuilding of the French colonial system in the West Indies and in Louisiana.

[1] Channing, IV.: 305, footnote.
[2] Ibid., IV.: 311.
[3] Cantillo, *Tradados de España*, 692; Malloy, *Treaties*, I.: 506.

In 1789 the combined imports and exports of the island were valued at more than one hundred forty million dollars, mostly sugar, coffee, indigo, and cotton. The population numbered six hundred thousand; less than forty thousand of these were white; and these held the economic and, therefore, the social and political control. Over five hundred thousand of the negroes were held in rigid slavery. The plantation owners had grown restive under pressure from two sources. One was due to the mercantilism of the French colonial system. Their exports had to be sold in France and their imports had to be bought there; and all goods had to be carried in French bottoms. But the greatest source of uneasiness sprang from the jealousy of the free mulattoes who had the conviction that a trifling difference in blood or color was an unreasonable basis for the social barriers. When the French revolution came these mulattoes claimed to own one third of the land and one fourth of the personal property and offered the revolutionists at home one fifth of their possessions if they could be relieved from the tyranny of the whites. The wealthy creoles of the island preferred death to sharing power with the inferior race, and therefore supported the Bourbon cause. The mulattoes supported the National Assembly. Both parties supplied themselves with arms. In the inevitable conflict the whites were almost exterminated with savage barbarism on a terrible night in August, 1791.[1] The slaves considered it a part of their newly won freedom to commit whatever excesses they pleased.

To add to the turmoil the Spaniards and the English organized bands of natives in the hope of thus conquering the island. One of these negroes in Spanish pay was destined for leadership and for becoming the instrument of defeating Napoleon's colonial ambitions and, consequently, of paving the way for the acquisition of Louisiana by the United States.[1] This was Toussaint Louverture, born a slave on the island in 1746.

Toussaint had the same abnormal physical and mental energy of Bonaparte; and he was always present where he was most needed. He deserted the Spanish service, joined the

[1] Stoddard, *French Revolution in San Domingo*, Chapter XI.

French, and quickly cleared the island of Spanish troops. The mulattoes hated him partly because he truckled to the whites and partly because of the strong support he received from the former slaves. At times he satisfied the demands of both the whites and the negroes at the expense of the mulattoes. Within two years, May, 1797, he held the military control over the whole colony.

When on June 13, 1798, the American Congress authorized the suspension of commercial relations with France and her dependencies Toussaint saw that the act meant a disturbance of the economic comforts of his people and possibly rebellion. He was the undisputed ruler of the island, owing only nominal allegiance to France. The combination of fear and ambition caused him to declare himself the "Bonaparte of San Domingo." He opened negotiations with the United States, assuring President Adams that if commercial intercourse were renewed American commerce would be protected by every means in his power. Adams asked Congress to modify the law accordingly and sent Edward Stevens as consul-general with diplomatic powers to San Domingo. Stevens assisted in negotiating an agreement, June 13, 1799, between Maitland, the British representative on the island, and Toussaint. Adequate supplies flowed in from the United States. By successfully laying siege to Jacmel he eliminated the French agent from the island. He then assumed both civil and military power; and he issued a constitution by which he was to hold power for life and to name his own successor. Bonaparte had to wait a year before he could imitate this step of the ex-slave; and he chafed under the comparison. Like Bonaparte again, Toussaint's power became his ruin.

The Treaty of 1800 implied that the United States must recognize San Domingo as a French colony. Stevens, the consul-general, foresaw difficulties and resigned because of ill health. Pichou, the new French representative in Washington, protested against any recognition of Toussaint. The preliminary peace of London removed the protection which the British had given Toussaint. "The gilded African," so dubbed by Napoleon, was isolated diplomatically. On December 30, 1801, Livingston wrote from Paris: "the armament, destined in the first instance for Hispaniola, is to proceed to Louisiana, provided Toussaint makes no opposition."[1] Napoleon intrusted the command of this armament to his brother in law, Leclerc.

Leclerc arrived with his ten thousand in San Domingo in the latter part of January, 1802. As instructed by Bonaparte, he stated in his first proclamation: "If you are told that these forces are destined to ravish your liberty, answer: The Republic has given us liberty, the Republic will not suffer it to be taken from us."[2] Bonaparte honored his victim with a personal letter in which he both flattered and threatened and closed with the following: "Assist the Captain-General with your counsels, your influence, and your talents. What can you desire?—the liberty of the blacks? You know that in all the countries where we have been, we have given it to the peoples who had it not."[3]

Toussaint knew intuitively Leclerc's mission. He offered the ablest resistance possible. In less than three months he swept away one French army and destroyed the industry of the island; the latter feat was an asset as a defensive measure, but it was also demoralizing to his followers. Several of his generals surrendered abjectly. And finally, Toussaint, betrayed on all sides committed the mistake of his life and surrendered, relying upon the honor of his captor. He died a captive in the fortress of Joux, near Besançon. Bonaparte directed the Minister of Marine to issue an order restoring the negroes to slavery and to prepare plans for the occupation of Louisiana.

Leclerc expelled the American consul, Lear, from the island, and condemned American ships that carried supplies to the opposing forces. These events together with the rumors about Louisiana made Jefferson suspicious. But Leclerc was to meet a new foe. Toussaint had disposed of 17,000 French soldiers. The yellow fever killed 7,000 more and struck an insidious terror into the entire French army. Leclerc sent such despatches as

[1] American State Papers, Foreign Relations, II.: 512.
[2] Adams, *History of the U. S.*, I.: 392.
[3] Ibid., I.: 393.

these: "Sacrifice six million francs at this time, Citizen Consul, that you may not have to spend sixty millions in the spring." "The rebellion grows, the disease continues." "I can reduce the the negroes only by force—and for this I must have an army and money." "These men may be killed, but will not surrender. They laugh at death; and it is the same with the women." "You will never subdue San Domingo without an army of twelve thousand acclimated troops besides the gendarmerie; and you will not have this army until you have sent seventy thousand men to San Domingo." Flushed with the fever which shortly took his life, Leclerc penned in his last despatch, October 7, 1802: "We must destroy all the mountain negroes, men and women, sparing only children under twelve years of age. We must destroy half the negroes of the plains, and not allow in the colony a single man who has worn an epaulette. Without these measures the colony will never be at peace." [1] Napoleon had already decided to abandon San Domingo.

The news of Leclerc's death and of the Spanish intendant's order denying the Americans the right of deposit at New Orleans reached Washington about the same time. The first indicated a halt in Napoleon's ambitions. The second was taken as a foretaste of what France would do. The ability of the French to control the Indians made Claiborne and the settlements along the Mississippi uneasy. Kentucky and Tennessee wanted war before Napoleon could fortify himself at New Orleans.

Jefferson wrote to Robert R. Livingston, the American minister in Paris on April 18, 1802: "The cession of Louisiana and the Floridas by Spain to France, works most sorely on the United States. On this subject the Secretary of State has written to you fully, yet I cannot forbear recurring to it personally, so deep is the impression it makes on my mind. It completely reverses all the political relations of the United States, and will form a new epoch in our political course. Of all nations of any consideration, France is the one which, hitherto, has offered the most points of a communion of interests. From these causes, we have ever looked to her as our natural friend, as one with which we

[1] Stoddard, *The French Revolution in San Domingo*, 334, 335, 342.

never could have an occasion of difference. Her growth, therefore, we viewed as our own, her misfortunes ours. There is on the globe one single spot, the possessor of which is our natural and habitual enemy. It is New Orleans, through which the produce of three-eighths of our territory must pass to market, and from its fertility it will ere long yield more than half of our whole produce, and contain more than half of our inhabitants. France, placing herself in that door, assumes to us the attitude of defiance.—The day that France takes possession of New Orleans, fixes the sentence which is to restrain her forever within her low-water mark. It seals the union of two nations, who, in conjunction, can maintain exclusive possession of the ocean. From that moment, we must marry ourselves to the British fleet and nation." In the same letter Jefferson instructed Livingston to broach to Napoleon the subject of the possible purchase by the United States of "the island of New Orleans and the Floridas." [1]

Early in 1803 Congress authorized the President to direct the governors to call out 80,000 militiamen and to hold them in readiness. Congress appropriated $2,000,000 for the purchase of the island of Orleans and adjacent lands. A considerable number of congressmen wanted to seize New Orleans outright and appropriate $15,000,000 for contingencies, but the moderate policy of Jefferson prevailed. Moreover, Livingston reported that Talleyrand had assured him that in Louisiana France would strictly observe the treaties existing between the United States and Spain. This report had a quieting effect upon the members of the two houses and especially upon those from Kentucky and Tennessee.

In order to palliate the opposition President Jefferson nominated James Monroe as minister extraordinary to aid Livingston in buying New Orleans and the Floridas. The Senate confirmed the nomination. And Jefferson wrote to Monroe January 13, 1803: "The measure has already silenced the Federalists here. Congress will no longer be agitated by them; and the country will become calm as fast as the information extends over it.

[1] Jefferson, *Works*, IV.: 431.

All eyes, all hopes, are fixed on you; and were you to decline, the chagrin would be universal, and would shake under your feet the high ground on which you stand with the public."[1] Monroe was appointed for the purpose of restoring political quiet at home rather than for the purpose of being of any material aid to Livingston in negotiating the purchase. And Jefferson had so explained in a letter to Livingston on February 3, 1803.

Monroe accepted the appointment. But not until March 2, 1803, when he was about to sail, did he receive the instructions.[2] For New Orleans and West Flordia, Monroe and Livingston could offer any amount up to $10,000,000. French citizens, vessels, and merchandise should be treated for ten years in this ceded territory on the same basis as American citizens, vessels, and merchandise; thereafter, the most favored nation principle should apply to the French. Frenchmen might have the right of deposit at New Orleans for ten years. The admission of the inhabitants to American citizenship would have to be left to Congress, but Monroe and Livingston could give the assurance that this would be done without unnecessary delay. The navigation of the Mississippi below the thirty-first parallel was to be free to the vessels and citizens of both parties, but "no other nation shall be allowed to exercise commerce to or at the same, or any other place on either shore below the said thirty-first degree of latitude for the term of ten years." The object of this provision was to give France the advantage over Englishmen and their vessels in the navigation of the river. There was no intention on the part of the United States to cancel Great Britain's right under the Treaty of 1783 to navigate the river above the thirty-first degree parallel. If France were to insist that her part of the cession from Spain be guaranteed to her, then Monroe and Livingston might as a last resort acquiesce. If France were disposed to sell only a part, then "the Floridas, together, are estimated at one fourth the value of the whole island of New Orleans, and East Florida at half that of West Florida."

[1] Jefferson, *Writings*, VIII.: 190.
[2] American State Papers, Foreign Relations, II.: 540

Monroe sailed on March 8, 1803. Spain had not yet delivered Louisiana to France. A few days later the Spanish minister, the Marquis of Casa Yrujo, informed Secretary of State Madison that the American right of deposit at New Orleans would be immediately restored. This removed the anxiety of the American settlers along the Ohio and the Mississippi.

Napoleon's expedition to Louisiana was to have sailed in the latter part of September, 1802. Marshal Victor had been given command. Laussat was to be prefect. The instructions to Victor gave the boundaries: "The extent of Louisiana is well determined on the south by the Gulf of Mexico. But bounded on the west by the river called Rio Bravo from its mouth to about thirty degrees parallel, the line of demarcation stops after reaching this point, and there seems never to have been any agreement in regard to this part of the frontier."—"There also exists none between Louisiana and Canada."[1] But the most important part of the boundary was that to the east of New Orleans. The instructions to Victor quoted from the treaty of 1763 by which Spain ceded Florida to Great Britain. Article VII of that treaty drew the boundary down the middle of the Mississippi to the river Iberville, and from that point down the middle of the river Iberville and of the lakes Maurepas and Pontchartrain to the sea. This gave New Orleans and the island on which it stood to France. The Iberville became, then, the eastern boundary of Louisiana. True Napoleon had bargained urgently with Charles IV. of Spain to have the Floridas turned over together with Louisiana and had offered Parma, Piacenza, and Guastalla; but Charles IV. refused and the Spanish minister, Godoy, would not permit the matter to be reopened.

Laussat reached Louisiana, but Marshal Victor never did. Napoleon's plans for reviving the French colonial empire had gone aground in San Domingo. He looked around for some dramatic enterprise under cover of which he might withdraw from a policy dear to the French. On March 12, 1803, Living-

[1] Adams, *History of the United States*, II.: 6.

ston witnessed a scene in Josephine's drawing room which left no doubt as to its meaning. Napoleon said to the British ambassador, Lord Whitworth: "I find, my Lord, your nation wants war again." "No sir, we are very desirous of peace" replied Whitworth. "I must either have Malta or war"[1] rejoined the First Consul. In the consequent alarm that spread throughout Europe, San Domingo and French colonial ambitions were forgotten. And it did not enter the thoughts of Americans that they might owe considerable to the dusky Toussaint and his five hundred thousand negroes who had fought desperately for freedom.

While Monroe was still on the ocean, Napoleon consulted with Talleyrand about selling Louisiana to the United States. Talleyrand did not approve. Napoleon consulted, thereupon, with his minister of finance, Barbê Marbois, who made his opinion that of his master. On Easter Sunday, April 10, 1803, Monroe left Havre for Paris. On that same Sunday Napoleon attended religious services at St. Cloud. That afternoon he had a conference with Marbois. He feared Great Britain would seize Louisiana as the first act of war; and he proposed to cede it to the United States. "I can scarcely say that I cede it to them, for it is not yet in our possession. If, however, I leave the least time to our enemies, I shall only transmit an empty title to those republicans whose friendship I seek. They only ask of me one town in Louisiana; but I already consider the colony as entirely lost; and it appears to me that in the hands of this growing Power it will be more useful to the policy, and even to the commerce, of France than if I should attempt to keep it."[2]

The next day, Monday, April 11, at daybreak, Napoleon summoned Marbois: "It is not only New Orleans that I cede; it is the whole colony without any reservation. Do not even await the arrival of Mr. Monroe; have an interview this very day with Mr. Livingston."[3] Curiously enough, it was not Marbois who approached Livingston that day but the astute

[1] American State Papers, Foreign Relations, II.: 547.
[2] Marbois, *History of Louisiana*: 264.
[3] Ibid., 274.

Talleyrand. In a letter of April 11, 1803, Livingston reported the interview to Madison: "M. Talleyrand asked me this day, when pressing the subject, whether we wished to have the whole of Louisiana. I told him no; that our wishes extended only to New Orleans and the Floridas; that the policy of France, however, should dictate (as I had shown in an official note) to give us the country above the River Arkansas, in order to place a barrier between them and Canada. He said that if they gave New Orleans the rest would be of little value, and that he would wish to know 'what we would give for the whole.' I told him it was a subject I had not thought of, but that I supposed we should not object to twenty million francs, provided our citizens were paid. He told me that this was too low an offer, and that he would be glad if I would reflect upon it and tell him tomorrow. I told him that as Mr. Monroe would be in town in two days, I would delay my further offer until I had the pleasure of introducing him."[1]

Livingston became insatiably anxious to reap the fruits of his labors alone, without the assistance of Monroe. For hours he waited his opportunity to see Talleyrand; and when he did succeed, that Prince assumed a coy attitude. "He told me he would answer my note," wrote Livingston to Madison "but that he must do it evasively, because Louisiana was not theirs. I smiled at this assertion, and told him that I had seen the treaty recognizing it.—He still persisted that they had it in contemplation to obtain it, but had it not."[2]

Monroe had arrived at St. Germain late Monday night; and within an hour after Livingston's interview with Talleyrand came a note announcing that Monroe would wait upon Livingston that night, Tuesday, April 12, 1803. On the afternoon of April 13, Livingston gave a dinner party in honor of Monroe. Marbois came and Livingston told him the news about Louisiana. Marbois said he had further information and asked Livingston to call after the dinner party was over. No sooner had Monroe gone than Livingston sought out Marbois. And in a conversa-

[1] American State Papers, Foreign Relations, II.: 552.
[2] Ibid., II.: 553.

tion which lasted till after midnight the bargain was virtually made; the first price mentioned by Marbois was 125,000,000 francs. Eager as Livingston may have been, yet he professed that the United States did not want territory beyond the Mississippi, that it was New Orleans and the Floridas that the Americans wanted. Marbois asked how much Livingston could give for the whole of Louisiana. Livingston replied that the United States could not and would not give a large sum. Both played the fencing game awhile longer. Finally Marbois dropped from 125,000,000 francs to 80,000,000 francs. Livingston told him that this was greatly beyond the means of the United States; but on leaving he promised that if the amount were made considerably less he would consult Monroe.

The exhilaration of buying an empire kept Livingston from going to sleep. Instead, he wrote a long despatch to Madison in which occurred the following: "The field open to us is infinitely larger than our instructions contemplated, the revenue increasing, and the land more than adequate to sink the capital, should we even go the sum proposed by Marbois,—nay, I persuade myself that the whole sum may be raised by the sale of the territory west of the Mississippi, with the right of sovereignty, to some power in Europe whose vicinity we should not fear. I speak now without reflection and without having seen Mr. Monroe, as it was midnight when I left the Treasury Office, and it is now near three o'clock. It is so very important that you should be apprised that a negotiation is actually opened, even before Mr. Monroe has been presented, in order to calm the tumult which the news of war will renew, that I have lost no time in communicating it. We shall do all we can to cheapen the purchase; but my present sentiment is that we shall buy." [1]

During the next two weeks Livingston did his utmost to reduce the amount. The first step toward breaking the deadlock appears to have been taken by the First Consul himself, who on April 23 drew up a project of a secret convention. This project specified that the whole of Louisiana should be ceded, that French commerce should enjoy all the rights of

[1] American State Papers, Foreign Relations, II.: 554.

American commerce within Louisiana, that the United States should allow the French six perpetual ports of deposit along the Mississippi; that the United States should assume all the debts due to American citizens under the second and fifth articles of the Convention of 1800; and that the United States should pay 100,000,000 francs to France.[1]

Marbois presented this project, but he was quite willing to substitute for it one of his own which he thought Napoleon would accept.[2] Thereupon, Livingston attempted to have the claims of the Americans settled by a separate convention, but Monroe did not approve of the plan. They then took up Marbois' project and each one of the American Commissioners drew a draft of his own, and each thought the other's was a poor one. The two agreed at last on the amount the United States could pay; fifty million to France and twenty million to American citizens for claims against France. Marbois replied that the negotiations would proceed only when the Americans had decided to accept eighty million francs as the price. Livingston yielded and Monroe did so readily. This occurred on April 29.

All the documents in the treaty bear the date of April 30, 1803, but the treaty of cession was not actually signed till May 2,[3] and the agreement on the American claims not till May 8 or 9. The negotiations appear to have been highly informal. No protocol was kept. And the writings of Monroe and Livingston furnish evidence that haste marked the close of the proceedings.

The introductory article to the treaty mentions that the motive is "to remove all source of misunderstanding relative to objects of discussion mentioned in the second and fifth articles of the Convention of the 30 September 1800 relative to the rights claimed by the United States in virtue of the treaty concluded at Madrid the 27 of October, 1795.—". With the second article of the convention of 1800 the treaty of 1803 had nothing whatsoever to do.

[1] Adams, *History of the United States*, II.: 40.
[2] Monroe, *Writings*, IV.: 12.
[3] Ibid., IV.: 17.

Article I contains a quotation from the Treaty of St. Ildefonso which constitutes the only description of the territory conveyed, namely: "His Catholic Majesty promises and engages on his part to cede to the French Republic six months after the full and entire execution of the conditions and stipulations herein relative to his Royal Highness the Duke of Parma, the Colony or Province of Louisiana with the same extent that it now has in the hands of Spain, and that it had when France possessed it; and such as it should be after the Treaties subsequently entered into between Spain and other States."

Livingston and Monroe had been instructed to obtain Florida, but neither of the Floridas was included in the purchase. Instead, they had acquired an area of vast but unknown dimensions to the west of the Mississippi. The American commissioners insisted at first upon defining the boundaries. Marbois took the matter up with Napoleon, who replied: "If an obscurity did not already exist, it would perhaps be good policy to put one there." He concealed a boundary which he had made definite in his orders to Marshal Victor. Livingston asked Marbois for these orders and for those given by Spain to the governors of Louisiana. Neither was forthcoming. He then called on Talleyrand.

"What are the eastern bounds of Louisiana?" asked Livingston.

"I do not know" replied Talleyrand.

"But what did you mean to take from Spain?"

"I do not know."

"Then you mean that we shall construe it our own way?"

"I can give you no direction. You have made a noble bargain for yourselves, and I suppose you will make the most of it." [1]

Napoleon and Talleyrand's cryptic replies probably meant that Spain in their estimation was already foredoomed to be conquered by the French and that what might happen to the Floridas so long as Great Britain did not get them mattered little. Livingston reported: "I asked him (Marbois) in case of

[1] American State Papers, Foreign Relations, II.: 561.

purchase, whether they would stipulate that France would never possess the Floridas, and that she would aid us to procure them, and relinquish all right which she might have to them. He told me that she would go thus far." [1] Napoleon gave a few days later oral assurance to the same effect. This much is definite; both parties realized that the Floridas were not included in the sale.[2]

But Livingston shortly convinced himself and Jefferson, too, by a piece of sophistry that West Florida had been included in the purchase. He reasoned that France had once owned nearly all of North America, and that the province of Louisiana included the Ohio and all the other rivers between the Great Lakes and the Gulf; hence, West Florida as well. This held true until the Treaty of Paris, 1763, when France ceded to Great Britain all of Quebec, the region around the Great Lakes and all of her claims to the land to the east of the Mississippi, Florida included, but with the exception of the Island of New Orleans. Almost simultaneously France ceded to Spain all of her claims to the west of the Mississippi. In 1783 the Floridas again became Spanish. So that at St. Ildefonso, when Spain receded Louisiana to France "with the same extent that it now has in the hands of Spain, and that it had when France possessed it,—" no one could deny that Spain had the right and the power to include West Florida; and apparently she had exercised that power. Spain, without knowing it, then, had receded West Florida to France; France, without exacting any pay for it, had implicitly sold it to the United States. All that the United States had to do was to step in and take possession. On May 20, 1803, Livingston wrote to Secretary Madison: "Now, it is well known that Louisiana as possessed by France, was bounded by the river Perdido, and that Mobile was the metropolis." And he continued: "Now sir, the sum of this business is to recommend to you in the strongest terms, after having obtained the possession that the French commissary will give you, to insist upon this as part of your right, and to take possession at all

[1] American State Papers, Foreign Relations, II.: 553.
[2] Ibid., II.: 558.

events to the river Perdido. I pledge myself that your right is good."[1]

Jefferson wrote to Breckinridge, August 12, 1803: "We have some claims, to extend on the seacoast westwardly to the Rio Norte or Bravo, and better, to go eastwardly to the Rio Perdido, between Mobile and Pensacola, the ancient boundary of Louisiana. These claims will be a subject of negotiation with Spain, and if, as soon as she is at war, we push them strongly with one hand, holding out a price in the other, we shall certainly obtain the Floridas, and all in good time."[2]

The second paragraph of the first article asserted that by Article III of the Treaty of St. Ildefonso "the French Republic has an incontestable title to the domain and to the possession of said territory;" and that the First Consul ceded the whole territory in full sovereignty to the United States. The American commissioners and apparently Marbois knew nothing of the pledge which Napoleon through his minister in Madrid, General St. Cyr, had made that France would never alienate Louisiana except to Spain. Nor did it concern the American negotiators that Napoleon afterward ratified the treaty without the consent of the legislative chambers and therefore omitted a requirement of the French Constitution. The American title to the territory was never questioned on that ground.

Article II provided for the transfer of public property and the archives.

By Article III the United States promised to incorporate the inhabitants of the ceded territory and admit them "as soon as possible according to the principles of the Federal Constitution to the enjoyment of all the rights, advantages and immunities of citizens of the United States." No separate act of Congress was thought necessary to execute this provision; the people of Louisiana by the above clause became citizens of the United States.

Articles IV and V provided for the delivery of the territory by France to the United States. The treaty was proclaimed on

[1] American State Papers, Foreign Relations, II.: 561.
[2] Jefferson, *Works*, IV.: 499.

October 21, 1803; but not until November 30 was the Spanish flag hauled down at New Orleans and the tri-color of France hoisted in its place. For twenty days did Louisiana remain under the jurisdiction of France with Laussat as governor. His act of greatest consequence consisted in the reëstablishment of the French legal system. On December 20, 1803, Governor Claiborne and General Wilkinson took over the province for the United States.

Article VI stipulated that the United States would observe the treaties entered into between Spain and the Indians until the United States and the tribes could make other agreements.

Article VII secured to French ships coming directly from France or her colonies and laden with French products and similarly Spanish ships coming directly from Spain or her colonies and laden with Spanish products the right to enter the port of New Orleans and all other ports of entry in the ceded territory for a period of twelve years on the same basis as American ships and merchandise. The commerce of no other foreign country was to enjoy these privileges. Article VIII provided that after the twelve year period the commerce of France should revert to the most favored nation basis.

Article IX stipulated that the convention providing for the payment of debts due American citizens under Article V of the Convention of 1800 was approved as if it had been a part of the treaty. Article X provided for ratification. The treaty was signed by Robert R. Livingston, James Monroe, and Barbé Marbois.

Another convention was entered into providing for the payment of sixty million francs by the United States. For this purpose the United States should issue bonds to the extent of $11,250,000 bearing interest at six per cent. The initial payment of the bonds was to be made fifteen years after the exchange of ratifications and the amount should not be less than three million dollars; and the payments were to continue annually thereafter.

A third convention provided for the payment of not to exceed twenty million francs by the United States to be applied to debts due by France to citizens of the United States as under the Convention of September 30, 1800. This sum could be applied to the debts specified in Article V of the Convention of 1800, which did not include any prizes condemned, or any indemnities claimed on account of captures or confiscations, nor did it include the claims of Americans who had houses of business outside the United States or who had entered into partnerships with foreigners. The sum did apply to claims for the delay of ships and goods captured, but which the French council of prizes had ordered restored; and it applied to debts contracted by France with American citizens.

Twenty million francs, or $3,750,000, did not cover the legitimate claims of American citizens by more than a fraction. No rule of apportionment was provided, consequently only the favored could be paid, which caused a great deal of criticism of Livingston on the part of those who received nothing. In addition the method of determining a claim and the mode of payment clouded the reputation of Livingston and even that of his successor, General Armstrong. According to Article VI of this claims convention the American minister in Paris should designate three persons to examine, without removing the documents, all the accounts of the different claims. And when these three persons should declare that the debt was due an American citizen and that it existed before September 30, 1800, then the American minister might draw an order on the United States Treasury, directing that the claim be paid. But Article X provided that the minister of the treasury of the French Republic should have supervision and final determination of every claim. This left the door open for all the venality and corruption possible in the French administration of that day. In addition the claims convention was an implicit agreement on the part of the United States not to press the claims of American citizens beyond the twenty million francs.

When Livingston had signed the treaty of cession, he rose and with tingling enthusiasm shook hands with Marbois and Monroe. "We have lived long, but this is the noblest work of our lives" [1] and, no doubt, the memory of his service on the

[1] Livingston, *The Livingstons of Livingston Manor*: 372.

committee which drafted the Declaration of Independence was clearly in his mind. "From this day" he continued "the United States take their place among the powers of the first rank—The instruments which we have just signed will cause no tears to be shed: they prepare ages of happiness for innumerable generations of human creatures."

Napoleon said: "The negotiation leaves me nothing to wish. Sixty millions for an occupation that will not perhaps last a day! I want France to have the good of this unexpected capital, and to employ it in works for the use of her marine."[1] The "works for the use of her marine" consisted in strengthening the French navy for a descent on the shores of England. Even in the failure of this object Bonaparte had the satisfaction of feeling that he had saved Louisiana from becoming a British province and that he had transferred whatever rights France had in New Orleans and in the region beyond the Mississippi to a power which would serve as a weight in the balance against Great Britain.

Spain felt outraged at the treaty; Godoy and King Charles knew they could do nothing beyond making useless protests to Bonaparte. Jefferson's first intention was that Monroe should go from Paris to Madrid to negotiate for the Floridas. Monroe did not go and the American minister at Madrid, Pinckney, failed to elicit friendly attention for the project. The Spanish minister in Washington, the Marquis de Casa Yrujo, opposed vigorously all American pretensions to either East or West Florida.

The treaty roused in the minds of statesmen at Washington an embarrassing number of constitutional questions. The party out of power had been unable to find any substantial grievances against the domestic policies of the administration. Gallatin's reduction of the taxes had brought an increase in the revenue. There had been few removals from office. The judiciary functioned well under Marshall. The chief cause of complaint by the Federalists seems to have been that Jefferson assumed more executive power than Washington and Adams had dreamed of

[1] Marbois, *History of Louisiana*: 312.

doing; and that the Louisiana purchase furnished the most alarming example.

Jefferson realized fully that he would have difficulty in harmonizing his actions with his previously expressed strict construction doctrines. Even before Monroe departed for France Jefferson asked Attorney General Lincoln for an opinion on what form the treaty should take. Lincoln advised that the treaty should not show that new territory was added to the United States, but that it should take the form of an adjustment of boundary with France.[1] As frequently happened, Jefferson wanted Gallatin's advice too. Gallatin wrote: "If the acquisition of territory is not warranted by the Constitution, it is not more legal to acquire for one State than for the United States.—To me it would appear, (1) that the. United States, as a nation, have an inherent right to acquire territory; (2) that whenever that acquisition is by treaty, the same constituted authorities in whom the treaty making power is vested have a constitutional right to sanction the acquisition." [2] Jefferson allowed Monroe to go to Paris free from any apprehensions about constitutionality; largely because he had small hope of acquiring even the island of New Orleans. Jefferson loved to tease the New England Federalists. Consequently, he honored the Boston Chronicle with the first news of the purchase, published June 30, 1803. Henry Adams, commenting upon it, says: "The great news had arrived; and the Federalist orators of July 4, 1803, set about their annual task of foreboding the ruin of society amid the cheers and congratulations of the happiest society the world then knew." [3]

Jefferson proposed to solve the difficulty by a constitutional amendment providing for a territorial form of government in the region south of the thirty-second degree parallel and reserving to the Indians the region to the north until another amendment should be passed providing for the right of whites to settle there. His object was to prevent Americans from scattering themselves

[1] Adams, *History of the United States*, II.: 78.
[2] Gallatin, *Works*, I.: 112.
[3] Adams, *History of the United States*, II.: 83.

over too much territory and thus by multiplicity of local interests endanger the union. He called a special session of Congress to meet October 17, 1803. His letter of August 12 to Senator Breckinridge of Kentucky, afterward Attorney General in Jefferson's cabinet, shows the mental processes of the President: "This treaty must of course be laid before both Houses, because both have important functions to exercise respecting it. They, I presume, will see their duty to their country in ratifying and paying for it, so as to secure a good which would otherwise probably be never again in their power. But I suppose they must then appeal to the nation for an additional article to the Constitution, approving and confirming an act which the nation had not previously authorized. The Constitution has made no provision for our holding foreign territory, still less for incorporating foreign nations into our Union. The executive in seizing the fugitive occurrence which so much advances the good of their country, have done an act beyond the Constitution. The Legislative in casting behind them metaphysical subtleties, and risking themselves like faithful servants, must ratify and pay for it, and throw themselves on their country for doing for them unauthorized, what we know they would have done for themselves had they been in a situation to do it." [1] Madison, at least later, held the same view.[2]

A few days later Jefferson received a letter from Livingston stating that he had reason to believe the First Consul might change his mind. Jefferson quickly changed his own and wrote to Breckinridge: "A letter received yesterday shows that nothing must be said on that subject (constitutional amendment) which may give pretext for retracting, but that we should do sub silentio what shall be found necessary." [3] Jefferson failed to find support for his scheme of an amendment, and he yielded to the opinion of the leaders within his party. Then too, Livingston's letters were filled with lack of confidence in Bonaparte; and the Marquis de Casa Yrujo protested that France had no right

[1] Jefferson, *Works*, IV.: 500.
[2] J. Q. Adams, *Diary*, I.: 267.
[3] Adams, *History of the United States*, II.: 86.

to transfer Louisiana, for she had not complied with the provisions regarding Tuscany in the Treaty of St. Ildefonso. In his message Jefferson threw the entire problem on "the wisdom of Congress."

The debate opened in the House first. On the question of carrying the treaty into effect Griswold of New York, a Federalist, argued almost identically in the language of Jefferson that the constitution did not authorize the acquisition of new territory; and, in addition, he pointed out that French and Spanish ships were to enjoy special privileges for twelve years in the ports of the acquired territory although the constitution prohibited Congress from granting any preference by regulation of commerce to the ports of one State over those of another.[1] John Randolph replied to the first point in the tenor of Attorney General Lincoln's advice to Jefferson that the United States had many doubtful boundaries, that the acquisition of Louisiana fell within the power to adjust a boundary, and that the proper organ for conducting these negotiations was the President. To the second point he replied that the favor given in the treaty to French and Spanish commerce in the ports of the purchase was "a part of the price of the territory."[2] Roger Griswold of Connecticut admitted that under the treaty making power and the war power the United States could acquire territory; but that such "new territory" and "new subjects" "must remain in the condition of colonies, and be governed accordingly."[3] Nicholson of Maryland replied for the Republicans by asserting that the right to acquire territory "must exist somewhere: it is essential to independent sovereignty.' And he pointed out that New Orleans was not a port within any State and therefore failed to come within the constitutional inhibition.[4] Cæsar Rodney maintained with him that the preference to New Orleans was indirectly a benefit to all the States and therefore a preference to none.

The Senate took up the debate November 2, 1803. That

[1] Annals of Congress, 13: 386, 432, 434.
[2] Ibid., 13: 434 ff.
[3] Ibid., 13: 463.
[4] Ibid., 13: 466, 471.

body had already approved the treaty on October 20, three days after the opening of the session. Several speeches were made to the question of carrying the treaty into effect. Timothy Pickering of Massachusetts was the first national figure for the Federalists to state his views. He affirmed that foreign soil could be acquired by conquest or by purchase and that such territory could be governed as a dependency. But the constitution did not give the President or Congress the power to incorporate such territory into the union; nor could an amendment lawfully effect such a purpose. Pickering clearly did not perceive it to be his business to help the Republicans out of their difficulties.[1]

John Taylor of Virginia followed. He began by regretting the enlargement of power by the federal government and the attempt to construe general phrases "so as to consolidate the States by degrees into one sovereignty." In purchasing Louisiana the United States had bought a foreign people without their consent and without the consent of the States, a wholly despotic act. But he recognized that the purchase came within the treaty and the war power. And curiously he came to the conclusion that Congress could provide for a government of the territory without an amendment to the constitution.[2] In reply Uriah Tracy of Connecticut made a point which reveals how vaguely citizenship was then understood. He did not doubt the power to acquire territory, but to admit the inhabitants to citizenship by treaty or by legislation or by constitutional amendment could not be done. Such an act would require the "universal consent of all the states or partners to our political association; and this universal consent I am positive can never be obtained to such a pernicious measure as the admission of Louisiana."[3] Breckinridge replied that the Federalists would hold the territory and the people as property of the government of the United States; but as such they might be used as a dangerous weapon against one of the States, and, therefore, he thought

[1] Annals of Congress, 13: 44.
[2] Ibid., 13: 50.
[3] Ibid., 13: 58.

it was more constitutional to admit the inhabitants to citizenship through the treaty making power. Evidently the Kentucky Resolutions did not haunt Breckinridge.[1]

Pickering's colleague, but not his friend, John Quincy Adams, believed that a constitutional amendment "amply sufficient for the accomplishment of everything for which we have contracted" was the rightful and legal way of solving the problem. And he believed that "the legislature of every State in the Union" would ratify.[2]

The bill to carry the treaty into effect passed the Senate by a vote of twenty-six to five. The House had voted for the same bill ninety to twenty-five. The vote meant that the largest transfer of territory by peaceful sale ever recorded had been accomplished, for without this bill the treaty would have been inoperative.

The next constitutional question that pressed itself upon Congress by reason of the purchase was: What power has Congress over the new territory?

An amendment was again proposed, but that proposition was rejected because it tended to show the incapacity of the United States to make the purchase. Another plan was to hold Louisiana forever as a dependency of the United States on the theory of an implied power of the federal government to govern what it had a right to buy. This plan conformed with the ideas of Pickering and Tracy. The third view consisted in treating the Louisiana Purchase in the same manner as the old Northwest Territory. In fact Congress adapted the Ordinance of 1787 for that purpose.[3]

BIBLIOGRAPHY

ADAMS, HENRY.—*History of the United States*, I. and II. New York, 1903.

American State Papers, Foreign Relations, Volume II. Washington, 1832.

Annals of Congress.—Volume 13. Washington, 1852.

CHANNING, EDWARD.—*History of the United States*, IV.: Chapters 11 and 12. New York, 1915.

[1] Annals of Congress, 13: 59 ff.
[2] Ibid., 13: 67.
[3] Ibid., 13: 1293.

FARRAND, MAX.—The Commercial Privileges of the Treaty of 1803. Am. Hist. Rev., VII.: 494.

GAYARRE, CHARLES.—*History of Louisiana*, 4 volumes. Third edition. New Orleans, 1885.

JEFFERSON, THOMAS.—*Works*. 9 volumes. Edited by P. L. Ford. New York, 1892–1898.

LIVINGSTON, E. B.—*The Livingstons of Livingston Manor*. New York, 1910

LYMAN, THEODORE.—*Diplomacy of the United States*, Vol. I. Boston, 1828.

MAHAN, A. T.—*The Influence of Sea Power upon the French Revolution and Empire*. Boston, 1898.

MARBOIS, FRANCOIS BARBE.—*History of Louisiana*, (translation). Philadelphia, 1830.

MONROE, JAMES.—*Writings*. Seven volumes. Edited by S. M. Hamilton. New York, 1898–1903.

PELZER, LOUIS.—*Economic Factors in the Acquisition of Louisiana*. Proceedings of the Mississippi Valley Historical Association, VI.: 109.

ROBERTSON, J. A.—*List of Documents in Spanish archives relating to the History of the United States, which have been printed or of which Transscripts are preserved in American Libraries*. Washington, 1910.

SLOANE, W. M.—*World Aspects of the Louisiana Purchase*. Am. Hist. Rev. IX.: 507.

State Papers and Correspondence bearing upon the Purchase of the Territory of Louisiana. House Doc., 57th Cong., 2nd Session, No. 431. Washington, 1903.

STODDARD, T. LOTHROP.—*French Revolution in San Domingo*. Boston, 1914.

TURNER, F. J.—*American Historical Review*, II.: 474; III.: 490, 650; VII.: 706; VIII.: 78; X.: 249, 574. Atlantic Monthly, 93: 676, 807.

CHAPTER VI

THE TREATY OF GHENT, 1814

"I only know of one principle to make a nation great, to produce in this country not the form but the real spirit of union, and that is, to protect every citizen in the lawful pursuit of his business."—JOHN C. CALHOUN.

Students frequently ask, Why did not the United States declare war on France in 1812 instead of on Great Britain? This attitude has an element of honest inquiry in it. And it becomes necessary to trace the causes of the War of 1812 in order to find an answer and to understand the issues that confronted the commissioners at Ghent in 1814.

The first of these causes was the impressment of American seamen into the British naval service. The British charged that certificates of protection to American seamen were frequently granted on fraudulent evidence by inferior magistrates and that British subjects who wished to desert the service of their country could easily procure such certificates. They pointed out that American as well as British judges recognized that a citizen could not change his citizenship at will but that the transfer required the consent of the home state. And this was no doubt true.[1] It must be acknowledged that after 1803 American tonnage increased about 70,000 tons annually, which required an annual increase of about 4,200 sailors; and of these Gallatin estimated that 2,500 were British;[2] either they were deserters or they had otherwise removed themselves from the British naval service. The chances of profit for the American shipowner were so great that he could and did pay high wages.

[1] See opinions of Justices Paterson and Iredell in Talbot v. Janson, 3 Dallas 133 (1795); that of Justice Washington in Murray v. The Charming Betsey, 2 Cranch 64 (1804) and in U. S. v. Gillies, 1 Peters' C. C. Rep. 159 (1815) and the decisions of Chief Justice Parsons in Ainslie v. Martin, 9 Mass. 461 (1813). Justice Story waived the decision of the question of indelible allegiance in the Santissima Trinidad, 7 Wheaton 283 (1822). See also Kent Commentaries on American Law, II.: 42. (N. Y. 1827).

[2] Gallatin, *Works*, I.: 335.

Jay had attempted in 1794 to incorporate in his treaty a clause limiting the practice of impressment. But Lord Grenville assured him that if Americans "had been impressed it was contrary to His Majesty's desire," [1] and, therefore, such a clause would be useless. Jay yielded and the impressments continued, Britain taking even Swedes, Danes, and Portuguese from American crews. In 1796 the American minister in London, Rufus King, presented a plan by which three classes of men should be immune, namely, native Americans, American citizens at the time of the treaty of peace, and foreigners other than British subjects. He defined a fourth class composed of British born subjects, who, subsequently to 1783, had satisfied the requirements of American law for citizenship, covering a period of five years, or who had sailed on American vessels for a period of three years.[2] Lord Grenville replied that such a method might lend itself to great abuse and lead to "the discharge at once of every British seaman on his own assertion, that he is an American citizen." [3]

Rufus King returned to the United States in the summer of 1803; and James Monroe was transferred from Paris to succeed him. He received instructions to limit his efforts to securing a treaty defining impressments, blockades, visit and search, contraband, and trade with the enemies' colonies.[4] Monroe informed Lord Hawkesbury about these instructions on April 2, 1804, and submitted a project of a treaty.[5] Monroe waited patiently; he saw one minister succeed another at the Foreign Office; and he observed that Great Britain took steps to conclude an alliance with Sweden and Russia against Napoleon and with the apparent intent to deal more rigorously than ever with neutral commerce. A year passed by and then Monroe spent another year at Madrid in adjusting boundary disputes with Spain. He returned and still the Foreign Office paid no attention to his proposals. In his despatches home

[1] American State Papers, Foreign Relations, I.: 481.
[2] Ibid., II.: 147.
[3] Ibid., II.: 148.
[4] Ibid., III.: 81.
[5] Ibid., III.: 91, 82.

Monroe urged resistance to British encroachments even at the risk of war. He recognized in France an able adversary to Great Britain and in the United States the only source of supply for many articles greatly needed by the English.

Due to the futility of the negotiations, the subject of impressments gradually dropped out of the diplomatic correspondence, but the practice of impressment grew by inverse ratio. British war vessels took their places off Sandy Hook, visited and searched every ship going in and coming out of New York, and impressed whomsoever they pleased. Impressments averaged as high as one thousand a year. Ships were left short-handed and some foundered in consequence. Exasperation grew among merchants and shipowners as well as among the families of the seafaring men.

A second cause for the War of 1812 was the rule of war of 1756, the purport of which was to deny neutral vessels the privilege of carrying a trade in time of war which had been closed in time of peace. Due to the mercantile policy of that period virtually all colonial trade belonged exclusively to the mother country. But the French and Spanish navies had been swept from the seas by the British. Consequently, France and Spain threw open to neutrals the carrying trade between themselves and their colonies, especially with the West Indies. They easily satisfied the literal meaning of the rule of 1756 by bringing the products of the French and Spanish West Indies into an American port, there paying the import duties, then transshipping the goods often in the same vessel to a French or Spanish port, and at the same time receiving a drawback on the import duties paid in the home port.

This device of the continuous voyage worked perfectly until the latter part of the year 1805, when the news reached America that the British High Court of Admiralty had condemned the ship and the cargo in the case of the "Essex." Sir William Scott gave the substance of the case in the following words: "It was the case of an American vessel which had gone from America to Lisbon, where finding the market bad she went on to Barcelona, and there took on a cargo of Spanish produce for the Havannah, under the direction of the agent in Europe, that she should go to the Havannah, first touching at Salem, in America, where the owner resided, who adopted the plan and sent the vessel on. It appeared clearly to the Court, that it was the intention, originating in the mind of an authorized agent, acting under full powers, that the vessel should go to the Havannah, and that this purpose was adopted by the owner; that it was in reality a continued voyage from Spain to the Havannah; that as to the intention all doubt was done away by the adoption on the part of the owner, who had the vessel in his own port, and was fully implicated in the engagement of sending her on, according to the projected voyage." [1]

The duties on the cargo at Salem amounted in this case to $5,278, but a drawback of $5,080 was permitted on exportation which made the real duty on the valuable cargo only $198. This and succeeding cases, notably the "William",[2] greatly curtailed the scope of American commercial ventures. A further extension of the rule of 1756 was made by an order in council, January 7, 1807, which forbade any neutral vessel to engage in the coastwise trade of France or of her allies. This prevented Americans from seeking the best market by going from one European port to another.

A third cause was the orders in council. These were dictated by British merchants and shipowners. The first one appeared on May 16, 1806, and it declared the coast from Brest to the river Elbe under blockade. On November 21, 1806, Napoleon issued his Berlin Decree which declared the British Isles in a state of blockade and rendered ships and goods going to or coming from them liable to condemnation. He did not enforce this decree against American commerce for almost a year. British merchants began to think that France and the United States had an understanding. Their effective advocate, James Stephen, had already published his "War in Disguise; or the Frauds of the Neutral Flags." He argued that America with her commerce aided England's enemies and that she should be treated accord-

[1] 5 C. Robinson, 369.
[2] Ibid., 385 (1806).

ingly.[1] The Chancellor of the Exchequer, Spencer Percival, drafted an order in council, approved November 11, 1807, which provided that American commerce destined for any region except the West Indies, Great Britain, and Sweden would have to enter a British port and take out a British license. This meant that no articles on the British prohibited list, cotton for example, would be permitted to enter the ports under Napoleon's domination. It meant that no articles from those ports could be taken to the United States. It meant also that license fees and taxes would have to be paid in British ports. In a sense Napoleon was right when he said that American commerce thereby denationalized itself and became British.

Percival's policy aimed to check American commerce and to stimulate English trade; only incidentally was it meant to retaliate for the Berlin Decree.[2] As an instance, the British Board of Trade in 1807 issued sixteen hundred licenses to enter the interdicted European ports mostly north of the Scheldt, but ports from Brest to Bayonne inclusive were specified in the licenses. From these ports the licensed vessels could export merchandise "to whomsoever the same may appear to belong," which words appeared in all of the licenses.[3] One of the best legal authorities of his day, Dr. Phillimore, stated that documents laid on the table of the House of Lords revealed "that upwards of fifteen thousand licenses were issued" in 1810 by the Privy Council, and that "forty-eight thousand foreign seamen" were employed in that year on the licensed vessels.[4] These vessels availed themselves of the so-called neutrals flags of Pappenberg, Kniphausen, and Varel. Frequently they carried licenses and papers from both the Board of Trade and the Minister of Marine in Paris and had them ready to show and to verify by oath as occasion demanded. Phillimore asked, "Is not Holland an integral part of the French Empire? . . .

[1] See introduction to Sir Francis Piggott's edition of "Stephen's, War in Disguise," London, 1917.

[2] Walpole, Life of Percival, II.: 280, 285, 287.

[3] See Phillimore, Joseph, Reflections on the Nature and Extent of the License Trade, 53, and copies of licenses in the appendix. (London, 1811).

[4] Phillimore, Reflections, 3.

Are not the Hans towns, Pappenberg, Kniphausen and Varel, precisely under similar circumstances? Are not the northern States of Europe . . . with the exception perhaps of Russia, who has no commercial marine, either the tributaries or feudatories of France? These mariners, then . . . are protected in their approach to this country, are convoyed to our very shores by our own fleets, are in the habit of receiving immense sums for freights from our merchants for the importation of enemies produce into our posts; and what is infinitely more alarming, are daily laying the foundation of a military marine, which will necessarily be under the influence and control of him, whose primary object is the humiliation of Great Britain." [1]

Thus the orders in council forbade the direct intercourse of American vessels with the countries under Napoleon's sway and left British trade largely open through the license system. These orders did not pretend to establish an effective blockade, but they rendered liable to condemnation any American vessel and her cargo that was destined for the forbidden ports. Englishmen themselves realized the suicidal effect of this clandestine trade with the enemy. The merchants and shipowners of Hull petitioned the Board of Trade to abolish the license system, which however beneficial it might be to them individually was pregnant with danger to the general interests of England. In addition to Dr. Phillimore, who published the first edition of his "Reflections" anonymously, such men as Alexander Baring, better known to Americans as Lord Ashburton, and William Wilberforce rose in the House of Commons and pointed out the danger to Britain of such indiscriminate issues of licenses and how war with America would be almost inevitable. But James Stephen and Spencer Percival refused to yield. British trade continued to increase as is shown by the following table.

Imports into Great Britain	*Exports from Great Britain*
1807—£25,326,845	£36,394,443
1808— 25,660,953	36,306,385
1809— 30,170,292	46,049,777
1810— 37,613,294	47,000,926

[1] Phillimore, *Reflections*, introduction v.

In spite of the orders in council the growth of British trade was probably more rapid than had ever been witnessed before.

Napoleon retaliated to Percival's order in council by issuing the Milan Decree, December 17, 1807. It declared that any neutral ship which submitted to search by an English vessel, paid any duty to Great Britain, or was destined for or came from a British port would be considered good prize. This decree became known only slowly among Americans. The more apparent and the more effective bar to their trade with the French dominions lay in the insolent British seadogs. To allay objections from the United States the cabinet modified the form of the orders in council, April 26, 1809, but the substance of the orders in council was not relinquished until two days before the United States declared war.

A fourth cause of the War of 1812 was the affair of the "Chesapeake" and the "Leopard." Early in 1807 a British squadron hovered outside of Hampton Roads for the purpose of searching American merchantmen going in and out and of making impressments. These British vessels came into port occasionally for supplies and at such times members of the crew occasionally deserted. On March 7, a whole boat's crew left the "Halifax." These deserters walked the streets of Norfolk with more security than did the British officers who met them and asked them to return. Four of these men enlisted on the American frigate "Chesapeake," under orders to go to the Mediterranean. The captain of the "Halifax" reported his grievances to Admiral Berkeley at Halifax. Berkeley did not wait to consult his superiors in London but issued an order that if the "Chesapeake" were met with at sea outside the limits of the United States a copy of the order should be shown to the captain and his vessel should thereupon be searched for the deserters. The frigate "Leopard," Captain Humphreys, brought this order from Halifax to the squadron off Hampton Roads June 21, 1807. It was the first time that a public ship of the United States was to be searched for deserters.

On June 22, 1807, the "Chesapeake," Commodore Barron commanding, started on what was thought to be her long voyage to the Mediterranean. No one on board had an inkling of an engagement unless it should be with the Barbary pirates after they had passed Gibraltar. The crew had never had a drill. The sick enjoyed the sun on the upper deck. Repairs and supplies cluttered the gun deck. As the "Chesapeake" stood out to sea the "Leopard" followed. But this caused no apprehension for it was the business of the British vessels to cruise up and down the coast. At 3:30 in the afternoon the "Leopard" bore down close to the windward, hailed, and said she had despatches for the commodore. Such conduct frequently happened as a courtesy, especially when a vessel was bound on a long voyage; and British vessels often assumed as their right the position to the windward. Commodore Barron returned the hail and hove to.

At 3:45 a British lieutenant came on board, delivered Admiral Berkeley's order together with a note stating that the captain of the "Leopard" would not presume to say anything in addition. Barron replied: "I know of no such men as you describe. The officers that were on the recruiting service for this ship were particularly instructed by the Government, through me, not to enter any deserters from his Britannic Majesty's ships, nor do I know of any being here. I am also instructed never to permit the crew of any ship that I command to be mustered by any other but their own officers. It is my disposition to preserve harmony, and I hope this answer to your despatch will prove satisfactory." [1]

The lieutenant left at 4:15. Commodore Barron ordered his officers to prepare the "Chesapeake" for action. The "Leopard" edged nearer. Captain Humphreys hailed and cried out that he was under necessity to comply with orders. Barron tried to gain time by saying he could not hear, for it would take half an hour to get his ship ready to fire. Humphreys repeated and forthwith fired a shot across the bow of the Chesapeake, another shot directly at her, and then three broadsides followed within pistol shot range during fifteen minutes. The officers of the "Chesapeake" conducted themselves gallantly and the

[1] Adams, *History of the United States*, IV.: 13.

crew behaved bravely, although there was, of necessity, considerable confusion. Barron endured the raking fire until he had been able to fire one gun for the honor of the ship. He then ordered the flag to be hauled down. The British recovered the four deserters. And Barron, disgraced, took the "Chesapeake" back to Norfolk to await orders.[1]

Mass meetings and newspapers throughout the United States condemned the outrage. On July 2, 1807, Jefferson issued a proclamation requiring all British armed vessels to leave American waters and forbidding Americans to have any relations with them. He requested the governors to hold their quotas of the militia in readiness. Madison and Gallatin favored preparations for war.

Canning at the Foreign Office did obtain the recall of Admiral Berkeley, and thereby roused a furious protest from English business men. To Monroe, Canning expressed himself willing to disavow the attack on the "Chesapeake." But Secretary Madison insisted in his instructions that, as a security for the future, an entire abolition of impressments from vessels under the flag of the United States be conceded.[2] This Canning could not concede, nor could anyone else in his place, for it would have brought a downfall of the cabinet. Canning sent George Rose as an envoy to Washington with instructions to condition his disavowal of the attack on the "Chesapeake" on a similar disavowal by Secretary Madison of the act of Commodore Barron in enticing British seamen to desert and in shielding them on board the "Chesapeake." [3] The consequence was that no disavowal took place on either side. But the fact remained that not since the battle of Lexington had the Americans received a blow which so united them in a national consciousness as did the attack of the "Leopard" on the "Chesapeake."

A fifth cause of the war was the American non-importation and embargo acts. Jefferson conceived and believed that he

[1] Niles, *Register*, I.: 49.
[2] American State Papers, Foreign Relations, III.: 183.
[3] Adams, *History of the United States*, IV.: 181.

might bring both the British and the French to a proper recognition of American neutral rights by an economic boycott. Both he and Congress had played with the proposition since April, 1806. After the "Chesapeake" affair Jefferson's conviction grew stronger. The non-importation act became effective on December 14, 1807. It barred British manufactures of leather, silk, hemp, glass, silver, paper, and many articles of wool from entry into the United States. But the measure appeared inadequate especially in view of Napoleon's intermittant seizures of American ships. Hence, Jefferson proposed and Congress passed an embargo act, December 22, 1807. It purported to hold American ships and goods in port indefinitely. A lack of public vessels and revenue cutters permitted evasions. Great Britain and France showed no signs of repealing the orders in council and the decrees. In fact, Napoleon approved of the embargo, for the British navy had been largely successful in keeping American ships away from his coasts; and he preferred to think that the United States had adopted his continental system. He went so far as to instruct his minister in Washington, Turreau, to propose an alliance. [1] In Great Britain prices of foodstuffs advanced considerably, but the chief effect of the embargo was to further antagonize the British. Secretary Madison instructed Pinkney in London to offer a withdrawal of the embargo if Great Britain would cancel her orders in council. Canning replied: "His Majesty cannot consent to buy off that hostility which America ought not to have extended to him, at the expense of a concession made, not to America, but to France." [2]

The embargo act recoiled most violently upon industry at home. The Federalists argued convincingly that the embargo cost more than war. True, citizens were not killed, but their productive power was paralyzed. The embargo threatened to bankrupt the government as well as the people, for the import duties fell off greatly. And the moral corruption caused by the measure was worse than that of war. Smuggling grew. Threats

[1] Adams, *History of the United States*, IV.: 310.
[2] American State Papers, Foreign Relations, III.: 231.

and acts of defiance against the government occurred. As an example, Amelia Island, lying off the coast between Florida and Georgia, became the center of an illicit trade of such volume as to arouse the envy of New York City. As another example, the Vermonters in April, 1808, constructed an immense raft of their surplus lumber on Lake Champlain, built thereon a ball proof fort, and placed on the raft their pork, beef, wheat, etc.—the whole worth over $300,000, bound for Canada. A crew of five hundred men defied the customs officers successfully. The governors of Vermont and New York had called out the militia to prevent its departure, but the raft escaped. Massachusetts under the administration of the Democratic Governor Sullivan openly defied the law by allowing coastwise ships to bring in flour, corn, rice, and rye. Jefferson took the governor to task; and Sullivan in reply pointed out the danger of insurrection. Jefferson conceded finally that the embargo might lead to war and asked Congress to authorize an increase in the regular army. His last important act as President was to sign a repeal of the embargo act.

Non-importation continued to pass through various stages, the most provocative being that under the Macon Bill No. 2, May, 1810. This law authorized the President to prohibit trade with the nation which did not repeal its decree or orders in council by March 3, 1811.

As soon as Napoleon heard of the Macon Bill he quickly instructed his minister of foreign affairs, Duc de Cadore, to write to the American minister in Paris, General Armstrong, August 5, 1810: "I am authorized to declare to you, sir, that the decrees of Berlin and Milan are revoked, and that after November 1 they will cease to have effect,—it being understood that in consequence of this declaration the English are to revoke their orders in council, and renounce the new principles of blockade which they have wished to establish; or that the United States will conformably to the act you have just communicated, cause their rights to be respected by the English." [1]

Madison accepted Cadore's letter as proof that the decrees

[1] American State Papers, Foreign Relations, III.: 386.

had been repealed. He may have suspected the wiliness of Napoleon's diplomacy, but he chose to refrain from expressing the thought that Napoleon meant to condition the repeal of the decrees on the cancellation of the orders in council by the British. On November 2, 1810, Madison issued a proclamation stating: "It has been officially made known to this Government that the edicts of France, violating the neutral commerce of the United States, have been so revoked as to cease to have effect on the first of the present month." [1] On the same day Gallatin issued an order to the collectors of customs providing for the cessation of commercial intercourse with Great Britain on and after February 2, 1811. Hundreds of American vessels willingly assumed the risk of capture by the British and set sail for France.

Napoleon received the news of Madison's proclamation with surprise and pleasure. At last the United States had adopted for itself his continental system. He had not repealed his decrees. Pending developments he permitted American vessels to obtain licenses for trade with France proper. He did nothing to make amends for past seizures. And he continued to sequester ship after ship on one pretext or another. Then, to perplex the Americans about his intentions, he would allow individual vessels to discharge their cargo on the condition that they would export its value in "national merchandise, of which two-thirds will be in silk." [2]

In Great Britain, Lord Wellesley, brother of the Duke of Wellington, had succeeded Canning at the Foreign Office. When Pinkney asked that the orders in council be repealed on the ground that Napoleon had revoked his decrees and that, therefore, retaliation would be no longer necessary, Wellesley replied that he could find no evidence that Napoleon had revoked his decrees and expressed a willingness to receive what information Pinkney had. Pinkney could furnish only the President's proclamation. By January 14, 1811, Pinkney's patience gave out. He asked for an audience of leave on the ground that after

[1] Richardson, *Messages*, I.: 482.
[2] American State Papers, Foreign Relations, III.: 505.

the lapse of many months Great Britain had taken no steps to send a minister to the United States. Wellesley wrote him a private letter announcing that A. J. Foster would be immediately gazetted as minister to the United States. Pinkney replied in an official note and therein presumed to ask, without waiting for instructions from home, what Mr. Foster was to do in Washington; whether the orders in council would be cancelled, the paper blockades be annulled, and the affair of the "Chesapeake" settled in accordance with American wishes.[1] Lord Wellesley replied by private letter that Great Britain could not yield. Pinkney thereupon renewed his request for an audience of leave on February 28, 1811, which the Prince Regent conceded.

A sixth cause of the war consisted in the trouble the American frontiersmen were having with the Indians in the North West. It is now clear that these troubles, including the battle of Tippecanoe, were due largely to the land hunger of the pioneers rather than to Indian hostility infused by the British.[2] But the Americans believed otherwise and their belief determined their actions.

A seventh cause of the war consisted in the peculiar character of the diplomats and of the diplomacy of the time. Napoleon was the shiftiest diplomat of his day if not of his century. He enforced the Berlin and Milan Decrees whenever such action promoted his interest. The Bayonne Decree of April, 1808, ordered the confiscation of all American vessels arriving in France. Napoleon issued and enforced it on the nice pretext that the Embargo Act permitted no American vessel lawfully to leave port, therefore, ships and cargoes entering French ports claiming to be American, had to be considered as British. The most atrocious of his decrees, that of Rambouillet, secretly issued, March 23, 1810, and published May 14, 1810, covered the seizure of American vessels in Portuguese, Spanish, Dutch, and Italian ports. But Macon's Bill, No. 2 passed Congress that same month, May, 1810. And when Napoleon heard of it he

[1] American State Papers, Foreign Relations, III.: 414.
[2] Adams, *History of the United States*. VI.: chapters 4 and 5.

scored through Cadore's letter a diplomatic victory. Whenever his seizures threatened a rupture with the United States he would either change his tactics or tatalizingly dangle the possibility of ceding Florida to the United States, a golden apple very much desired by both Jefferson and Madison.

Pinkney took his departure from London in February, 1811. At no time was America more in need of a minister at the Court of St. James than during the next sixteen months. And yet no one can have any feeling but admiration for Pinkney. He had done his utmost during five years. As an interpreter of political events and as a negotiator he had to match both Canning and Wellesley and he did. [1]

The British diplomats in Washington conducted themselves with a consciousness that the United States lay at the mercy of the British navy. Erskine forgot it temporarily by placing a conciliatory interpretation upon his instructions from Canning, which brought his peremptory recall and a prompt repudiation of the agreement to revoke the orders in council he had reached with President Madison. Francis James Jackson succeeded Erskine. Canning instructed him to point out that "The American government cannot have believed that such an arrangement as Mr. Erskine consented to accept was conformable to his instructions." This imputation of bad faith was one which Madison only had a full warrant to make. Jackson had applied for the mission to Washington. He had been successful on similar occassions before. It was he who carried the demand to the Danish Prince Royal at Kiel to deliver the fleet which led to the bombardment of Copenhagen in September of 1807. Even King George III thought the manner of presenting that demand deserved a rebuke. When Jackson was presented at court on his return the King asked: "Was the Prince Royal upstairs or down, when he received you?" "He was on the ground floor," replied Jackson. "I am glad of it! I am glad of it! for if he had half the spirit of his uncle George III, he would have infallibly kicked you down stairs." [2]

[1] See Wheaton, *Life, Writings, etc., of William Pinkney.*
[2] Adams, *History of the United States*, IV.: 65.

According to his instructions, Jackson charged the American government with fraud. His insolence brought out the fine temper of President Madison who mentioned that when Great Britain refused to fulfill her pledge a formal and frank disclosure of her reasons became her duty and that the United States had a right to look to Jackson for this disclosure.[1] Jackson fenced at first and then sulked. Finally, Madison instructed the Secretary of State to inform Jackson that no further communication would be received from him, November 8, 1809. From this time until the arrival of Foster, July 2, 1811, Great Britain had no minister in Washington. Beyond making the tardy disavowal for the attack on the "Chesapeake," November 1, 1811, Foster could do nothing but express diplomatic threats.

The younger element in the Congress that met in December, 1811, felt that their country had been humiliated long enough. Impressments, the captures off the American coast, the rule of war of 1756, the orders in council, the "Chesapeake," Jackson's haughty diplomacy, the return of Pinkney, the Indian troubles, all flamed the desire for war. Madison, Monroe, and Gallatin had no well defined plan. This made it all the easier for the "war hawks," Henry Clay of Kentucky, John C. Calhoun of South Carolina, Peter B. Porter of New York and Felix Grundy of Tennessee, to assume the leadership. They advocated redress for wrongs endured, and they wanted to incorporate Canada and the Floridas. They assumed the Floridas to be under British control. No one struck the keynote better than Calhoun in his first set speech before the House, December 12, 1811. "Sir, I only know of one principle to make a nation great, to produce in this country not the form but the real spirit of union; and that is to protect every citizen in the lawful pursuit of his business. He will then feel that he is backed by the Government; that its arm is his arms; and will rejoice in its increased strength and prosperity. Protection and patriotism are reciprocal."[2]

Congress declared war June 18, 1812. Aside from Perry's victory on Lake Erie, September 10, 1813, and Jackson's victory

[1] American State Papers, Foreign Relations, III.: 311.
[2] Annals of Congress, 23.: 479.

at New Orleans after the treaty of peace had been signed, no outstanding action of signal credit to either side could be boasted. British and Americans grew to know each other better in war than they had in peace. British contempt for American seamanship changed to respect. Michæl Scott of Glasgow, who wrote from first hand knowledge as a lieutenant in the British navy, expressed this sentiment best in his Tom Cringles' Log: "I don't like Americans, I never did and never shall like them. I have seldom met an American gentleman in the large and complete sense of the term. I have no wish to eat with them, drink with them, deal with or consort with them in any way; but let me tell the whole truth,—nor fight with them, were it not for the laurels to be acquired by overcoming an enemy so brave, determined, alert, and every way so worthy of one's steel as they have always proved."[1] Again Scott said: "In the field or grappling in mortal combat on the blood-slippery quarter-deck of an enemy's vessel, a British soldier or sailor is the bravest of the brave. No soldier or sailor of any other country, saving and excepting those damned Yankees, can stand against them."

In the Revolution the American struggle brought on a European war. In 1812 the Americans were drawn into a European war. Russia had become the ally of Great Britain; and Czar Alexander disliked the American war because it weakened England at the moment when Russia was about to be invaded by Napoleon and his armies. Four months after the United States had declared war Alexander prepared to offer mediation. The offer reached Secretary Monroe on March 8, 1813. Madison directed Monroe to accept the offer promptly; and they assumed that the offer would not have been made without the consent of Great Britain. They consulted Jefferson and decided to appoint a commission to go to St. Petersburg for the negotiations. John Quincy Adams was already there as American minister. Albert Gallatin and James A. Bayard, a Federalist from Delaware, were the other members. While Gallatin and Bayard were on their voyage Lord Castlereagh

[1] *Tom Cringle's Log*: 179, (New York, 1895).

came to the conclusion to reject the Czar's offer of mediation. Consequently, the American commission waited in St. Petersburg from July, 1813, to January, 1814.

Czar Alexander renewed the tender of his good offices. Castlereagh declined again to accept them on the ground that the dispute with America invoked domestic questions, but he announced his willingness to negotiate directly with the Americans. He suggested London or Gottenburg as the place of meeting. President Madison appointed a new commission composed of J. Q. Adams, J. A. Bayard, Henry Clay, and Jonathan Russell. Madison omitted Gallatin on the assumption that he was on his way home to resume his duties at the Treasury. Gallatin had, however, gone to London to facilitate the opening of direct negotiations; and on hearing of it Madison quickly appointed Gallatin a member of the commission. Clay and Russell sailed for Gottenburg. Gallatin preferred London because the commission could meet personally the Secretary of State for Foreign Affairs and because Gallatin knew several of the leading men. But Clay and Adams refused to sit in London, stating that "they were plain Americans and that in England they would only be snubbed and treated as colonists." [1] They compromised on Ghent, where the Americans waited long and impatiently for the British delegates to arrive.

On March 8, 1813, the United States had accepted the Russian offer of mediation and shortly afterward appointed a commission. One year and five months later the three British commissioners reached Ghent. It was Lord Gambier's first venture in diplomacy; he had been an officer in the navy. Henry Goulburn was Under-Secretary of State for the Colonies; and it was his first essay in foreign affairs. And William Adams, an admiralty lawyer, was the third, whose chief claim to fame was that he served on this commission.

They were instructed to insist on the rule of uti possidetis as the starting point of the negotiation. This point furnished the key to the lengthy delays by the British. Napoleon had been beaten in his Russian campaign of 1812–13. And at Leipzig,

[1] *Diary of James Gallatin*: 21.

October, 1813, he received such a crushing defeat that he felt compelled to abdicate and retire to the island of Elba under the provisions of the first peace of Paris, May 13, 1814. Great Britain was thus left largely free to prosecute the war against the United States. She had sent Wellington's brother in law, Pakenham, with a fine body of veterans from the campaign in Portugal and Spain to take New Orleans. General Ross with his army had good chances of success against Baltimore and Washington. Sir George Prevost in Canada was receiving large reinforcements; and it was expected that a large part of Maine, New Hampshire, Vermont, New York, and the territory to the south of the Great Lakes would be added to Canada by this principle of military possession. Having obtained a recognition by the Americas of the rule of uti possidetis, the English commissioners were to stipulate that the Northwest Territory should be set aside as a state for the Indian tribes; this state would serve the advantage of a buffer state as well. And the inshore fisheries off the Canadian and Newfoundland coasts were to be considered as forfeited by the war.[1]

The American commissioners received their instructions in two groups: those of April 15 and 27, 1813, and those of January 28 and 30, February 10 and 14, and March 22, 1814. The instructions of April 15, 1813 stated that as soon as Great Britain would give assurance that she had abandoned the principles of impressment and of paper blockades the United States would order a cessation of hostilities. The definition of a blockade announced by Great Britain in 1803 was held to be satisfactory: "that no blockade would be legal, which was not supported by an adequate force . . ." Other points of less importance stressed a recognition of the right to trade with the colonies of an enemy of Great Britain, and agreement upon regulations for visit and search, restriction on the list of contraband goods, prohibition on British trade with the Indians on American soil, and a stipulation that the increase of American naval power on the Great Lakes would meet with no objection from Great Britain. There was also to be a mutual restoration of occupied territory, and an

[1] Castlereagh, *Memoirs and Correspondence*, X.: 67.

effort to obtain all of Canada.[1] Secretary Monroe's letter of April 27, 1813, instructed the commissioners that if the subject of claims to Florida should enter the discussions the claim to West Florida should be based on the cession from France in 1803 and that to East Florida on the right to indemnity for spoliations.[2] The express relinquishment of impressments was a sine qua non.[3]

In the second group of instructions, beginning with the letter of January 28, 1814, Monroe stated that there had been no change in American sentiment on impressments. "Our flag must protect the crew" he said. Sailors already impressed should be paid the wages by Great Britain which they would have earned on American merchantmen. Slaves seized by the British forces should be either returned or paid for. He pointed out that it would do away with friction and conform with the best interests of both parties for Great Britain to cede all of Canada to the United States.[4]

The instruction of January 30, 1814, mentioned that Great Britain had condemned the American vessels and cargoes in her ports at the opening of the war, while the United States had given British vessels six months in which to withdraw. Compensation by Great Britain should therefore be conceded in the treaty.[5] In a letter dated February 10, 1814, Monroe receded somewhat from his firm stand on a recognition of neutral rights and permitted the commissioners to agree to a provision that the United States in the matter of neutral rights should be given most favored nation treatment.[6] On February 14, 1814, Monroe grew concerned about impressments again, fearing no doubt that the provision for most favored nation treatment in the previous despatch was too general. He wanted an express renunciation of impressment by Great Britain. He wrote: "To withdraw from the war without it, would be to subject the

[1] American State Papers, Foreign Relations, III.: 695.
[2] Gallatin, *Writings*, I.: 539.
[3] Ibid., I.: 542.
[4] American State Papers, Foreign Relations, III.: 701; see Updyke, Diplomacy of the War of 1812: 178.
[5] American State Papers, Foreign Relations, III.: 702.
[6] Ibid., III.: 703.

United States to all the expense in blood and treasure which has been and may be incurred without obtaining the security for which we have contended. . . ." And in the last letter, March 22, 1814, Monroe revealed concern not about a possible failure to acquire Canada but about the claims which the British might make to the territory south of the then northern boundary of the United States. And under no pretext were the American commissioners to yield or to recognize British claims to the Pacific coast near the Columbia River.[1]

The two commissions met at one o'clock in the Hotel des Pays-Bas on August 8, 1814. The members exchanged their full powers. Lord Gambier made the opening speech in which he hoped for a restoration of amicable relations. John Quincy Adams responded with a disposition to reciprocate every sentiment of candor and conciliation. Henry Goulburn then rose and indicated the four points upon which the British commissioners had been instructed. 1. Impressment involved the claim of His Britannic Majesty to the allegiance of all the native subjects of Great Britain. 2. Peace with the Indians should be included and a definite boundary agreed upon for their territory. This point Goulburn made a sine qua non. 3. The boundary between the United States and the adjacent British colonies should be revised; and 4, The fishing privileges of the United States within British jurisdiction would not be renewed without an equivalent.[2]

Adams asked whether the British government thought it proper to discuss impressment and British allegiance. Goulburn replied that his government did not think it necessary but had included the point as one likely to arise. Bayard asked what their intention was in revising the boundary. Goulburn said they did not have in mind the acquisition of territory but the removal of causes for dispute. Adams reviewed each point and asked permission to confer with his colleagues before making a reply. Goulburn wanted an immediate answer as to whether the American instructions permitted negotiations on a separate

[1] Updyke, *Diplomacy of the War of 1812*: 185.
[2] American State Papers, Foreign Relations, III.: 705.

territory for the Indians. Adams perferred not to reply; whereupon the conference adjourned until eleven o'clock the next day.[1]

The point about a separate territory for the Indians had considerable significance for the British, because the fur trade with them had averaged before the war £250,000 in value annually. The interest in the British American inshore fisheries had grown greatly during the war; and the people of Nova Scotia had petitioned Lord Bathurst to have the Americans excluded in the forthcoming treaty.

When the Americans reached their rooms they found two despatches from Secretary Monroe, dated June 25 and 27, directing the commissioners to refuse to allow the fisheries to be brought into the discussion, and, if they found it necessary, to omit impressments altogether from the treaty. The Secretary of State assumed that the rights to the fisheries had not been abrogated by the war.

At the second conference Adams stated that the American commissioners had instructions on impressments but none on the second point, the Indians. However, he had good reason for believing that peace negotiations with the Indians had already begun; and both he and Gallatin assured the British that peace with the Indians would quickly follow peace with Great Britain. On the subject of the boundaries, Adams stated the Americans had instructions, but on the fisheries they had none. He stated further that they had instructions to obtain a definition of blockade, an agreement on neutral and belligerent rights, and to secure an indemnity for captures made before and during the war. He mentioned also that there were numerous other points on which they had power to negotiate either in the treaty of peace or in a separate treaty of commerce. On the sceond and fourth points, the separate Indian state and the Newfoundland fisheries, he reiterated that the British could not expect the Americans to have instructions for they were in no way connected with the causes of the war. The British commissioners asked if these two points could not be made the subject of an arrangement

[1] J. Q. Adams, *Memoirs*, III.: 6.

sub spe rati. The Americans thought not. The British stated that they could not go beyond their instructions and, therefore, would have to refer the whole matter back to the Foreign Office. The Americans proposed that a protocol should be kept to which the British agreed.[1]

That evening Adams drafted a protocol which Bayard, Gallatin, and Clay revised. The next day the two commissions met to prepare drafts. The British objected strenuously to the American draft on the ground that it was too explanatory and too argumentative. The Americans yielded; but they were determined that if the negotiations failed, the world should know upon whom the responsibility rested. The British commissioners sent a messenger to London to find out whether the negotiations should continue.

Lord Castlereagh, himself, brought the new instructions on August 18, while on his way to the Congress of Vienna via Paris. At the next conference the British still insisted that a provisional article on the Indian state should be inserted. They took up next the subject of the boundary. The United States should agree not to keep naval forces on the Great Lakes or maintain or build any fortifications on the shores. And sufficient territory should be ceded in Maine to allow a direct line of communication between Halifax and Quebec.

The Americans spent four days in drafting the reply to these demands; and in the process they brought out the fact that they had more differences to settle among themselves than with the British. Clay, Russell, and Bayard riddled the draft drawn by Adams, which, as head of the commission, he had a right to make, with the result that Gallatin, the ablest of them all but who was at the foot, drafted the reply. This reply stated that the Indians could not be considered as an independent people and that for Great Britain to do so would be a violation of the Treaty of 1783, which acknowledged the disputed region to be within the boundaries of the United States. The Americans did, however, concede that they would include the Indians in the peace; which was eventually done in Article IX of the treaty. The

[1] American State Papers, Foreign Relations, III.: 705, 708.

restriction on the military defense of the Great Lakes could not be accepted. To the point of ceding part of Maine for a road between Halifax and Quebec the American commissioners stated they had no instructions and that they would not subscribe to a cession of any part of the territory of the United States. They renewed their protest that the propositions made by Great Britain had no relation to the differences between the two countries and that they had no foundation in the principles of uti possidetis or of status quo ante bellum. Instead of settling differences these propositions gave rise to new ones. At the end of the note the Americans offered to negotiate on the basis of status quo ante bellum with a reservation to both parties of their rights pertaining to their respective seamen.[1] The reply was sent to the British on the evening of August 25, 1814. If cables had been in existence both parties would have known that General Ross had taken Washington the day before. But their despair of concluding a treaty could hardly have been greater. They prepared to leave by the end of the month.

As before the British commissioners could exercise no discretionary powers but had to send copies of the American reply to Paris, where Castlereagh and Wellington then were, and to London, where Lord Bathurst had been given supervision over the negotiations at Ghent. Both Castlereagh and Bathurst felt irritated because the Americans had been so deft in throwing the responsibility for a possible rupture in the negotiations on the British. The note of September 2 constituted an effort to shift that responsibility.[2] It had become more evident daily that the British people wanted complete peace.

The American commissioners skilfully refused to assume responsibility for a break; and by their arguments made the burden doubly heavy on the British.[3] The note of September 9 was also referred to the British government. Lord Bathurst authorized his commissioners to abandon the demands for an Indian state and for the exclusive control of the Great Lakes. This

[1] American State Papers, Foreign Relations, III.: 711.
[2] Ibid., III.: 713.
[3] Ibid., III.: 715.

concession made the Americans feel that negotiations had seriously begun. And they intimated that the time had arrived for an exchange of projects for a proposed treaty.[1] But Lord Bathurst was not yet ready for such a move, for after half a dozen minor despatches had passed back and forth he instructed his commissioners, October 18, to secure a recognition of the principle of uti possidetis as a basis for boundary negotiations. He instructed them also to omit mention in the treaty of naturalization, impressments, and topics relating to maritime laws if the Americans so desired, otherwise Great Britain could not yield from her position repeatedly declared on these points. In their reply the American commissioners rejected the principle of uti possidetis categorically and substituted that of status quo ante bellum,[2] October 24, 1814.

In the meantime, the temporary capture of Washington had stiffened American resistance. The British had been defeated in Canada. Early in October George M. Dallas had brought despatches from Ghent, which Secretary Monroe released. The newspapers [3] expressed themselves unanimously that the British terms were unendurable and advocated a vigorous prosecution of the war. The demands for northern territory and for a cancellation of the fishing rights roused New England furiously. The despatches helped to give Madison a united country. And the later news of that fact caused Great Britain to incline favorably.

In their note of October 31 the British stated that they had no further points to consider and asked the Americans to present their objections and "such further points as the government of the United States consider to be material." [4] The Americans took this to be a suggestion for them to submit a project of a treaty. And with the task of drafting this project they battled for the next ten days. Gallatin and Adams prepared complete drafts; the others prepared notes. But the drafts of Gallatin and Adams became basic for discussion. Gallatin provided for a

[1] American State Papers, Foreign Relations, III.: 723.
[2] Ibid., III.: 725.
[3] Providence Patriot, October 24, Philadelphia Aurora, October 24, New York Spectator, October 29, Norfolk Ledger, October 22, 1814.
[4] American State Papers, Foreign Relations, III.: 726.

renewal of the rights to the fisheries by conceding to the British the free navigation of the Mississippi. Clay would not permit the British on the Mississippi; the exclusive right to navigate that river was far more important than the fisheries. Adams contended as ably for the fisheries as his father had done in 1782; this right was a part of American independence, he claimed, and could not be cancelled by war. The majority of the commission favored Gallatin's article, with Clay and Russell dissenting. But Clay's persistence won and the fisheries were left out except for an explanatory clause in a note accompanying the draft that they were "not authorized to bring into discussion any of the rights or liberties which the United States have hitherto enjoyed in relation thereto." The boundary line west of the Lake of the Woods was omitted. Other boundary disputes were to be submitted to commissions. The principle of the status quo ante bellum was inserted. And so was a provision prohibiting impressment and excluding from the merchant marine service of either party persons belonging to the other. A legal blockade was defined. Indemnities were provided for, those for captures and condemnations made in violation of the law of nations before the war were to be paid by Great Britain, and those made after the war began were to be examined by a commission and paid by either party in accordance with the findings.[1] The British commissioners sent this project to London the next day.

During this ten day period the Cabinet had urged the Duke of Wellington to take command of the British forces in Canada. He replied: "I have already told you (Lord Liverpool) and Lord Bathurst that I feel no objection to going to America, though I don't promise to myself much success there." Another sentence from the same reply: "That which appears to me to be wanting in America is not a general, or a general officer and troops, but a naval superiority on the Lakes." Commenting on the negotiations at Ghent he wrote: "Why stipulate for the uti possidetis? You can get no territory; indeed, the state of your military operations, however creditable, does not entitle you to demand

[1] American State Papers, Foreign Relations, III.: 733.

any."[1] Wellington's letter was dated at Paris, November 9. On November 18 the Cabinet decided to abandon the claim to territory.

The British commissioners replied to the American project of a treaty on November 26. They made no mention of the fisheries, but they stipulated for the old right of navigating the Mississippi. Adams favored immediate acceptance, but Clay would rather have no treaty at all than accept this provision. Gallatin then brought forth his proposition that the right to navigate the Mississippi be conceded if the British would expressly recognize the old right to fish. Clay lost his temper and pronounced the whole "a damned bad treaty."[2] But after three days Gallatin dominated. And the renewal of both rights was proposed to the British.[3]

Bathurst instructed the British commissioners to propose that both subjects be left to future negotiation.[4] This implied that both rights had been cancelled by the war; something which Adams could not admit. But he found himself alone; which for an Adams meant a redoubling of energy, with the result that the American commissioners agreed to make another effort to have the British concede that the Treaty of 1783 should govern the right to the fisheries or at least agree not to mention them. Due to the ability and the patience of the American commissioners the British had been driven to concede point after point. So Lord Bathurst consented to omit all mention of the fisheries and of the navigation of the Mississippi.[5]

It has been frequently remarked that the treaty of Ghent settled nothing. This is largely true so far as the causes of the war were concerned. But a summary of the treaty shows that considerable was accomplished; and another summary will show that the presentation of divergent views at Ghent in 1814 greatly facilitated future negotiations.

Article I provided for the cessation of hostilities on the

[1] Wellington, *Supplementary Despataches*, I.: 426.
[2] J. Q. Adams, *Diary*, III.: 118.
[3] American State Papers, Foreign Relations, III.: 742.
[4] Castlereagh, *Correspondence*, X.: 214.
[5] Ibid., X.: 221.

exchange of ratifications and for the mutual restoration of territory, records, and property, including slaves captured on land. This article was brought into dispute by Great Britain refusing to order her naval commanders to deliver the slaves which had been received on board her war vessels. The matter was submitted to the Czar of Russia, who decided in favor of the interpretation made by the United States, 1822.[1] And in 1826 Great Britain agreed to pay an indemnity of $1,204,960.

Article II provided for a mutual restoration of prizes taken after a specified time, which varied with the length of time necessary to inform war vessels in different parts of the world.

Article III provided for the mutual restoration of prisoners of war. The United States took this to mean that cost of transportation should be borne by the party that held the prisoners. This caused delay which, in turn, led the Americans at Dartmoor prison to revolt. British troops fired indiscriminately at them and killed many before order was restored. The United States finally accepted the offer of Great Britain that the transportation costs should be borne jointly by the two states.

The injection of the argument on uti possidetis and status quo ante bellum caused the commissioners on both sides to make an effort to settle boundary disputes. They provided for reference to a commission in each of four sectors. Article IV dealt with the disputed islands in the Bay of Passamaquoddy. John Holmes, American, and Thomas Barclay, British, made up this commission. They decided in 1817 that Moose Island, Dudley Island, and Frederick Island belonged to the United States and that all the others in dispute belonged to Great Britain.[2] Not until 1892 was provision made for marking this boundary.

Article V covered the stretch from the source of the St. Croix to the river St. Lawrence. C. P. Van Ness for the United States and Thomas Barclay were appointed. They failed to agree. The matter was submitted to the King of the Netherlands for arbitration in 1828, but he went beyond his powers as stated

[1] Moore, *International Arbitrations*, I.: 360.

[2] Malloy, *Treaties*, I.: 619. See Rives, *Correspondence of Thomas Barclay*, chap. VIII.

in the convention; and, hence, the United States refused to be bound by the award. The controversy was finally settled by the Webster-Ashburton Treaty.

Article VI provided for a third boundary commission to determine the line through the St. Lawrence, the lakes Ontario, Erie, Huron, and the connecting rivers. Peter B. Porter for the United States and John Ogilvy, and later Anthony Barclay, for Great Britain were appointed. They reached an agreement on June 18, 1822.[1]

Article VII provided for the determination of the boundary from Lake Huron to the northwestern point of the Lake of the Woods. This was left to Porter and Anthony Barclay. They failed to agree. The matter was later settled by the Webster-Ashburton Treaty.

Article VIII provided for the filling of vacancies, filing of reports, and so on, in connection with the boundary commissions.

Article IX provided for mutual peace with the Indians, if the red men were willing, on the exchange of ratifications.

Article X expressed what had come to be pronounced British sentiment in favor of suppressing the slave trade. The article stated: "It is hereby agreed that both the contracting parties shall use their best endeavors to accomplish so desirable an object." Congress had already in 1807 forbidden the importation of African slaves; but the trade continued in a small and clandestine manner. Congress acted again on May 15, 1820, by declaring slave trading to be piracy, punishable with the death penalty. This did not help greatly because the United States refused to permit the merchantmen that flew her flag to be visited and searched by foreign war vessels. The slave trade appeared again in the Webster-Ashburton negotiations.

On Christmas Eve, 1814, the commissioners signed the treaty in triplicate. The treaty reached London on December 26, and while there were some mutterings in the press that the members of the cabinet had humbled themselves and discredited the country, yet the satisfaction was general that the war was over. On March 9, 1815, two news items silenced all criticism; Jackson

[1] Malloy, *Treaties*, I.: 620.

had defeated General Pakenham at New Orleans and Napoleon was making a triumphal return towards Paris from the Island of Elba.

A copy of the treaty reached Washington on February 14, 1815. That evening Madison considered the treaty with his cabinet. The next day he sent it to the Senate. And on that same day the Senate approved it by a unanimous vote. On February 17 the ratifications were exchanged between Mr. Baker, the British agent, and Secretary Monroe. On February 18, the President proclaimed the treaty. The market responded immediately. In New York brown sugar fell from $26 to $12.50 a hundred pounds; tea from $2.25 to $1 a pound; tin from $80 to $25 a box. Cotton fabrics declined 50 per cent. Specie dropped from 22 per cent. to 2 per cent. above par. Wheat, cotton, and tobacco rose rapidly. All in all the Treaty of Ghent was the most popular agreement the United States has ever made, and the news of the victory at New Orleans, January 8, 1815, contributed to that end. That victory meant that Great Britain would respect the principles for which the United States went to war. It was therefore of small consequence whether they were included in the treaty or not.

The United States had not obtained a renunciation of impressments; but Great Britain never assumed to exercise it again; and the last mention of the subject was made by Webster in 1842. Blockade was not defined; and when it finally was in the Declaration of Paris, 1856, the United States revealed slight desire to ratify. Mutual respect for naturalization processes was obtained by the Clarendon-Motley Convention of 1870; but ever since the War of 1812 Great Britain has respected the principle that the flag covers the crew. The American right to the inshore fisheries off Newfoundland was renewed by the Treaty of 1818.

At Ghent nothing had been done with commerce and navigation; although the American commissioners had expressed a willingness to negotiate. These two subjects were reserved for a special convention, signed at London, July 3, 1815. J. Q. Adams, Clay, and Gallatin represented the United States. F. J. Robinson, H. Goulburn, and William Adams represented Great Britain.

Robinson had replaced Gambier at the head of the British commission; and he was a man of quite different qualifications. He was vice-president of the committee of the privy council for trade and plantations, and he had accompanied Castlereagh during the recent negotiations at Paris. Later he and Huskisson coöperated in favor of a reduction of import duties and of the removal of restrictions on navigation. He treated the American commissioners with courtesy and sympathy.

As for trade with the United Kingdom the British commissioners conceded quickly that there should be a reciprocal liberty of commerce between the two countries and that ships and cargoes belonging to the nationals of either party should be given permission to enter the ports and rivers to which other foreigners were permitted to come. They conceded also that discriminating duties on tonnage and merchandize should be mutually abolished.[1] Gallatin declared afterward that this was the only portion of the treaty that was of value;[2] which reveals, no doubt, what his attitude would have been on such a measure as the merchant marine act of 1920.

There were three other groups of questions which the Americans wanted to settle. The first one related to the right to trade with the British provinces on the northern frontier of the United States and that included the free navigation of the St. Lawrence River. The second group of questions related to the opening of direct trade with the British West Indies and to the right to carry goods between the British West Indies and Nova Scotia. Robinson recognized the fairness of the American argument on these questions; but the cabinet was not yet prepared nor were the merchants of Great Britain ready to give up the mercantile colonial system. The United States had to engage in a series of embargoes on Canadian and West Indian goods brought in British vessels, and in tariff and tonnage duties' wars before Great Britain became convinced of the folly of her position. The two countries reached an informal agreement in 1830, which was just as effectual as a treaty; and it has worked well ever since.

[1] American State Papers, Foreign Relations, IV.: 8, 11.
[2] Gallatin, *Writings*, I.: 665.

Great Britain by an order in council and the United States by an act of Congress, May 29, 1830, removed the old restrictions; and thus permitted American vessels to engage in trade with the British colonies anywhere, and this applied to trade between the colonies as well. But British vessels were not and never have been permitted to engage in the American coastwise trade.

The third group of questions which the Americans wanted to settle at London related to the East Indian trade. Direct intercourse only was obtained. American ships and cargoes, however, were granted most favored nation treatment in the East Indian ports.[1] The convention of 1815 was concluded for only four years, but it was renewed for ten years in 1818, and extended indefinitely in 1827 until the merchant marine act of 1920 caused its denunciation by the United States.

In the negotiations at Ghent, the English had attempted to bar the Americans from keeping any ships of war on the Great Lakes or to maintain any fortifications on the shores thereof. This the Americans virtually conceded in the Rush-Bagot agreement of 1817 on the condition that Great Britain should do likewise.[2] Each party could maintain on Lake Ontario one vessel not exceeding one hundred tons burden, armed with one eighteen pound cannon; on the three upper lakes two such vessels; and on Lake Champlain one such vessel. Of some consequence industrially is the fact "that no other vessels of war shall be there built or armed."[3] This has prevented the shipyards on the Great Lakes from competing in the building of war vessels with the yards on the seaboard. But the whole convention is an excellent example of what good faith between two nations, unsupported by military force, can achieve.

In the end, then, the United States had to yield on only one point which she had hoped to secure at Ghent and that was indemnity for the captures of American ships and goods under the orders in council. Great Britain yielded on point after point at Ghent and continued to do so down through the century

[1] See Treaty in Malloy, *Treaties*, I.: 624.
[2] J. M. Callahan, *Agreement of 1817*, Am. Hist. Assoc. Report, 1895:369.
[3] Malloy, *Treaties*, I.: 628.

much to the promotion of solidarity among the English speaking peoples of the world.

BIBLIOGRAPHY

Adams, Henry.—History of the United States, volumes III—IX. New York, 1903–1904.

Adams, Henry.—*Life of Albert Gallatin.* Philadelphia, 1879.

Adams, J. Q.—*Memoirs,* 12 volumes. Edited by Charles Francis Adams. Philadelphia, 1874–1877.

Adams, J. Q.—*Writings,* 7 volumes. Edited by W. C. Ford, New York 1913–1917.

American State Papers, Foreign Relations. Volume III. Washington, 1832.

Bayard, James A.—"*Papers.*" Report of American Historical Association, 1913. Volume II.

Callahan, J. M.—*The Neutrality of the American Lakes and Anglo-American Relations.* J. H. U. Studies, Series XVI numbers 1–4. Baltimore, 1898.

Castlereagh, Viscount.—*Memoirs and Correspondence of Robert Stewart, Viscount Castlereagh,* 12 volumes. London, 1851–1853.

Channing, Edward.—*History of the United States.* Volume IV. New York, 1917.

Clay, Henry.—*Works.* Edited by C. Colton, 10 volumes. New York, 1904.

Gallatin, Albert.—*Writings,* 3 volumes. Edited by Henry Adams. Philadelphia.

Gallatin, James.—*Diary.* New York, 1916.

Hunt, Gaillard.—*Life in America One Hundred Years Ago.* New York, 1914.

Lamson, Captain Zachary G.—*Autobiography,* (Introduction by O. T. Horoe). (Good account of commercial troubles leading to War of 1812).

Lyman, Theodore.—*The Diplomacy of the United States.* Volume II. Boston, 1828.

Mahan, A. T.—*The Influence of Sea Power upon the French Revolution and Empire,* 2 volumes. Boston, 1898.

Mahan, A. T.—*Sea Power in its Relation to the War of 1812.* Boston, 1905.

Malloy, W. M.—*Treaties,* 1776–1909. Volume I. Washington, 1910.

Moore, J. B.—*International Arbitrations,* 6 volumes. Washington, 1898.

Phillimore, Joseph.—*Reflections on the Nature and Extent of the License Trade.* London, 1811.

Rives, George L.—*Correspondence of Thomas Barclay.* New York, 1894.

Scott, Michael.—*Tom Cringle's Log.* New York, 1895.

Updyke, F. A.—*The Diplomacy of the War of 1812.* Baltimore, 1915.

WALPOLE, SPENCER.—*Life of Spencer Perceval*, 2 volumes. London, 1874.

WELLINGTON, DUKE OF—*Supplementary Despatches, and Memoranda*, 15 volumes. Edited by his son.

BARING, A.—*Inquiry into the causes and consequences of the orders in council and an examination of the conduct of Great Britain towards the neutral commerce of America.* London, 1808.

CHAPTER VII

THE CONVENTION OF 1818 WITH GREAT BRITAIN

"We thought it safer to err on our own side of the question, and to ask for more than perhaps under all circumstances we expected to obtain, rather than to limit our demands to less than might be intended by our Government."—GALLATIN AND RUSH TO J. Q. ADAMS.

This convention is one of the shortest and also one of the most important to which the United States has become a party. It has five provisions; the two minor may be disposed of quickly. Article IX renewed for a ten year period the commercial convention of July 3, 1815. In 1827 this same convention was renewed for an indefinite period and was in effect until the merchant marine act of 1920 caused its denunciation. By Article V the two parties agreed to submit for arbitration to a friendly power whether Article I of the Treaty of Ghent included the restoration of the slaves received on board English war vessels. The two parties agreed later upon the Czar of Russia, who decided in favor of the United States. The three major provisions related to the northeastern fisheries, the boundary from the Lake of the Woods to the Rocky Mountains, and to the joint occupation of the Oregon country for a ten year period.

Even before the Treaty of 1783 the fisheries had shown themselves to be of international importance. The trade and navigation acts of 1764 and 1775 had for their purpose to limit New England trade to the United Kingdom and the British West Indies, to cut off the great fish trade with France, Holland, Spain, and Portugal, and to stop all fishing on the banks of Newfoundland. Men from the four northern colonies testified repeatedly before the House of Commons that the fisheries furnished the life blood of New England. Massachusetts claimed that the loss of the fisheries would deprive of the means of living six thousand of her fishermen and would compel ten thousand of her other citizens to find employment elsewhere. Rhode Island pointed out that of 14,000 hogshead of molasses imported into that colony in one year only 2500 were of British production, and that molasses produced within British dominion could not supply the needs of the distillers of that little colony. Consequently the duty on molasses should be lowered, the right to fish off the Newfoundland banks should be continued, and the right to transport fish to be used in exchange for foreign commodities, especially molasses, should be unlimited. The restrictions on the fisheries assisted materially in bringing on the Revolution. And after the war had begun the leading question which Vergennes asked of Silas Deane before French aid could be granted was whether the revolutionary forces could maintain themselves without the fisheries.[1] During the war Congress expressed time and again its anxieties about preserving the ancient fishing privileges.[2] Although Congress weakened in July, 1781, by resolving that an equality with Englishmen in the fisheries need not be a sine qua non in the peace negotiations; yet John Adams used utmost zeal in securing the fishing rights in the Treaty of 1783.

Article III of the Treaty of 1783 specified that "the people of the United States shall continue to enjoy unmolested the right to take fish of every kind on the Grand Bank, and on all other banks of Newfoundland; also in the Gulf of St. Lawrence, and at all other places in the sea where the inhabitants of both countries used at any time heretofore to fish." In other words, the deep sea fisheries outside the three mile limit came within the scope of a right of the American people; while the next two provisions of this article came within the scope of a liberty of the American people. "And also that the inhabitants of the United States shall have liberty to take fish of every kind on such part of the coast of Newfoundland as British fishermen shall use (but not to dry or cure the same on the island) and also on the coasts, bays, and creeks of all other of His Britannic Majesty's dominions in America." This second provision specified the "liberty" to the inshore fisheries; and the third provision specified the

[1] Wharton, *Diplomatic Correspondence of the American Revolution*, II.: 115.
[2] Journals of the Continental Congress, V.: 771; VI.: 1056; XII.: 1041.

"liberty" to dry and cure fish on certain shores: "and that American fishermen shall have liberty to dry and cure fish in any of the unsettled bays, harbours, and creeks of Nova Scotia, Magdalen Islands, and Labrador, so long as the same shall remain unsettled; but so soon as the same or either of them shall be settled, it shall not be lawful for the said fishermen to dry or cure fish at such settlements, without a previous agreement for that purpose with the inhabitants, proprietors or possessors of the ground."[1]

During the succeeding years the fishing industry declined until in 1789 the estimate was an average yearly earning for each vessel of $273 with an average yearly expenditure of $416. Congress came to the relief of the industry with a bounty on fish and a subsidy on vessels. But the French revolution and the Napoleonic wars greatly stimulated the industry so that by 1801 the people of Nova Scotia and Newfoundland protested to Parliament that the Yankees were ruining them. But Jefferson's long embargo gave, in turn, relief to the British colonists. And the War of 1812 made these colonists doubly eager to obtain the inshore fisheries as a monopoly.[2] In New England the feeling was just as strong on the other side; the cry became "No peace without the fisheries." But Henry Clay's constituents claimed that "peace was better than codfish."

The Treaty of Ghent said nothing about the fisheries. The understanding among the British negotiators was that the War of 1812 had abrogated the two "liberty" clauses in Article III of the Treaty of 1783. The understanding among the American negotiators was, with a reservation by Gallatin, that the whole of Article III carried with it a permanent character and could not be affected by war. They thought it would be advantageous to have a continuation of the right expressed in the Treaty of Ghent, but there was no necessity for such action.

However, the British government and the people of Newfoundland and Nova Scotia quickly adopted the understanding of the British negotiators. In July of 1815 an American codfish-

[1] Malloy, *Treaties*, I.: 588.
[2] Niles' *Weekly Register*, June 11, 1814.

ing vessel entered the port of Barnstable with the following endorsement on its license: "Warned off the coast by His Majesty's sloop Jaseur, not to come within sixty miles. N. Lock, Captain."[1] This endorsement had been made while the vessel was lying forty-five miles off the coast of Nova Scotia. Other vessels were ordered off in a similar manner. The State Department protested to Lord Bathurst, who explained in due time that the action of the British naval officer was unauthorized. But the catch for that season had been lost.

President Madison sent America's ablest man on the fisheries as minister to London, John Quincy Adams. No one in Washington thought it would be necessary to endow Adams with full power to negotiate a treaty. Adams reviewed the negotiations at Ghent before Bathurst and Castlereagh; and he argued American rights so ably and pertinaceously[2] that those two gentlemen felt quite relieved to find that he had no full power to negotiate an agreement, and, therefore, they transferred the negotiations on that subject to Mr. Bagot, the British minister in Washington. Bagot evinced a conciliatory disposition and negotiated directly with Monroe as Secretary of State and later as President. Monroe acknowledged that some concessions on the provisions of Article III, 1783, could and would be made. Meanwhile, President Monroe decided that he needed the services of John Quincy Adams as Secretary of State and appointed Richard Rush, who had been Acting Secretary, as American minister to London. The result was that, under the circumstances, the British would rather negotiate in London.

During the summer of 1817 several incidents occurred which made action necessary. On May 12, 1817, Rear Admiral Sir David Milne at Bermuda had issued an order to the ships under his command to seize all foreign vessels fishing or at anchor within His Majesty's North American provinces and send them to Halifax for adjudication. The Americans had been in the habit of going within the three mile limit to procure bait, wood,

[1] American State Papers, Foreign Relations, IV.: 349.
[2] Ibid., IV.: 352.

and water, and to clean their fish. They were sent to Halifax in such numbers that the saying "Gone to Halifax" became a byword. Frequently these vessels were condemned and had to give bond, pending an appeal to the vice-admiralty court in London.[1] On August 4, 1817, twenty American fishing vessels sought refuge from a storm in the harbor of Ragged Island and were compelled to pay light dues, which was contrary to what the Americans termed their rights.

By May, 1818, Castlereagh displayed eagerness to renew the commercial convention of 1815. Such unexampled readiness by the Foreign Office caused Rush to be suspicious, but he advised the State Department that the occasion be used to settle the outstanding differences. Monroe transferred Gallatin from Paris temporarily to assist Rush in the negotiations. Secretary Adams wrote to Gallatin and Rush, July 28, 1818: "The President authorizes you to agree to an article whereby the United States will desist from the liberty of fishing, and curing and drying fish, within the British jurisdiction generally, upon condition that it shall be secured as a permanent right, not liable to be impaired by any future war, from Cape Ray to the Rameau Islands, and from Mount Joli, on the Labrador coast, through the strait of Bellisle, indefinitely north, along the coast; the right to extend as well to curing and drying the fish as to fishing." [2]

Gallatin and Rush succeeded in acquiring far more than this right to fish and to dry fish on the Labrador coast and on the western one-third of the southern coast of Newfoundland. In addition it was provided that the inhabitants of the United States might forever catch fish on the shores of the Magdalen Islands and along the entire west coast of Newfoundland from Cape Ray to Quirpon Island. The "liberty" "forever" to cure fish was limited to the unsettled bays, harbors, or creeks of Labrador above Mount Joli and of the south coast of Newfoundland from Cape Ray to Rameau Islands. An immense amount of discussion centered on the words "liberty" and "forever." Gallatin and Rush preferred "right" to "liberty" but Robinson

[1] American State Papers, Foreign Relations, VI.: 369.
[2] Ibid., IV.: 378.

and Goulburn had the advantage of pleading the wording in Article III of the Treaty of 1783. The British objected strenuously to the use of the word "forever," but the Americans declared they would not agree to the article at all unless the word were inserted three times.[1]

The liberty of fishing or drying fish forever renounced "within three marine miles of any of the coasts, bays, creeks, or harbors" not above mentioned was inserted for the purpose of making it clear that the liberties acquired by this treaty were not new ones and that express renunciation was necessary.[2] It was agreed that American fishermen could enter any harbor or bay for shelter, repairs, wood, and water, but "for no other purpose whatever."

The British attempted to revive their treaty right to navigate the Mississippi; but were unsuccessful.

It was likewise agreed that nothing in the article should be considered prejudicial to "the exclusive rights of the Hudson Bay Company." Gallatin and Rush's comment on this clause is of interest as regards the "liberty" to the fisheries and also as regards Canada's occasional claim to exclusive jurisdiction over Hudson Bay as a closed sea. "To the exception of the exclusive rights of the Hudson Bay Company we did not object, as it was virtually implied in the treaty of 1783, and we had never, any more than the British subjects, enjoyed any right there; the charter of that company having been granted in the year 1670. The exception applies only to the coasts and their harbors, and does not affect the right of fishing in Hudson Bay beyond three miles from the shores, a right which would not exclusively belong to, or be granted by, any nation." [3]

Gallatin and Rush made a curious mistake in assuming that the cod and halibut fishing beyond the three marine miles off Nova Scotia were the only valuable fisheries there. It has turned out since that the mackerel fisheries have been equally valuable, and that the schools of mackerel take refuge under

[1] R. Rush, *Residence at the Court of London:* 334.
[2] American State Papers, Foreign Relations, IV.: 380.
[3] Ibid., IV.: 380.

the Treaty of 1818. The temptation to follow the mackerel within the three mile limit has caused numerous seizures of American fishing vessels by Canadian revenue cutters and even by British war vessels. At times the governments of the United States and Great Britain have had to use great tact to avoid hostilities,—notably so in 1852.

The first article of the Treaty of 1818 regulates the inshore fisheries at present. For about twenty years few misunderstandings concerning the treaty arose. From March 16, 1855, to March 17, 1866, the Elgin-Marcy reciprocity treaty revived for American fishermen their old rights under the Treaty of 1783. Except for these two periods, 1818 to 1836 and 1855 to 1866, the first article of the Treaty of 1818 has been subjected to constant dispute and contention until the decision of the Hague tribunal made the meaning clear in 1910.

Without analyzing the various projects of treaties, modi vivendi, and measures of retaliation intended to bring about a settlement of disputes, it will be sufficient to state that on January 27, 1909, it was agreed to submit the whole matter to the Hague Court for arbitration. Five eminent jurists were chosen to sit on the bench: Dr. H. Lammasch of Austria, Jonkheer A. F. de Savornin Lohman of the Netherlands, Dr. Luis M. Drago of Argentina, Sir Charles Fitzpatrick of Canada, and Mr. George Gray of the United States. Seven questions were presented to this court for decision.

The first question resolved itself into two parts: a. "Whether the right of regulating reasonably the liberties conferred by the Treaty of 1818 resides in Great Britain." b. "And if such right does so exist, whether such reasonable exercise of the right is permitted to Great Britain without the accord and concurrence of the United States."

A few examples will show the purport of these questions. Newfoundland Statutes, 39 Victoria, ch. 6, sect. 4, provided "No person shall, between the hours of twelve o'clock on Saturday night and twelve o'clock on Sunday night, haul or take any herring, caplin or squids, with nets, seines, bunts, or any such contrivance. . . ." And the next year this act was amended to "include and apply to the jigging of squids, and to the use of any contrivance whatever, and to any mode of taking and obtaining fish for bait." [1] Americans claimed this regulation to be an unreasonable interference with their right to fish within the three mile limit on the treaty coast. The Newfoundland Sabbath had not been provided for in the treaty. The British claimed that the regulation was reasonable and designed to promote public order and morality. Other regulations prescribed minutely where and during what seasons seines or other means of fishing might or might not be used and prescribed the size of the meshes of nets. Occasionally these regulations were changed suddenly so that the American fishermen could not know about them. The British claimed that these regulations were for the protection and preservation of fish and also equitable and fair as between local fishermen and the inhabitants of the United States exercising their liberty under the treaty. The Americans claimed that these regulations were designed to discriminate against them and were in violation of their treaty rights.

The tribunal decided that the words "in common with British subjects" meant that the inhabitants of the United States were admitted to a regulated fishery; [2] that, therefore, Great Britain had a right to make and to enforce regulations. But in reply to the second part of the question whether the reasonable exercise of the right was permitted to Great Britain without the concurrence of the United States, the tribunal decided that whatever may have been the situation under the Treaty of 1818, standing alone, Great Britain had repeatedly recognized in practice that there were limitations on the exercise of the right of regulating, bounded by reason. In accordance with its power under the agreement, submitting the whole dispute to arbitration, the tribunal created a commission of experts on fisheries and called on each party to designate one commissioner from its own nationals. As the third non-national commissioner the tribunal designated Dr. P. P. C. Hoek of the Netherlands to act as umpire.

[1] North Atlantic Coast Fisheries Arbitration, I.: 181.
[2] Foreign Relations, 1910: 549.

This commission was to pass upon the reasonableness of British fishing regulations and to hear objections advanced by the United States.[1] On the first question, then, both parties could claim a victory.

Question two. "Have the inhabitants of the United States, while exercising the liberties referred to in said article, a right to employ as members of the fishing crews of their vessels persons not inhabitants of the United States?"

Great Britain claimed that the treaty conferred the liberty to fish on the inhabitants of the United States exclusively. But the tribunal decided that the inhabitants of the United States had a right to employ as members of their fishing crews on American vessels persons not inhabitants of the United States. However, these non-inhabitants so employed could derive no benefit or immunity from the treaty.[2] The United States won the decision on this point.

Question three. "Can the exercise by the inhabitants of the United States of the liberties referred to in the said article be subjected, without the consent of the United States, to the requirements of entry or report at custom houses or the payment of light or harbor or other dues or to any other similar requirement or condition or exaction?"

This question related to the liberty to take fish and to dry and cure fish on the treaty coasts specified in 1818 and therefore could not apply to the privileges of commercial vessels. The United States argued for a complete exemption for her fishing vessels. The tribunal based its decision on the words "in common with the subjects of His Britannic Majesty;" hence American fishing vessels would have to pay the same light and harbor dues as those imposed on Newfoundland fisherman. But "the inhabitants of the United States should not be subjected to the purely commercial formalities of report, entry, and clearance at a customhouse, nor to light, harbor, or other dues not imposed upon Newfoundland fishermen." [3] However, Newfoundlanders

[1] Foreign Relations, 1910: 556–7.
[2] Ibid., 1910: 559.
[3] Ibid., 1910: 560.

had been generally exempt; so that the decision on this point might be considered as a victory for the United States.

Question four, epitomized. Must American fishing vessels pay light or harbor or other dues or report at custom houses in order to enter for shelter, repairs, wood, and water?

The tribunal stated: "And it is decided and awarded that such restrictions are not permissible." The court explained that the right of entry for the four above purposes constituted in large measure those duties of hospitality and humanity which all civilized nations impose upon themselves and expect the performance of from others. But if American fishermen remained more than forty-eight hours, they should report to a customs official, "if reasonably convenient opportunity therefor is afforded." [1]

Question five. "From where must be measured the 'three marines miles of any of the coasts, bays, creeks, or harbors' referred to in the said article?"

The United States claimed that all bays, creeks, or harbors six miles or less wide might be considered closed, but all those wider than six miles should be considered open sea. The tribunal concluded that no evidence had been furnished which proved that the application of the three mile rule to bays was present in the minds of the negotiators in 1818 and that they could not reasonably have been expected either to presume it or to provide against its presumption. In answering this question, then, the tribunal recognized established usage and it took into consideration especially the practice of Great Britain in maintaining her jurisdiction in these bays and also the practice of other countries in recognizing such enforcement of jurisdiction in the bays in question by Great Britain. The tribunal found also that Article IV of the special agreement in regard to the arbitration provided that the judges should keep in mind the removal of future differences. Therefore, the tribunal announced the headland to headland theory with the provision that those bays which were ten miles or less in width should be considered closed. "In every bay not hereinafter specifically provided for

[1] Foreign Relations, 1910: 561.

the limits of exclusion shall be drawn 3 miles seaward from a straight line across the bay in the part nearest the entrance at the first point where the width does not exceed 10 miles." [1] Dr. Luis Drago gave a dissenting opinion on this question, based chiefly on the renunciatory provision of the Treaty of 1818. Great Britain won the decision on this point.[2]

Question six. "Have the inhabitants of the United States the liberty under the said article or otherwise to take fish in the bays, harbors, and creeks on that part of the southern coast of Newfoundland which extends from Cape Ray to Rameau Islands, or on the western and northern coast of Newfoundland from Cape Ray to Quirpon Islands, or on the Magdalen Islands?"

Great Britain contended that American fishermen had no such liberty. The tribunal held that the word "coast" in the treaty included harbors, bays, and creeks. On this point the United States won.

Question seven. "Are the inhabitants of the United States whose vessels resort to the treaty coasts for the purpose of exercising the liberties referred to in Article I of the Treaty of 1818 entitled to have for those vessels, when duly authorized by the United States in that behalf, the commercial privileges on the treaty coasts accorded by agreement or otherwise to United States trading vessels generally?"

The tribunal answered this question affirmatively, with the qualification that American fishing vessels "cannot at the same time and during the same voyage exercise their treaty rights and enjoy their commercial privileges, because treaty rights and commercial privileges are submitted to different rules, regulations, and restraints." [3]

This arbitration settled remarkably well, if not perfectly, the long and vexed dispute between the United States and Great Britain on behalf of her two North American dominions.

The second major dispute settled by the Treaty of 1818 was

[1] Foreign Relations, 1910: 566.
[2] Ibid., 1910: 569.
[3] Ibid., 1910: 569.

the northern boundary from the Lake of the Woods to the Rocky Mountains. The Treaty of 1783 provided that this boundary should run from the northwestern point of the Lake of the Woods to the source of the Mississippi River, then supposed to be in British America. Jay's Treaty provided for a joint survey of the Mississippi but this survey was never made. Monroe and Pinkney during their negotiations in London in 1806 had offered to take a line running north and south through the northwestern corner of the Lake of the Woods and on the intersection of that line by the forty-ninth parallel, run the boundary along that parallel to the "Stony Mountains." This was the boundary adopted in Article II of the Treaty of 1818.

The third and last major dispute partially settled by the Treaty of 1818 related to the Oregon country. Gallatin and Rush proposed an extension of the boundary from the Rocky Mountains along the forty-ninth parallel to the Pacific Ocean. They said: "We did not assert that the United States had a perfect right to that country, but insisted that their claim was at least good against Great Britain. The forty-ninth degree of north latitude had, in pursuance of the treaty of Utrecht, been fixed, indefinitely, as the line between the northern British possessions and those of France, including Louisiana, now a part of our territories." [1]

But the British negotiators were not ready to reach an agreement on the definitive disposition of the territory in that region. They had, as they considered, good claims to the whole region down to the Columbia River. These claims were based on the explorations of the coast by Captain Cook in 1778 and by Mackenzie and Vancouver in 1793, on the settlements at Nootka Sound on the western coast of Vancouver Island, recognized by Spain in the Nootka Sound Convention of 1790, on purchases made from the Indians, and on trading posts established by the Hudson Bay Company.[2]

The Americans had similar and, what seemed to them, better claims to the region. Captain Gray had entered and explored

[1] American State Papers, Foreign Relations, IV.: 381.
[2] Ibid., IV.: 381.

the Columbia River in 1792, the year before Vancouver had appeared. Lewis and Clark had entered the region from the east and explored it in Jefferson's first administration. When these two explorers returned to St. Louis in 1806, Manuel Lisa, Pierre Chouteau, and Governor William Clark organized the Missouri Fur Company. Within two years this company had established the earliest known posts on the upper Missouri and in the region drained by the Columbia and its tributaries.

John Jacob Astor of New York organized the Pacific Fur Company and brought into his employment Americans familiar with the fur trade and Canadians and Scotchmen long in the service of the British fur trading interests. They established their headquarters at the mouth of the Columbia in March, 1811, and named the place Astoria. The British acquired the property of the Pacific Fur Company during the War of 1812. But Article I of the Treaty of Ghent provided for restoration without delay of all territory and places taken by either party during or after the war. Due to the slowness of means of communication and of mental slowness as well the Americans did not retake possession of Astoria, with Lord Bathurst's consent, until October 6, 1818. This was just two weeks before the Treaty of 1818 was signed. So that the American argument as well as the trend of events sustained the recognition of American supremacy on the Columbia River.

However, the proposal of Rush and Gallatin to extend the boundary along the forty-ninth parallel to the Pacific Ocean met with a counter project from Robinson and Goulburn. This project specified substantially what was afterward agreed to in the treaty, that the country "claimed by either party on the northwest coast of America, westward of the Stony Mountains, shall, together with its harbors, bays, and creeks, and the navigation of all rivers within the same, be free and open, for the term of ten years from the date of the signature of the present convention, to the vessels, citizens, and subjects of the two Powers." This was agreed to with the reservation that the treaty should be construed without prejudice to the claims of either party in that region.

The so-called joint occupation of Oregon continued until the Treaty of 1846, which embodied the proposal made by Gallatin and Rush in 1818. Great Britain secured the free navigation of the Columbia River. The United States agreed to recognize the possessory rights of the Hudson Bay Company and of British subjects.[1]

A dispute arose later about the channel between Vancouver Island and the mainland. San Juan is an island which divides this channel, so that the question became: which branch of the channel is the boundary to follow. The United States claimed that the western arm or the Haro Channel was the channel intended by the treaty, because it was the larger and the deeper. Great Britain contended for the other arm or the Rosario Channel. American citizens and British subjects had settled on San Juan. Armed conflict threatened. General Scott succeeded in preventing a collision. But the dispute dragged on until in the Treaty of Washington, 1871, the two parties agreed to submit the matter to the German Emperor for arbitration. He decided in favor of the American claim.[2]

Other matters discussed in the negotiations at London in 1818 were: impressment, blockade, contraband, the right of Americans to navigate the St. Lawrence, and trade with the British West Indies. No agreement could be reached, although the British commissioners argued in a much more liberal manner than ever before. It should be stated also that Gallatin admitted to John Quincy Adams that the critical situation with Spain in respect to Florida made Rush and himself more anxious to reach a settlement with Great Britain than they otherwise would have been.[3]

[1] Malloy, *Treaties*, I.: 656.
[2] Moore, *International Arbitrations*, I.: 227.
[3] Gallatin, *Writings*, II.: 84.

BIBLIOGRAPHY

ADAMS, HENRY.—*Life of Albert Gallatin.* Philadelphia, 1879.

ADAMS, J. Q.—*Memoirs,* 12 volumes. Edited by Charles Francis Adams. Philadelphia, 1874–77.

ADAMS, J. Q.—*Writings,* 7 volumes. Edited by W. C. Ford. New York, 1913–1917.

American State Papers, Foreign Relations, IV.: 348–407. Washington, 1834.

Foreign Relations of the United States, 1910. Washington, 1915.

GALLATIN, ALBERT.—*The Oregon Question,* 1846. Writings, III.: 491–536.

LYMAN, THEODORE.—*The Diplomacy of the United States,* 1778–1828. Vol. II. Boston, 1828.

Proceedings in the North Atlantic Coast Fisheries Arbitration, 1910; 12 volumes Washington, 1912.

RUSH, RICHARD.—1. *Narrative of a Residence at the Court of London,* 1817–1825. London, 1833. 2. *Occasional Productions, etc.,* Philadelphia, 1860.

WILSON, G. G.—*The Hague Arbitration Cases*: 134–205. North Atlantic Coast Fisheries. Boston, 1915.

CHAPTER VIII

THE FLORIDA PURCHASE, 1819

"As there is no court of chancery between nations their differences can be settled only by agreement or by force. The resort to force is justifiable only when justice cannot be obtained by negotiation; and the resort to force is limited to the attainment of justice. The wrong received marks the boundaries of the right to be obtained."—JOHN QUINCY ADAMS.

Florida had been Spanish from the days of Ponce de Leon to the Treaty of Paris, 1763. That treaty closed what in America was called the French and Indian War; but it had been a European war as well, with Spain fighting as an ally of France. During that war Great Britain had captured Havanna, with which Spain in the peace negotiations would not part. Consequently, she ceded Florida to Great Britain in return for the best port in the Antilles.

During the latter part of the American Revolution France and Spain fought Great Britain again. Under the terms of the peace negotiations at Paris, Great Britain ceded Florida back to Spain. In the treaty between the United States and Great Britain, the second article provided that the southern boundary of the United States should run from the middle of the Mississippi River along the thirty-first parallel to the middle of the Apalachicola, thence midstream to the junction with the Flint River, and then straight to the head of the St. Mary's River and down the middle of the St. Mary's to the Atlantic. Thomas Pinckney's treaty with Spain, 1795, incorporated this same southern boundary provision in its second article.

Because of the increasing number of American settlers near the rivers that flowed into the Gulf of Mexico and of their need to use those rivers to float their products to a market, Adams and especially Jefferson grew anxious to acquire the Floridas. Jefferson directed the Secretary of State, Madison, to instruct Charles Pinckney at Madrid to sound Spain on the possibility of acquiring New Orleans and the Floridas. If this proposition should fail to meet with favor, he was empowered to negotiate for the free navigation of the Mobile, the Chattahoochee, and other rivers running through the Floridas.[1] But Pinckney could obtain no definite statement from the Spanish ministers, not even as to whether West Florida was included in the secret Treaty of St. Ildefonso, 1800.

Meanwhile, Madison had instructed Livingston at Paris to obtain what information he could from Talleyrand. Talleyrand gave him to understand that the Floridas were not included in the cession. Jefferson decided to appoint Monroe to join with Livingston as a commission extraordinary to treat with Napoleon at Paris, and he authorized Monroe to join with Pinckney as a similar commission to treat at Madrid. Madison wrote to both Pinckney and Livingston, February 23, 1803, stating that the object of Monroe's instructions would be to procure a cession of New Orleans and the Floridas to the United States.[2] Before Pinckney received this letter he had made a strong effort at Madrid to obtain a reply to his proposition on New Orleans and the Floridas. In the conference which followed, Cevallos informed Pinckney that Louisiana had been ceded to the French, including the town of New Orleans. Shortly afterward, May 4, 1803, Cevallos stated that Spain would not dispossess herself of any territory in favor of the United States. And he referred the United States to France in the following words: "By the retrocession made to France of Louisiana, that power regains the said province with the limits it had saving the rights acquired by other powers. The United States can address themselves to the French government to negotiate the acquisition of territories which may suit their interest.[3]

Madison had, March 2, 1803, instructed Livingston and Monroe to obtain from France "the two Floridas, the Island of Orleans. . . ."[4] The course of these negotiations with Marbois has been described in chapter V. Livingston and Monroe knew

[1] American State Papers, Foreign Relations, II.: 515, 517.
[2] Ibid., II.: 535, 537.
[3] Ibid., II.: 557.
[4] Ibid., II.: 540.

and Marbois knew that West Florida was not included in the Louisiana Purchase. Scarcely had the treaty been signed when a new chain of thought occurred to Livingston. West Florida to the river Perdido belonged to the United States. Without knowing it Napoleon had a good title to West Florida and he had sold that region to America. Why? Did not the first article of the Treaty of 1803 stipulate that the French Republic ceded forever and in full sovereignty the province of Louisiana, and quoting from the Treaty of St. Ildefonso, "with the same extent that it now has in the hands of Spain, and that it had when France possessed it; . . ."? Of course Spain had always held East Florida. But had not France from the beginning claimed as Louisiana all of the Mississippi Valley up to the Appalachian mountain system, down along the Perdido River to the Gulf of Mexico? This possession lasted until 1763, when France among other cessions ceded West Florida to Great Britain with the Iberville River as the western boundary. In 1783 it was ceded back to Spain, and from then on Spain held West Florida and Louisiana. Therefore, the words in the Treaty of St. Ildefonso meant that Bonaparte might have claimed West Florida; and since he transferred all of his rights to the United States, all that the United States had to do was to make good the claim. Said Livingston in his report to Madison, " . . . insist upon this as a part of your right, and to take possession at all events to the river Perdido. I pledge myself that your right is good." [1]

Madison and Jefferson were delighted to accept Livingston's interpretation. Madison wrote back to Livingston, March 31, 1804: "It is not denied," by Spain, "that the Perdido was once the east limit of Louisiana. It is not denied that the territory now possessed by Spain extends to the river Perdido. The river Perdido we may say then is the limit to the east extent of Louisiana ceded to the United States. This construction gives an obvious and pertinent meaning to the term 'now' and to the expression 'in the hands of Spain,' which can be found in no other construction." [2]

[1] American State Papers, Foreign Relations, II.: 561.
[2] Ibid., II.: 575.

And Congress accepted Livingston's interpretation with alacrity. On February 24, 1804, an act, championed by John Randolph, was passed, providing for "laying and collecting duties on Imports and the Tonnage within the territory ceded to the United States by the Treaty of April 30, 1803." The eleventh section of this act authorized the President "whenever he shall deem it expedient to erect the Shores, Waters and Inlets of the Bay and River Mobile and of the other Rivers, Creeks, Inlets and Bays emptying into the Gulf of Mexico, east of the said River Mobile and west thereof to the Pascagoula, inclusive, into a separate District and to establish such place within the same, as he shall deem expedient, to be the Port of Entry and Delivery for such District. . ." [1]

The Spanish minister in Washington, d'Yrujo, took a copy of this act with him to the Secretary of State and objected strenuously, March 7, 1804. Said he: "The authority given to the president is unlimited, east of the River Mobile, and comprehends indirectly the power of declaring or rather making war since it is not to be presumed that any nation will patiently permit another to make laws within its territories without its consent." [2] D'Yrujo weakened his objection by giving special point to the territory east of the Mobile River, for there was a very small patch of territory on that side, stretching to the Perdido, which the United States claimed under the treaty. Spanish objections grew weaker also because of the precarious condition in which Spain was placed by Napoleon's strategy.

In 1804 Monroe proceeded on a special mission to Madrid for the purpose of obtaining East Florida, a settlement of spoliation claims, and a determination of boundaries. He proposed to Cevallos that His Catholic Majesty should cede the territory east of the Mississippi; arbitrate the claims of American citizens and Spanish subjects in accordance with a convention agreed to in 1802, but as yet unratified by Spain; and the United States would limit its western boundary by the Colorado. Under no circumstances should he yield any territory east of the

[1] 2 Statutes at Large, 254.
[2] H. B. Fuller, *The Purchase of Florida*: 124.

Rio Grande.[1] By the end of May, 1805, Spain had totally rejected this proposition,[2] and thereby terminated Monroe's special mission. In April Monroe had joined with Pinckney in asking for the recall from Washington of d'Yrujo for engaging in undue newspaper propaganda in behalf of Spain. D'Yrujo was accordingly recalled.

The United States continued eager for Florida. General Armstrong in Paris was directed to sound Talleyrand on the possibility of obtaining French aid. Talleyrand offered in his equivocal manner to accomplish the result for $7,000,000, if the United States would cancel the claim for spoliations committed by the French in Spanish ports. Jefferson was ready to pay $5,000,000; but Congress opposed this amount and authorized only $2,000,000.[3] By 1806, May 2, Napoleon refused to sell.[4]

Two years later Napoleon acknowledged that England had placed the continent in such a condition that he could not doubt that the United States would declare war on her. And whenever the United States did so he would approve the sending of American troops into Florida.[5] Madison replied that should a precautionary occupation become necessary against the hostile designs of Great Britain "it will be recollected with satisfaction that the measure has received his Majesty's approbation."[6] When these words were conveyed to Napoleon by his minister, the military situation had changed and with it Napoleon had changed his mind. Said he: "Answer the American minister that you do not know what he means about the occupation of the Floridas; and that the Americans, being at peace with the Spaniards, cannot occupy the Floridas without the permission or the request of the King of Spain."[7]

In 1810 a revolution occurred in West Florida. Americans were the leaders, but they acted with the consent of the Spanish governor. Having exhausted the use of the governor as a tool,

[1] American State Papers, Foreign Relations, II.: 627.
[2] Ibid., II.: 666.
[3] Adams, History of the United States, III.: Chapters 5 and 6
[4] Ibid., III.: 376.
[5] Ibid., IV.: 293.
[6] Ibid., IV.: 307.
[7] Ibid., IV.: 311.

they disposed of him, assembled in convention, and declared "West Florida to be a free and independent State." Thereupon, they urged annexation to the United States. President Madison boldly issued a proclamation annexing West Florida to Louisiana and ordering Governor Claiborne to take possession to the Perdido and govern it as a part of the territory of Orleans.[1] Madison reasserted that the territory had been acquired under the Louisiana Purchase. Great Britain had no minister in Washington, but she instructed her chargé d'affaires to protest. Spain had scarcely a mouthpiece either at home or in Washington to voice a protest.

When Congress met in December, Florida received immediate attention. Senator Giles reported a bill extending the territory of Orleans to include West Florida, but Henry Clay pointed out that this had already been done by the President's proclamation. Macon in the House wanted to admit Orleans and West Florida together as one State. Before his measure got through both houses, it provided for the admission of Louisiana with the Iberville as the eastern boundary; and West Florida remained as Orleans Territory until April 14, 1812, when Congress divided the territory at the Pearl River. The western half was then added to the State of Louisiana and the eastern half became on May 14, 1813, a part of the territory of Mississippi.

Rarely has the advice of a lawyer, like that of Livingston at Paris in 1803, been acted upon more assiduously by a client, than did the United States toward West Florida. In 1819, however, the treaty with Spain tended to discredit the advice of Livingston, the laws of Congress relating to West Florida, and the acts of the President relating thereto by recognizing that Spain then ceded West Florida to the United States.[2] It is worthy of note also that the recent maps published by the authority of the United States do not include West Florida as being in the Louisiana Purchase.

Madison expected Congress during the session of 1812–1813 to approve the seizure of East Florida as well, and he took

[1] Richardson, *Messages*, etc., I.: 480.
[2] See Article II of the treaty in Malloy, *Treaties*, II.: 1652.

measures accordingly. Indeed, the inhabitants or patriots of East Florida virtually seized the region for themselves. Commander Campbell with nine American gunboats and General Matthews with a body of American troops assisted them. The Spanish governor, Lopez, surrendered. Amelia Island was occupied. St. Augustine was about to be taken. And General Andrew Jackson was on the way with 2,000 Tennesseans.

But Madison had overreached the desire of the Senate for more territory. That body refused twenty-one to eleven to approve the invasion of Florida. Generals Matthews and Jackson had to be recalled. Then, the old Spanish leaders and the British emissaries roused the Indians to attack the patriots and the remaining Americans, and for several years spasmodic warfare continued.

Spain voiced her protest against the American invasion through the British minister, Foster. Monroe replied that Spain owed America more for spoliations than the whole of East Florida was worth. And he authorized Joel Barlow to give out the same information in Paris.[1] Spain could not maintain order in the province; hence, it had become the breeding ground for smugglers, marauders, and buccaneers. However, on March 8, 1813, the Czar's offer of mediation arrived. This was accepted. And Madison and Monroe decided that it would be unwise diplomatically to procede further with intervention in Florida.

Not until December, 1815, did the United States recognize the government of Ferdinand VII. in Spain, when the President received Don Luis de Onis as minister. A wide variety of questions came up for settlement. Don Luis demanded the return of West Florida. He pointed out that filibustering expeditions into East Florida and Mexico had their origin in Georgia, and sometimes in New Orleans and Norfolk. He assumed that Spain could still enforce her old colonial policy in South and Central America if the United States would observe strict neutrality. He asked, therefore, that vessels sailing under the insurgent flags of Cartagena, of Mexico, and of Buenos Ayres be excluded from American ports, that American vessels be pre-

[1] American State Papers, Foreign Relations, III.: 515.

vented from sailing to Spanish America, and that the Mexican insurgents under the leadership of Toledo and Herrera be barred from recruiting soldiers on American soil.[1]

Secretary Monroe replied with a review of the spoliations committed by Spain and of the treaty agreed to in 1802 for arbitrating the respective claims, but which Spain had not yet ratified. Spain had herself referred the United States to France when Pinckney had been authorized to buy the Floridas. The American ministers in Madrid had repeatedly made overtures for the settlement of the boundary of Louisiana and for the establishment of a neutral belt between the two parties; but Spain had rejected all of them and made none in return. The action of the Spanish government had invited "the most decisive measures on the part of the United States." He spoke of "the breaches of the neutrality of Spain, which her Government permitted, if it did not authorize, by British troops and British agents in Florida, and, through that province, with the Creeks and other Indian tribes, in the late war with Great Britain, to the great injury of the United States. The United States held Louisiana as it had been held by France prior to 1763, extending from the Perdido to the Rio Grande;" and the United States considered her "right established by well-known facts and the fair interpretation of treaties." Monroe asked for more definite information about the collection of troops on American soil by Toledo and Herrera, and if the statement were true the offenders would be prosecuted. With respect to the revolutionists in Spanish America, Monroe stated: "All that your Government had a right to claim of the United States was, that they should not interfere in the contest, or promote, by any active service, the success of the revolution, admitting that they continued to overlook the injuries received from Spain and remained at peace. This right was common to the colonists. With equal justice might they claim that we would interfere to their disadvantage; that our ports should remain open to both parties, as they were before the commencement of the struggle; that our laws regulating commerce with foreign nations should

[1] American State Papers, Foreign Relations, IV.: 422.

not be changed to their injury. On these principles the United States have acted."[1]

The President and Congress did make an effort to strengthen the neutrality law of 1794. The act of March 3, 1817, provided that persons engaged in fitting out vessels in American ports for the purpose of cruising against powers with which the United States was at peace should, upon conviction, be fined as high as $10,000, imprisoned not more than ten years, and the vessel itself might be condemned. During the next year the neutrality laws were revised and embodied in the comprehensive statute of April 20, 1818, which is substantially the present law on the subject.[2] But the law written and the law observed were two different propositions. John Quincy Adams in his "Memoirs" paid particular respect to conditions in Baltimore. "They are all fanatics of the South American cause. Skinner, the postmaster, has been indicted for being concerned in the piratical privateers. Glenn, the district attorney, besides being a weak incompetent man, has a son said to be concerned in the privateers. [3] Adams continued: "The district judge, Houston, and the circuit judge, Duval, are both feeble, inefficient men over whom William Pinkney, employed by all the pirates as their counsel, domineers like a slave driver over his negroes."[4]

As usual, Spain put forth feelers for the best possible place to conduct the negotiations. At first she decided on Washington in order to test Secretary Monroe; then she shifted to Madrid to try the American minister, George W. Erving. Her next move was to make an effort to find upon what conditions Great Britain could be induced to offer mediation. Spain sent another full power to Don Luis de Onis in Washington. This was recalled and negotiations began in Madrid. Finally she decided on Washington. The result was that the best trained man in the United States for the purpose became the American negotiator, John Quincy Adams, President Monroe's Secretary of State.

[1] American State Papers, Foreign Relations, IV.: 425.
[2] See C. G. Fenwick, *The Neutrality Laws of the United States*.
[3] J. Q. Adams, *Memoirs*, IV.: 318.
[4] Ibid., *Memoirs*, IV.: 318.

On December 10, 1817, Don Luis notified Adams that he had received full power and instructions to begin and conclude an agreement. He reviewed and argued at length the claims of Spain in four letters of December 29, 1817, January 5, 8, and 8, 1818.[1] Adams replied on January 16: "I am instructed by the President to propose to you an adjustment of all the differences between the two countries, by an arrangement on the following terms:

1. Spain to cede all her territory eastward of the Mississippi.

2. The Colorado, from its mouth to its source, and from thence to the northern limits of Louisiana, to be the western boundary; or, to leave that boundary unsettled for future arrangement.

3. The claim of indemnities for spoliations, whether Spanish, or French within Spanish jurisdiction, and for the suppression of deposit at New Orleans, to be arbitrated and settled by commissioners, in the manner agreed upon in the unratified convention of 1802.

4. The lands in East Florida, and in West Florida, to the Perdido, to be made answerable for the amount of the indemnities which may be awarded by the commissioners under this arbitration; with an option to the United States to take the lands and pay the debts, or to sell the amount received equally according to the amount of their respective liquidated claims, among the claimants. No grants of land subsequent to the 11th of August, 1802, to be valid.

5. Spain to be exonerated from the payment of the debts, or any part of them."[2]

Adams added that the events on Amelia Island and those which were threatening along the Florida border constituted sufficient motive for the elimination of all delay.

Don Luis de Onis replied on January 24, 1818. He assumed that it was the river Colorado of Natchitoches and not the one of the same name "still farther within the limits of the Spanish provinces" that Adams had in mind. He pointed out that

[1] American State Papers, Foreign Relations, IV.: 452, 455, 460, 463.
[2] Ibid., IV.: 464.

Spaniards held claims for indemnities from the United States; but these Adams had wholly omitted; while both the Floridas were to be ceded by Spain to satisfy American claims. This he held to be offensive to the dignity and honor of His Catholic Majesty as well as unjust. Spain could not possibly be held responsible for the spoliations committed by France within Spanish jurisdiction; moreover, France had assumed that responsibility. Nor would he admit the annullment of grants of land in Florida since August, 1802.

De Onis proposed that Spain should cede the Floridas in return for territory on the west side of but bordering on the Mississippi; that both Spanish and American claims for indemnity be left to the commission mentioned in the unratified agreement of 1802; that Spain and the United States join in their endeavor to obtain from France indemnity for spoliations committed by that state within Spanish jurisdiction; and that the United States should take effective measures to prevent expeditions being fitted out in her ports or territory against the commerce and possessions of Spain.[1]

The events along the Florida border were rapidly reaching a crisis and thus interrupted the negotiations. General Jackson had been directed in January, 1818, to take command of the forces on the border and conclude the war against the Seminoles, half breeds, runaways, slaves, and a motley crew of brigands. He crossed into East Florida, marched to Fowlton, where he found a thousand head of cattle marked with the brands of Georgians. He set fire to the town, and proceeded to St. Marks, which he reached on April 6. He informed the Spanish governor that in order to prevent further breaches of neutrality, United States troops would occupy the fort until the end of hostilities. It was at St. Marks that he captured the English Indian trader Arbuthnot. Jackson marched to Suwanee from which the Indians had fled, due largely to information furnished by a letter from Arbuthnot. While there, he captured another Englishman, Robert C. Ambrister. Jackson returned to St. Marks. The two Englishmen were summoned before a court-martial, charged

[1] American State Papers, Foreign Relations, IV.: 464.

with aiding and comforting the enemy and waging war against the United States, and convicted. Ambrister was shot and Arbuthnot hanged.

Jackson marched back to Fort Gadsden. Toward the end of May news reached him that over five hundred Indians had gathered at Pensacola, were fed by the Spanish governor; and from there they conducted raids upon American settlers. Jackson hurried off for Pensacola. The Spanish governor sent him a message to turn back or he would be driven out. Such threats never failed to enrage Jackson. He took Pensacola without opposition, May 24, 1818; the governor had fled to Barrancas. And there Jackson captured fort, governor, garrison, and all, and sent them off to Havana. He left a small body of troops to hold Pensacola and Barrancas and returned the hero of the Florida border and once more the hero of the nation.

Don Luis de Onis promptly demanded reparation. "The Governor of Pensacola," said he, "had conducted himself with the most scrupulous circumspection, to avoid giving the slightest ground of complaint to General Jackson, his officers, and troops. Neither he nor the Governor of East Florida was notified of the war against the Seminole Indians, nor were they informed of the just causes of that war; nor was any call made upon them to seek and punish those Indians in case of their having committed aggressions upon the lands or citizens of this republic.". . ."I am persuaded that the Government of the United States cannot have authorized this hostile, bloody, and ferocious invasion of the dominions of Spain, . . . In the President's message to Congress of the 25th of March last, I observe that orders have been given to pursue and chastise the Seminole Indians; and that if, in the course of the war, it should be necessary to enter the Spanish territory, the authorities of Spain are to be respected and the territory evacuated the moment the war is at an end." De Onis concluded by demanding a restitution of the places taken and occupied by General Jackson, the delivery of artillery, warlike stores, and public and private property, indemnity for the crown and subjects of Spain, "together with the lawful punishment of the general and the officers of this republic by whom they were committed."[1]

Adams replied that the character of the Indian hostilities could not be unknown to Spain, that in the fifth article of the Treaty of 1795 both parties agreed "to restrain by force all hostilities on the part of Indian nations living within their boundaries," that General Jackson had at one time called on the Governor of Pensacola to comply with the provisions in this treaty, that the answer acknowledged the obligation but pleaded incompetency of force, and that depredations on and massacres of Americans had continued. Said Adams: "By the ordinary laws and usages of nations, the right of pursuing an enemy, who seeks refuge from actual conflict within neutral territory, is incontestable." He concluded, "I am instructed by the President to inform you that Pensacola will be restored to the possession of any person duly authorized on the part of Spain to receive it; that the fort of St. Mark, being in the heart of the Indian country, and remote from any Spanish settlement, can be surrendered only to a force sufficiently strong to hold it against the attack of the hostile Indians, . . ."[2]

Don Luis de Onis forwarded Adams' reply by special messenger to Madrid. The Minister of Foreign Affairs, Don José Pizarro, wrote a note ordering a suspension of diplomatic negotiations and including a threat of war unless suitable termination were put to "an incident which, from its transcendent moment, is capable of producing an essential and thorough change in the political relations of the two countries."[3]

This despatch brought a masterly reply from Adams, November 28, 1818. He reviewed the incidents that led to the war with the Seminoles. He pointed out that Robert C. Ambrister had been a lieutenant in a British force of colonial marines, commanded by Colonel Nicholls, which had landed in Florida. Spain had formally declared herself neutral. The hostility of these British forces had not ceased with the Treaty of Ghent;

[1] American State Papers, Foreign Relations, IV.: 496.
[2] Ibid., IV.: 497
[3] Ibid., IV.: 523.

they continued to sally forth with their black, white, and red combatants against the defenseless borders of the United States. In due time Lord Bathurst and Lord Castlereagh had disavowed the conduct of Colonel Nicholls. But in 1817 Arbuthnot had succeeded Nicholls as the mentor for the Indians and Ambrister had continued his activities among the red men. Jackson had taken action,"not in a spirit of hostility to Spain, but as a necessary measure of self defence; giving notice that they (the forts) should be restored whenever Spain should place commanders and a force there able and willing to fulfil the engagements of Spain towards the United States." He demanded that an enquiry be instituted by Spain into the conduct of her governors in Florida. He returned to the subject of Colonel Nicholls and asked, "Has his Majesty suspended formally all negotiation with the sovereign of Colonel Nicholls for this shameful invasion of his territory, without color or provocation, without pretence of necessity, without shadow or even the avowal of a pretext? Has his Majesty given solemn warning to the British Government that these were incidents of transcendent moment, capable of producing an essential and thorough change in the political relations of the two countries?" Later in the same paragraph: "But against the shameful invasion of the territory; against the violent seizure of forts and places; against the blowing up of the Barrancas and the erection and maintenance, under British banners, of the negro fort on Spanish soil; against the negotiation by a British officer, in the midst of peace, of pretended treaties, offensive and defensive, and of navigation and commerce, upon Spanish territory, between Great Britain and Spanish Indians, whom Spain was bound to control and restrain—if a whisper of expostulation was ever wafted from Madrid to London, it was not loud enough to be heard across the Atlantic nor energetic enough to transpire beyond the walls of the palaces from which it issued and to which it was borne." [1]

Adams wrote this note for Minister Erving to transmit to Don José Pizarro. In addition Adams had in mind the whole

[1] American State Papers, Foreign Relations, IV.: 539.

European situation; and a copy of the note was sent to every American diplomat abroad. The members of the Holy Alliance were particularly interested in the quieting of revolutionary efforts and in the restoration to Spain of her rebellious colonies. Gallatin had written from Paris that the affair at St. Marks had made upon France and other parts of Europe sensations peculiarly unfavorable to the United States.[1] Rush in London had gone to a dinner at the French embassy on July 30, 1818, where foreign diplomats had eagerly inquired whether the seizure of St. Marks and Pensacola meant war with Spain.[2] In the British market the price of stocks fell and newspaper opinion favored retribution for the execution of Arbuthnot and Ambrister.[3] It needs to be said that Adams' grip on the situation did much to place the United States in the right light before the world.

Before this note was written Pizarro had decided to reopen negotiations for a definitive treaty. Jackson's episode had made the need for ceding the Floridas to the United States so apparent that this point required no further argument. De Onis showed a disposition to be content with a boundary slightly farther west than the Mississippi.[4] Thereupon, Adams made an immense concession on the western boundary: beginning at the mouth of the river Sabine, following that river to latitude 32 degrees, thence north to the Red River, up that stream to its source, touching the chain of the Snow Mountains, thence to the summit of those mountains and following the chain to the forty-first parallel, and thence along that parallel to the "South Sea," a quaint term for the Pacific first used by Balboa. Adams had proposed to give up the claim to Texas. No doubt he acted on the advice of President Monroe and the cabinet, for he states in his Memoirs "in all negotiations conducted by me while secretary of state, whether with Spain, France, or England, I insisted invariably upon all the claims of the United States to their utmost extent; and whenever anything was conceded, it was by

[1] Gallatin, *Writings*, II.: 69, 74.
[2] R. Rush, *Residence at the Court of London*, 291 (London, 1833).
[3] Ibid., 412
[4] American State Papers, Foreign Relations, IV.: 526.

direction of the President himself, and always after consultation in cabinet meetings, and that it was especially so in the negotiation of the Florida treaty."[1]

Adams agreed that both parties should renounce claims for damages until the date of the treaty. He still insisted that grants of land in Florida made by Spain since 1802 should be void. For this contention he would have had new facts if he had read the correspondence from Madrid. Erving had discovered in February, 1818, that the King had made three huge land grants in Florida, one to the Duke of Alagon, captain of the bodyguards, another to Count of Punon Rostro, one of his Majesty's chamberlains, and the third to Don Pedro de Vargas, treasurer of the household. It was believed that these grants encompassed all of the remaining crown lands.[2] On the remaining points contained in the treaty there was no serious difference.

Don Luis de Onis replied that he could not agree to have the boundary follow the Red River or the forty-first parallel. Adams thereupon reserved American rights to the Rio Grande.[3] Don Luis sent to Madrid for further instructions on the western boundary. On January 6, 1819, he proposed that the northern boundary should extend from the source of the Missouri, westward to the Columbia River and thence to the sea. Adams rejected it. Don Luis yielded by running the boundary from the Red River to the Arkansas at the one-hundredth meridian and by accepting the forty-first parallel to the San Clemente River, and thence to the Pacific; and he included a project of a treaty.[4] Adams submitted a counter project which approved the shift to the Arkansas but still insisted on the forty-first parallel. It recognized Spanish land grants in Florida up to January 24, 1818.[5]

On February 16, 1819, the French minister in Washington, M. de Neuville, brought to Adams copies of the treaties in parallel

[1] J. Q. Adams, *Memoirs*, VIII.: 186.
[2] American State Papers, Foreign Relations, IV.: 509.
[3] Ibid. IV.: 545.
[4] Ibid., IV.: 617.
[5] Ibid., IV.: 619.

columns, annotated with the differences between the parties. He conducted conversations with Adams and then with Don Luis. The latter yielded to the forty-second parallel. Adams and Don Luis thereupon exchanged full powers, and on Washington's birthday, 1819, signed the treaty.[1] Two days later the Senate advised ratification; and on February 25, 1819, the President signed the document.

Summary of the treaty.

Article I. There was to be a firm and inviolable peace between the parties.

Article II. East and West Florida were ceded to the United States.

Article III. The western boundary of the United States should begin "in the sea" at the mouth of the Sabine, up that river along the western bank to the thirty-second parallel, thence due north to the Red River, up that river to the one-hundredth meridian, thence due north to the Arkansas, up that river along its southern bank to its source, thence due north to the forty-second parallel and then along that parallel to the "South Sea." By this article the United States acquired whatever claim Spain had to the Oregon country.

Article IV. A survey of the western boundary was provided for.

Article V. The inhabitants of the ceded territories should enjoy "free exercise of their religion" and should have the right to emigrate.

Article VI. The inhabitants of the territories ceded to the United States should be incorporated in the union as soon as consistent with the principles of the constitution. This article contained only slight verbal changes as compared with the much debated Article III in the Louisiana Treaty.

Article VII. Possession of ceded territories should be given within six months after the exchange of ratifications. Due to difficulties described later the United States did not receive possession until July 10, 1821.

Article VIII. All grants of land in the ceded territories made

[1] American State Papers, Foreign Relations, IV.: 621–625.

by Spain before January 24, 1818, should be recognized by the United States. All grants made after that date "are hereby declared and agreed to be null and void." Adams had failed to read carefully the Erving correspondence concerning the three huge land grants dated February 6, 1818, until after the treaty was signed.[1] He therefore asked that Spain should expressly cancel those in her ratification.

Article IX. The United States renounced its claims mentioned in the convention of 1802; those based on French seizures, within the jurisdiction of Spain, on the suspension of the right of deposit at New Orleans in 1802, on Spanish seizures either at home or in the colonies; and all other claims filed by American citizens up to the signature of the treaty.

Spain renounced her claims mentioned in the convention of 1802; those based on sums advanced to Captain Pike; on the expedition of Miranda, fitted out in New York; on unlawful seizures by the United States; and all other filed claims of Spanish subjects up to the signature of the treaty.

Article X. The convention of 1802 was annulled.

Article XI. The United States assumed the claims of its own citizens against Spain to the extent of $5,000,000. A special commission was created by this article to hear these claims. Spain agreed to furnish whatever pertinent documents she possessed. And the Spanish minister could ask for the records and proceedings of the commission. Claims to the extent of $5,454,545.13 were later allowed by this commission; and these claims were paid pro rata.[2]

Article XII. The principle that "the flag shall cover the property," mentioned in the Treaty of 1795, "the two high contracting parties agree that this shall be so understood with respect to those Powers who recognize this principle; but if either of the two contracting parties shall be at war with a third party, and the other neutral, the flag of the neutral shall cover the property of enemies whose Government acknowledge this principle, and not of others."

[1] J. Q. Adams, *Memoirs*, IV.: 291.
[2] Moore, *International Arbitrations*, V.: 4517.

Article XIII. Deserters from merchant vessels should be mutually arrested and delivered at the instance of consuls of the respective parties.

Article XIV. The United States certified that it had not received compensation from France for seizures made by French privateers and condemnations made by French tribunals on the coasts and in the ports of Spain. This article had a special point inasmuch as the French minister, M. de Neuville, acted as unofficial mediator toward the close of the negotiations. France agreed to pay these claims in 1831.

Article XV. For a term of twelve years the ports of Pensacola and St. Augustine should be open to Spanish vessels laden with goods of Spanish production "without paying other or higher duties on their cargoes, or of tonnage, than will be paid by the vessels of the United States." No other nation was to enjoy this same privilege.

Article XVI. Ratifications should be exchanged within six months.[1]

The President commissioned John Forsyth as minister to Spain in March, 1819. Secretary Adams instructed him to obtain an expressed renunciation of the grants of Florida lands to the three court favorites and to preserve the right of the United States to be first named in one of the certificates of ratification and the right of the representative of the United States to sign first, one of these certificates.[2]

By a curious turn in political fortune Don Casa d' Yrujo had become the leading minister in Madrid. He had not forgotten his efforts to convince Madison that Livingston's interpretation of the first article in the Louisiana Treaty as including West Florida was a figment of the imagination and his subsequent recall from Washington at the request of Madison. Forsyth's request that the three land grants be expressly cancelled appeared to him to be mere cavil and to have been disposed of by Article VIII of the treaty. This appeared to M. de Neuville, also, to be a fair interpretation.[3] However, Adams did not have

[1] Malloy, *Treaties*, II.: 1651.
[2] American State Papers, Foreign Relations, IV.: 650, 652.
[3] Ibid., IV.: 653.

the authenticated dates of these grants; and he had had considerable experience with tricks in diplomacy.

But the point of vital importance to the Spanish government was the fear that as soon as the treaty had been ratified by Spain, the United States would feel free to recognize the independence of the South American republics; a fear which had considerable reason back of it.[1] Mr. Forsyth waited a month for a reply to his urgent communication. And when it came, June 19, 1819, the reply stated "His Majesty has, in consequence, commanded me to inform you, in reply, that, on reflecting on the great importance and interest of the treaty in question, he is under the indispensable necessity of examining it with the greatest caution and deliberation before he proceeds to ratify it.[2]

Forsyth protested zealously on the delay in ratification. Two months later, August 10, 1819, he was informed that several explanations must be made with the United States and that a person high in the confidence of his Majesty would be despatched to Washington.[3] The time for ratifying the treaty expired on August 22, 1819. On October 2, Forsyth announced to the first minister of state that he had been authorized to receive the ratification by Spain on two conditions; ratification to take place within ten days and disavowal of the three land grants.[4] The first minister continued his dilatory tactics and returned Forsyth's note of October 18, with the explanation that its language would not permit the note to be laid before the King.[5]

The situation grew so strained that the first minister asked the Russian chargé d'affaires, Count Bulgary, to call on Forsyth and state that General Vives would proceed immediately to Washington with competent powers to reach an amicable settlement with the Secretary of State.[6] General Vives was appointed. He travelled leisurely by coach to Bayonne, thence to Paris

[1] See W. F. Johnson, *America's Foreign Relations*, I.: 320 ff. and F. E. Chadwick, *United States and Spain*, Chapter VIII.
[2] American State Papers, Foreign Relations, IV.: 654.
[3] Ibid., IV.: 656.
[4] Ibid., IV.: 662.
[5] Ibid., IV.: 672.
[6] Ibid., IV.: 675.

where he saw Gallatin, from Paris to London where he saw Rush, and began negotiations in Washington on April 14, 1820.

In the meantime Adams had communicated, December 16, 1819, with William Lowndes, chairman of the Senate committee on foreign relations. "As there is no court of chancery between nations" wrote Adams, "their differences can be settled only by agreement or by force. The resort to force is justifiable only when justice cannot be obtained by negotiation; and the resort to force is limited to the attainment of justice. The wrong received marks the boundaries of the right to be obtained." He wrote further that the United States "cannot compel the King of Spain to sign the act of ratification, and, therefore cannot make the instrument a perfect treaty; but they can, and are justifiable in so doing, take that which the treaty, if perfect would have bound Spain to deliver up to them; and they are further entitled to indemnity for all the expenses and damages, which they may sustain by consequence of the refusal of Spain to ratify." [1]

Adams did not have back of this recommendation to use force the unanimous support of the President and the cabinet; nor is it likely that he wanted more than a show of eagerness on the part of Congress to use force. In this he was justified. He aroused public opinion. The hero, Jackson, had no reservations. He wrote to Senator Eaton, December 28, 1819, "Under the bad faith of Spain, as I believe, the only good explanation that can be given is from the mouth of American cannon."

This concentration of American desire together with the successful cultivation of European opinion by the State Department brought the friendly interposition of the Russian, French, and British ministers in Washington. The first letter of General Vives to Adams revealed the causes for Spanish delay, Vives dwelt on the scandalous system of piracy that had been carried on from the ports of the United States against Spain and her possessions and on the spirit of hostility displayed everywhere as being sufficient "imperiously to dictate the propriety of suspending the ratification of the treaty." He proposed that the

[1] American State Papers, Foreign Relations, IV.: 673.

United States prohibit in the future the departure of piratical or hostile expeditions against the Spanish possessions and that the United States should "agree to offer a pledge that their integrity shall be respected."[1] This meant that the United States should bind itself not to recognize the independence of the South American countries.

Adams asked Vives for a copy of his full powers and for a copy of the act of ratification before he would reply. Vives furnished the copy of full powers but not the latter. Adams expressed his surprize and noted that the full power of Don Luis de Onis was identical with that of Vives, in which his Catholic Majesty had promised "on the faith and word of a King, to approve, ratify, and fulfil whatsoever might be stipulated and signed by him." Adams continued, "By the universal law of nations, nothing can release a sovereign from the obligation of a promise thus made, except the proof that his minister, so empowered, has been faithless to his trust, by transcending his instructions." No such proof had been furnished nor had it even been alleged that Don Luis de Onis had violated his instructions. The proposals made in Vives' letter Adams refused to consider "in the present state of relations between the two countries, as points for discussion," until after the Floridas had been delivered.[2]

General Vives had no power to deliver the Floridas, but the French and Russian ministers arranged a conference for him with Secretary Adams; and Adam's letter to Vives of May 3, 1820,[3] shows that at the conference differences had been completely removed. The imputations of hostility to Spain and of violation of neutrality with respect to the Spanish provinces Adams maintained were wholly unfounded. On the last point Adams stated: "As a necessary consequence of the neutrality between Spain and the South American provinces, the United States can contract no engagement not to form any relations with those provinces." In reply Vives expressed satisfaction with

[1] American State Papers, Foreign Relations, IV.: 680.
[2] Ibid., IV.: 682.
[3] Ibid., IV.: 683.

the contents of Adams' letter, except on the last point, the reply to which he would have to refer to Madrid. Vives informed Adams also of the current intelligence that the constitution of 1812 had been sworn to by the King and that, therefore, the ratification of the treaty would have to be approved by the Cortes.[1]

Adams wrote a sharp reply. He quoted Vattel and Martens to show the obligation of the King to ratify. And he informed Vives that the correspondence would be turned over to Congress "to whom it will belong to decide how far the United States can yet, consistently with their duties to themselves, and the rights of their citizens, authorize the further delay requested in your note of the 5th instant."[2] The President sent the papers to Congress the next day, May 9, 1820. Both houses adjourned a week later without taking action.

Forsyth put forth his best efforts during the summer to obtain the approval of the treaty by the Cortes and the ratification by the King. The Spanish government yielded on Vives' third point. And on October 5, 1820, the Cortes advised the King to ratify the treaty with an expressed renunciation of the three land grants. Ferdinand VII. ratified as advised on October 24, 1820. With the certificate of ratification of the treaty an order was included to General Vives for the evacuation and delivery of the Floridas.[3]

When these documents reached General Vives in Washington, he notified Adams to that effect; and he had sufficient pertinacity to plead consideration of indemnity to certain Spaniards and compensation for the benefit of the grantees of Florida lands whose title had been recognized as cancelled. Adams replied characteristically that the former was covered by the treaty and on the later "no indemnity can be due, because no injury was done." [4]

The President resubmitted the treaty to the Senate. That body advised ratification February 19, 1821. The President

[1] American State Papers, Foreign Relations, IV.: 684, 688.
[2] Ibid., IV.: 685.
[3] Ibid., IV.: 696, 702.
[4] Ibid., IV.: 703.

signed it, the ratifications were exchanged, and the President proclaimed the treaty on February 22, 1822; exactly two years after the treaty had been signed by Adams and Don Luis de Onis.

BIBLIOGRAPHY

ADAMS, J. Q.—*Memoirs*, 12 volumes. Edited by Charles Francis Adams Philadelphia, 1874–1877.

ADAMS, J. Q.—*Writings*, 7 volumes. Edited by W. C. Ford. New York, 1913–1917.

American State Papers, Foreign Relations, IV. Washington, 1834.

CHADWICK, F. E.—*The Relations of the United States and Spain, Diplomacy.* Chapter VII. New York, 1909.

COX, ISAAC J.—*The West Florida Controversy.* 1798–1813. Baltimore, 1918.

Executive Journal of the United States Senate, 1819. Volume III. Washington, 1828.

FULLER, H. B.—*The Purchase of Florida.* Cleveland, 1906.

CHAPTER IX

THE WEBSTER-ASHBURTON TREATY, 1842

"It will be for Her Majesty's Government to show upon what rules of national law the destruction of the "Caroline" is to be defended. It will be for that government to show a necessity of self-defence, instant, overwhelming, leaving no choice of means, and no moment for deliberation."—DANIEL WEBSTER.

The issues of paramount importance that passed through Webster's hands during his first term as Secretary of State were those with Great Britain. These issues had led more than once to open hostilities locally and had threatened to involve the two countries in war. These issues may be divided into three parts; those connected with the northeastern boundaries, including the Aroostook War; those connected with the relations between American citizens and the insurgents during the Canadian rebellion of 1837, including the Caroline affair, the case of McLeod, and the need of a provision for extradition; and those connected with the suppression of the international slave trade, including the right of visit and search. Webster argued and presented diplomatically the rights of the United States in the case of the "Creole." And in a dignified and summary manner he reached an understanding with Great Britain, once and for all time, in regard to impressments. All of these issues were merged in the discussions leading to the Webster-Ashburton Treaty.

The negotiators were peculiarly well fitted for reaching an agreement. Before his elevation to the peerage Lord Ashburton bore the name of Alexander Baring. He had been, since 1810, the head of the banking house of Baring Brothers, which held extensive investments in various parts of the world and particularly in the United States. While a resident and in business in America, he had listened to the debates in Congress on Jay's Treaty,[1] and he had married, 1798, the eldest daughter of U. S.

[1] H. Adams, *Life of Gallatin*: 669.

Senator Bingham of Pennsylvania. After his return to London he continued his friendly relations with many American families. He held a seat in the House of Commons for thirty years and served as Chancellor of the Exchequer in the cabinet of the Duke of Wellington. When the aggressive Lord Palmerston ceased to be Secretary of State for Foreign Affairs and Lord Aberdeen succeeded him, the latter looked around for a suitable man to head a special mission to the United States; the choice fell on Lord Ashburton. Webster described him as a good man to deal with, who could see that there were two sides to a question. "He was fully acquainted with the subject, and always, on all occasions, as far as his allegiance and duty permitted felt and manifested good will towards this country." [1]

Daniel Webster had long been the political leader of New England, and he had become nationally known both at the bar and in Congress as the expounder of the constitution. Several times he had been mentioned for the post of minister to London. The summer and fall of 1839 he had spent in the United Kingdom and had been showered with hospitalities. He met the leading men, among them Carlyle, Dickens, Hallam, Canning, and Lord Ashburton. Carlyle's description of him is often quoted. "Not many days ago I saw at breakfast the notablest of your notabilities, Daniel Webster. He is a magnificent specimen. You might say to all the world, 'This is our Yankee Englishman; such limbs we make in Yankee land!" As a logic fencer, or parliamentary Hercules, one would be inclined to back him at first sight against all the extant world. The tanned complexion, that amorphous crag-like face; the dull black eyes under the precipice of brows, like dull anthracite furnaces, needing only to be blown; the mastiff mouth accurately closed; I have not traced so much of silent Berserkir rage that I remember in any man."

President Harrison offered Webster the choice of Secretary of State or Secretary of the Treasury. Webster chose the former. When Harrison died, and Tyler was shortly afterward read out of the Whig party, the members of the cabinet resigned except

[1] Webster, *Works*, II.: 122.

Webster. And it was largely a high sense of patriotism and a desire to settle outstanding difficulties with Great Britain that caused him to remain.

Lord Ashburton arrived in Washington on April 4, 1842. The negotiations were conducted throughout informally; no protocols were kept; and not many letters were exchanged. The first subject to come up was that of the northeastern boundaries. For over half a century the description of the boundary in the Treaty of 1783 had been in dispute. Which was the real river St. Croix therein mentioned? Where was the "northwest angle of Nova Scotia?" What and where were the "Highlands" along which the boundary was to run? Which stream should be regarded as the "northwesternmost head of the Connecticut River?"

Jay's Treaty had provided for a commission to settle the dispute on the St. Croix River. This commission reported in 1798 that it had decided upon the stream and had placed a marker at its source.[1] So that much of the boundary was settled.

The Treaty of Ghent provided for several boundary commissions. Each commission was to be composed of one national of each party to the treaty. And if these commissioners should fail to agree the whole dispute should be referred to "some friendly sovereign or State" for decision. One commission passed upon the boundary in Passamaquoddy Bay; with the result that the islands to the left, including Moose, Dudley, and Frederick passed to the United States, and those to the right, including Grand Manan, passed to Great Britain.[2]

Another commission was to pass upon the boundary from the marker at the head of the St. Croix River to "the northwesternmost head of the Connecticut River, thence down along the middle of that river to the forty fifth degree of north latitude." This commission failed to agree, October 4, 1821; and it developed another source of dispute. Up to that time a survey made of the forty-fifth parallel in 1774 had been accepted as accurate; but this commission found that the true line should run three-

[1] Moore, *International Arbitrations*, I.: 30.
[2] Ibid., I.: 61.

quarters of a mile farther south. To the north of this corrected line, on Rouse's Point, the United States had erected costly fortifications, which controlled navigation northward to the St. Lawrence at that point. The dispute was then submitted to the King of the Netherlands for arbitration. The King refused, however, to abide by the limitations prescribed in the agreement. He had, therefore, in his award, January 10, 1831, exceeded his powers; and for that reason the United States protested.[1] Great Britain recognized likewise that the award was recommendatory rather than decisive; so both parties agreed that the award should not be binding.

President Jackson tried for five years to reach an agreement with Great Britain but failed. Van Buren proposed two methods of reaching the desired result; a commission composed of an equal number of nationals "with an umpire to be selected by some friendly European power, or a commission composed of scientific Europeans." [2] But the suggestions were too indefinite. Great Britain could not accept. In the meantime surveys had been made by Maine and Massachusetts and by New Brunswick. The State and provincial authorities had become exacting on questions of land titles, in the collection of taxes on the fertile farm lands, and of supervising timber rights in the disputed areas. The New Brunswick officials arrested some Americans, which caused the governor of Maine to order out the militia and take possession of the debatable territory. This military occupation became known as the Aroostook War. President Van Buren sent General Winfield Scott to mediate. And he succeeded remarkably in persuading the authorities of Maine and New Brunswick to withdraw their armed forces pending further negotiations.

Secretary of State Forsyth had sought the opinion of the government of Maine on the adoption of a new boundary to be decided upon by diplomatic negotiation rather than by arbitration. Governor Kent submitted the matter to the legislature, which resolved, March 23, 1838, first, that it was inexpedient to

[1] Moore, *International Arbitrations*, I.: 119, 137.
[2] Message of March 20, 1838.

approve the negotiation for a conventional line; but that the State would insist on the line established by the Treaty of 1783; second, that the State had not assented to the appointment of an arbitrator under the Treaty of Ghent, and was not prepared to consent to the appointment of a new one; and third, that the senators and representatives of Maine in Congress should urge the government of the United States to make the survey and to carry the boundary thus determined into operation.

When Webster became Secretary of State he decided not to dally with the slow processes of arbitration in a matter that contained so many explosive elements, but to negotiate directly for a boundary. He might have assumed that the treaty making power of the United States extended to the disposition of land in the questionable possession of a State without the consent of that State, but he did not. Not only were the jurisdictional rights of Maine involved; but when Maine had been separated from Massachusetts and admitted to statehood, the agreement was that the public lands should be held in common and the proceeds from their sale divided equally. A considerable portion of these public lands lay within the disputed region. Webster had, therefore, three parties to negotiate with rather than one.

Webster asked Senator Williams of Maine to consult with the governor and the leading men of the State and to find out what concessions Maine might want in order to agree to a conventional line. Williams found a disposition on the part of the leading men to yield, if suitable reimbursement for expenses were made and the free navigation of the St. John's River were conceded.[1] But Maine would not appoint commissioners until her government should receive information that Lord Ashburton had power to agree to a conventional line.

Webster wrote to the governors of Maine and Massachusetts, April 11, 1842, stating that Lord Ashburton had full power to agree to a boundary and proposing that those States send commissioners "empowered to confer with the authorities of this government upon a conventional line, or line by agreement, with its terms, conditions, considerations, and equivalents;

[1] C. H. Van Tyne, *Letters of Daniel Webster*, 256.

with an understanding, that no such line will be agreed upon without the assent of such commissioners."[1]

A curious incident occurred of which Webster availed himself in persuading the government of Maine to overcome its inertia. In 1814 Jared Sparks had been searching the archives of Paris for papers relating to the Revolution. He found a letter from Franklin to Vergennes, dated December 6, 1782, with a map enclosed. Said Franklin: "I have marked with a strong red line, according to your desire, the limits of the United States as settled by the preliminaries between the British and American plenipotentiaries." Sparks discovered that this strong red line passed westward from the source of the St. Croix River in such a manner as to exclude all the territory drained by streams flowing into the St. John's River.[2] The map supported almost exactly the claim made by Great Britain. Should the map prove to be the one mentioned by Franklin, Maine would lose all of the territory in dispute. Sparks reported the fact to Webster. Accordingly, Webster asked Sparks to go to Augusta and show the map to the governor.[3] The governor declared in favor of a conventional line; and the legislature chose the commissioners. Massachusetts appointed her commissioners soon afterward. On June 12, 1842, those from Maine arrived in Washington and on June 13, those from Massachusetts. On the latter day Lord Ashburton addressed his first note to Webster on the boundary.

Lord Ashburton proposed that the boundary should run due north from the marker at the source of the St. Croix to the river St. John, then follow the channel of that river, except for the Madawaska settlement on the south side of the St. John, which should remain with Great Britain. If this were conceded he would accept the old survey of the forty-fifth parallel, made in 1774, and thus concede to the United States Rouse's Point and add to the States of New York, Vermont, and New Hampshire considerable strips of land which they would not possess if the parallel were corrected. Ashburton expressed himself as willing

[1] Webster, *Works*, VI.: 274.
[2] H. B. Adams, *Life and Letters of Jared Sparks*, II.: 394, 411.
[3] For a discussion of this map, see Moore, *International Arbitrations*, I.: 154.

to concede to the United States the privilege of floating timber down the St. John to the ocean free of duty.

The commissioners from Maine declined this offer and proposed to include the Madawaska settlement on the south side of the St. John and also a large stretch of territory to the north of the St. John beyond the mouth of the Madawaska. For several weeks the negotiations became what Ashburton called "the battle of the maps." Indeed, if it had not been for the persistence of the Maine commissioners, Webster would have been willing to yield the Madawaska settlement on the south of the St. John.[1]

On July 27, 1842, Webster put into the form of a memorandum a description of the boundaries agreed upon in the oral discussions. The boundary should begin with the marker at the source of the St. Croix; thence due north on the line run by the surveyors in 1817 and 1818, provided for in the Treaty of Ghent, to the middle of the channel of the St. John; up the middle of the main channel of that river to the mouth of the river St. Francis; thence up the middle of the channel of the St. Francis and the lakes through which it flows to the outlet of Lake Pohenagamook; thence southwesterly in a straight line to a point on the northwest branch of the river St. John, which point was to be ten miles from the main stream of the St. John; thence, in a straight line eight degrees west of south to the point where the parallel of latitude of 46 degrees 25 minutes intersects the southwest branch of the St. John; thence southerly by that branch to its source in the Metjarmette portage; thence down along the highlands which divide the waters that empty themselves into the St. Lawrence from those which fall into the Atlantic, to the head of Hall's Stream; "thence, down the middle of said stream, till the line thus run intersects the old line of boundary surveyed and marked by Valentine and Collins, previously to the year 1774, as the 45th degree of north latitude;" thence west along that old boundary line to the St. Lawrence River.[2]

Lord Ashburton replied on July 29: "This settlement appears

[1] Webster, *Private Correspondence*, II.: 120, 122.
[2] Webster, *Works*, VI.: 285.

substantially correct in all its parts, and we may now proceed without further delay to draw up the treaty." [1] As a matter of fact, this part of the boundary was incorporated into Article I of the treaty exactly as Webster had described it.[2]

The disputed territory had comprised 12,027 square miles, or 7,697,280 acres. Of this amount Article I of the treaty assigned to the United States 7,015 square miles, or 4,489,600 acres, and to Great Britain 5,012 square miles or 3,207,680 acres.[3] It would appear that such an arrangement should have brought with it universal satisfaction, even in Maine. But for several years this part of the treaty was attacked chiefly on the ground that the award of the King of the Netherlands had conceded to the United States a larger area, namely, 7,908 square miles, or 893 square miles more than under the Webster-Ashburton Treaty. These attacks brought from Webster a masterly two days speech in the Senate, four years later, in defense of the treaty.[4] However, the Dutch award would not, even though accepted, have brought with it the numerous advantages to the people of Maine that this treaty provided.

Article III provided for the free navigation of the river St. John to both parties. The unmanufactured products of forest and farm from the parts of Maine watered by the St. John or its tributaries should, when going down that river to the seaport of St. John, be treated as though they were the goods of New Brunswick. A reciprocal privilege through Maine was granted to similar New Brunswick products in the region watered by the St. John or its tributaries. This privilege increased immediately the value of forest and farm lands in Maine. Great Britain placed a liberal construction on this privilege, and treated the specified products of Maine in the region described, when they reached the ports of the United Kingdom, as though they were the products of New Brunswick.

Article IV made provision for the confirmation of land grants made by either party in the hitherto disputed region provided

[1] Webster, *Works*, VI.: 288.
[2] See maps in Moore, *International Arbitrations*, I.: 85, 143, 149, 156.
[3] Webster, *Works*, VI.: 276.
[4] Ibid., V.: 78.

the claimant had been in possession for more than six years. All other equitable possessory claims were to be recognized and adjudicated "upon the most liberal principles of equity."

Article V provided for the disposition of the so-called "disputed territory fund" and for the payment by the United States to Maine and Massachusetts of $300,000, "in equal moieties." To the latter provision Lord Ashburton protested as "irregular and inadmissible" and wanted it understood that his government incurred "no responsibility for these engagements."[1] The disputed territory fund consisted of money received by the officers of New Brunswick for licenses issued to cut timber in the disputed territory. This fund was now to be divided between the United States and Great Britain "in proportions to be determined by a final settlement of boundaries." The United States agreed to pay over its share to the States of Maine and Massachusetts. The United States agreed further "to pay and satisfy said States, respectively, for all claims for expenses incurred by them in protecting the said heretofore disputed territory and making a survey thereof in 1838." Lord Ashburton objected again; and no doubt properly so, for the agreement partook of the nature of domestic legislation.

Article VI provided for the surveying and marking of the boundaries.

These articles disposed of the troublesome dispute over the northeastern boundary. From July 29 to August 8, 1842, the negotiations progressed rapidly on the remaining points.

It was agreed that the channels in the St. Lawrence on both sides of the Long Sault Islands and of Barnhart Island, off northern New York, and a part of that State, and of the Detroit and St. Clair rivers as well as of St. Clair Lake should be free and open to the navigation of both parties. (Article VI).

The commission appointed under Article VI of the Treaty of Ghent to determine the boundary from Lake Huron to the most northwestern point of the Lake of the Woods could not agree. Instead of submitting the dispute to arbitration, the matter was left for Webster and Ashburton to agree upon. They agreed to

[1] Webster, *Works*, VI.: 289.

draw the boundary so as to assign the disputed Sugar Island to the United States. Lord Ashburton made this concession on the condition that the channels mentioned in the preceding paragraph should be open to British navigation.

The next subject to be taken up was the inviolability of national territory. In 1837 a rebellion had broken out in Canada. It was suppressed, and many of the persons engaged in it had fled to the United States. These associated themselves with several American adventurers and carried on hostilities against Great Britain. They seized Navy Island in the Niagara River, which belonged to Canada. President Van Buren described the situation in his annual message of December, 1838, as follows: "Information has been given to me, derived from official and other sources, that many citizens of the United States have associated together to make hostile incursions from our territory into Canada, and to aid and abet insurrection there, in violation of the obligations and laws of the United States, and in open disregard of their own duties as citizens. This information has been in part confirmed by a hostile invasion actually made by citizens of the United States, in conjunction with Canadians and others, and accompanied by the forcible seizure of the property of our citizens, and an application thereof to the prosecution of military operations against the authorities and people of Canada."[1]

These daredevils and fanatics engaged the steamboat "Caroline," owned by a resident of Buffalo, to carry their supplies from the town of Schlosser, New York, to Navy Island. Canadian troops guarded the opposite shore. On the night of December 29, 1837, a body of volunteers from these troops crossed the river to Navy Island with the hope of finding the "Caroline" there. Being disappointed, they crossed to Schlosser in New York; took forcible possession of the steamer; killed one of the crew, Durfree by name; tugged the vessel out into the current; and left it to drift over Niagara Falls.

The British and Canadian governments approved the action of the volunteers. Colonel McNab, who had ordered the attack,

[1] Richardson, *Messages*, etc., III.: 485.

was knighted. The Secretary of State, Forsyth, protested to the British minister, H. S. Fox, against this "extraordinary outrage committed . . . on the persons and property of citizens of the United States within the jurisdiction of the State of New York."[1] In reply Lord Palmerston asserted that the destruction of the vessel would turn out to be justifiable, and he assumed for the British government full responsibility.[2]

Although frequent expressions of local sympathy for the rebels occurred in New York, Vermont, and Michigan, no further diplomatic action was taken until November, 1840. At that time a former deputy sheriff in Canada, Alexander McLeod, crossed over to New York and boasted that he had been one of the volunteers that attacked the "Caroline" and that he had killed one of her crew. He was arrested by New York State officials and indicted for murder under the laws of New York. He was admitted to bail; but the threat of violence by a mob overawed the court and he was sent back to jail. The British minister, Fox, demanded McLeod's immediate release on the ground that if he had committed the act as charged, he had done so as one of the armed forces of Great Britain and that Great Britain assumed full responsibility. Secretary Forsyth replied that it would be for the courts to decide upon the validity of the defense. The feeling in Great Britain grew intense. Palmerston informed the American minister in London, Stevenson, that if McLeod were executed, that would be the signal for war.[3] Such was the situation when Webster became Secretary of State in the spring of 1841.

Webster was inclined to accept the British view;[4] and if McLeod had been in the custody of federal officials, he would, no doubt, have been set free. But McLeod was in the hands of the authorities of New York. The best that Webster could do was to inform the Attorney General, John J. Crittenden, as to the facts in the case, to advise him to see the governor of New York with the intimation that if the indictment were pending in the

[1] Richardson, *Messages*, etc., III.: 404.
[2] Webster, *Works*, V.: 119.
[3] Bulwer, *Palmerston*, III.: 46, 49.
[4] Webster, *Works*, VI.: 251.

courts of the United States, the President would direct that a nolle prosequi be entered. He advised the Attorney General, further, to go to Lockport where the trial was to be held and to see to it that the prisoner had "skilful and eminent counsel" and that the counsel would be furnished with the material evidence. But he was not to act as counsel himself. If the defense should be overruled by the court, Crittenden should then inform the counsel that it was the wish of the government of the United States that "proper steps be taken immediately for removing the cause, by writ of error, to the Supreme Court of the United States." [1] Crittenden proceeded as he had been advised; and it is probable that no other Attorney General has ever gone on a similar errand.

The counsel asked for McLeod's release on a writ of habeas corpus before the supreme court of New York on the ground that if he had any part in the killing of Durfree, he had acted as a soldier under orders in an expedition sanctioned by the government of Great Britain. McLeod's release was denied.[2] The trial proceeded. The counsel undertook to prove that McLeod had not been present during the attack upon the "Caroline." They were successful, and McLeod was acquitted.

This case led Congress to pass an act, August 29, 1842, drafted by Webster, granting power to justices of the Supreme and district courts of the United States "to grant writs of habeas corpus in all cases of any prisoner or prisoners in jail or confinement, where he, she, or they, being subjects or citizens of a foreign state, and domiciled therein, shall be committed or confined, or in custody, under or by any authority or law, or process founded thereon, of the United States, or of any one of them, for or on account of any act done or omitted under any alleged right, title, authority, privilege, protection, or exemption, set up or claimed under the commission, or order, or sanction of any foreign state or sovereignty, the validity and effect whereof depend upon the law of nations, or under color thereof." The

[1] Webster, *Works*, VI.: 262.
[2] 25 Wendell 482; and for a criticism of the opinion, see 26 Wendell, appendix.

act authorized these judges to hear such cases and upon the presentation of sufficient proof to release.[1]

The attack upon the "Caroline" had two important results. It caused Webster to express in what has become classic form the principle of the right of intervention for national self defense. He used the expression first in a note to the British minister, Fox, and he repeated it to Lord Ashburton on July 27, 1842. "The undersigned trusts that, when her Britannic Majesty's government shall present the grounds at length on which they justify the local authorities of Canada in attacking and destroying the "Caroline," they will consider that the laws of the United States are such as the undersigned has now represented them, and that the government of the United States has always manifested a sincere disposition to see those laws effectually and impartially administered. If there have been cases in which individuals, justly obnoxious to punishment, have escaped, this is no more than happens in regard to other laws. Under these circumstances, and under those immediately connected with the transaction itself, it will be for Her Majesty's government to show upon what state of facts and what rules of national law the destruction of the "Caroline" is to be defended. It will be for that government to show a necessity of self-defence, instant, overwhelming, leaving no choice of means, and no moment for deliberation." [2] The last sentence contains the statement of the principle. Webster continued: "It will be for it to show, also, that the local authorities of Canada, even supposing the necessity of the moment authorized them to enter the territories of the United States at all, did nothing unreasonable or excessive; since the act, justified by the necessity of self-defence, must be limited by that necessity, and kept clearly within it."

Lord Ashburton replied that he agreed as to the principles of international law applicable to the unfortunate case. But, in his estimation, the dispute was not of a kind to be susceptible of any settlement by a convention or treaty. Said he: "Respect for the inviolable character of the territory of independent nations is the

[1] Webster, *Works*, VI.: 267

[2] Ibid., VI.: 261, 293.

most essential foundation of civilization." Being in accord with Webster as to principles, he undertook by a recital of facts, taken largely from American sources, to show that the action of Great Britain in the "Caroline" affair came within the limits prescribed by those principles. "Looking back to what passed at this distance of time," wrote Ashburton, "what is, perhaps, most to be regretted is, that some explanation and apology was not immediately made; this, with a frank explanation of the necessity of the case, might, and probably would, have prevented much of the exasperation, and of the subsequent complaints and recriminations to which it gave rise." [1] This quotation has at times been interpreted as an apology; which it was not; nor was it so received by Webster.

Said Webster in reply, "the President is content to receive these acknowledgements and assurances in the conciliatory spirit which marks your Lordship's letter, and will make this subject, as a complaint of violation of territory, the topic of no further discussion between the two governments." [2]

The second great result of the "Caroline" affair led to the embodiment in the treaty of an article on extradition, as a means of checking the lawless elements along the border. The suggestion of this remedy appears to have been due to Senator Woodbridge of Michigan; [3] but the drafting of the article itself was left to Webster.

Jay's Treaty had provided for the return of fugitives charged with murder or forgery; but that article expired by limitation on October 28, 1807. For many years previous to the Webster-Ashburton Treaty, a condition had existed, such as Senator Woodbridge put it in the Senate, April 7, 1849: "If the perpetrator of a crime can reach a bark canoe or a light skiff, and detach himself from the shore, he may in a few minutes defy pursuit, for he will be within a foreign jurisdiction."

The Treaty of 1842, Article X, provided for the extradition of all fugitives from justice charged with "murder, or assault with

[1] Webster, *Works*, VI.: 294.
[2] Ibid., VI.: 302.
[3] Ibid., V.: 140.

intent to commit murder, or piracy, or arson, or robbery, or forgery, or the utterance of forged paper, committed within the jurisdiction of either."

This article was later amended to include, in 1889, manslaughter, when voluntary; counterfeiting or altering money; uttering or bringing into circulation counterfeit or altered money; embezzlement; larceny; receiving any money, valuable security, or other property, knowing the same to have been embezzled, stolen, or fraudulently obtained; fraud by a bailee, banker, agent, factor, trustee, or director or member or officer of any company, made criminal by the laws of both countries; perjury or subornation of perjury; rape; abduction; child stealing; kidnapping; burglary; housebreaking or shop breaking; piracy by the law of nations; revolt, or conspiracy to revolt by two or more persons on board a ship on the high seas, against the authority of the master; wrongfully sinking or destroying a vessel at sea, or attempting to do so; assaults on board a ship on the high seas, with intent to do grievous bodily harm; crimes and offenses against the laws of both countries for the suppression of slavery and slavetrading. But no fugitive criminal was to be surrendered for an offense of a political character.[1]

In 1900 the list was amended to include: obtaining money, valuable securities or other property by false pretenses; wilful and unlawful destruction or obstruction of railroads which endangers human life; and procuring abortion.[2] The list was further amended in 1905 to include: bribery, defined to be the offering, giving, or receiving of bribes made criminal by the laws of both countries; and offenses, if made criminal by the laws of both countries, against bankruptcy law.[3]

The third series of difficulties with Great Britain that the Webster-Ashburton Treaty settled, or paved the way for settlement, was that arising out of the status of the international slave trade. Both countries had long been interested in the suppression of this trade. The source of this nefarious traffic lay

[1] Malloy, *Treaties*, I.: 740.
[2] Ibid., I.: 781.
[3] Ibid., I.: 799. On the general subject of extradition, see J. B. Moore, *A Treatise on Extradition and Interstate Rendition.*

along three thousand miles of African coast line between Senegal and Cape Frio. Dotting this line were numerous stations, to which the nearby chiefs brought their captives and sold them for some finery or firewater. The slaves were there confined in pens, holding a ship load or more, and were held ready to be loaded on a slaver at a moment's notice. These vessels looked like ordinary vessels from a distance, but they carried concealed slave decks, and had on board large boilers to cook rice for the slaves, extra water casks, numerous shackles, and a large crew. They carried two sets of papers, flags of all nations, and officers ready to adapt themselves to an emergency. The destination of the cargo was usually Porto Rico, Cuba, Brazil, or even some port in southern United States.

As early as June, 1818, Castlereagh had turned to the American minister, Richard Rush, with a project of a convention. This provided for mixed courts to sit on British colonial soil and the reciprocal right of visit and search of suspected slavers flying the British or American flags. Secretary of State Adams doubted the constitutionality of the former and, as for the latter, he knew full well that the American people had had enough of British visit and search before the War of 1812.[1] The United States did, however, show its willingness to coöperate by passing several laws. By the act of April 20, 1818, the burden of proof was thrown on the person detected bringing in negroes that he did so lawfully. By the act of March 3, 1819, the President was authorized to use naval vessels to seize and to bring into port ships engaged in the slave trade if under the control of Americans; he was authorized to send back negroes brought in illegally, and to appoint persons to receive such negroes on the coast of Africa. The act of May 15, 1820, made the slave trade piracy. But the slave trade continued to grow. It was estimated that over three hundred vessels were busily engaged in the traffic. Negotiations were resumed in London and a convention signed, March 13, 1824. But the Senate tinkered the provisions on the reciprocal right of visit and search in such a manner that Great Britain refused to approve the amendments.

[1] American State Papers, Foreign Relations, V.: 70.

By 1840 the American flag had become the protector of every slaver bold enough to fly it. Webster and Ashburton took up the matter and came to the agreement stated in Article VIII of the treaty. Each party was to maintain an adequate naval force off the coast of Africa. It was understood that the vessels of the American navy were to visit and search suspected slavers flying the American flag and to take charge of the offenders in accordance with American laws. The consequent appearance of American war vessels off the African coast had the effect of making the stars and stripes appear less frequently at the mast head of slavers. The United States failed to lend its full coöperation in the suppression of the slave traffic until after the Civil War had begun.[1]

Merged with this negotiation on the slave trade occurred an effort to settle the case of the "Creole." This American brig sailed from Hampton Roads on October 27, 1841, with a cargo of 135 slaves, bound for New Orleans. While at sea, on November 7, the slaves mutinied, killed one of the owners of the cargo, secured possession of the vessel, and ordered the mate under threat of death to steer for Nassau in the Bahama Islands. There the slaves, except those implicated in the murder, were released by the British authorities on the ground that slavery did not exist in the Bahamas. The United States asked for their surrender for the reason that the ship had entered in distress, that such an entrance into a foreign port did not suspend the operation of the laws of the United States, or affect in any way the legal relations of the persons on board. Webster argued ably the rights of the United States in a long letter to Lord Ashburton on August 1, 1842.[2] Ashburton replied that the news of the "Creole" had reached London only a few days before his departure. He urged, therefore, that the matter be omitted from the treaty and referred to London for adjustment. In the meantime, he agreed "that there shall be no officious interference with American vessels driven by accident or by violence" into the ports of the British possessions on the southern borders

[1] See treaties of 1862, 1863, 1870, and 1890 in Malloy, *Treaties*.
[2] Webster, *Works*, VI.: 303.

of the United States.[1] Webster expressed regret but acquiesced.[2] In 1853 the case was submitted to arbitration; and the umpire, Joshua Bates of the firm of Baring Brothers, London, sustained the argument that Webster had made in 1842, and awarded to the United States the sum of $110,330.[3]

There was one other point mentioned in the negotiations, but omitted from the treaty, on which Webster achieved definite results. And that was on the question of the impressment of American sailors. Ashburton pleaded that he had no instructions on that subject. Nevertheless, Webster reviewed the American argument. He repeated the principle laid down by Jefferson, that "the simplest rule will be, that the vessel being American shall be evidence that the seamen on board are such."

Webster continued: "Fifty years' experience, the utter failure of many negotiations, and a careful reconsideration, now had, of the whole subject, at a moment when passions are laid, and no present interest or emergency exists to bias the judgment, have fully convinced this government that this is not only the simplest and best, but the only rule, which can be adopted and observed, consistently with the rights and honor of the United States and the security of their citizens. That rule announces, therefore, what will hereafter be the principle maintained by their government. In every regularly documented American merchant vessel the crew who navigate it will find their protection in the flag which is over them." [4]

Ashburton replied that the note would be transmitted without delay to his government. It need hardly be said that Webster's statement became just as binding upon Great Britain as any separate article in the treaty could possibly have made it.

On August 9, 1842, the treaty was signed. The Senate advised ratification on August 20; the President ratified on August 22; the ratifications were exchanged on October 13; and on November 10, the President proclaimed the treaty.

Never have diplomatic negotiations been conducted on a

[1] Webster, *Works*, VI.: 313.
[2] Ibid., VI.: 317.
[3] Moore, *International Arbitrations*, I.: 417.
[4] Webster, *Works*, VI.: 325.

higher plane than between Webster and Ashburton. Each was actuated with a genuinely friendly spirit toward the other; and each was actuated with the deepest patriotic motives toward his country. Both knew thoroughly the subject matter committed to their charge; and both were well versed in the principles of international law. They sat as judges endeavoring to reach a just conclusion, rather than as partisans attempting to over-reach each other and to win their case.

BIBLIOGRAPHY

CURTIS, GEORGE TICKNOR.—*Life of Daniel Webster*, 2 volumes, New York, 1870.

McINTIRE, J.W.—*The Writings and Speeches of Daniel Webster*, 18 volumes, Boston, 1903.

McMASTER, J. B.—*History of the United States*, volume VII. New York, 1910

MOORE, J. B.—*International Arbitrations*, volume I. Washington, 1898.

TIFFANY, ORRIN E.—*Relations of the United States to the Canadian Rebellion of 1837*–1838. Ann Arbor, 1905.

WEBSTER, DANIEL.—*Letters*. Edited by C. H. Van Tyne. New York, 1902.

WEBSTER, DANIEL.—*Private Correspondence*. 2 volumes. Edited by Fletcher Webster. Boston, 1857.

WEBSTER, DANIEL.—*Works*, volumes II, V, and VI. Boston, 1851.

CHAPTER X

THE TREATY OF GUADALUPE HIDALGO, 1848

"Sister republics, may the two countries ever maintain the most friendly relations in all their intercourse."—CLIFFORD AND SEVIER TO PRESIDENT PENA Y PENA.

"I desire nothing more ardently than that our treaty may be the immutable base of that constant harmony and good understanding which should prevail with sincerity between the two republics, for the advancement of their happiness, their greatness, and their respectability in the universal society of nations."—FROM THE REPLY OF PENA Y PENA.

President Tyler signed the joint resolution of Congress for the admission into the union of the republic of Texas March 1, 1845. Three days later Polk was inaugurated. The part of his address that people at home and abroad read with greatest interest related to Texas. He asserted that the Lone Star State had once been a part of the United States; that the region had been unwisely ceded to Spain in 1819; that Texas had been independent since 1836; and that she had a complete right to dispose of her territory and to merge her sovereignty with that of the United States. "I regard the question of annexation as belonging exclusively to the United States and Texas. They are independent powers competent to contract, and foreign nations have no right to interfere with them or to take exceptions to their reunion." [1]

But the Mexican minister in Washington, Señor Almonte, addressed to the Secretary of State, March 6, 1845, a vehement protest against the joint resolution. The United States had committed the most unjust act of aggression against a friendly state that could be found in the annals of modern history. The United States had despoiled Mexico of a large part of her territory by admitting into the union Texas, "an integrant portion of the Mexican territory." And he demanded his passports.[2]

[1] Richardson, *Messages*, etc., IV.: 380.
[2] Sen. Doc. I, 29 Congress, 1 sess., 38.

Polk chose for his Secretary of State, James Buchanan, who entered upon his duties March 10, 1845. On that very day he replied to Almonte's protest. The admission of Texas was, he stated, "irrevocably decided, so far as the United States are concerned." He repeated that Texas had long since achieved her independence of Mexico, and that, therefore, Mexico had no just cause of complaint. He added that the President regretted that the government of Mexico should have taken offense; and he assured Almonte that the President would make strenuous efforts to reach an amicable adjustment of outstanding disputes.[1]

The Mexican government had virtually decided to recognize the independence of Texas; but to tolerate her annexation to the United States might endanger the existence of Mexico herself; so thought Cuevas, the Minister of Foreign Relations, in March, 1845. On March 28, Cuevas wrote to the American minister in Mexico, Wilson Shannon, that diplomatic relations could not continue between the two countries. What could he add to what had already been said in protest? "Nothing more than to lament that free and republican nations, neighbors worthy of a fraternal union founded in mutual interest and a common and noble loyalty, should sever their relations by reason of an event which Mexico has endeavored to forestall, but which the United States had carried through and which is as offensive to the first as it is unworthy of the good name of the American union." He added that Mexico would oppose the annexation of Texas "with all the earnestness which becomes its honor and sovereignty." [2] Such words threatened war.

The President, Herrera, called a special session of Congress to meet on July 1, 1845, for the purpose of considering among other subjects those relative to the United States and the department of Texas. Congress met; and on July 21, 1845, Cuevas proposed the following resolution: "As soon as the government ascertains that the department of Texas has united itself to the American Union, or that the troops of the latter have invaded it,

[1] Sen. Doc. I, 29 Congress, 1 sess., 39.
[2] Rives, *United States and Mexico*, I.: 697, 701.

it shall declare that the nation is at war with the United States of North America. This war shall be conducted for the purpose of saving the integrity of the Mexican territory within its ancient limits—recognized by the United States in the treaties from the year 1828 to 1836—and for the purpose of assuring the threatened independence of the nation."[1]

On that same day the Minister of Finance asked the Mexican Congress to authorize a loan of $15,000,000. Congress did authorize the loan on September 15, 1845; but it failed to authorize the declaration of war. By the end of July, 1845, General Taylor had arrived at Corpus Christi and proceeded to occupy the territory between the Neuces and the Rio Grande.

But a war with Mexico was not what President Polk wanted. He had the Oregon dispute with Great Britain on his hands. The support of Congress in favor of a war policy toward Mexico would be doubtful. And the only valid reason for war consisted in the failure of Mexico to satisfy the claims of Americans. He decided to attempt to reëstablish diplomatic relations. But the news of the warlike spirit of the Mexican government made him uncertain as to whether an American minister would be received. He instructed Secretary Buchanan to write to the American consul, John Black, in the city of Mexico, September 17, 1845, to ascertain whether the Mexican government would receive "an envoy from the United States, intrusted with full power to adjust all the questions between the two governments. Should the answer be in the affirmative, such an envoy will be immediately despatched to Mexico."[2]

On the strength of the information furnished by Polk's secret agent in Mexico, W. S. Parrott, the President had conferred with John Slidell of New Orleans and asked him to undertake the mission.[3] Consul Black's reply did not reach Washington until November 9, 1845, when Parrott appeared with it in person. The Mexican Minister of Foreign Relations had expressed in equivocal terms that Mexico would receive a "commissioner"

[1] Rives, *United States and Mexico*, II.: 59.
[2] H. R. Doc. 60, 30 Cong., 1 sess., 12.
[3] Polk, *Diary*, I.: 34.

with full powers to settle the "present dispute." And he made this disposition on the part of Mexico conditional upon "the previous recall of the whole naval force now lying in sight of our port of Vera Cruz." [1]

Polk directed Slidell to go to Pensacola and there await instructions. The first subject which was to engage Slidell's attention was the claims of American citizens against Mexico. "The history of no civilized nation presents," wrote Secretary Buchanan, "in so short a period of time, so many wanton attacks upon the rights of persons and property as have been endured by citizens of the United States from the Mexican authorities." Ten years before, Jackson had sent a special message to the Senate on this subject, in which he had mentioned that the conduct of Mexico "would justify, in the eyes of all nations, immediate war." Jackson had asked for an act authorizing reprisals by the use of naval force. Both the Senate and the House recommended that another effort be made to obtain a just settlement. This was done. Mexico made fair promises, but evaded all compliance with them. On April 11, 1839, an agreement was reached to arbitrate these claims. By 1841, February, the commission had awarded to the United States on behalf of American claimants $2,026,139; and had not then disposed of all of the claims. Mexico found it inconvenient to comply with the award. Again the United States agreed to a convention, January 30, 1843, by which the interest on the sum awarded should be paid annually and the principal by installments. Mexico paid these up to April 30, 1843, and since that time she had paid neither. Still another convention was entered into in regard to American claims; but Mexico had "interposed the same evasions, difficulties, and delays." It became, therefore, Slidell's duty to impress upon the Mexican government the grave injustice of their conduct, the patient forbearance of the United States, and the need for a speedy adjustment.

"But," said Buchanan, "in what manner can this duty be performed consistently with the amicable spirit of your mission? The fact is but too well known to the world, that the Mexican

[1] H. R. Doc. 60, 30 Cong., 1 sess., 16.

government are not now in a condition to satisfy these claims by the payment of money. Unless the debt should be assumed by the government of the United States, the claimants cannot receive what is justly their due. Fortunately, the joint resolution of Congress, approved 1st March, 1845, 'for annexing Texas to the United States,' presents the means of satisfying these claims in perfect consistency with the interests, as well as the honor, of both republics. It has reserved to this government the adjustment 'of all questions of boundary that may arise with other governments.' This question of boundary may, therefore, be adjusted in such a manner between the two republics as to cast the burden of the debt due to American claimants upon their own government, whilst it will do no injury to Mexico."

Buchanan pointed out the reasons for the claim of Texas to the Rio Grande from its mouth to its source as the boundary. The western boundary of the Louisiana Purchase had been the Rio Grande. This had been given up in 1819; but when Texas achieved her independence by the battle of San Jacinto, April, 1836, her jurisdiction extended to the Rio Grande. Representatives of the people in the region between the Nueces and the Rio Grande had taken part in the legislative and constitutional deliberations of Texas. The United States desired to deal liberally with Mexico; and Slidell was empowered to offer that the United States would assume all the just claims of American citizens against Mexico for the boundary established by the Congress of Texas, beginning at "the mouth of the Rio Grande; thence up the principal stream of said river to its source; thence due north to the forty-second degree of north latitude." If Mexico would add "the narrow strip of territory in the valley of New Mexico, west of the Rio Grande," Slidell might agree to pay $5,000,000 for it.

The last subject in the instructions related to California. Information possessed by the State Department led to the apprehension that both Great Britain and France had "designs upon California." Slidell should ascertain whether Mexico had any intention of ceding it. The government of California was only nominally dependent on Mexico; and this was especially true since the recent rebellion, which had sent back to Mexico Governor Micheltorena with his convict soldiers. Slidell was informed that "Money would be no object, when compared with the value of the acquisition." For any line running due west from the Rio Grande so as to include Monterey, Slidell might offer $25,000,000. And for any line running due west so as to include the harbor and bay of San Francisco, he might offer $20,000,000. Full powers for the concluding of a treaty were enclosed with the instructions. Finally, Slidell was informed "Your mission is one of the most delicate and important which has ever been confided to a citizen of the United States." [1]

These instructions had been approved at a cabinet meeting on November 8, 1845.[2] Supplementary letters from Buchanan to Slidell show that Polk was willing to forego the acquisition of California if it should appear possible only to adjust the claims and to settle the boundary of Texas.[3] Slidell stepped ashore at Vera Cruz on November 29, 1845; and within a week the American consul announced his arrival to the Minister of Foreign Relations. Just seven weeks had passed since that minister had consented to receive a commissioner from the United States.

The minister procrastinated. He had not expected an envoy until January. The opposition was calling him a traitor for entering into the arrangement with the United States; and the opening of negotiations might provoke a revolution and destroy Herrera's administration.[4] On December 6, 1845, Slidell wrote the usual formal note to the Minister of Foreign Relations asking when he might be received by the President, and he enclosed a copy of his credentials. He received no reply. On December 15, he wrote again. The minister replied that the matter was under consideration by the council. And on December 17 the council published its decision: "The Supreme Government is advised that the agreement which it entered

[1] Sen. Doc. 52, 30 Cong., 1 sess., 51.
[2] Polk, *Diary*, I.: 93.
[3] Buchanan, *Works*, VI.: 311, 345.
[4] H. R. Doc. 60, 30 Cong., 1 sess., 23.

into to admit a plenipotentiary of the United States with special powers to treat of the affairs of Texas, does not compel it to receive an Envoy Extraordinary and Minister Plenipotentiary to reside near the Government, in which character Mr. Slidell comes according to his credentials." [1] On December 20, Slidell was informed officially that he could not be received.[2]

Slidell decided to await further instructions from home. While waiting he witnessed a bloodless and successful revolution staged by General Paredes on the basis that President Herrera had lost public confidence, because he had tried to evade war with the United States. Slidell hoped that the need for money might make the new administration more tractable. New instructions arrived in March, 1846; and these directed Slidell to apply to the new Minister of Foreign Relations. If he met with refusal, he was to return home. Slidell applied; and he was not received, because the United States maintained a threat of force by land and sea; because the United States had annexed Texas; and because a minister instead of a "commissioner" had been sent; and because the President of the United States had exceeded his constitutional powers in accrediting Slidell as a minister without having the appointment ratified by the Senate.[3] The Mexicans felt encouraged inasmuch as war appeared probable between the United States and Great Britain over the Oregon dispute. Slidell asked for his passports and returned home.

By this time Polk had received another suggestion that might solve the Mexican problem. Colonel Atocha of New Orleans had called on the President Friday, February 13, 1846. He was a Spaniard by birth; he had lived for many years in Mexico and had supported the sinister Santa Anna, who was now in exile at Havana. Polk confided freely to his diary what took place at this interview. Atocha had recently come from Havana, where he had seen Santa Anna, who was in constant communication with his friends in Mexico. The revolution by Paredes had Santa

[1] Rives, *United States and Mexico*, II.: 71.
[2] H. R. Doc. 60, 30 Cong., 1 sess., 37.
[3] Ibid., 67.

Anna's approval; and the latter had strong hopes of returning to power. Santa Anna favored a treaty with the United States with the Rio Grande as the boundary for Texas. He favored the cession to the United States of the territory lying north of a line beginning at San Francisco Bay and running due east to the Colorado. For this cession the United States should pay $30,000,000. This sum would enable Santa Anna to place the government of Mexico on a firm footing. Santa Anna was surprised that General Taylor's army was kept at Corpus Christi instead of on the Rio Grande. And he had expressed the opinion that the United States "would never be able to treat with Mexico, without the presence of an imposing force by land and sea." [1] General Taylor had already received orders to occupy the east bank of the Rio Grande.

Colonel Atocha called again the following Monday; and the President made another entry. He repeated Santa Anna's assurances about a treaty, but no "administration in Mexico dared to make such a proposition, for if they did so there would be another revolution by which they would be overthrown. He said they must appear to be forced to agree to such a proposition. He went on to give his own opinion and, as he said, that of General Santa Anna, that the United States should take strong measures before any settlement could be effected. He said our army should be marched at once from Corpus Christi to the Del Norte, and a strong naval force assembled at Vera Cruz, that Mr. Slidell, the U. S. Minister, should withdraw from Jalappa, and go on board one of our ships of war at Vera Cruz and in that position should demand the payment of the amount due our citizens; that it was well known the Mexican Government was unable to pay in money, and that when they saw a strong force ready to strike on their coasts and border, they would, he had no doubt, feel their danger and agree to the boundary suggested. He said that Paredes, Almonte, and General Santa Anna were all willing for such an arrangement, but that they dare not make it until it was made apparent to the Archbishop of Mexico and the people generally that it was

[1] Polk, *Diary*, I.: 224.

necessary to save their country from a war with the United States."[1]

On the day after each of these interviews, the President held a cabinet meeting. At the first he proposed to send a confidential agent to Santa Anna; but the cabinet did not approve, so that matter was dropped. At the second he proposed sending a strong message to Congress asking that the President be given authority to secure a redress of grievances "by aggressive measures."[1] Nothing more appears to have been done in regard to Mexico until after Slidell's return to Washington, May 8, 1846. In the meantime, the Oregon dispute had been as good as settled.

The President did most ardently want California and he still thought that it might be had through negotiation. All the information at hand tended to show that the region was virtually independent of Mexico. The Mexicans there had gradually become degenerate. They made no new settlements. They robbed the missions. Agriculture withered under their ravages. With numerous cattle at their doors, they had neither milk, butter, nor cheese. The trade, including that in hides, was in the hands of foreigners like Sutter; so was the trapping of fur bearing animals. The Mexicans made no surveys and no explorations. No one knew of the mineral resources as yet; but it was generally known that California was a garden spot, splendidly adapted for agriculture and grazing. The Mexican had ceased to keep step with the progress of civilization. He was impotent to govern the territory. And it followed as a consequence that he could not long retain possession. Efficient colonists percolated into the region. With this movement of population the American government had nothing to do; it neither encouraged nor discouraged. However, Americans had made emphatic appeals to Polk's administration when their property had been destroyed or confiscated and their relatives had been killed.

Polk did not have great confidence in Congress on the Mexi-

[1] Polk, *Diary*, I.: 228.
[2] Ibid., I.: 233.

can issue. The northeastern states could not look with favor upon the extension of what they believed would be slave territory. Their representatives in Congress had barely consented to the annexation of Texas. The northwest could hardly be assumed to be in favor of an aggressive war. And later Lincoln's spot resolution confirmed that assumption. As a Tennessean Polk knew the South and the southwest. The people had favored the annexation of Texas; but leading southerners knew that the region was ill adapted to slavery. Polk had even kept secret the orders to General Taylor to advance to the Rio Grande. Moreover, he recognized that the right of the United States to the strip between the Neuces and the Rio Grande was in question, or he would not have consented to bargain for it by assuming the claims of American citizens against Mexico.

In Polk's mind the actions of Mexico left no recourse but war. And war he had decided upon even before he heard that the Mexicans had crossed the Rio Grande to attack General Taylor. At the cabinet meeting on Saturday, May 9, 1846, Polk stated that he had no new advices from the border, but he could not maintain silence much longer. He expected to send a message to Congress the following Tuesday; and he asked the members of the cabinet if he should recommend a declaration of war. All replied yes, except Bancroft, who explained that he would feel better satisfied if the Mexicans committed the first overt act. Polk decided to send the war message on Tuesday. But on the evening of the same day, Polk received the information that hostilities had been opened by the Mexicans under General Arista. This satisfied Bancroft's scruples; and Polk decided to send the war message on Monday.[1] Polk and Bancroft spent the entire day of Sunday, May 10, in preparing the message. Polk made the following entry in his diary: "At 10½ o'clock I retired to rest. It was a day of great anxiety to me, and I regretted the necessity which had existed, to make it necessary for me to spend the Sabbath in the manner I have." [2]

[1] Polk, *Diary*, I.: 384.
[2] Ibid., I.: 389.

Polk did not recommend to Congress that war be declared. The message stated that "war exists by the act of Mexico." He reviewed the treatment by Mexico of the claims of American citizens, the double refusal to receive Slidell, the rights of Texas to the Rio Grande as a boundary, the warlike proclamations of the Mexican government, and the destruction of commerce. "In the meantime we have tried every effort at reconciliation. The cup of forbearance had been exhausted even before the recent information from the frontier of the Del Norte. But now, after reiterated menaces, Mexico has passed the boundary of the United States, has invaded our territory and shed American blood upon American soil. She has proclaimed that hostilites have commenced, and that the two nations are now at war." And he recommended that Congress make liberal provision for raising and sustaining adequate military forces.[1]

Congress supported the President promptly. News arrived of General Taylor's series of victories; a series too brilliant for Polk's approval, for he did not intend that presidential candidates should be made in Mexico. Fremont and Kearny took gradually possession of the then almost isolated region of California. After some doubts and misgivings, covering six months, Polk ordered General Scott to command the expedition to Vera Cruz. But the move that the President expected most from was based on the information received from Colonel Atocha. He thought correctly that Santa Anna would have considerable influence in Mexico, but incorrectly that Santa Anna would live up to his implied promises. Secretary of the Navy Bancroft sent a confidential message to Commodore Conner, who commanded the naval forces before Vera Cruz: "If Santa Anna endeavors to enter the Mexican ports, you will allow him to pass freely."[2]

So much significance did Polk attach to Santa Anna that he designated a special agent to confer with the fugitive at Havana. This agent was Commander Alexander Slidell Mackenzie, a nephew of John Slidell. Mackenzie reached Havana on July

[1] Richardson, *Messages, etc.*, IV.: 437.
[2] Reeves, *American Diplomacy under Tyler and Polk:* 298.

5, 1846, and, two days later, had a long interview with Santa Anna. He informed Santa Anna that the United States naval vessels off Mexico would permit him to return, that the President wanted the government of Paredes overthrown, that the United States would agree to no armistice with Paredes, and that as soon as Santa Anna should return to power and announce his readiness to treat, the President would agree to a suspension of hostilities by land but the blockade would be maintained. American claims being recognized, the President would ask for no indemnity, and he would pay liberally for the cession of northern Mexico.

Santa Anna expressed gratitude for the order to Commander Conner to let him pass, and drafted a note, which he asked Mackenzie to copy. In this note Santa Anna enjoined the greatest secrecy and promised that being restored to his country he would enter into negotiations and agree to such a peace as had been described. He preferred a friendly arrangement to the ravages of war. To attain this object he considered it necessary that General Taylor should advance to the city of Saltillo; thus compelling Paredes to fight or withdraw. Taylor could then advance to San Luis Potosi which would compel Mexicans of all parties to recall Santa Anna.[1]

On Sunday morning, August 16, 1846, the British war vessel, "Arab," passed by the American vessels off Vera Cruz into the port. The senior British officer had informed Commodore Conner that the vessel carried no cargo and if permitted to go into port would take none on her return. "I could easily have boarded the Arab," Conner reported to Bancroft, "but I deemed it most proper not to do so, allowing it to appear as if he had entered without my concurrence."[2] Santa Anna had landed at Vera Cruz, and he proceeded to the capital in triumph.

Hardly had Santa Anna reached the city of Mexico before a note from Buchanan arrived, dated July 27, 1846, offering to send a minister with full power to conclude a treaty of peace. The offer was rejected. Santa Anna as "general-in-chief of

[1] Reeves, *American Diplomacy under Tyler and Polk:* 299.
[2] H. R. Doc. 60, 30 Cong., 1 sess., 776.

the liberating army" was not the same as Santa Anna in exile.

In January, 1847, Polk made another effort to open negotiations. This time he sent the renowned Colonel Atocha himself. But the Mexicans spurned the overtures. Polk's disappointment was tempered by the news of Taylor's victory over Santa Anna's forces at Buena Vista and of the surrender of Vera Cruz to Scott. Again the subject of peace negotiations came before a cabinet meeting on April 10, 1847. Polk recorded in his diary that he had emphasized the need of having a commissioner with full powers, "who should attend the head-quarters of the army ready to take advantage of the circumstances as they might arise to negotiate for peace." All the members of the cabinet had concurred in his opinion. But his embarrassment consisted in the selection of a suitable commissioner. Thomas H. Benton had asked for the position with the proviso that he be given chief command of the army as well.[1] The diary states: "Such is the jealousy of the different factions of the Democratic party in reference to the next Presidential Election towards each other that it is impossible to appoint any prominent man or men without giving extensive dissatisfaction to others, and thus jeopardizing the ratification of any Treaty they might make. In this also the Cabinet were agreed." [2] Polk had stated that he preferred Buchanan, but he could not be spared for an indefinite period. Buchanan concurred in this view and had suggested the chief clerk of the State Department, Nicholas P. Trist. After much conversation the cabinet unanimously agreed that it would be proper to send Trist with a project of a treaty drawn by Buchanan and approved by the cabinet.

In a week the cabinet had before it the project of a treaty. This provided that the boundary should "commence in the Gulf of Mexico, three leagues from the land opposite the mouth of the Rio Grande." Nothing in the correspondence indicates why the nine instead of the three mile limit was inserted in the project and finally accepted in the treaty. The boundary should follow

[1] Polk, *Diary,* II.: 352.
[2] Ibid., II.: 466.

the Rio Grande to the point where it strikes the southern line of New Mexico; thence west in such a manner as to convey to the United States all of New Mexico and Upper and Lower California. In consideration of this extension of boundary the United States agreed to pay $15,000,000 in five equal annual installments, the first one to be paid immediately after the treaty had been ratified by Mexico. And the United States agreed to assume the just claims of American citizens up to $3,000,000. Mexico should agree to grant and guarantee forever to the government and citizens of the United States the right of transport across the isthmus of Tehuantepec. Mexico should not confiscate or impose any additional duty upon goods imported through ports that had been under American occupation. The Treaty of Commerce of 1831 was to be revived for eight years.[1]

In the accompanying instructions Trist was directed to communicate a copy of the project and of the instructions to General Scott. If it should appear necessary during the negotiations with the Mexican plenipotentiary Trist might offer as high as $30,000,000 for Upper and Lower California, New Mexico, and the right of transit across Tehuantepec. The sine qua non of any treaty consisted in "the extension of our boundaries over New Mexico and Upper California, for a sum not exceeding twenty millions of dollars." Should the Mexican agent insist that some provision be inserted in the treaty assuring the rights of persons and property in the ceded territory, then Trist might consent to the insertion of the substance of the third article of the Louisiana Treaty. This provided for incorporation in the United States and admission to citizenship of the inhabitants as soon as the principles of the constitution would permit. In the meantime there should be free enjoyment of property and of religious worship. But all titles to land issued by Mexico since May 13, 1846, should be null and void. As soon as the treaty should be signed and ratified by Mexico Trist was empowered to communicate that fact to the American military and naval commanders, who had received orders from the Secretary of War and Secretary of the Navy to suspend hostilities

[1] Sen. Doc. 52, 30 Cong., 1 sess., 85.

upon receipt of such notice. In other words, the chief clerk of the State Department was given large discretionary power as to when hostilities should cease. Trist was equipped with a draft for $3,000,000 in favor of Mexico; and he was enjoined to use every precaution that the draft be made out to the proper Mexican functionaries.[1]

Nicholas P. Trist was a Virginian. He had entered West Point, but resigned before graduation in order to study law. He married Jefferson's granddaughter. He served successively as a clerk in the Treasury, as private secretary to President Jackson, and as consul in Havana. He knew Spanish. And he was a mature man, forty-seven years of age. His record and his character indicated that he possessed excellent qualifications for the mission.

The cabinet approved the project, the instructions, the full power, and the orders to General Scott and Commodore Perry on April 15, 1847. The next day, Trist started on his mission. He reached Vera Cruz on May 6; and he wrote a letter informing Scott of his presence, inclosed the order from the Secretary of War and a letter addressed by Buchanan to the Mexican Minister of Foreign Relations to be forwarded by a flag of truce. But Trist failed to inform Scott of the real object of his mission. Two sentences from Secretary of War Marcy's order will show why the proud and suspicious nature of General Scott should be set on fire. "Mr. Trist is clothed with such diplomatic powers as will authorize him to enter into arrangements with the government of Mexico for the suspension of hostilities. Should he make known to you in writing that the contingency has occurred, in consequence of which the President is willing that further active military operations should cease, you will regard such notice as a direction from the President to suspend them until further orders . . ."[2]

General Scott had his worries about means of transport and supply. He knew that he did not possess the confidence of the administration and he was continually looking for signs

[1] Sen. Doc. 52, 30 Cong., 1 sess., 81.
[2] H. R. Doc. 60, 30 Cong., 1 sess., 940.

of distrust. Circumstances excused what would have otherwise constituted a puerile reply to Trist. He refused to forward the sealed note from Secretary Buchanan to the Mexican Minister of Foreign Relations. Said he: "I see that the Secretary of War proposes to degrade me, by requiring that I, the commander of this army, shall defer to you, the chief clerk of the Department of State, the question of continuing or discontinuing hostilities." He assured Trist that the question of an armistice was a military question merely. Unless Trist possessed military rank above him, all overtures for an armistice would have to be made through Scott.[1]

Trist wrote a rejoinder of thirty pages with innuendos on "wanton contempt of orders" and "contumacy sought to be covered up." He explained for the first time to Scott that the suspension of hostilities should occur only after Mexico had ratified the treaty, which was "what any man of plain, unsophisticated common sense would take for granted that it must be; and it is not what your exuberant fancy and overcultivated imagination would make."[2] Scott never opened or read this communication himself, but ordered a subordinate to open and read it to him in the presence of several staff officers. "My first impulse," wrote Scott, "was to return the farrago of insolence, conceit, and arrogance to the author, but, on reflection, I have determined to preserve the letters as a choice specimen of diplomatic literature and manners."[3] The whole correspondence was submitted by Secretaries Marcy and Buchanan to Polk who advised them to caution Scott and Trist on endangering public interests in the enemy's country by "a violent and embittered personal quarrel."[4]

In order to convey the note from Buchanan to the Minister of Foreign Relations Trist managed to communicate with the British legation. The British minister, Bankhead, sent out a fine young gentleman, Edward Thornton, to confer with Trist. Thornton took back with him much gossipy news

[1] H. R. Doc. 60, 30 Cong., 1 sess., 814.
[2] Ibid., 818, 816.
[3] Ibid., 996.
[4] Ibid., 975.

and also Buchanan's despatch, which was duly delivered to Ibarra, the Minister of Foreign Relations. Santa Anna expressed to Thornton a desire for an arrangement of difficulties with the United States, and Ibarra transmitted a very courteous letter through his hands for Secretary Buchanan. Thornton visited the American camp at Puebla again on June 24, 1847, delivered the letter, mentioned that the Mexican Congress sat in special session" to consider negotiations for peace; and he was no doubt instrumental in reconciling Scott and Trist.

Purported agents from Santa Anna appeared in the American camp and stated that if their chief were paid $10,000 immediately to be used in overcoming resistance in the Mexican Congress, the peace commissioners would be named. The agents represented also that it would be well to make a secret payment of $1,000,000, which would not be mentioned in the treaty. These suggestions appealed to Scott and Trist. They consulted several officers. General Pillow, a personal friend of Polk, favored the bribe. General Twiggs approved. Generals Quitman and Shields dissented; and Cadwalader said nothing. Thereupon, Scott paid over the stipulated $10,000 from the secret service fund which was at his disposal. Whereupon, Santa Anna hesitated to carry out his part of the understanding and advised that the American army should take a position near the city of Mexico.[1]

Scott advanced slowly but surely. He won the victories of Contreras and Churubusco in the latter part of August, 1847. Santa Anna fled to Mexico City and forthwith asked the British legation to prepare the way for peace. Bankhead wrote two notes to Trist assuring him that the Mexicans earnestly desired peace. The Minister of Foreign Relations, Pacheco, wrote another expressing a desire to listen to and discuss whatever propositions the United States had to offer. In form this note was a reply to Buchanan's note of April 15, for the Mexican officials did not want to appear to be initiating the negotiations.[2]

[1] Buchanan, *Works*, VII.: 484; Polk, *Diary*, III: 245, 251, 261, 341, 384, 388; Hitchcock, E. A., *Fifty Years in Camp and Field:* 267.

[2] Sen. Doc. 52, 30 Cong., 1 sess., 189.

The three notes were entrusted to General Mora y Villamil who found Scott at the village of Coyoacan.

Scott had now complied with Santa Anna's previous suggestion of defeating the Mexican army and of occupying a position within sight of the capital. The notes from Bankhead and a visit from Thornton convinced him that the Mexicans desired peace. Moreover, Scott was himself actuated with a desire to end the war. Disease and guerrilla warfare diminished the fighting strength of the army and caused much worry. Mora proposed a truce on his own authority with nothing in writing from Santa Anna to support the proposal. Scott refused; but he wrote a note to Santa Anna, stating that "too much blood had already been shed in this unnatural war;" that the United States had a peace commissioner with the army; and that "In order to open the way for the two republics to enter into negotiations, I desire to execute, on reasonable terms, a short armistice." [1]

This apparently spontaneous request for an armistice by Scott appears to have been exactly what the adroit Santa Anna wanted. He replied through his Minister of War, Alcorta: "It is certainly lamentable that an inconsiderate regard for the rights of the Mexican republic has led to the shedding of blood by the two first republics of this American continent, and with great exactness Your Excellency has characterized this war as unnatural—not alone for its motives, but likewise on account of its being produced by two nations whose interests and relations are identified with each other. The proposition of an armistice to terminate this scandal has been acceded to with pleasure by His Excellency, the President and General in Chief, because it will open a way through which the propositions of the commissioner of the President of the United States of America for the decorous termination of this war may be listened to." Two Mexican generals had been nominated to agree on the terms of an armistice. And the President-General had expressed "his willingness that the army of the United States shall take commodious and furnished quarters, hoping they will be found

[1] Sen. Doc. 52, 30 Cong., 1 sess., 308.

without the range of shot from the Mexican fortifications." [1] This reply appeared conspicuously in the Mexican newspapers.

The armistice was agreed to on August 24, 1847. It was to continue during the period of the negotiations or until forty-eight hours' notice had been given by either party. Scott did not require a single material guarantee. He and Trist believed fully in the sincerity of Santa Anna and felt confident of success. Trist wrote the Minister of Foreign Relations to name time and place of meeting. Pacheco replied that the commissioners had not yet been chosen. Santa Anna and Congress were endeavoring to shove the responsibility for the negotiations on the other. Congress could not summon even a quorum. Santa Anna appointed the commissioners, who declined promptly. Finally he persuaded four prominent Mexicans to accept, among them ex-President Herrera. But he did not confer upon them full power; they could merely accept and transmit the American proposals. Trist pointed out this defect and at the same time delivered to them the project of the treaty.[2]

In reply Pacheco instructed the Mexican commissioners to insist upon the Neuces River as the boundary, the release of Mexico from all claims, and an indemnity for the loss of Texas. The United States should pay the expenses of the war and withdraw the American troops as soon as the treaty was signed.[3] The commissioners found these terms so impossible that they offered their resignation immediately. But Santa Anna had not yet reaped the full benefit of the armistice, and directed Pacheco to inform the commissioners that the instructions should be followed as far as possible. They succeeded marvelously. Trist gave up Lower California, the right of transit across Tehuantepec; he offered to submit the question of the Neuces to Washington; and he promised to propose to Scott a continuance of the armistice until a reply should be received.[4] But Trist was saved the trouble of waiting for a reply from Buchanan for Santa Anna

[1] Sen. Doc. 52, 30 Cong., 1 sess., 308, 350.
[2] Ibid., 191.
[3] Ibid., 369.
[4] Ibid., 195.

rejected the terms. And on September 6, the Mexicans handed Trist a counter project of a treaty, in which New Mexico was retained and likewise California as far north as latitude thirty-seven, or up to San Francisco. The project proposed also that Great Britain should guarantee the observance of the treaty.[1] Under his instructions, Trist could not accept these terms, and he declared the negotiations at an end. Thereupon, Scott gave notice of the termination of the armistice not because the negotiations had failed, but on the ground that new fortifications had been erected.[2] And Santa Anna resumed his fusillade of belligerent proclamations and heinous charges against the American troops. Grant states in his "Memoirs" that the Mexican officers "simply quit, without being particularly whipped, but because they had fought enough." Scott began to evolve his plan for capturing Chapultepec and Mexico City.

The news of the armistice reached Washington in the middle of September. Polk registered a fear in his diary that Santa Anna needed time to reorganize his defeated army.[3] Not until the first week in October did the news of the termination of the armistice and the diplomatic correspondence reach the President. He directed that Scott should levy contributions on the enemy and that Trist be recalled, because his remaining longer might create the impression in Mexico that the United States would accept Santa Anna's terms. "Mexico must now sue for peace" wrote Polk.[4] Trist's recall bore the date of October 6, 1847; and it reached him on November 16.

By the latter date numerous events had occurred in Mexico. Scott had taken possession of Mexico City on September 14. Santa Anna had resigned the presidency and on October 7, turned over the command of the army to General Reyes; and thereafter spent several months as a fugitive until on April 5, 1848, he departed from Mexico under an American safe conduct for Jamaica. The American squadron under Commodore Perry continued to maintain a blockade of all the Gulf ports. The

[1] Sen. Doc. 52, 30 Cong., 1 sess., 378.
[2] Ibid., 346.
[3] Polk, *Diary*, III.: 172.
[4] Ibid., III.: 186.

presidency had temporarily devolved upon Manuel de la Pena y Pena, the presiding judge of the Supreme Court, who had always favored a straightforward settlement of disputes with the United States. He appointed as Minister of Foreign Relations, Luis de la Rosa, a well known advocate of peace. The capital had been moved to Queretaro where Congress was to assemble; and a quorum of that body appeared on November 2. Trist had grown impatient with his enforced idleness and with the volatile condition of Mexican politics. On October 2, he sent a note through the British legation to Rosa.

This note contained no offer to reopen negotiations but it presented the American argument for the Rio Grande as the boundary in reply to the former Mexican claim of the Neuces.[1] Rosa wrote a brief and direct reply to the effect that commissioners would be appointed in a few days to continue the negotiations.[1]

When Congress mustered a quorum, it proceeded to elect General Anaya as President ad interim, and he appointed Pena y Pena as Minister of Foreign Relations. On November 22, the latter sent a note to Trist through the British legation, announcing that the President had appointed commissioners. And this was done in spite of the fact that the Minister of Foreign Relations had been informed through Thornton of Trist's recall. Pena y Pena wrote a private letter to Trist imploring him to remain and to take into consideration the difficulties of the Mexican government. He reminded Trist that he had reopened negotiations under full powers and that it was now too late to withdraw. Moreover, Scott urged Trist to stay and finish the work he had begun. On November 27 he was apparently still firm in his decision to heed the recall, and so wrote to Buchanan. He stated: "The only possible way in which a treaty can be made is, to have the work done on the spot—negotiation and ratification to take place at one dash." [3] But every attention and flattery which the Latin mind could devise was showered upon

[1] Sen. Doc. 52, 30 Cong., 1 sess., 214.
[2] Ibid., 227.
[3] Ibid., 228.

him. And Scott was confident that any treaty which he might negotiate would be ratified in Washington. By December 3, Trist yielded; and he gave the Mexican commissioners to understand that he would assume responsibility for a treaty, which he could take with him to Washington.

Having obtained their immediate object in this decision of Trist, the Mexicans proceeded to dally again. Their commissioners had not been confirmed by the Senate, which was a pretext for compelling that body to share in the responsibility for the inevitably unpopular treaty. Three weeks were thus consumed. Finally, under pressure from the British legation, Pena y Pena yielded and instructed the commissioners to go on with the negotiations, December 30, 1847.

Thereupon, the serious negotiations began in Mexico City. Trist immediately laid down as a sine qua non the Rio Grande as the boundary and the inclusion of San Diego in the cession to the United States. He stated also that he would not consent to pay more than $15,000,000. The Mexicans objected to the boundary and asked for $30,000,000. Trist possessed a decided advantage in having Scott's efficient army near, also in the fact that he was acting in defiance of orders and could drop negotiations at any time. The disputes that appear to have consumed the most time concerned the form of phraseology rather than the substance of the meaning. By January 25, 1848, the treaty was complete, except for the signatures. The Minister of Foreign Relations authorized the signature on condition that Lower California be connected by land with Sonora and that no part of Sonora or Chihuahua be included in the cession. Trist and the Mexican commissioners were able to reassure him on that score. His next move was to ask for immediate cash. Trist threatened to break off negotiations; and Scott announced his intention to march to Queretaro. The British legation assisted with its influence. Finally, the government yielded; and the treaty was signed, February 2, 1848, not at Mexico City, but at the neighboring town of Guadalupe Hidalgo, which held the shrine of a virgin greatly worshipped by the Mexicans. During this week gold had been discovered in California near Sutter's mill. Fortunately, there were no telegraphic connections or further delays might have resulted.

In the meantime, the news had arrived in Washington that Scott and Trist had at one time thought of paying Santa Anna a million dollars as a bribe. Various generals in Scott's army published letters claiming undue credit for themselves. The President believed these jealousies had been produced by "the vanity and tyrannical temper of General Scott, and his want of prudence and common sense." [1] He ordered that General William O. Butler should take command of the army and that Scott should appear before a court of inquiry to sit in Mexico. Trist's determination to disregard the order of recall from the Secretary of State appeared to Polk most surprising. He wrote in his diary, "I directed the Secretary of War to write at once to Major General Butler, directing him, if Mr. Trist was still with the Head Quarters of the army, to order him off, and to inform the authorities of Mexico that he had no authority to treat. If there was any legal provision for his punishment he ought to be severely handled. He has acted worse than any man in the public employ whom I have ever known." [2] Before this order could be delivered to Butler Trist had started home.

A despatch bearer arrived with the treaty on the evening of Saturday, February 19, 1848. The President spent the Sabbath with members of the cabinet examining the secular document. It opened significantly with the words, "In the name of Almighty God:" Article I provided for a "firm and universal peace." Article II provided for the appointment of commissioners to agree upon a truce as soon as the treaty was signed. Article III: Upon the exchange of ratifications, the United States should order the lifting of the blockade and should at the earliest moment practicable withdraw the troops to within thirty leagues of the coast. The customs houses should be delivered to the Mexican authorities together with all bonds and evidences of debt for duties. All duties collected after the ratification by Mexico should be delivered minus the

[1] Polk, *Diary*, III.: 266.
[2] Ibid., III.: 301.

cost of collection. Article IV: The evacuation of Mexican territory should be completed within three months of the exchange of ratifications. The mutual restoration of prisoners of war; and the restoration by the United States to Mexico of all forts, apparatus of war therein, and of public property was provided for. Article V: The boundary began in the Gulf of Mexico, "three leagues from land," opposite the mouth of the Rio Grande; thence up the middle of that river, following the deepest channel, to the point where it struck the southern boundary of New Mexico; thence along the southern and western boundary of New Mexico, according to Disturnell's map, published in New York, 1847, until it intersected the first branch of the Gila River; thence down the middle of that stream to its juncture with the Colorado; thence across the Colorado, following the boundary between Upper and Lower California to the Pacific. Except for the change made by the Gadsden Purchase, this line remains the boundary today. Article VI provided for the free navigation of the Gulf of Lower California, the Colorado, and the Gila to the vessels and citizens of the United States. And Article VII provided for the reciprocal free navigation of the Rio Grande.

Article VIII allowed the Mexicans in the ceded territory one year in which to elect to remain Mexican citizens or become Americans. If they had made no choice by the end of the year they should be considered Americans. The property of all was to be fully respected. Article IX: Those Mexicans who should become Americans were to "be admitted at the proper time (to be judged of by the Congress of the United States) to the enjoyment of all the rights of citizens of the United States, according to the principles of the constitution." In the meantime they were to enjoy freely their liberty, property, and the exercise of their religion. This was the substance of Article III of the Louisiana Purchase Treaty. Trist had amplified it, but the amplifying words were eliminated by the American Senate.

In Article X Trist went beyond his instructions. Mexico declared therein that she had made no land grants in Texas since March 2, 1836, nor in New Mexico and California since May 13, 1846. But she stipulated that previous grants in the above mentioned regions, on which the grantees had not complied with all the conditions, should revive as of the date of the exchange of ratifications of the treaty.[1] The President and his cabinet reached the conclusion that he should recommend to the Senate that this article be stricken from the treaty. He gave as his reason: "The public lands within the limits of Texas belong to that State, and this Government has no power to dispose of them or to change the conditions of grants already made. All valid titles to lands within the other territories ceded to the United States will remain unaffected by the change of sovereignty; . . ."[2] The Senate complied.

Article XI: The United States agreed to restrain the Indians in the cession to the same extent as it did those in the remainder of the American territory. It was declared unlawful for an American to purchase Mexicans held captive by the Indians or to buy Mexican property stolen by the Indians.

Article XII: For the extension of boundaries the United States agreed to pay $15,000,000; $3,000,000 of which should be paid immediately upon ratification of the treaty by Mexico, and the remainder in four equal annual installments with interest at six per cent. Polk had authorized Trist to go as high as $20,000,000.

Articles XIII, XIV, and XV related to the claims of Americans against Mexico. The United States agreed to pay all those of Americans that had been decided against Mexico and not yet liquidated. The United States agreed to discharge those claims of citizens not heretofore decided up to the amount of $3,250,000. The exoneration of Mexico from these demands of American citizens should be complete. Mexico agreed to furnish any documents in her possession necessary for the adjustment of these claims. The American commission created for this purpose by Congress, March 3, 1849, did allow claims to the extent of $3,208,314.96.

Article XVI: Complete right of fortification along the boundary was reserved by both parties. Article XVII: The Commer-

[1] Sen. Doc. 52, 30 Cong., 1 sess., 49.
[2] Richardson, *Messages*, etc., IV.: 573.

cial Treaty of 1831 was revived for eight years and indefinitely thereafter subject to termination on one year's notice from either party. Mexico gave such notice on November 30, 1880.

Articles XVIII, XIX, and XX related to the exemption from customs duties of supplies for the American army and to penalties in case of fraudulent use of this privilege.

Article XXI stipulated that in case of dispute between the two parties concerning "political or commercial relations," they would endeavor to preserve peace and friendship by using "mutual representations and pacific negotiations." And if they could not thus settle their differences, resort should not on that account be had to reprisals, aggression, or hostility of any kind; but the one aggrieved should consider in a spirit of peace whether it might not be better to submit the dispute to arbitration. And should such a proposal be made by either party, the other would accede to it, unless deemed "incompatible with the nature of the difference, or the circumstances of the case."

Article XXII contained restrictions to apply in case war should break out between the two republics, "absolutely where the nature of the subject permits, and as closely as possible in all cases where such absolute observance shall be impossible," merchants of either party residing in the territory of the other were allowed twelve months if living in the interior and six months if living in the seaports to collect their debts, settle their affairs, and freely depart. In case of invasion the following should "be allowed to continue their respective employments, unmolested in their persons," "women and children, scholars of every faculty, cultivators of the earth, merchants, artisans, manufacturers, and fishermen, unarmed and inhabiting unfortified towns, villages or places." The houses and goods of these should not be destroyed; and if necessity should arise to take anything from them for the use of the armed forces, it should be paid for at an equitable price. All charitable institutions should be respected. Prisoners of war should not be confined in prisons, nor be put in irons, or "restrained in the use of their limbs;" they should be placed in cantonments and "lodged in barracks as roomy and good as are provided by the party in whose power they are for its own troops." Officers should be given liberty on parole "within convenient districts." If these prisoners should escape and be caught in arms, they could be dealt with "according to the established laws of war." Officers were to be daily furnished with as many rations, and of the same articles, as might be allowed in kind or commutation to officers of equal rank in the army of the captor state and the ordinary prisoner should have the same rations as the common soldier. These rations should be paid for by the home state of the prisoner of war when peace was to be reëstablished.

Article XXIII allowed four months in which to bring about ratification by the two parties and an exchange of ratifications. A secret article extended this term to eight months; but this was stricken out by the United States Senate.

On that Sunday, February 20, 1848, "The question to be decided," the President noted, "was stated, viz., whether the treaty should be rejected by me or sent to the Senate for ratification. A free discussion ensued. I took the advice of the Cabinet separately and individually. Mr. Buchanan and Mr. Walker advised that I should reject it. Mr. Mason, Mr. Marcy, Mr. Johnson, and Mr. Clifford advised that I should accept it and send it for ratification to the Senate."[1] All agreed that Article X should be rejected.

Buchanan's negative advice nettled the President. "I cannot help laboring under the conviction," he wrote, "that the true reason of Mr. Buchanan's present course is that he is now a candidate for the Presidency, and he does not wish to incur the displeasure of those who are in favour of the conquest of all Mexico. That he earnestly wishes me to send the treaty to the Senate against his advice, I am fully convinced, not from anything he has said, but from circumstances and his general bearing I do not doubt. No candidate for the presidency ought ever to remain in the Cabinet. He is an unsafe adviser."[2]

On the next day, Polk called the cabinet together again and for the first time informed them that he had decided to

[1] Polk, *Diary*, III.: 347.
[2] Ibid., III.: 350.

submit the treaty to the Senate. He gave as his reasons that on the boundary Trist had adhered to his instructions; that it was doubtful whether more territory could be obtained; that if he should reject the treaty, Congress might refuse to authorize men and money for the prosecution of the war; and that if he should reject his own terms, offered the April before, he feared the results upon his own political party.[1]

On that same day John Quincy Adams in the House of Representatives suffered a paralytic stroke, which caused the adjournment of both Houses until Wednesday. In the brief message delivered to the Senate on that day, Polk reviewed the actions of Trist and recommended the ratification of the treaty. On February 28, the Senate committee on foreign relations decided to report the treaty adversely, not because of the treaty itself, but because of it having been negotiated by Trist after his recall. The President informed Chairman Sevier that it was the treaty and not the conduct of Trist that was before them for their approval. Thereupon, the committee changed its decision and reported the treaty without recommendation. Webster opposed the treaty, for the reason that it was presumed to extend slave territory. Houston opposed it because the boundary was not stretched southward to include Tampico; and he had the support of Jefferson Davis. Baldwin of Connecticut failed in his attempt to insert the Wilmot proviso. The final vote on advising ratification took place on March 10, 1848, with 38 in favor and 14 opposed to the treaty.

Polk appointed Senator Sevier and his Attorney General, Nathan Clifford, as commissioners to go to Mexico, and there in accordance with the provisions of the treaty obtain an exchange of ratifications. They were also charged with the task of explaining the amendments made by the American Senate.

During the two months since the signature of the treaty political conditions in Mexico had been in a state of flux but the sum total of change had been small. Butler had superseded Scott as commander of the American army. Colonel Sterling Price had captured Chihuahua in March, 1848. Butler had

[1] Polk, *Diary*, III.: 347.

entered into a formal armistice. The Mexican Congress had been unable to summon a quorum. That a treaty had been signed the Mexicans knew; but the government maintained a policy of secrecy as to its terms. The Puros, or the radical faction, were opposed to any treaty, and wanted the complete annexation of entire Mexico to the United States; hence, they urged the continuance of anarchy and of the war. The Mexicans of the property class had gloomy forebodings about conditions when the American army should withdraw. They had confidence in Scott and they urged him to issue a proclamation declaring himself dictator, when the treaty should be ratified. Scott acknowledged afterward that these proffers had been "highly seductive both as to power and fortune."[1] The royalist group under Paredes renewed its activity and used opposition to the treaty as a rallying cry. But these were rather factions than parties. The great body of Mexicans realized that there was nothing to do but to ratify the treaty, no matter what the terms. The difficulty that Sevier and Clifford found was that no leaders wished to assume responsibility and act.

Finally, President Pena y Pena brought himself to review in his message to Congress the heroic efforts of Mexico in achieving her independence and of the courage and firmness of the soldiers in the present war. "I have never believed," said he, "neither do I now believe, that the republic is absolutely incapable of continuing the war, and affording an example which might be transmitted with glory to posterity. But with the same frankness and good faith, I must say that I am convinced that the condition in which we are, with all its attendant circumstances, imperiously calls for peace." He enumerated the advantages which Mexico obtained by the treaty, the guaranty by the United States of liberty and property to those Mexicans who lived in the territory ceded. The cession was small compared to what they might have lost. The $15,000,000 which the United States was to pay he spoke of as an "indemnity." The release from American claims was a considerable item. The alleviation of the calamities of war, if it should again occur,

[1] Scott, *Autobiography:* 581.

and the obligation on the part of the United States to restrain the Indian tribes constituted great advantages. He expressed regret that the American Senate had seen fit to make amendments; but these were not of sufficient importance to warrant rejection of the treaty.[1] The Minister of War furnished Congress with a report that if the treaty were rejected it would be impossible to continue hostilities. The Minister of Foreign Relations, who had also charge of the treasury, pointed out the financial straits of the country and his reasons for ratification. The Deputies approved on May 19, 1848, by a vote of 51 to 35; and the Senate approved on May 25 by a vote of 33 to 4. Not until May 30, 1848, were the ratifications exchanged; and the American commissioners turned over the stipulated $3,000,000.

Trist had reached Washington in due time, and found all doors at the State Department closed to him. At the time of his recall, his salary and allowances had been canceled. In vain did he attempt to secure a hearing. On August 7, he addressed a long communication to the Speaker of the House, asking for redress and for the impeachment of the President. The Speaker referred the letter to the committee on foreign affairs where it was pigeonholed. Anxious as officials appear to have been to forget him, Trist would not be forgotten. At last he obtained the ear of Senator Sumner at whose instance Congress appropriated $14,560, April 20, 1871. Trist could feel in the closing years of his life that he had been vindicated.

BIBLIOGRAPHY

BUCHANAN, JAMES.—*Works*, VI, VII, VIII. Edited by J. B. Moore. Philadelphia, 1909.

POLK, JAMES K.—*Diary*. 4 volumes. Edited by Milo M. Quaife. Chicago, 1910.

REEVES, J. S.—*American Diplomacy under Tyler and Polk*. Baltimore, 1907.

RICHARDSON, JAMES D.—*Messages and Papers of the Presidents*, Vol. IV. Washington, 1897.

RIVES, GEORGE L.—*The United States and Mexico*, 1821–1848. 2 volumes.. New York, 1913.

[1] H. R. Doc. 50, 30 Cong., 2 sess., 62.

SMITH, E. KIRBY.—*To Mexico with Scott.* Cambridge, 1917.
SMITH, JUSTIN H.—*The War with Mexico.* 2 volumes. New York, 1919.
United States. House Executive Documents: 38, 40, 56, 60, 30 Cong., 1 sess. 50, 30 Cong., 2 sess. Washington, 1849.
United States. Senate Executive Document: 52, 30 Cong., 1 sess. Washington, 1848.

CHAPTER XI

THE PERRY AND HARRIS TREATIES WITH JAPAN, 1854 AND 1858

"Nippon and America, all the same heart."—MATSUSAKI TO PERRY.

American naval officers render services daily in the promotion of international good will. The services may consist of a salute, an exchange of visits, the quieting of a disturbance which might lead to war, or even of the negotiation of agreements, conventions, and treaties. As yet no officer has performed his pacific mission with greater distinction nor with more far-reaching results than Commodore Matthew Calbraith Perry. His name is better known today among the school children of Japan than among those of his native land.

He was born in Newport, Rhode Island, in 1794. At fifteen, he entered the navy. During the war of 1812 he served first on the frigate, "President, " and later on the "United States," which was blockaded in the harbor of New London for the greater part of the war. His older brother won the decisive victory on Lake Erie. The succeeding years M. C. Perry spent in the merchant service; but by 1819 he had reëntered the navy. He served as executive officer on the "Cyane," which convoyed the "Elizabeth" with her pioneers to Liberia. On his return he assisted to extirpate piracy in the West Indies. From 1833 to 1843 he was stationed at the Brooklyn Navy Yard, and during that time demonstrated the use of steam as a motive power for war vessels. Then he commanded the squadron on the African coast, in the interest of destroying the international slave trade. And during the Mexican war he enforced the blockade off the Gulf ports. He was fifty-eight years of age, in the very prime of life intellectually.

His new task consisted in reopening Japan to foreign intercourse. Japan at one time, 1550 to 1620, welcomed western commerce and western ideas. But religious zealots and sharp traders had caused a revulsion of feeling. The English East India Company had to abandon its factory in 1623; the Spaniards had to leave in 1624; and the Portuguese in 1638. The Dutch alone were permitted to remain. They had conducted no religious propaganda, and their commercial dealings had been marked with honesty and fairness. Even the Dutch were confined, 1641, to the little island of Dejima in the harbor of Nagasaki. And their number of ships was limited at first to six, then to two, and in 1790, to one a year. The Chinese were restricted to the same port, with a maximum after 1740 of ten junks a year. So that for more than two centuries Japan had remained virtually a hermit nation.

Other nations had made unsuccessful efforts to reopen Japan. Russia's jurisdiction had been extended across Siberia to the Pacific by 1638. The Russians made repeated attempts to secure admission to Japan; the most noteworthy being that of Lieutenant Laxman in 1792, who carried on some friendly negotiations. In 1808 the British frigate, "Phaeton," sailed into Nagasaki in search of Dutch merchantmen, with the result that several Japanese officers, responsible for the port, found it necessary to commit hara-kiri.[1] The Dutch had tried to open negotiations for a treaty in 1844 and again in 1852.

Americans had likewise made several attempts. During the Napoleonic wars they had taken over the Dutch carrying trade. Several American vessels under Dutch charters entered the port of Nagasaki and discharged their cargoes. The captain of one of these vessels, Stewart, appeared later with a cargo on his own account; but he was refused permission to land. D. W. C. Olyphant of New York planned the second serious attempt in 1837. Seven shipwrecked Japanese had been picked up off the coast of Vancouver. Olyphant had for years carried on trade with China, and he fitted out a special ship for the return of these Japanese. With them he sent the famous German

[1] F. L. Hawk's *Narrative* or Sen. Doc. 79, 33 Cong., 2 sess., part I.: 42.

missionary, Dr. Gutzlaff, and two American missionaries, Dr. Peter Parker and Reverend S. Wells Williams, and also a member of Olyphant's commercial house, Mr. King. He placed on board a considerable collection of presents, among them a telescope, a barometer, a set of United States' coins, a portrait of Washington, and a memorial, written in Chinese, setting forth that the object of the expedition was the return of the shipwrecked Japanese and an opening of friendly relations. The vessel sailed with confidence directly for the capital, Yedo, where the batteries on the shore opened fire upon it. No one was permitted to land there or anywhere along the coast; and the expedition ended at Macao. The only result in Japan of this and similar missions was the issuance of an edict that shipwrecked Japanese could be returned only in Dutch or Chinese vessels to the port of Nagasaki.[1]

The third effort had an official character, in that the American diplomatic representative to China, Edward Everett, entrusted to Commodore Biddle the duty of ascertaining whether the ports of Japan were accessible. Biddle sailed for Yedo with two naval vessels and cast anchor there July 20, 1846. He was honored with a reply seven days later stating that communications from foreigners could be received only at Nagasaki; that the Japanese ports were not and would not be opened to Americans; and that he must depart immediately and never return.

Besides the desire for commercial intercourse with Japan, another motive actuated the United States. Since 1820 the interest of Americans in the Pacific whale fisheries had grown greatly. In several instances the fishermen had suffered shipwreck on the Japanese coasts and had been treated with indignities and cruelties. Throughout their stay they were held as prisoners with only one port of exit, Nagasaki, and with only one Dutch vessel a year leaving. Commander Glynn of the "Preble" obtained information at Canton in 1849 that fifteen shipwrecked Americans were in desperate straits at Nagasaki. He set sail forthwith and rather unceremoniously rescued them.[2]

[1] Sen. Doc. 59, 32 Cong., 1 sess., 78.
[2] Ibid., 1.

It was also urgent that these Pacific fishermen should have the right in case of distress to obtain water, food, and fuel from the Japanese.[1]

Perry received the command of what was then called the East India squadron, consisting of three war vessels and two transports; and to these were to be added eight other vessels. During the nine months of waiting for the equipment of the latter vessels, Perry made careful preparations for the execution of his mission. At his instance the government purchased charts to the value of $30,000 from the Netherlands. A considerable library on Japan was collected from European as well as American bookstalls. Applications for permission to join the expedition came pouring in from all parts of the world; but Perry refused them all. He prepared a long list of presents, including samples of various fire arms, a barrel of whiskey, a cask of wine, and quantities of cordials and champagne, a telescope, a set of telegraph instruments, a miniature railway train, Audubon's Birds and Quadrupeds, eight baskets of Irish potatoes, and the not to be forgotten garden seeds.[2]

His instructions were drafted by C. M. Conrad, Secretary of War and Acting Secretary of State, and were addressed to John P. Kennedy, the Secretary of the Navy, who conveyed them to Commodore Perry, November 13, 1852. He was to obtain humane treatment in the future for shipwrecked Americans, to secure permission for American vessels to enter for food, fuel, and supplies, and the permission of American "vessels to enter one or more ports for the purpose of disposing of their cargoes by sale or barter." He was not to mention the grievances of other nations, nor was he to seek any exclusive commercial advantage for the United States. The instructions expressed the desire that whatever advantages might be gained by the expedition would "ultimately be shared by the civilized world." It was pointed out that the discovery of gold in California, the railway across the isthmus of Panama, and the navigation of the ocean by steam had brought the two countries

[1] Sen. Doc. 34, 33 Cong., 2 sess., 6.
[2] Hawk's *Narrative*, Pt. I.: 356.

closer and made the need for friendly and peaceful intercourse imperative.

But the question was how were these objects to be attained. Commodore Perry was directed to proceed with his squadron to whatever port in Japan he deemed most advisable; ask to see the Emperor in person, if possible; and deliver to him the letter from the President. He could assure the Japanese that the United States, unlike other Christian countries, did not interfere with the religion of its people, much less with that of other nations. He should explain that although Americans spoke the same language as the English, they were not British subjects, and also that the United States had no connection with any European government.

The peaceful character of the mission was emphasized throughout the instructions. Perry was to bear in mind that "as the President has no power to declare war, his mission is necessarily of a pacific character, and will not resort to force unless in self-defence in the protection of the vessels and crews under his command, or to resent an act of personal violence offered to himself or to one of his officers." Again the instructions stated: "In his intercourse with this people, who are said to be proud and vindictive in their character, he should be courteous and conciliatory, but at the same time, firm and decided. He will, therefore, submit with patience and forbearance to acts of discourtesy to which he may be subjected, by a people to whose usages it will not do to test by our standard of propriety, but, at the same time, will be careful to do nothing that may compromise, in their eyes, his own dignity or that of the country. He will, on the contrary, do everything to impress them with a just sense of the power and greatness of this country, and to satisfy them that its past forbearance has been the result, not of timidity, but of a desire to be on friendly terms with them."

An impression exists that Perry went to Japan to obtain a concession by force, if necessary. To remove it, one more quotation from the instructions is here given. "If, after having exhausted every argument and every means of persuasion, the commodore should fail to obtain from the government any relaxation of their system of exclusion, or even any assurance of humane treatment of our shipwrecked seamen, he will then change his tone, and inform them in the most unequivocal terms that it is the determination of this government to insist, that hereafter all citizens or vessels of the United States that may be wrecked on their coasts, or driven by stress of weather into their harbors shall, so long as they are compelled to remain there, be treated with humanity; and that if any acts of cruelty should hereafter be practised upon citizens of this country, whether by the government or by the inhabitants of Japan, they will be severely chastised." And in the supplementary instructions of February 15, 1853, Edward Everett stated, "Make no use of force, except in the last resort for defence, if attacked, and self preservation."

Perry was then invested with large discretionary powers, and informed that so far as the main object of his mission permitted, he might explore the coasts of Japan and gather all the knowledge possible.[1] How wisely the American government chose its agent and how well he executed his mission remains to be seen.

Tired of delays and having made arrangements for the other vessels of his squadron to join him later, Commodore Perry set sail from Norfolk in the steam frigate "Mississippi" on November 24, 1852. He reached Madeira in seventeen days; Jamestown, St. Helena on January 10, 1853; Cape Town on January 24; Mauritius on February 18; Point de Galle, Ceylon, on March 10; Singapore on March 25; Hong Kong on April 6, where the sloops of war "Plymouth" and "Saratoga" and the store ship "Supply" were waiting; Napha in the Lew Chew Islands on May 26, where the "Susquehanna" joined the squadron with the well known traveler, Bayard Taylor, on board; and finally, with four war vessels, instead of twelve as promised, he entered the bay of Yedo on July 8, 1853. At five o'clock in the afternoon the squadron cast anchor off the town of Uraga with the lofty cone of Fujiyama in the distance. Hundreds of small craft surrounded the vessels; but Perry had ordered that no one should

[1] Sen. Doc. 34, 33 Cong., 2 sess., 2, 4.

be permitted to come on board. Several attempted to climb the anchor chains, but they were warned off with pikes and pistols.

A conspicuous boat with a distinguished looking person came alongside Perry's ship, the "Susquehanna". Neither was this person received. He unrolled a scroll of paper on which was written in French that the ships had anchored at their peril and should depart. Mr. S. Wells Williams informed him in Chinese that the Commodore would receive no one but a functionary of the highest rank. They seemed to have difficulty in understanding the language. One man in the boat said in good English, "I talk Dutch."[1] The Dutch interpreter, Mr. Portman, took up the conversation. The Japanese asked if the vessels were American; he appeared to have knowledge that they might be coming. He urged pertinaciously that he be allowed to come on board. But Portman refused and informed him that the commander of the squadron was of the highest rank and could confer only with the highest in rank at Uraga. The Japanese, who spoke Dutch, said that the vice-governor of Uraga was in the boat and was the proper person to be received. Portman asked why the governor did not come. The laws of Japan would not permit him to step on board foreign vessels was the reply; and he proposed that the commodore should appoint an officer of corresponding rank to the vice-governor for a conference. After a proper delay Perry granted the request and appointed Lieutenant Contee to receive the vice-governor, Nagazima Saburosuke. Perry kept himself secluded in his own cabin and communicated with the Japanese representative through his aid only.

Perry directed that the dignitary be informed that he had come on a friendly mission, that he had a letter from the President of the United States to the Emperor; and he hoped that a suitable officer would be appointed to receive a copy of the letter and to set a day for the delivery of the original. Nagazima replied that Nagasaki was the only place for the negotiation of foreign business and that the squadron would need to go there. Perry replied from his sanctum through his aid that he had

[1] Williams, *Journal of the Perry Expedition*, 48.

purposely chosen Uraga because of its nearness to Yedo; that he would not go to Nagasaki; that he expected the letter to be properly received; that his intentions were friendly, but he would permit no indignity, and that the guard boats which had been collecting around the vessels should be immediately removed or he would disperse them by force. The vice-governor stepped quickly to the gangway and gave an order which caused the guard boats to return to the shore. Perry considered this his first point gained. The vice-governor took his leave, saying that he had no authority to make any promises, but that an officer of high rank would call in the morning. Thus ended Perry's first day in Japanese waters.[1] He had thus far successfully carried out his resolve "to demand as a right, and not to solicit as a favor, those acts of courtesy which are due from one civilized nation to another."[2]

On the following morning the governor himself appeared. Perry directed that he be received by Commanders Buchanan and Adams and Lieutenant Contee. Perry noted, "I was well aware that the more exclusive I should make myself, and the more exacting I might be, the more respect these people of forms and ceremonies would be disposed to award me . . ."[3] The governor declared that Japanese law made it impossible to receive the President's letter except at Nagasaki. He was informed that the commodore would not consent to this proposal; that if a suitable person were not appointed to receive the documents, he would go on shore with a sufficient force and deliver them in person. The governor promised to communicate with Yedo for further instructions. The officers announced that the commodore would wait three days for a reply. The governor had on this visit offered water and supplies, which were courteously refused. He had been permitted to take a look at the magnificent box which contained the letter of the President but not to touch or examine it.

While waiting Perry directed that a survey be made of the

[1] Hawks, *Narrative*, Pt. I.: 232.
[2] Perry, *Notes*, Sen. Doc. 34, 33 Cong., 2 sess., 45.
[3] Ibid., 45.

harbor. The governor appeared and voiced a protest. He received the reply that the commodore was complying with American law which was for him as inviolable as Japanese law for the governor. Perry considered this his second point gained.[1]

Promptly on the third day, July 12, 1853, at 10 o'clock in the morning, the governor came on board and said that a special building would be erected on shore for the reception of the commodore and his suite and for the delivery of the President's letter to a high official designated by the Shogun. But no reply would be given in Uraga; it would be transmitted to Nagasaki through the Dutch superintendent. He was informed that the commodore would receive the reply nowhere except in that neighborhood. The governor said he would return the next morning with more definite information. He failed to return until the next afternoon, apologized for his tardiness, vouched for the high character of the officer who should receive the commodore, and exhibited a copy of the instructions from the Shogun to the Prince of Idzu, who would bring the President's letter to Yedo.

On July 14 Perry landed with 400 officers and men, well armed and equipped, and marched to the building erected for his reception. Five to seven thousand Japanese troops surrounded the spot, which was also covered by the guns of the American ships in the harbor. Perry delivered the President's letter, his letter of credence, and three communications from himself. The Prince of Idzu gave him a receipt, which mentioned that since the place was not designed to treat with foreigners neither conference nor entertainment could take place and requested Perry to depart. Perry continued the survey of the harbor for several days. The governor of Uraga came alongside with presents. He was told that these would be accepted on condition that he would receive presents in return. He gave the then familiar excuse that Japanese law forbade the reception of presents. He was told that American law enjoined reciprocity of courtesies. He yielded. But when he saw the amount he begged to be permitted to take only what he could

[1] Perry, *Notes*, Sen. Doc. 34, 33 Cong., 2 sess., 47.

conceal. Perry directed that if he did not take all the articles in an open manner his own presents would be returned. Again he yielded. Perry counted this exchange of presents as another point gained.[1]

Perry had been assured by the governor and he knew beforehand that a reply to the President's letter would require time for deliberation and if acceded to would alter many laws and traditions of the empire. He had also found his supply of water short. For those two reasons he had mentioned in one of his communications to the Shogun that he would await the reply on his return to Yedo Bay in the spring.[2] Consequently, after a ten day stay in the bay, Perry departed for Hong Kong.

A Russian squadron under Admiral Pontiatine had offered to coöperate with Perry; and it visited Nagasaki twice during the winter of 1853 and 1854. Perry had reason to think a French squadron was on its way to Japanese waters. He feared that his opportunity might fall into other hands, and left Hong Kong, therefore, on January 14, 1854. At the Lew Chew Islands, the Dutch agent met him with a letter from the Japanese authorities, stating that the Shogun had died, and asking Perry to delay his return until after the period of mourning. But Perry's squadron of seven ships put in its appearance at Yedo Bay on February 13.

Perry received the news that the fleet would be treated with courtesy, that the Shogun would appoint a suitable person to confer with him, and that Kamakura in the outer bay had been designated as the place for the negotiations. To the latter Perry objected. The Japanese proposed Uraga. Perry wanted to go to Yedo. They compromised on Yokohama. After many formalities in the observance of which Perry easily equalled the Japanese, the five Japanese commissioners received Perry at noon on March 8. Refreshments were served. The courteous reply to the President's letter was received by Perry. He replied orally, and at the close handed the Japanese a draft of a treaty similar to the American treaty with China in 1844.

[1] Perry, *Notes*, Sen. Doc. 34, 33 Cong., 2 sess., 53.
[2] Ibid., 54.

An American seaman having died on board the "Mississippi" Perry asked for the right of burial. The Japanese replied that the body could be sent to Nagasaki. Perry insisted on burial on shore there; and the Japanese yielded. They then agreed upon March 13 for the reception of the presents from the President to the Emperor. The Japanese were duly surprised at the telegraph instruments conveying instantly messages even in their own language. They rode on top of the Lilleputian railway train, examined the fire arms with intense curiosity, and made some notes and sketches of the various articles.

On March 17 the negotiations began in earnest. To Perry's project of a treaty the Japanese replied that they were not ready to make such concessions. Instead, they came with an informal project of their own, in which the word Nagasaki appeared in nearly every proposition. They conceded that food and fuel could be obtained by American ships at Nagasaki at the same prices paid by the Dutch and Chinese and to be paid for in silver or gold. After five years another port might be opened for a similar purpose. Perry replied that this was well enough, but that one or more ports must be substituted for Nagasaki, which was out of the route of American commerce, and that these ports must be opened within sixty days. The manner of payment for the articles received should be arranged by treaty. The Japanese proposed that American shipwrecked sailors and their property should be sent to Nagasaki by sea. Perry agreed except as to the port.

The Japanese stated that they could not possibly distinguish between foreign sailors who were pirates and those who were not; hence these sailors should not be allowed to walk about wherever they pleased. Perry replied that shipwrecked men and others who resorted to the ports of Japan should not be confined, but should be granted the same freedom granted to Japanese. They should, however, be amenable to such laws as might be agreed upon by treaty.

The fourth Japanese proposal specified that at Nagasaki Americans should have no intercourse with the Dutch or the

Chinese. Perry replied that Americans would never submit to such restrictions as had been imposed upon the Dutch or the Chinese and that any further allusion to such restraints would be considered offensive.

Perry had asked for the opening of a port in the Lew Chew Islands. The Japanese said that these islands constituted a very distant country and that they could not discuss the opening of a harbor. Perry replied that there was no good reason for excluding the Americans; therefore, the point would be insisted upon. In regard to the port of Matsumai on the island of Yezo, the Japanese made a similar statement; and Perry made a similar reply.[1]

These propositions were not discussed in as summary a manner as here indicated. The Japanese commissioners interposed all possible difficulties, especially that the laws of the empire forbade the granting of the concessions. The negotiations were conducted largely through oral discussions by means of interpreters. At the end of each session Perry and the Japanese negotiators would exchange statements on the points agreed upon. These statements were usually written in three different languages, Japanese, Chinese, and Dutch.

When the main points of the treaty had been quite definitely settled, the Japanese commissioners invited Perry on March 24 to receive the gifts from the Shogun. These consisted of specimens of rich brocades and silks, lacquered boxes, trays, and tables, porcelain ware of wonderful lightness and artistic workmanship, fans, and articles of apparel. A set of Japanese coins Perry appreciated greatly, because the law against the export of coins had been suspended for the occasion. Perry had previously invited the commissioners with their attendants to dine with him on board the flag ship. This they accepted and mentioned Saturday, March 25, as the date. Perry suggested that Saturday might prove stormy, that the next day was his Sabbath when he could not receive company, and that he preferred to have the honor of their presence on Monday. It was so arranged.

And a great dinner it must have been, for Hawks in his

[1] Perry, *Notes*, Sen. Doc. 34, 33 Cong., 2 sess., 128.

"Narrative" devotes three quarto pages to its description. Hayashi, the leading commissioner, ate and drank sparingly, but tasted of every dish and sipped of every kind of wine. Says Hawks: "The others proved themselves famous trenchermen, and entered more heartily than their chief into the conviviality of the occasion. Matsusaki was the soul of the party. . ." "In the eagerness of the Japanese appetite, there was but little discrimination in the choice of dishes and in the order of courses, and the most startling heterodoxy was exhibited in the confused commingling of fish, flesh, and fowl, soups and syrups, fruits and fricassees, roast and boiled, pickles and preserves. As a most generous supply had been provided, there were still some remnants of the feast left, after the guests had satisfied their voracity, and most of these, the Japanese in accordance with their usual custom, stowed away about their persons to carry off with them. The Japanese always have an abundant supply of paper within the left bosom of their loose robes in a capacious pocket." Toward the close of his description Hawks states: "It was now sunset, and the Japanese prepared to depart with quite as much wine in them as they could well bear. The jovial Matsusaki threw his arms about the Commodore's neck, crushing, in his tipsy embrace, a pair of new epaulettes, and repeating, in Japanese, with maudlin affection, these words, as interpreted into English: "Nippon and America, all the same heart."[1] As the last boat pulled off a salute of seventeen guns was fired. And the day was done.

The next morning Perry met the Japanese in conference on the remaining details of the treaty. He found them more sober than usual and also more willing to make concessions. They agreed upon the opening of two ports in Japan proper, Shimoda and Hakodate, and of Napha in the Lew Chew Islands; although Napha was not mentioned in the treaty, for it was a question whether the Lew Chew Islands belonged to Japan. Perry named the distance in the country to which Americans might go around the Japanese ports, and it was accepted. But Americans were not to have permanent residence with their

[1] Sen. Doc. 79, 33 Cong., 2 sess., Pt. I.: 374.

families in these ports. Perry's proposition on consular agents caused the Japanese great anxiety. He maintained firmly that these agents would serve for the protection of the Japanese as well as for his own countrymen. They conceded that one such might live at Shimoda, but not until eighteen months after the date of the treaty had elapsed. Another point made the Japanese apprehensive. Perry explained that in accordance with American law the treaty could not be considered binding as soon as signed by the plenipotentiaries. Perry proceeded thereupon to allay their fears, knowing that all the concessions agreed to were to come from them. And he promised them the friendship and forbearance of the United States. Finally, on Friday, March 31, 1854, the treaty was signed with proper ceremonies. Perry signed three copies in the English language, accompanied by translations in the Dutch and Chinese languages. The Japanese signed and delivered to Perry three drafts written in Japanese, Chinese, and the Dutch languages.

The treaty consisted of twelve articles. Article I established a perfect and permanent peace between the two countries. Article II opened the port of Shimoda at once to American vessels for the purchase of fuel and necessities, and the port of Hakodate one year later. Payment for the goods was to be in gold or silver in accordance with a schedule of prices furnished by the Japanese. Articles III, IV, and V assured assistance to American shipwrecked sailors, security for their property, and humane treatment during their stay. And their movements should be free within seven Japanese miles of the two ports. The reciprocal assistance of the United States to Japanese shipwrecked was likewise provided for. Article VI called for careful deliberation between the parties if any other goods were needed or any other business had to be arranged. By this provision Perry opened the way for Harris' commercial treaties. In the meantime Americans should have the right to trade under such regulations as the Japanese government might establish (Article VII). Article VIII specified that all food, fuel, and necessities should be obtained through the agency of Japanese officers. Article IX granted to the United States and its citizens most favored nation treatment. Article X limited the visit of American vessels to the ports of Shimoda and Hakodate except when in distress. Article XI permitted the residence in Shimoda of an American consul after the lapse of eighteen months from the signing of the treaty. And Article XII provided for the exchange of ratifications within eighteen months. These were exchanged on February 21, 1855; and the treaty was proclaimed in the United States on June 22, 1855.[1]

Those were the terms of the first modern treaty negotiated with Japan. Perry recognized fully its limitations. But he had succeeded in rousing Japan from her more than two centuries of seclusion. At his instance she had set aside immemorial laws and customs. She had recognized humane principles in the treatment of foreigners. The shipwrecked were no longer to be treated as criminals. Ports had been opened for the purchase of food and supplies. The most favored nation clause had been inserted. The beginnings of commerce were recognized. In short, Perry had awakened the latent powers of a nation, which was to forge its way faster than any other in the world's history to the forefront among the states of the world.

Great causes had no doubt been at work for a long time in paving the way for the opening of Japan. Perry recognized that the time was imminent or he would not have hurried away from Hong Kong in January of that year. Among these causes needs to be mentioned the presence of the Dutch in the port of Nagasaki. They had educated Japanese opinion on the progress of events outside the small empire, such as steam navigation and Britain's forceful opening of China to trade. The repeated visits of Russian, French, and British vessels, public and private, to Japanese waters may have been another cause. A third cause consisted in the advance of Russian jurisdiction down the Asiatic coast. Even to the Japanese, seclusion could hardly mean self defense. There had been and were Japanese leaders who advocated foreign intercourse. They may have been persecuted as were Watanabe, Takano, Sakuma, and others; but their influence lived on.

[1] Malloy, *Treaties*, etc., I.: 998.

Neither party to the treaty received it with great favor. In Japan it tended to draw the issues more sharply between the supporters of the Shogun and those of the Mikado. In the United States the business men felt disappointed. They had already in 1852 estimated the direct annual trade at $200,000,000.[1] And Edward Everett Hale noted facetiously that a filibustering expedition in the Gulf of Mexico awakened far more interest among the people than did the opening by peaceful diplomacy of an empire in the Far East to the intercourse of the world.[2]

The British appreciated quickly the importance of Perry's treaty and sent Admiral Sir James Stirling with a squadron of four vessels to obtain a similar pact. He reached Nagasaki on September 7, 1854; and, no doubt, Great Britain's war with Russia at the time helped him. The ports specified were Nagasaki and Hakodate. Like a good Englishman he obtained the concession that if British officers violated Japanese law on shore the port might be closed to them and if British sailors committed such violations they were to be turned over to the commander of their vessel for punishment. This constituted a kind of extraterritorial jurisdiction. The convention bore the date of October 14, 1854. Two months later, the Russian admiral, Pontiatine, appeared and obtained the treaty of February 7, 1855. It resembled Perry's. Three ports were opened, Nagasaki being the third. And the principle of extraterritoriality was fully recognized. The treaty had a boundary provision in it as well. The Dutch entered into negotiations for enlarged privileges. Theirs was an elaborate document, dated January 30, 1856. It had to provide for a cancellation of the restrictions which the Dutch had labored under for centuries. And they obtained some slight trading concessions which by the most favored nation clause inured to the United States also. A French vessel appeared in February, 1855, at Shimoda; but it was turned away, because Japan had no treaty with France.

[1] De Bow's *Review*, XIII.: 561.
[2] *North American Review*, 83: 236.

The United States permitted the lapse of only sixteen months, instead of eighteen as specified in Article XI of the treaty, before Townsend Harris was appointed consul-general to reside at Shimoda, July 31, 1855. He came of a New England family that had emigrated to New York long before the Revolution occurred. Burgoyne had burned the home of his grandmother, Thankful Townsend Harris. And she taught him "to tell the truth, fear God, and hate the British." As a young man he set up in the china and crockery business in New York City. He had traveled as a supercargo to the Far East and had become acquainted with oriental manners. He had also found time to acquire a mastery of the French, Spanish, and Italian languages, and to serve as one of the founders of the Free Academy, which grew later into the College of the City of New York. He was a personal friend of Marcy and of Seward. On the way to his destination he negotiated a treaty with Siam, based on the British treaty of April 18, 1855. Not until August 21, 1856, did he reach Shimoda. The Japanese made a good impression upon him, for the last sentence of the entry in his journal for August 25 runs, "I repeat they are superior to any people east of the Cape of Good Hope."[1]

They would rather Harris had not come. Shimoda had not, they said, recovered from the disastrous earthquake of the year before; they had no place ready; could he not go away and come again another year. He and they agreed finally upon a temporary residence. Japanese officers lived in the house with him. To this surveillance he protested, and they were removed. He had to exercise great patience and endurance with the officials in the matter of social courtesies, securing written replies to his communications, proper recognition of the value of American money; but friendly relations grew steadily. His disappointments he confided to his diary. "They are the greatest liars on earth" he concluded on January 8, 1857.

Harris' chief purpose was to obtain a commercial treaty. He succeeded in securing considerable concessions by June, 1857; which, in order to clinch, he incorporated into the form

[1] Griffis, *Townsend Harris:* 42.

of a convention and signed together with the Japanese commissioners under due formalities on June 17. He summarized the main provisions in his journal. 1. Nagasaki opened to American ships. 2. Permanent residence granted to Americans at Shimoda and Hakodate. 3. American currency was given approximately three times the value it formerly had. 4. Americans were to be tried by their own law in American consular courts. 5. The consul-general could go wherever he pleased in Japan.[1] The fact that under Article II missionaries could come and reside permanently pleased Harris immensely. He wrote further in his journal that day. "Am I elated by this success? Not a whit; I know my dear countrymen but too well to expect any praise for what I have done, and I shall esteem myself lucky if I am not removed from office; not for what I have done, but because I have not made a commercial treaty that would open Japan as freely as England is open to us."

He continued to preach the good will of the United States and by contrast pointed to the attitude of Great Britain, Russia, and France in their dealings with China and in their attitude toward Japan. He argued that Japan would set a good example before the world by entering freely into a liberal commercial treaty with him, while unattended by fleets or soldiers. Such action would prove to the other powers that a display of force was unnecessary in Japan. He presented these arguments skilfully in person before Lord Hotta at the Foreign Office. He outlined a treaty in which he asked for the unrestricted privilege of trade and pointed to the manner in which Great Britain had conducted the Opium War in China and quoted from Sir John Bowring to the effect that Great Britain could tolerate no longer the condition of affairs in Japan. He asked also for the right to have an American minister in Japan.[2]

After months of coaxing, cajolery, and anxiety, he and the Japanese commissioners, Inouye, Lord of Shinano, and Iwase, Lord of Higo, agreed on a draft of a treaty, February 26, 1858. The Japanese asked for approximately two months, until April

[1] Griffis, *Townsend Harris:* 160. Compare Malloy, *Treaties*, etc., I.: 998.
[2] Griffis, *Townsend Harris:* Chapter 13.

21, in which to discuss the treaty among themselves and attempt to harmonize various factions before they would sign. Harris returned to Shimoda where he suffered an attack of "nervous fever." The Emperor and his councillors expressed the deepest sympathy. His Majesty sent him two of his best physicians, daily messages of cheer, and presents of fruit, arrowroot, and so on. Harris returned to Yedo by April 2 for the signing; but Lord Hotta had been unable to obtain the support of the various factions for the treaty; nor was he able to do so by June 1. Harris agreed to give them until September 4, 1858, on the condition that the Japanese would refrain from entering into any kind of treaty with another foreign power until thirty days after the American treaty had been signed. The treaty bore the date of July 29, 1858.

The treaty contained fourteen articles with seven regulations appended. Article I granted a reciprocal right to each party to maintain a diplomatic agent in the capital of the other. American consuls could reside in the ports of Japan opened to American commerce. Japanese consuls could reside in any or all ports of the United States. Reciprocal freedom of travel for diplomats and consuls was included.

By Article II the President agreed to act as a mediator between Japan and any European power whenever requested by Japan. American ships of war should extend friendly assistance to all Japanese vessels upon the high seas, so far as laws of neutrality would permit. And American consuls throughout the world should give friendly aid to Japanese vessels.

Article III opened the following ports in addition to Shimoda and Hakodate, Kanagawa and Nagasaki on July 4, 1859, Niigata on January 1, 1860, and Hiogo on January 1, 1863. Six months after the opening of Kanagawa the port of Shimoda should be closed as a place of residence and trade. This was at the instance of Harris, for the harbor of Shimoda had proved ill protected. In all of these ports American citizens might reside permanently. They could lease land, purchase the buildings thereon, and erect dwellings and warehouses. This clause furnished the basis for the only arbitration to which Japan has become a party.[1] No fortifications could be erected, and the right of inspection was reserved. Japan agreed to place no restrictions on the free ingress or egress of Americans to their places of business or abode. Yedo and Osaka were opened to residence only for American traders. Americans might freely buy from and sell to the Japanese directly, without the intervention of Japanese officers as heretofore. But munitions of war could be sold to the Japanese government and to foreigners only. No rice or wheat could be exported as cargo from Japan; this permitted of buying sufficient provisions for a ship's crew. Copper was apparently mined on government account; for it was stipulated that the government should sell the surplus at public auction. Harris had had difficulty in obtaining Japanese servants; so he inserted a provision that Americans should have the right to employ them.

By Article IV duties on imports and exports should be paid in accordance with the tariff appended. Harris attempted to secure the cancellation of export duties but without success. If the Japanese customs officers should be dissatisfied with the value of an article placed by the owner, they might fix the value with the understanding that if the owner objected they could purchase the goods at the valuation fixed. The United States obtained the privilege of landing and keeping naval stores at three ports without payment of duty. The importation of opium was forbidden; and if an American vessel had more than four pounds avoirdupois on board, the Japanese customs officers could destroy the excess. This salutary provision had been first inserted in the Dutch treaty. On goods imported under the treaty, the Japanese could levy no excise or transit duties. This was a wise provision which it would have been well for the English to have inserted in the Chinese treaty. No higher duties were to be levied than those specified in the tariff, nor higher than those on goods imported in Japanese vessels or in the vessels of any other nation.

Article V permitted coins of all description, except Japanese copper coins, to be exported from Japan. Moreover, foreign coin

[1] See Japanese House Tax Arbitration, Wilson, *The Hague Cases:* 46.

should pass freely in Japan for the corresponding weight of similar Japanese coins. This provision virtually drained Japan of her own coins and made difficult the detection of counterfeit in foreign coins. This article was amended by Article VI of the convention of June 25, 1866, which restored to Japan her own coinage.

Article VI established American consular courts which were to administer American law. Americans charged with criminal offenses should be there tried. Japanese charged with offenses against Americans should be tried in Japanese courts. The consular courts were to be open to Japanese creditors for the recovery of claims against Americans and reciprocally the Japanese courts to American creditors of the Japanese. Neither government was to be held responsible for the payment of debts contracted by its citizens.

Article VII defined the limits within which, at the various ports, Americans might travel and the penalties, usually expulsion, for violation.

Article VIII granted to Americans the freedom of religious worship and the right to erect suitable places for worship. Harris took great pride in this article, for it permitted the residence of American missionaries. The freedom of worship had been inserted in the Dutch treaty; but the right to build churches was an addition.

Article IX provided for the arrest and the return to the consul by the Japanese of American deserters and fugitives from justice. For such services the consul was to pay a just compensation.

Under Article X Japan should have the privilege, so far as neutrality laws would permit, of obtaining by purchase or construction ships of war, merchant vessels, munitions, and of securing the services of experts.

Article XI stipulated that the regulations added to the treaty should have the same binding effect as the treaty.

Article XII revoked the conflicting clauses in the treaties of 1854 and 1857.

Article XIII provided that after July 4, 1872, either party

could give one year's notice of a desire for a revision of the treaty. Harris' intent was, and no doubt that of the Japanese, that in fourteen years time permission should be granted to either party to profit by experience. But in 1866 and in 1872 the Japanese found themselves greatly restricted by the operations of the most favored nation clause. The consent of all the treaty powers had to be obtained. This was accomplished only by 1894, becoming effective in 1899.

Article XIV stipulated that the treaty should become effective on July 4, 1859; that the ratifications should be exchanged at Washington; that the treaty should be executed in quadruple and that each copy should be written in the English, Japanese, and Dutch languages of which the Dutch should be considered the original.

The regulations appended to the treaty were more liberal than any before granted. Tonnage duties were eliminated. Penalties were reduced. But on the whole they were based on the regulations which the Dutch had previously obtained.

The seventh regulation contained the tariff provisions. Under the Dutch and Russian treaties of 1857, the import duties had been fixed temporarily at 35 per cent. ad valorem. Harris obtained rather quickly a reduction to 12½ per cent. ad valorem on both imports and exports; but he wanted a complete abolition of export duties. One of the last features of the negotiation consisted in the agreement on the seventh regulation. Class 1 included free imports, gold and silver, coined and uncoined; wearing apparel in actual use; household furniture and books, the property of persons who came to reside in Japan, and which was not for sale.

Class 2 included imports with a 5 per cent. duty; ship-repairing materials, salted provisions, breadstuffs, live animals, coal, rice, paddy, steam machinery, zinc, lead, tin, raw silk.

Class 3 included imports with a 35 per cent. duty; all kinds of intoxicating liquors.

Class 4 included unenumerated imports with a duty of 20 per cent.

The last class included all articles of Japanese production

exported as cargo, and these were to pay 5 per cent., except gold and silver coin and copper in bars, which should be free.[1]

Townsend Harris had won a great diplomatic victory. He wrote to a friend: "The pleasure I feel in having made the treaty is enhanced by the reflection that there has been no show of coercion, nor was menace in the least used by me to obtain it. There was no American man of war within one thousand miles of me for months before and after the negotiations. I told the Japanese at the outset that my mission was a friendly one; that I was not authorized to use any threats; that all I wished was that they would listen to the truth that I would lay before them." [2]

The Japanese did not wait thirty days after the signature of the American treaty before they entered into treaties with other powers; and, in all likelihood, Harris absolved them from this promise. The Dutch signed a treaty with Japan on August 18, 1858; Russia on August 19; Great Britain on August 26; and France on October 7, 1858. All of them used the Harris Treaty as a basis. Lord Elgin obtained two modifications for Great Britain. The British treaty should become effective on July 1 instead of July 4, 1859; so that this treaty had the honor of being the first to become effective; and the change in date removed an unpleasant reminder of what July 4 meant to an Englishman. The other modification consisted in the shifting of woolen and cotton goods from the class paying 20 per cent. duty to the class that paid 5 per cent. duty. Baron Gros tried to secure a reduction for France in the duties on wines. The Japanese replied that if they realized a need for the wines they would revise the schedule five years later. The most favored nation clause extended the reductions on woolen and cotton goods to the United States as well.

The distinguished Japanese scholar, Inazo Nitobe, estimates the work of Perry and of Harris as follows: "The expedition of Perry was heralded with a loud blare of trumpets, while the coming of Harris was attended with no demonstration. Four

[1] Malloy, *Treaties*, etc., I.: 1000.
[2] Letter in *Living Age*, February, 1859: 572.

thick quarto volumes made known to the world the minutest details of Perry's expedition, while Harris even forbade the publication of his papers, until twenty-five years after his decease." "Thus has it always been. An oak falls noisily crashing through the forest; the acorns drop with scarce a sound. To generations after the acorns prove the greater blessing." [1]

When Harris obtained the consent of the Japanese to have the ratifications exchanged in Washington he secured therewith the acceptance of an invitation to send their first diplomatic mission. Owing partly to internal differences in Japan and to the delay of the United States in furnishing transportation, which had been arranged for through diplomatic channels, the going into effect of the treaty was postponed for almost a year. The embassy consisted of eighteen persons of rank, two with the rank of envoys, and fifty-three servants. Flag-officer Josiah Tattarall of the U. S. S. "Powhatan" regretted the number of servants; and the officials he had to stow away two and three in a state room.[2] The mission traveled by way of Panama, reached Washington, was properly entertained, and exchanged the ratifications on May 22, 1860. On the next day the President proclaimed the treaty.

A slight reduction in the import duties was arranged in 1864. A revision of duties took place in 1866, together with an amendment of Article V of Harris' Treaty affecting Japanese coin. The Treaty of 1878 contained further modifications. It abolished discriminatory duties in Japan on American imports or exports and cancelled the Japanese export duties. The regulation of the coasting trade was reserved to Japan. All fines imposed and collected by the American consular courts for violation of treaties should be turned over to the Japanese authorities. And Article V of the Harris' Treaty, 1858, was cancelled. In 1886 an extradition treaty was negotiated. And in 1894 the two countries negotiated a treaty, effective July 17, 1899, revising completely the commercial relations between them. By Article XVIII, that treaty superseded the Perry Treaty of 1854 and the

[1] Nitobe, *Intercourse between the United States and Japan:* 116.
[2] Sen. Doc. 25, 36 Cong., 1 sess., 12.

Harris Treaty of 1858 and, in consequence, abolished the judicial functions of American consuls in Japan.[1]

BIBLIOGRAPHY.

FOSTER, JOHN W.—*American Diplomacy in the Orient.* Boston, 1903.

GRIFFIS, W. E.—*Life of Townsend Harris,* Boston, 1895.

GRIFFIS, W. E.—*Matthew C. Perry.* Boston, 1887.

HARRIS, TOWNSEND.—*Journal.* (The major part is found in Griffis' Townsend Harris.) (Typewritten transcript from the original manuscript is in the Library of Congress).

HAWKS, F. L.—*Narrative of the Expedition of an American Squadron to the China Seas and Japan.* Sen. Doc. 79, 33 Cong., 2 sess. Washington, 1856.

Littell's Living Age, 1859. New York.

NITOBE, INAZO. *Intercourse between the United States and Japan.* J. H. U. Studies in History and Political Science, extra volume number 8. Baltimore, 1891.

PAULLIN, C. O. *Diplomatic Negotiations of American Naval Officers,* 1778–1883. Baltimore, 1912.

Sen. Ex. Doc. 25, 36 Cong., 1 session. (Serial No. 1031). Washington, 1860.

Sen. Ex. Doc. 34, 33 Cong., 2 sess. (Serial No. 751). Washington, 1855.

TREAT, PAYSON J.—*The Early Diplomatic Relations between the United States and Japan, 1853–1865.* Baltimore, 1917.

WILLIAMS, S. WELLS.—*Journal of the Perry Expedition to Japan* (in Transactions of the Asiatic Society of Japan, Volume 37, part II). Yokohama, 1910.

[1] See Malloy, *Treaties,* etc., I.: 1028.

CHAPTER XII

THE ALASKA PURCHASE, 1867

"International law, properly so-called, is only so much of the principles of morality and justice as the nations have agreed shall be part of those rules of conduct which shall govern their relations one with another."—Sir Charles Russell.

Alaska fails to comprise an area as large as the Louisiana Purchase; nevertheless, its extent is significant. The New England states, New York, New Jersey, Delaware, Maryland, Pennsylvania, the five great states in the old Northwest Territory, Minnesota, Iowa, and one-half of Missouri could be placed within the confines of Alaska. The known resources in fish, copper, gold, silver, other minerals, fur-bearing animals, and forests are large; and the prospective resources are immense.

Vitus Bering explored the St. Elias region for Russia in 1741. The survivors of his expedition brought back with them tales of wealth to be made in furs. Numerous fur trading companies were organized. By an imperial ukase of August 11, 1799, these were either eliminated or merged in the Russian American Company. In this ukase Paul I stated: "The benefits and advantages resulting to our empire from the hunting and trading carried on by our loyal subjects in the northeastern seas and along the coasts of America have attracted our royal attention and consideration; therefore, having taken under our immediate protection a company organized for the above named purpose of carrying on hunting and trading, we allow it to assume the appellation of "Russian American Company;" and for the purposes of aiding the company in its enterprises, we allow the commanders of our land and sea forces to employ said forces in the company's aid if occasion requires it, while for further relief and assistance of said company, and having examined their rules and regulations, we hereby declare it to be our highest imperial will to grant to this company for a period of twenty years the following rights and privileges."

1. The fifty-fifth degree of north latitude was taken as the starting point. From there the rights of the company extended to the exclusive use of the coasts of America north and south of that line and of the "Aleutian, Kurile, and other islands situated in the northeastern ocean." 2. All new discoveries north and south of this line made by the company could be occupied as Russian possessions, "if they had not been previously occupied by any other nation." 3. The company could "use and profit by everything which has been or shall be discovered in those localities, on the surface and in the bosom of the earth, without any competition by others." 4. The company could establish settlements and fortify them. 5. It might enjoy freedom of navigation and commerce with "all surrounding powers." 6. It could employ for hunting, navigation, and trade any free person and also serfs and house-servants with the consent of their land holders. 7. Government timber might be cut. 8. The company could buy powder and lead at the government magazines at cost price. 9. A partner's share in the company could not be seized for debt. 10. The rights of the company were made a monopoly. 11. Paul conferred judicial powers in minor cases upon the company.[1]

Investors in St. Petersburg absorbed quickly the capital stock of 1,238,740 rubles. The Czar, the Czarina, and the Grand Duke Constantine subscribed for large sums, and directed that the dividends should be devoted to charity. During the first twenty year period of the company the net earnings were 7,685,608 rubles. Of this amount 4,250,000 rubles were distributed as dividends and the remainder was added to the capital.

The ukase mentioned nothing on the treatment of the natives. Nor would any philanthropic stipulations have been observed if they had been inserted. Baronof's rule during the first eighteen years of the century tolerated the work of missionaries insofar as they promoted peace and respect for his authority among the natives; but his chief function consisted in obtaining

[1] H. H. Bancroft, *History of Alaska:* 379.

furs from the natives and in stimulating them to bring larger quantities. His methods did not differ essentially from those of Cortez, Alvarado, and Pizarro in an earlier day in other sections of the Cordillera. Indeed, a cargo of furs enriched the owner in Russia as much as a cargo of the precious metals the owners in Spain. Successful frontiersmen in such regions place small value upon their own lives and less upon the lives of others. The Russians in Alaska had no fear of punishment. They could commit robbery, rape, and murder with impunity, for, to use their own phrase, "God is high above and the Czar is far away."

Fortunately for the progress of civilization, business must conform to moral standards or perish by the wayside, as did piracy, slavery; and as have several of the colonial trading companies. The Hudson Bay Company has kept step with progress and consequently enjoys still great prosperity. The Russian American Company founded settlements at Yakutat Bay and Sitka; kept up those at Unalaska and Kodiak; took a census of the fur seals which led to a conservation of the herd; made surveys of the seacoast; started ship building projects; kept watch on Astor's enterprise on the Columbia River; warned off American expeditions to Alaska, which, in some instances, were successful in obtaining cargoes of fur from the Indians at higher prices than the Russians offered; and established farming communities on the California coast to supplement the insecure and hazardous supply of foodstuffs from St. Petersburg, such as wheat, potatoes, vegetables, some fruit, beef and hides. This gradual occupation and claim to the whole of the Pacific coast from San Francisco northward furnished the administration at Washington with one of the motives for the Monroe Doctrine.

The Russian American Company came in conflict with the claims of the Hudson Bay Company, of Astor's company, and with the rights of Spain. Spain refused to sell the Russians any tracts of land; and such as they held rested on titles acquired from the Indians only. The Russian company could obtain no favorable intervention with the authorities at Madrid through the offices of the home government at St. Petersburg. This compelled the company to offer for sale its entire California property at Ross and Bodega to the Hudson Bay Company; but no agreement could be reached. They offered it next to General Vallejo; and he refused to buy. Finally, in September, 1841, they reached an agreement with John A. Sutter. They turned over to him all improvements, implements, 1700 head of cattle, 940 horses, and 900 sheep for $30,000.[1]

At the end of its first twenty year period the company applied for a renewal of its exclusive privileges. This was provided for in the imperial ukase of September, 1821. The limits of the jurisdiction of the company over the Pacific coast of America had become more definite. The southern extremity rested on latitude fifty-one degrees north, or the northern cape of Vancouver Island and stretched to Bering Strait and beyond. The company could exercise exclusive jurisdiction over a belt of the marginal sea one hundred miles wide. The manager was placed on the same official footing as the governors of the Siberian provinces. Government officials, including those in the army and the navy, could enter the service of the company on half pay and without losing their turn for promotion. All servants of the company were exempted from conscription. Attempts were made to safeguard against abuse and injustice. If the company's shares should fall fifty per cent. in value, the government would assume the loss, and might sell the shares at auction.[2]

Diplomatic difficulties arose with Great Britain and with the United States, due to the protests of British and American traders. The United States reached an agreement first, 1824; Henry Middleton acted as negotiator and Nesselrode and Poletica for Russia. Article I provided for the freedom of navigation and fishing upon the Pacific Ocean and for the freedom to resort to the unoccupied coasts for the purpose of trading with the natives. The interpretation of this article came up in the later fur seals arbitration. By Article III the United States agreed that none of its citizens should form any establishment north of 54° 40′ north latitude and Russia agreed that no Russians should form any establishment south of that point. The two parties

[1] H. H. Bancroft, *History of Alaska:* 489.
[2] Ibid.: 531.

agreed reciprocally not to furnish the natives north or south of 54° 40 with spirituous liquors, fire-arms, powder, or any munitions of war or to permit their respective citizens or subjects to do so. Each party reserved to itself the right to punish its own citizens or subjects committing such offenses; and there was to be no search or detention of vessels on account of such offenses.[1]

The same Russian commissioners negotiated a convention with Great Britain, 1825; Lord Stratford Canning representing Great Britain. The third and fourth articles described the boundary between the British North American possessions and those of Russia. This was afterward inserted in Article I of the treaty ceding Alaska to the United States and became the basis for the Alaska boundary arbitration, 1903, which will be described later. Article X provided for the reciprocal right of British and Russian ships in distress to enter any harbor for repairs and provisions, without payment of duty or port charges. Otherwise the treaty contained substantially the same provisions as the American.

The news of the treaties aroused indignation and remonstrance on the part of the Russian American Company. Its right had been violated by taking away the exclusive jurisdiction over the marginal sea, one hundred miles from the coast, and by permitting foreigners to trade on the uninhabited shores belonging to the company. This foreboded, the representatives claimed, the ruin and the dissolution of the company. Czar Alexander paid no attention to the complaints; but Nicholas did make a futile effort to have the treaties cancelled. The Hudson Bay Company gradually made serious inroads upon the former monopolies of the Russian company, with the result that the yield of the hunting grounds was considerably less for the second period of twenty years than the first period. However, the dividends declared were almost double those in the first term; in several instances they were charged on the earnings of future years.

The charter was duly renewed for a third term of twenty years on March 5, 1841. The boundary was changed in accord-

[1] Malloy, *Treaties*, etc., II.: 1512.

ance with the American and British treaties. Not any of the company's rights were curtailed. It was given the monopoly of Russian trade with certain ports in China, for example, all tea going from Shanghai to St. Petersburg had to pass through the company's hands. No liquor could be sold to the natives. And an order was soon afterward proclaimed from St. Petersburg that no liquor could be sold to anybody.

As soon as the company felt the forebodings of the Crimean War, its representatives approached those of the Hudson Bay Company. The two agreed to petition their governments to consider the regions occupied by these two trading companies as neutral. Great Britain and Russia acceded to this request with the understanding that neither company should assist in the belligerent actions of its home government. And this agreement was respected by all the parties concerned. Several British cruisers visited the harbor of Sitka; but they found no evidence of violation of the agreement and they inflicted no damage. They did bombard two ports, Petropavlosk and the Russian settlement on Ourup on the Asiatic coast, which were within the jurisdiction of the Russian American Company. Russia protested; but Great Britain justified the attacks on the ground that the ports did not lie on the northwest coast of America. Though the Alaskan settlements met with no direct British attack, they did suffer greatly. As usual the British patrolled the sea lanes. Food and clothing became scarce, to say nothing about the inability to sell the furs and the consequent lack of power to buy the products of the hunt from the Indians. The Indians conducted raids on the posts and even committed massacres.

American interest in the Alaskan fisheries and the fur trade had been steadily growing. And during the Crimean War their opportunities multiplied. Another project assisted in stimulating American interest. Scientists foresaw small hope of making a successful project of an Atlantic cable. Several men, but notably Major P. M. Collins, had played with the idea of constructing a land line via Bering Strait. Major Collins obtained from Russia the right to build such a line on through

Siberia. He secured the coöperation of the Western Union Telegraph Company. The United States instructed its minister in St. Petersburg to favor the project. Great Britain made the necessary concessions through the western part of British America. And as soon as Cyrus Field's venture with the Atlantic cable failed in 1858, the Western Union began operations in earnest.

The American Civil War interrupted its efforts; but by the latter part of 1866, thousands of miles of survey had been made, the material for the entire line had been purchased and even distributed at convenient points. The line had been erected to New Westminster, the capital of British Columbia, and 850 miles of line beyond to the banks of the Simpson River were erected and connected. A great deal of work had been done through Siberia. The Western Union felt certain that by the end of 1867 the whole line would be completed. But an unforeseen event occurred. The double success of the "Great Eastern" in 1866 in laying two cables from Valencia Bay to Heart's Content eliminated all need of the Western Union Telegraph Company line by way of Alaska, Bering Strait, and Siberia.[1]

In 1860 the directors of the Russian American Company had submitted a revised draft of the charter to be renewed for another twenty years. The Czar's government ordered an investigation of the company's conduct and affairs. Pending a report the charter expired; and the company continued to do business on the tolerance of the imperial will alone. As a result of the investigation the imperial council recommended in 1865 that the charter be renewed on two conditions, one, that all Aleuts and native tribes should be exempt from involuntary servitude and that all the inhabitants of Russian America should be permitted to engage in whatever industry they pleased; two, that the government should assume no liability for the decrease in the value of the company's shares. The directors of the company failed to meet these conditions.

Russia had never taken formal possession of Alaska; that region had not been incorporated or thought of as a province

[1] Diplomatic Correspondence, 1867, Part I.: 385.

of the empire. The Czar had extended his protection to the traders there. Through an ukase he had incorporated the Russian American Company in which several members of the royal family were stockholders; and twice he had renewed the charter. The Crimean War had made evident how easily Russian America might fall into the hands of a hostile power and how imminent the possibility was of the British lion and the Russian bear facing each other on opposite shores of Bering Strait. Since the Russian American Company refused to accept a third renewal of its charter on the conditions proposed, would it not be wise to cede the Russian rights in America to a friendly power and thus obtain the advantages of a buffer state and place a barrier to British expansion?

The United States had shown considerable interest in the activities of the Russian American Company as evidenced by one principle in the Monroe Doctrine; by the Treaty of 1824; by interceding in behalf of American fishermen and traders, who had continuously been growing more numerous; and by assisting to make smooth the course for the project of the Western Union Telegraph Company. Moreover, the discovery of gold in California had made closer relations with Alaska imperative; for example, Sanderson and Moss of San Francisco ordered 250 tons of ice from Alaska in 1851 at $75 a ton. And the people of Washington Territory wanted the right to take part in the rich salmon, cod, and halibut fisheries off Alaska.

Senator William M. Gwin of California and the Assistant Secretary of State broached the subject of a purchase of Alaska to the Russian minister, Baron Edward de Stoeckl, in 1859, and mentioned $5,000,000 as the price; but nothing came of it.[1] From 1861 on, the talk became common among the Russians in Alaska and the Americans interested in the region that the United States would some day acquire it. Negotiations for the adjustment of the rights of American fishermen and traders in Alaska continued. Indeed, when Baron Stoeckl left Washington in the latter part of 1866 for a short visit to St. Petersburg, he promised to use his efforts to obtain favorable action on the

[1] F. Bancroft, *Life of Seward*, II.: 474.

requests of the State Department in behalf of Americans. And it was while in St. Petersburg, February, 1867, that Baron Stoeckl received direct authority to treat for the sale of the territory.

As soon as he arrived in Washington he opened informal negotiations with William H. Seward, an ardent expansionist, then Secretary of State. Stoeckl named ten million dollars as a reasonable price; Seward bid five million. Then both worked toward $7,500,000. Seward proved the ablest bargainer; they agreed on $7,000,000, with the reservation by Stoeckl that all the rights and properties of the Russian American Company should be respected. On March 23, 1867, Seward sent Baron Stoeckl a message stipulating that the President would pay $7,200,000 if the cession of Alaska were made free and unencumbered of all reservations, franchises or grants.[1] On March 25, 1867, Stoeckl replied: "I believe myself authorized, Mr. Secretary of State, to accede literally to this request on the conditions indicated in your note." He did, however, cable St. Petersburg for definite approval. On the evening of March 29, 1867, the Russian minister called at Seward's home and found the Secretary of State engaged in his usual game of whist. Stoeckl reported the receipt of a cablegram giving the Czar's consent to the cession and suggested that he would be ready to proceed with the final touches the next day. Seward retorted, "Why wait till tomorrow? Let us make the treaty tonight." He sent out messengers to summon the necessary clerks for immediate duty at the State Department. The Assistant Secretary of State called for Charles Sumner, chairman of the senate committee on foreign relations. Stoeckl ordered his assistants to appear. By midnight the necessary parties and persons had gathered at the State Department. And by four o'clock in the morning the treaty was signed. At noon President Johnson sent the treaty to the Senate with a message advising ratification.

No one expressed much opposition to the treaty; but a great deal of good natured raillery found expression both in the

[1] Diplomatic Correspondence, 1867, Part I.: 399.

newspapers and in the Senate. It was "Seward's folly," "Johnson's polar bear garden." It was a bad bargain palmed off on a silly administration by the shrewd Russians. The ground was frozen six feet deep; no useful animals could live there.[1] But Sumner made a thorough study of the resources of Alaska, which he presented convincingly to the Senate on April 9.[2] The Senate advised ratification on the same day by a vote of 37 to 2, Fessenden and Morrill constituted the minority. The President ratified on May 28. The ratifications were exchanged on June 20, 1867; and the President proclaimed the treaty the same day. All of these actions took place before the House of Representatives had given its consent to the appropriation of the money stipulated. And more than that, both sides appointed commissioners [3] for the delivery of Alaska to the United States, which was accomplished on October 11, 1867.

When the House took up the question of the appropriation, it had been placed in such a position that it could not well refuse. Members expressed freely their views on the limitations of the treaty making power of the executive and of the Senate. But they complied finally with what was expected of them and passed the appropriation by a vote of 113 to 43.[4]

The treaty contained seven articles. The first laid the basis for two famous boundary arbitrations. The boundary on the west consisted of a water line passing "through a point in Behring's straits on the parallel of sixty-five degrees thirty minutes north latitude, at its intersection by the meridian which passes midway between the islands of Krusenstern, or Ignalook, and the island of Ratmanoff, or Noonarbook, and proceeds due north, without limitation, into the same Frozen Ocean. The same western limit, beginning at the same initial point, proceeds thence in a course nearly southwest, through Behring's straits and Behring's sea, so as to pass midway between the northwest point of the island of St. Lawrence and the southeast point of Cape Choukotski, to the meridian of one hun-

[1] F. W. Seward, *Seward at Washington*, III.: 367.
[2] Sumner, *Works*, XI.: 186.
[3] Diplomatic Correspondence, Pt. I.: 404.
[4] Congressional Globe, 1867–1868: 4055.

dred and seventy-two west longitude; thence, from the intersection of that meridian, in a southwesterly direction, so as to pass midway between the island of Atton and the Copper island of the Kormandorski couplet or group, in the North Pacific ocean, to the meridian of one hundred and ninety-three degrees west longitude, so as to include in the territory conveyed the whole of the Aleutian islands east of the meridian." [1]

The first act of Congress relating to Alaska was passed July 27, 1868. It created a customs' district out of the territory and made it the duty of the Secretary of the Treasury to prevent the killing of any fur seal until Congress should otherwise provide. By the act of July 1, 1870, the Secretary of the Treasury was directed to lease for a term of twenty years the right to take fur seals on the islands of St. Paul and St. George in the Pribilof group for an annual rental of not less than $50,000 and a tax of $2 on each fur-seal skin taken. The number that could be taken was limited to 100,000 and the season for taking the skins was limited to June, July, September, and October. Special regulations were authorized for the Indians to capture young seals at any time for purposes of food and clothing. Mr. Boutwell leased, accordingly, this privilege to a corporation chartered under the laws of California, the Alaska Commercial Company, John F. Miller. President. The rental was fixed at $55,000.

The above statute made no provision for protecting the seals in the surrounding waters, although it was generally known that the seals traveled far out at sea in search of food and resorted to the Pribilof Islands mainly during the breeding season and the season for bearing the young. But no international controversies arose until 1868. In that year Sir Lionel Sackville-West, the British minister in Washington, informed the Secretary of State, Bayard, that his government had received a telegram from the commander of the British naval force in the north Pacific announcing that three Canadian sealing schooners had been seized by the United States revenue cutter "Corwin" while sailing the Bering Sea more than sixty miles from the nearest land. The master and one of the crew of each vessel were placed

[1] Malloy, *Treaties*, etc., II.: 522.

under arrest and the remainder were taken to San Francisco and there left to shift for themselves. Judge Dawson of the United States condemned the vessels and sentenced the captains and the members of the crews to a fine and imprisonment for thirty days. It appeared to Sackville-West that the United States was asserting a claim to the sole sovereignty of Bering Sea stretching 600 and 700 miles west of the mainland of Alaska. His government had no doubt, he wrote, that the United States would admit the illegality of the proceedings against the British subjects and vessels concerned and make reasonable reparation.[1]

The State Department did not possess the information required at the time. But it afterward turned out that the British minister had been correctly informed. Judge Dawson had based his condemnation of the vessels and the conviction of the members of the crew on the understanding that Russia had claimed and exercised jurisdiction over that part of Bering Sea afterward ceded to the United States and that the United States had succeeded to this right; hence "all the penalties prescribed by law against the killing of fur bearing animals must therefore attach against any violation of law within the limits before described."[2] Bayard assured Sackville-West that he need have no apprehension that the United States would avoid its international obligations and that new regulations for the fur seal fisheries were under consideration by the Treasury Department. But during the next year, 1887, three more Canadian sealing schooners were seized by an American revenue cutter; and Judge Dawson promptly declared them forfeited. He stated that for the want of books at his command he had to rely upon a brief prepared by N. L. Jeffries, the attorney for the Alaska Commercial Company, for collection of historical events and the citation of authorities. As might be inferred, this brief was devoted to a maintenance of the claim that the Bering Sea within the American boundary was a mare clausum.[3] Again, the British minister received the first information in Wash-

[1] Sen. Ex. Doc. 106, 50 Cong., 2 sess.: 7.
[2] Ibid.: 49.
[3] Moore, *International Arbitrations*. I.: 775.

ington of the event. Attorney General Garland directed by telegraph that the vessels be released. The marshal at Sitka wrote a letter in reply expressing the belief that the telegram had been thought to be not genuine. Garland helped to settle the aggravated situation by repeating the order to release the schooners.

Various proposals for saving the fur seals from extinction were brought forward both by the Foreign Office and the State Department. But no agreement could be reached, partly because of friction over the treaty rights of Americans to engage in the northeastern inshore fisheries off Canada and Newfoundland. More seizures of Canadian sealing vessels were made in 1889. The new Secretary of State, James G. Blaine, defended the seizures on the ground that the vessels had been engaged in a pursuit that was contra bonos mores, which involved serious and permanent injury to the rights of the government and the people of the United States. To establish this ground, it was unnecessary, said Blaine, to argue the sovereignty of the United States over Bering Sea or to define what powers had been acquired from Russia. The fur seals constituted the most valuable source of revenue from the Alaskan possessions. Russia had exercised a recognized full control over the seal fisheries to 1867; and since the cession the United States had controlled these fisheries without dispute till 1886. Vessels of other nations had been permitted to engage in the whale fisheries in Bering Sea, but they had uniformly abstained from engaging in the fur seal fisheries. The United States had made careful regulations for the protection of the seal with the object of thereby benefiting mankind. During the four years from 1886 to 1889, the seal herds had decreased by forty per cent. because of the incursions made by Canadian vessels, while the seals were swimming on the high seas in search of food.

Blaine continued, "In the judgment of this Government the law of the sea is not lawlessness. Nor can the law of the sea and the liberty which it confers and which it protects, be perverted to justify acts which are immoral in themselves, which inevitably tend to results against the interests and against the welfare of mankind. One step beyond which Her Majesty's Government has taken in this contention, and piracy finds its justification." [1]

Lord Salisbury through the British minister, Sir Julian Pauncefote, denied that the United States had any property right in the seals and asserted that until they were caught they belonged to nobody. He denied likewise that Russia had wielded any exclusive protection over the seals to 1867 and cited a protest by John Quincy Adams against the ukase of 1821, which forbade foreigners to engage in whaling or fishing within one hundred miles of the coast.[2] Blaine replied that J. Q. Adams had protested against the application of the ukase of 1821 in the Pacific Ocean; but that it could not be and was not applied to Bering Sea.[3] Salisbury replied in turn that Bering Sea was not known by that name in 1824; he quoted from contemporary correspondence to show that it was considered a part of the Pacific Ocean; and he closed by offering to submit the dispute to arbitration.[4]

Thereupon, Blaine submitted five questions which should form the basis for the arbitration. Salisbury suggested a few modifications; and the questions were ready for incorporation in the agreement providing for arbitration. This was concluded on February 29, 1892. Seven arbitrators should sit, two to be named by the Queen of Great Britain, two by the President of the United States, and one each by the President of France, the King of Italy, and the King of Sweden and Norway. Article VI contained the five questions; and Article VII specified that if the answers to the questions left the subject of the protection of the fur seals in such a condition that the concurrence of Great Britain was necessary for the establishment of regulations, the arbitrators could then determine what these concurrent regulations should be.

The arbitrators were Justice John M. Harlan and Senator John I. Morgan of the United States; Lord Hannen of the High Court of Appeal and Sir John Thompson, the Canadian

[1] Foreign Relations, 1890: 366.
[2] Ibid., 419.
[3] Ibid., 437.
[4] Ibid., 456.

Minister of Justice, of Great Britain; Baron Alphonse de Courcel of France, who was later chosen president of the tribunal; Marquis Emilio Visconti Venosta of Italy; and Gregers Gram of Norway. John W. Foster acted as agent for the United States and Charles H. Tupper as agent for Great Britain. Among the counsel for the United States were Edward J. Phelps, James C. Carter, Henry W. Blodgett, F. R. Coudert, and Robert Lansing. For Great Britain, Sir Charles Russell, Her Majesty's Attorney General, Sir Richard Webster, and Christopher Robinson of Canada served as counsel. The submission of cases, counter cases, and arguments had been provided for in the treaty. These fill sixteen substantial volumes. It will be sufficient here to repeat the five questions submitted to the tribunal, to indicate the trend of the argument, and to summarize the answer of the tribunal to each of the questions.

Question 1. What exclusive jurisdiction in the sea now known as the Bering Sea, and what exclusive rights in the seal fisheries therein, did Russia assert and exercise prior and up to the time of the cession of Alaska to the United States?

In support of the first part of this question, that of exclusive jurisdiction in the sea, the United States had relied upon documentary evidence obtained from the archives in Alaska at the time of the purchase. A native Russian, Ivan Petroff, had been employed to translate these documents. For some reason, he perverted the meaning of various phrases to favor greatly the cause of the United States. Count Nesselrode was made to say in 1824 that the Czar would protect the Russian American Company's interests "in the catch and preservation of all marine animals;" whereas he actually said that "the government has never lost sight of its interests." In another instance Nesselrode was made to say, "the sovereignty of Russia over the shores of Siberia and America, as well as over the Aleutian Islands and the intervening sea, has long since been acknowledged by all the powers;" while in the correct translation he mentioned only "the coasts of Siberia and the Aleutian Islands." Facsimile copies of the original documents had been furnished the British agent, but as soon as these errors were discovered John W.

Foster communicated the fact to Mr. Tupper, November 2, 1892.[1]

Six of the judges concurring,[2] the tribunal decided that by the ukase of 1821, Russia had claimed jurisdiction in Bering Sea to the extent of 100 Italian miles from the coasts and islands belonging to her. But in the negotiations leading up to the treaty with the United States in 1824 and with Great Britain in 1825, Russia had admitted her jurisdiction in that sea should be restricted to the reach of a cannon shot from the shore. And it appeared to the court that from 1824 to 1867, Russia had "never asserted in fact or exercised any exclusive jurisdiction in Bering's Sea or any exclusive rights in the seal fisheries therein beyond the ordinary limits of territorial waters." [3]

Question 2. How far were claims of jurisdiction as to the seal fisheries recognized and conceded by Great Britain?

The first question having been answered in the way it was, the second admitted of but one reply, the same six judges concurring, that Great Britain had not recognized or conceded any exclusive jurisdiction on the part of Russia in the seal fisheries outside of ordinary territorial waters.

Question 3. Was the body of water now known as the Bering Sea included in the phrase Pacific Ocean, as used in the Treaty of 1825 between Great Britain and Russia; and what rights, if any, in Bering Sea were held and exclusively exercised by Russia after said treaty?

The answer to this question depended upon the interpretation of documents submitted by both parties. These consisted of treaties, protocols, reports of directors of the Russian American Company, reports of officials of the Czar, and the writings of navigators. The British counsel were able to prove that the body of water known as Bering Sea was included in the phrase "Pacific Ocean" as used in the Treaty of 1825; and six of the judges so decided. The British counsel were likewise able to prove to the satisfaction of the same six judges that Russia had

[1] Case of the United States, 54, 61, and Counter Case of the United States, 151, 153, 147.

[2] Senator Morgan did not concur in the answer to any of the five questions.

[3] Fur Seal Arbitration, I.: 77 contains the award.

held no exclusive rights of jurisdiction in Bering Sea and had exercised no exclusive rights in the seal fisheries outside of the ordinary territorial waters after the Treaty of 1825.

Question 4. Did not all the rights of Russia as to jurisdiction and as to the seal fisheries in Bering Sea east of the water boundary, in the treaty between the United States and Russia of the 30th of March, 1867, pass unimpaired to the United States under that treaty?

The rights of Russia having been defined by the answers to the previous three questions, the same six judges had no difficulty in agreeing that those rights did pass unimpaired to the United States.

Question 5. Had the United States any right, and if so, what right of protection or property in the fur seals frequenting the islands of the United States in Bering Sea when such seals were found outside the ordinary three-mile limit?

In his written argument James C. Carter for the United States asked what law was to govern the decision. He concluded that the tribunal was to be guided by the law of nations; the sources of which were, first, the actual practice and usages of nations; second, the judgments of courts which administer the law of nations, such as prize courts and courts of admiralty; third, if the two previous sources should fail to furnish a rule, then resort should be had to the source from which all law flows, the dictates of right reason, natural justice, or the law of nature; fourth, and in ascertaining what the law of nature is upon any particular question, the municipal law of states, so far as it speaks with a concurring voice, is a prime fountain of knowledge; and fifth, the concurring authority of jurists of established reputation.[1]

Carter took up next the question of protection and property in the seal herd. He denied the contention of Great Britain that the seals were res communes or res nullius. Blackstone made a distinct consideration of what wild animals were the subject of property. The essential characteristics which rendered such animals subject to property were "that the care and industry of

[1] Argument of the United States: 7.

man acting upon a natural disposition of the animals to return to a place of wonted resort secures their voluntary and habitual return to his custody and power, so as to enable him to deal with them in a similar manner and to obtain from them similar benefits as in the case of domestic animals." [1] The fur seals furnished an excellent example. "They are by the imperious and unchangeable instincts of their nature impelled to return from their wanderings to the same place; they are defenseless against man, and in returning to the same place voluntarily subject themselves to his power, and enable him to treat them in the same way and to obtain from them the same benefits as may be had in the case of domestic animals. They thus become the subjects of ordinary husbandry as much as sheep or any other cattle. All that is needed to secure this return, is the exercise of care and industry on the part of the human owner of the place of resort." [2] Carter claimed that in the case of bees their nature is no more changed by man than that of the seals. This held true of pigeons, deer, wild geese, or swans; and yet property in these was universally recognized so long as they retained the animum revertendi. But what was the extent of such ownership? Carter replied that the property of the United States in the seal herd was coupled with a trust for the benefit of mankind and that it was the usufruct or the increase that belonged to the United States.[3]

Mr. Phelps presented the arguments for the United States on the freedom of the sea and on the right to protect the fur seals on the high seas. He held that the sea was free only for innocent and inoffensive use. In using the sea nations submit to principles of law and pay due regard to the rights of others. But the right of self defence had never been given up by any state. "Instead of taking its defence into its own hands, the Government of the United States had refrained from the exercise of that right, has submitted itself to the judgment of this Tribunal, and has agreed to abide the result." Phelps stated

[1] Argument of the United States: 47.
[2] Ibid.: 47.
[3] Ibid.: 51.

further, "If by the judgment of this high and distinguished Tribunal the Alaskan seal herd is sentenced to be exterminated, a result which the United States Government has been unable to anticipate, it must submit, because it has so agreed." [1]

How the British counsel met the claims of the Americans may be seen in the oral argument of Sir Charles Russell. He referred to the interchangeable use by Carter of the moral law and the law of nature for international law. "It may be admitted," said Sir Charles, "that all systems of law prevailing, I care not in what country, profess to be founded upon principles of justice. Does it follow from that that every principle of justice, as one nation or another may view it, or every principle of morality as one nation or another may view it, forms part of international law? By no means. International law, properly so-called, is only so much of the principles of morality and justice as the nations have agreed shall be part of those rules of conduct which shall govern their relations one with another. . . . In other words, international law, as there exists no superior external power to impose it, rests upon the principle of consent. In the words of Grotius, Placuitne Gentibus? is there the consent of nations. If there is not this consent of nations, then it is not international law." [2]

On the subject of property rights in the seal, Sir Charles paid his respects to the trusteeship of the United States, mentioned by Mr. Carter. The United States asked the tribunal to put an end to pelagic sealing in the Bering Sea and in the Pacific Ocean, to authorize the visit and search of foreign vessels engaged in sealing and their confiscation, if necessary, and the United States would then recognize its duty as trustee to mankind for the benefit of the fur seal at the market price enhanced by duties imposed on the business and by the fact that the business itself was a monopoly.[3]

"Now, it is said" continued Sir Charles "that these animals resort to the islands to breed, and resort there in compliance

[1] Argument of the United States: 178.
[2] Oral Arguments of Great Britain: 8.
[3] Ibid.: 29.

with what has been picturesquely described as the 'imperious instincts of their nature.' They do.

"And when they get there what do the representatives of the United States do? Can they do anything to improve the breed? Nothing. . . . What do they do? They do two things, one positive the other negative, and two things only. The positive thing is that they do what a game preserver does; he has a game keeper to prevent poaching; they have people on the islands to prevent raiding. The negative thing that they do is that they do not kill all. They knock on the head a certain number, but exercise a certain amount of discrimination, ... Let me illustrate my meaning. Suppose the existence, which there may well be in some undiscovered region, of an island where there are seals; what does the United States do on the Pribiloff Islands that Nature, unassisted, does not do on the undiscovered island?

"The only thing that nature does not do is to knock them on the head. . . . . .

"Do they do anything to induce them to go there? No, they do not. On the contrary, if they were to attempt by any kind of artificial means to provide for the reception of the seals, it would have the effect of driving them away, not of inducing them to come. Unlike the case of the bees,—the wild hive of bees, for which the man desiring that hive provides a mechanical contrivance, and also the beginning of a supply of food for them to induce them to form their combs of honey,—unlike the case of the doves, for which the owner supplies food and a dovecote where they get shelter from the weather, the owners of the Pribiloff Islands do nothing; and if they were to do anything it would have the effect of repelling rather than of inducing them to come." [1]

Sir Charles admitted that the seals have, "by this imperious and unchangeable instinct of their nature, the animus revertendi." But he knew of no instance, and the American counsel had cited none, in which this doctrine had given a property right in migratory animals.[2]

[1] Oral arguments of Great Britain, 208.
[2] Ibid.: 208.

"Am I not well founded," asked Sir Charles, "in saying that by the municipal law of every country in the world, the right to property in things must be made out according to the municipal law of the place where the property is situated, subject always to certain rules as to devolution, etc., with which we are not now concerned, founded upon the principle that mobilia sequuntur personam. They must have their right of title by municipal law. Does the United States municipal law give them property? No. The legislative even of the United States has not affected to give property." [1] He pointed out that the United States had extended only game laws to the area in question. The United States did not assume to grant any property right in the seals to the lessees; the only right given was the license to kill within specified restrictions. He pointed out further that game laws were not predicated upon the ownership by the state in the game; they operated merely to stay the hand of the slayer.

Phelps' argument on the freedom of the sea was met in the British written argument.

"What is the freedom of the sea?

"The right to come and go upon the high sea without let or hindrance, and to take therefrom at will and pleasure the produce of the sea. It is the right which the United States and Great Britain endeavoured, and endeavoured successfully, to maintain against the claim of Russia seventy years ago. It is the right in defence of which, against excessive claims of other nations, the arguments of the United States have in former times held so prominent a place.

"And what is this claim to protect the seal in the high sea? It is, as of right and for all time, to let and hinder the vessels of all nations in their pursuit of seals upon the high sea; to forbid them entrance to those vast seas which the United States have included in the denomination of the 'waters of Alaska;' to take from these vessels the seals they have lawfully obtained; and to search, seize, and condemn the vessels and crews, or with show of force to send them back to the ports from which they set out.

[1] Oral Arguments of Great Britain: 226.

"From giving its high sanction to these views this Tribunal may well shrink; and it is with no mere idle use of high-sounding phrases that Great Britain once more appears to vindicate the freedom of the sea."[1]

In reply to the fifth question, then, a majority of the arbitrators, Baron de Courcel, Lord Hannen, Sir John Thompson, Marquis Visconti Venosta, and Mr. Gregers Gram agreed to "decide and determine that the United States has not any right of protection or property in the fur seals frequenting the islands of the United States in Bering Sea, when such seals are found outside the ordinary three mile limit."

In accordance with powers conferred by the treaty providing for the arbitration, the tribunal recommended legislation to be enacted by the two governments for the protection of the fur seals within sixty miles of the Pribilof Islands. The two governments complied; but it was found that the number in the seal herds steadily diminished. Long and, at times, tedious negotiations for further protection of the seals followed. Finally, a treaty was concluded in Washington on July 7, 1911, between the United States, Great Britain, Japan, and Russia. The parties agreed to prohibit all persons subject to their jurisdictions from engaging in pelagic sealing in the Pacific Ocean, north of 30 degrees latitude; and the seas of Bering, Kamchatka, Okhotsk, and Japan were definitely included. Sea otters were likewise included in this protection. The killing of seals on land was subjected to definite proportions and the distribution of seal skins should take place in accordance with understandings, reached chiefly through concessions made by the United States.[2]

It needs be said that Great Britain obtained compensation for the Canadian owners whose sealing schooners had been seized in the eighties and for the members of the crews who had been subjected to fine and imprisonment. The arbitration commission created by the treaty of February 8, 1896, awarded $473,151.26 for this purpose, which the United States paid.

The other great arbitration which found its basis in article one

[1] Argument of Great Britain: 10.
[2] See treaty in Charles, *Treaties*, etc., 84.

of the Treaty of 1867 was that relating to the eastern boundary of Alaska. This dispute was precipitated by the discovery of gold in the Klondyke in 1896. The treaty between Russia and Great Britain in 1825 specified that the boundary should begin at the southernmost point of Prince of Wales Island, thence northward "along the channel called Portland channel, as far as the point of the continent where it strikes the 56th degree of north latitude; from this last mentioned point, the line of demarcation shall follow the summit of the mountains situated parallel to the coast as far as the point of intersection of the 141st degree of west longitude;" and thence follow that meridian to the "Frozen ocean." This provision was followed with an explanation that wherever the summit of the mountains, situated parallel to the coast, should "prove to be at the distance of more than ten marine leagues from the ocean, the limit between the British possessions and the line of coast which is to belong to Russia as above mentioned shall be formed by a line parallel to the winding of the coast, and which shall never exceed the distance of ten marine leagues therefrom." [1]

This description shut the Canadians out from the coast lands and the waters of the Pacific from the Portland Channel northward. In 1898 Great Britain on behalf of Canada laid claim to the ports of Dyea and Skagway on the Lynn Channel and based the claim on a novel construction of the treaty. Britain contended that the line defined as running ten leagues parallel with the sinuosities of the coast or heads to tidewater inlets should run parallel to the general trend of the coast itself. Britain offered arbitration but the United States held back, because it wanted other and earlier disputes cleared away, such as the protection to the seals, the northeastern fisheries, the Venezuela dispute, and the cancellation of the Clayton-Bulwer Treaty. Finally, the United States agreed to refer the dispute to a joint commission of "impartial jurists of repute," January 24, 1903; Secretary Hay signed for the United States and Michael H. Herbert for Great Britain. The tribunal was to be composed of six jurists. The United States chose Secretary of War Elihu

[1] Malloy, *Treaties*, II.: 1522.

Root, Senator H. C. Lodge, and Senator George Turner. Great Britain chose Baron Alverstone, Lord Chief Justice of England, Sir Louis Jette, Lieutenant Governor of Quebec, and Mr. A. B. Aylesworth.

The tribunal met in London, September 3, 1903. Except for the islands of Pearse and Wales in the Portland Channel the United States won its case completely. American counsel relied in their argument upon the undisputed possession by Russia from 1825 to 1867 and by the United States until the discovery of gold in the Klondyke; upon British and Canadian official acts; upon maps drawn by the British admiralty; upon the location of American postoffices, customs houses, and mission schools, and their maintenance for twenty years within the disputed areas. Britain rested her contention primarily on the impossibility of drawing the line thirty miles inland parallel to the sinuous edge of salt water; it should therefore cut across the deeper inlets. The rush to the Klondyke had demonstrated that there was no inland chain of mountains near the coast but a number of peaks, hence the line should follow the general direction of these peaks; which would likewise cut across the deeper inlets.

The two Canadian jurists could not agree with the majority. A few excerpts from the opinion of Lord Alverstone will indicate the trend of his reasoning and the character of the dispute.

"In ordinary parlance no one would call the waters of any of these channels or inlets between the islands, or between the islands and the mainland, 'ocean'. I agree with the view presented on behalf of Great Britain, that no one coming from the interior and reaching any of these channels, and particularly the head of Lynn Canal or Taku Inlet, would describe himself as being upon the ocean, but, on the other hand, it is quite clear that the Treaty does regard some of these channels as the ocean. . . . This consideration, however, is not sufficient to solve the question of the word 'coast' to which the mountains were to be parallel,. . . . . . ." [1]

"There is, so far as I know, no recognized rule of international

[1] Alaskan Boundary Tribunal, I.: 38.

law, which would by implication give a recognized meaning to the word 'coast' as applied to such sinuosities and such waters different from the coast itself."

"As I have said more than once, the locus in quo to which the Treaty was referring precludes the possibility of construing the word 'coast' in any particular article in any special way, if it does not refer to the coast line of the continent. I think the words 'upon the border of the continent comprised within the limits of the Russian possessions' in Article V rather confirm the view that Russia was to get a strip all along the continent, but I do not think that much reliance can be placed upon this because of the provision as to rivers and streams in Article VI.[1]

"Turning now from a consideration of the language of the Treaty alone, what light is thrown upon this question by reference to the negotiations?

"After most careful examination, I have been unable to find any passage which supports the view that Great Britain was directly or indirectly putting forward a claim to the shores or ports at the head of the inlets. This is not remarkable, inasmuch as no one at the time had any idea that they would become of any importance." [2]

By Article II of the Treaty of 1867, the United States succeeded to all the public buildings and lands in Alaska, the archives included, with the exception of the churches, which should remain the property of the resident members of the Greek Oriental Church.

Article III. The Inhabitants of the region might reserve their natural allegiance and they were given three years in which to return to Russia; but if they preferred to remain in the territory they should be admitted to American citizenship. No restriction was placed upon the control by the United States over the aboriginal tribes.

Article IV provided that the cession should be considered complete upon the exchange of ratifications. Agents should be appointed to arrange for the transfer of the territory.

[1] Alaskan Boundary Tribunal, I.: 39.
[2] Ibid., I.: 40.

Article V stipulated that the Russian troops should be withdrawn immediately upon the exchange of ratifications.

Article VI stipulated the price, $7,200,000 in gold, payable within ten months after the exchange of ratifications. The cession was declared to be "free and unincumbered by any reservations, privileges, franchises, grants, or possessions, by any associated companies, whether corporate or incorporate, Russian or any other, or by any parties, except merely private individual property holders; . . . ." It was for the insertion of this clause that Seward agreed to pay $200,000.

Article VII provided for the exchange of ratifications in Washington within three months after the President had ratified with the advice and consent of the Senate.[1]

BIBLIOGRAPHY

Alaskan Boundary Tribunal, *Proceedings*. 8 volumes. Washington, 1904.

BANCROFT, FREDERICK.—*The Life of William H. Seward*. Two volumes, New York, 1900.

BANCROFT, H. H.—*History of Alaska, 1730–1885*. Works, XXXIII. San Francisco, 1886.

Diplomatic Correspondence, 1867, Part I. or House Doc. 1, 40 Cong., 2 session, part 1. Washington, 1868.

Fur Seal Arbitration. Proceedings of the Tribunal. 15 volumes and a supplementary one. Washington, 1895.

SEWARD, FREDERICK W.—*Seward at Washington*. Volume II. New York, 1891.

[1] Malloy, *Treaties*, etc., II.: 1521.

CHAPTER XIII

THE TREATY OF WASHINGTON, 1871

"I trust I need not express how profound is my regret at the conclusion to which her Majesty's government have arrived. . . . . It would be superfluous in me to point out to your lordship that this is war. No matter what may be the theory adopted of neutrality in a struggle, when this process is carried on in the manner indicated, from a territory and with the aid of the subjects of a third party, that third party to all intents and purposes ceases to be a neutral."—CHARLES FRANCIS ADAMS TO LORD RUSSELL.

During the Civil War, several leading English politicians had, as Lord Salisbury expressed it, put their money on the wrong horse. Even as astute a man as Gladstone anticipated with certainty the success of the Southern States. In his speech at Newcastle, October 7, 1862, he declared "there is no doubt that Jefferson Davis and other leaders of the South have made an army; they are making, it appears, a navy; and they have made what is more than either, they have made a nation." [1] On the eve of Vicksburg and Gettysburg, June 30, 1863, he stated in the House of Commons, "We do not believe that the restoration of the American Union by force is attainable. I believe that the public opinion of this country is unanimous upon that subject." Lord Palmerston, Prime Minister, desired the division of the republic as a diminution of a dangerous power [2] and argued openly that Great Britain had a right to furnish both belligerents "with ships destined for warlike purposes." [3] Earl Russell, the Secretary of State for Foreign Affairs, looked upon it as a duty of the British government to preserve for his countrymen "the legitimate and lucrative trade of ship building." These men could lay claim to statesmanship. For the politicians the opinion of G. W. P. Bentinck, M. P., will suffice. In a speech at Kings Lynn he gave his sympathy to the Southerners, for they

[1] Morley, *Gladstone*, II.: 79.
[2] Ibid., II.: 82.
[3] House of Commons, July 23, 1863.

were fighting against "one of the most grinding, one of the most galling, one of the most irritating attempts to establish tyrannical government that ever disgraced the history of the world." He went on, "But there is a further lesson to be learned. The result of these much vaunted institutions, which we have heard praised before, and which we shall again hear praised by the hired spouters of associations, is this, that the nation becomes so brutalized that the civilized man disappears; he is afraid to put himself forward; he is ashamed of his country; he has no voice in the conduct of her affairs; and the whole nation is turned over to the control of men such as Lincoln and Butler, whom I do not hesitate to denounce, after their conduct in the last few months, as men who are a disgrace to civilization." [1]

The strange feature of this attitude taken by statesmen and politicians is that they voiced public opinion. Richard Cobden stood on the other side. He commented tersely in the House of Commons, April 24, 1863, "We generally sympathize with everybody's rebels but our own;" and he estimated that nineteen-twentieths of the members of English society felt firmly convinced that the Civil War could end only in separation.[2] Captain James D. Bulloch, the naval representative of the Confederate States in Europe, wrote in his book in 1884 that the great majority of the people of Great Britain were on the Southern side and the men in the army and the navy unanimously so.[3] Charles Francis Adams Jr. who was with his father, then American minister in London, agrees that sympathy for the Southern cause pervaded the members of the learned professions, the commercial, financial, and banking circles, and the officers of the army and navy.[4] A noted Frenchman, who was then in exile in England, Louis Blanc,[5] compared the sympathy for the North to a dam and the sympathy for the South to a torrent.

The Confederacy had anticipated this situation in Great Britain and counted heavily upon it for support. Senator J. H.

[1] London Morning Post, November 4, 1862.
[2] Cobden, *Speeches*, II.: 103.
[3] Bulloch, *Secret Service of the Confederate States*, II: 303.
[4] C. F. Adams, *The Treaty of Washington:* 34.
[5] Blanc, *Letters on England:* 146.

Hammond of South Carolina struck the keynote in a speech in the Senate, March 4, 1858: "Without firing a gun, without drawing a sword, should the North make war on us, we could bring the whole world to our feet. What would happen if no cotton was furnished for three years? I will not stop to depict what everyone can imagine; but this is certain, England would topple headlong, and carry the whole civilized world with her. No, you dare not make war on cotton. No power on earth dares to make war on it—Cotton is King."

Besides this dependence of Great Britain upon the South for cotton, British bankers loaned heavily to the Southerners. Britons and Southerners held a common dislike of the tariff imposed by the Northerners, which had for one of its purposes to compel the Southerners to buy their machinery, clothing, and foodstuffs in the North and consequently to sell the cotton there as well. Moreover, the goods from the North and the cotton from the South would have to be shipped in New England vessels, for the coastwise trade was not open to foreign ships. Great Britain and the Confederacy had, then, mutual and reciprocal economic interests. Traditionally, it was with the Yankees that Great Britain had had friction. This was true in the Revolution, in the War of 1812, in the relations with Canada, in the northeastern fisheries, in the rivalry for sea carrying trade, and in a prospective competition in manufactures.

When hostilities opened in April, 1861, the Confederacy had no navy and had no means with which to build a navy. If the cotton was to find a market and if the Confederacy was to obtain military supplies, a navy would be a matter of prime necessity. James D. Bulloch of Georgia had been a lieutenant in the United States Navy; and the government at Montgomery decided upon him as a competent man to undertake the acquisition of a navy in England. He reached Liverpool on June 4, 1861. Before the end of the month and before his government had placed any funds in Europe, he had contracted with William C. Miller and Sons of Liverpool for the building of the cruiser "Oreto," afterward famous as the "Florida." Fawcett, Preston and Co. of the same port agreed to furnish the engines. Within another month, he had contracted with Lairds at Birkenhead to build "No. 290," afterward the "Alabama." Bulloch contracted with Lairds in his own name as a private individual.[1] Fraser, Trenholm and Co., fiscal agents of the Confederacy, furnished the security.

Bulloch explained later that it was not the object of his government to obtain one or two ships merely, but "to get ships and naval supplies without hindrance as long as the war lasted." [2] He acted with prudence and caution and he desired to do nothing in violation of British law. He engaged as his legal adviser F. S. Hull, "who piloted me safely," says Bulloch, "through the mazes of the Foreign Enlistment Act." With reference to this act, the crafty solicitor furnished the following rules for Bulloch's guidance.

"1. It is no offense (under the Act) for British subjects to equip, etc. a ship at some country without her Majesty's dominions, though the intent be to cruise against a friendly State.

"2. It is no offence for any person (subject or no subject) to equip a ship within her Majesty's dominions, if it be not done with the intent to cruise against a friendly State.

"3. The mere building of a ship within her Majesty's dominions by any person (subject or no subject) is no offence, whatever may be the intent of the parties, because the offence is not the building but the equipping.

"Therefore any shipbuilder may build any ship in her Majesty's dominions, provided he does not equip her within her Majesty's dominions, and he has nothing to do with the acts of the purchasers done within her Majesty's dominions without his concurrence, nor without her Majesty's dominions even with his concurrence." [3]

In connection with this opinion, Bulloch states that he always kept the foregoing deductions rigidly in mind and that he took every precaution for the protection of the builders and for safeguarding the ships against forfeiture. "No ship was ever

[1] Bulloch, *Secret Service*, I.: 60.
[2] Ibid., I: 65.
[3] Ibid., I.: 67.

supplied with any portion of her equipment within her Majesty's dominions, nor was the builder or vendor of any ship employed to assist in the equipment without her Majesty's dominions."[1] By complying with the letter of the Foreign Enlistment Act, Bulloch was able to make of British ports naval bases for the Confederacy; those ports furnished the shipyards and the arsenals.

The foreign enlistment act had been passed in 1819, at the time when the former colonies of Spain were achieving their independence. Its chief purpose was to prevent the agents of these potential states from delivering letters of marque and reprisal to British vessels so that they might go out and capture Spanish merchantmen. No forfeiture of a vessel had ever been decreed under the act. It had been permitted to slumber undisturbed on the statute books.

The American minister in London, Charles Francis Adams, protested at the Foreign Office against allowing the "Oreto" and the "No. 290," building at Liverpool, to leave port. He fairly bombarded the Foreign Office with depositions and evidence on the hostile purpose of those vessels. Earl Russell replied by submitting a report of the British commissioners of customs showing that the "Oreto" was pierced for four guns but that she had taken nothing on board but coal and ballast, that the expense of her construction had been paid, and that the builders believed that she was destined for the service of the Italian government.[2]

On March 22, 1862, the "Oreto" sailed from Liverpool, under British registry, with clearance papers for Palermo and Jamaica in ballast. She carried a crew of fifty-two, all British except for two or three.[3] She sailed for Nassau as did the schooner "Prince Alfred" from London with her armament and stores as cargo. The American consul instituted proceedings against the "Oreto" in the vice admiralty court at Nassau; she was seized temporarily, and then restored. Both vessels proceeded to Green Cay, a

[1] Bulloch, *Secret Service*, I.: 68.
[2] Diplomatic Correspondence, 1862: 40.
[3] Ibid., 1862: 66.

desert island about sixty miles from Nassau. There the "Oreto" took on her armament, changed her name to "Florida," hoisted the Confederate flag, and put to sea.

Repeatedly she took on coal in British ports in excess of what would be necessary to carry her to the nearest port of her own country or some nearer destination. She also took on a supply of coal with the full knowledge and consent of the port officials at Barbadoes without allowing three months to lapse since her last coaling in a British port. Both of these rules had been incorporated in the instructions from the British government, January 31, 1862,[1] for the guidance of port authorities in dealing with belligerent vessels. Only once did the "Florida" touch a Confederate port, and that was at Mobile in 1862. She enlisted men at New Providence, British West Indies, and repeatedly she remained in port more than twenty-four hours. She captured three Yankee merchantmen; fitted them out with guns, officers, and men; commissioned them as tenders; and these received the hospitalities of Confederate vessels in British ports.[2] Overcoming nigh insuperable difficulties, even to combatting yellow fever among the crew, the "Florida" in her career up to the time of her capture in the harbor of Bahia, Brazil, 1864, burned or bonded over forty vessels carrying the United States flag.

The "No. 290" was launched on May 15, 1862, and christened the "Enrica." On June 15, she took her trial trip.[3] She returned, was taken into dock to complete her outfit and to take on board coal and stores. Bulloch employed Captain Butcher, then serving with the Cunard Line, to take the "Enrica" to Terceira. Captain Semmes had taken the C. S. S. "Sumter" into Gibraltar, where he was being watched by two union vessels. Rather than assume any risks, Bulloch ordered that the "Sumter" be sold to an English firm. This was done technically; the "Sumter" was then brought to the Mersey, flying the British flag, and there converted into a blockade runner. Captain

[1] Geneva Arbitration, I.: 226.
[2] Ibid., I: 133 ff.
[3] Bulloch, *Secret Service*, I.: 230.

Semmes was thereupon ordered to take command of the "Enrica" at Terceira.

The arguments of Adams had become so persistent and convincing at the Foreign Office, that on Saturday, July 26, 1862, Bulloch received information "from a private but most reliable source, that it would not be safe to leave the ship in Liverpool another forty-eight hours."[1] He decided accordingly to make an all day trial trip on Tuesday and so informed the Lairds. He ordered Captain Butcher to ship a few more hands and lay in some additional coal and stores. On Monday the "Enrica" came out of dock; on Tuesday morning she got under weigh; the invited guests on board. The guests returned in a tug at three in the afternoon; but the "Enrica," never; she was on her way to the Azores, without registry and without clearance papers. During those same days, on the Thames, at London, lay a barque, the "Agrippina," which took on board gun-carriages, guns, shot, and all necessary munitions and equipment, and sailed for desolate Praya Bay. There, on the east side of Terceira, the two vessels met. The "Enrica" took on board her equipment, mounted her guns, changed her name to "Alabama," and, on August 24, 1863, sailed out, flying the Confederate ensign, Captain Semmes in command.

In May, 1863, Semmes wrote from Bahia to Bulloch, "We are having capital success. That 'little bill' which the Yankees threaten to present to our Uncle John Bull, for the depredations of the Alabama, is growing apace, and already reaches $3,100,000."[2] She never touched at a Confederate port; and she had no difficulty in replenishing her supply of coal and food from the merchantmen she captured. She followed purposely the shipping lanes in every sea and every climate. She remained as long as it was deemed prudent in the icy fogs off the Newfoundland Bank; then she harried and burned amid the steaming moisture of the West Indies; next, she might be heard of in the Pacific; and she surprised American shipping in the China Sea and in the Strait of Malacca.

[1] Bulloch, *Secret Service,* I.: 238.
[2] Ibid., I.: 267.

From English vessels that she met, the "Alabama" received every courtesy and rousing cheers, for was she not English built, were there not Englishmen on board, had she not outwitted even the Yankee, and was she not driving the Yankee merchant marine from the seas? The President of the Board of Trade, Milner Gibson, stated in a speech at Ashton-under-Lyne, January 20, 1864, that for the year 1863-64, the number of British ships clearing had increased to 14,000,000 tons as against 7,000,000 for all foreign tonnage and he gave the decrease in American tonnage between Great Britain and the United States at about forty-seven percent.[1]

The "Alabama" took on coal at Singapore. American merchantmen had been sufficiently driven from the Indian Ocean, so she had to coal again, within three months, at Capetown. At Capetown, too, her tender, the "Tuscaloosa," was received as a belligerent vessel, although she had been an old Yankee merchantman, captured at sea, never condemned by a prize court, and commissioned at sea as well. The "Alabama's" last cruise took her through the Atlantic, along the coast of Africa and Europe to Cherbourg, France. There she accepted the challenge of the union vessel, the "Kearsarge," and after a gallant fight, went down, June 19, 1864.

Since his visit to Terceira in August, 1862, when he saw the "Alabama" safely started on her mission, Bulloch had devoted his energies to the buying of vessels, of naval supplies, and to the so-called Laird ironclads. It had become the purpose of the Confederacy to build a whole fleet of armored vessels capable of opening and defending the ports under blockade. The escape of the "Florida" and the "Alabama" had increased the vigilance of the American consul in Liverpool, T. H. Dudley, and of

[1] Table of Transfers of American shipping to Englishmen.

Year	*Vessels*	*Tonnage*
1858	33	12,684
1859	49	21,308
1860	41	13,638
1861	126	71,673
1862	135	64,578
1863	348	252,579
1864	166	92,052

the American minister in London, Mr. Adams. Lord Russell acknowledged repeatedly that the foreign enlistment act might be evaded by subtle contrivances; "but her Majesty's government cannot, on that account go beyond the letter of the existing law." [1] For him and for British public opinon at the time there was no international law on the obligations of neutrals. He had no vision of what might have been the effect upon British commerce in the Boer War had President Kruger been able to obtain a "Florida" and an "Alabama" in the United States or in Germany; or in the Great War had Germany been able to obtain cruisers from the United States in 1916 under similar circumstances to the "Alabama." Adams pointed to the handwriting on the wall; and several Britons could read it; among them Cobden, Sir George C. Lewis and W. E. Forster; but the cabinet could not. Said Lord Palmerston, premier, in the House of Commons, July 23, 1863, "I cannot, in the abstract, concur with my honourable friend (Cobden) in thinking there is any distinction in principle between muskets, gunpowder, bullets and cannon on the one side, and ships on the other." He maintained that merchants had the right to supply "one of the belligerents, not only with arms and cannon, but also with ships destined for warlike purposes." [2]

The Laird iron-clads were in an advanced stage of construction, when Adams and Dudley decided to test their status and that of similar vessels under the foreign enlistment act before a British judge and jury. For this purpose the "Alexandra" was chosen. She had been built by Miller and Co., who had also built the "Florida." She had been launched on the day that the Danish Princess Alexandra entered London, previous to her marriage to the Prince of Wales. And she was lying in dock to have her engines placed by Sillim and others of Fawcett and Co. On March 28, 1863, Dudley made a formal affirmation that he had reason to believe that the "Alexandra" was intended for the Confederacy in violation of the foreign enlistment act. This affirmation together with several affidavits were forwarded to

[1] Diplomatic Correspondence, 1862: 223.
[2] Hansard, 172: 1269.

Adams, who presented them to Lord Russell. Adams was determined to push the case even though the officers of the crown could not be moved to act, and for that reason had asked for and obtained the services of William M. Evarts. But the cabinet yielded.

On April 5, 1863, the surveyor of customs seized the "Alexandra." On June 22 the case of the Attorney General vs. Sillim and others, claiming the "Alexandra," came up before the court of exchequer at Westminster, the Lord Chief Baron, Sir Frederick Pollock, presiding. Distinguished counsel appeared on both sides. For the crown, Sir William Atherton, her Majesty's Attorney General; Sir Roundell Palmer, her Majesty's Solicitor General, and Sir Robert Phillimore. For the owners Sir Hugh Cairns, J. B. Harslake, George Mellish, and James Kemplay. The information contained ninety-eight counts, charging that the defendants did attempt or endeavor to equip, furnish, and fit out the vessel to serve against a power at peace with Great Britain. The arming of the vessel was not charged at all. The vessel had been built under contract with Charles K. Prioleau of Liverpool at his own cost and risk. When seized the engineers, Sillim and others, had claimed her as being in their possession. The character of her design and construction proved that she had a warlike destination. Evidence revealed that Bulloch had shown keen interest in her construction as had other Confederate naval and military officers. A good deal of information was revealed about the "Florida" and the "Alabama;" but it could have only a moral effect as far as the "Alexandra" was concerned. It was shown that the builders had stated in conversation that she was intended for the Confederate service.

In charging the jury, the judge read passages from Story and Kent to show that powder and arms might be shipped by the nationals of a neutral country to belligerents. Then he asked, "Why should ships be an exception? I am of opinion, in point of law, they are not." He pointed out that it was admitted that the "Alexandra" was not armed. "It appears to me" he continued "that if true that the 'Alabama' sailed away from Liverpool without any arms at all as a mere ship in ballast, and that her armament was put on board at Terceira, which is not in her Majesty's dominions, then the foreign enlistment act was not violated at all." The jury returned a verdict immediately for the defendants.[1] C. F. Adams Jr. reports that the listeners in the courtroom cheered. The counsel for the crown tendered a bill of exceptions, on which the case was appealed to the court of exchequer chamber and finally to the House of Lords; the crown losing in every instance.

Charles Francis Adams had now exhausted all lawful means provided by Great Britain to save the United States from having its rights infringed by Great Britain allowing her ports to become naval bases for the enemy, and to save Britain herself in some future day when the tables should be turned, to say nothing of the award of $15,500,000 by the Geneva tribunal, which Great Britain had to pay because she did not have adequate legislation upon her statute books. Like a good diplomat, Adams, cheerful and undaunted, expressed his appreciation of the efforts of the British government in the case of the "Alexandra" and proceeded to bring every possible influence to bear upon Lord John Russell, who held the key to the situation.

By June, 1863, the fortunes of the Confederacy had reached their height both at home and abroad. It looked as though there could be no restrictions placed upon the construction of naval vessels in Great Britain. Indeed, on July 4, 1863, the first of the Laird ironclads took the water. In the latter part of 1862 Mason and Slidell had promoted a proposal by Napoleon III to the courts of Britain and Russia to join in offering mediation in the American struggle, with an armistice of six months as a preliminary. The Czar refused to join and the British reply meant the same as a refusal. In June, 1863, Napoleon III had invited two members of the House of Commons, Lindsay and Roebuck, to dine with him at the Tuileries. He declared himself ready to coöperate with Britain in an immediate recognition of the independence of the Confederate States. And Roebuck was to force the hand of the cabinet by a motion to that effect in

[1] Diplomatic Correspondence, 1863: 281.

the House of Commons. Fortunately, Roebuck bungled. The Emperor denied the statements imputed to him. And Roebuck withdrew his motion on July 13.

In the meantime Adams had presented to Lord Russell the claims of American citizens for depredations committed by the "Alabama" and the "Florida." Russell disclaimed all responsibility for the acts of these vessels.[1] However, telling events in America had occurred. On the morning of July 16, Adams received news of the victory at Gettysburg and three days later came the news of the surrender of Vicksburg. The emancipation proclamation had received the most vindictive denunciation by the press in the latter part of 1862;[2] but this in itself caused wide reading of the proclamation and a revulsion of popular feeling against the institution of slavery. After Vicksburg and Gettysburg this feeling nurtured by Cobden and Bright became more manifest. But night and day shifts worked on the iron-clads in the Mersey. The Confederate agents attempted to conceal their trepidation by transferring the contract to a French banker, Bravay, who professed to act for the Egyptian government. They paid Lairds a gratuity of £5,000 for the consent to this transfer.[3]

In August Adams became the guest of the Duke of Argyll at Inverary, a union sympathizer. The Duke was a member of the cabinet and believed that the iron-clads were built on French account. Adams disillusioned him. That evening the Duke wrote letters; one may have gone to Lord Russell. When Adams returned to London Russell desired earnestly to comply with whatever the international obligations demanded.[4] On September 4 Consul Dudley notified Adams that one of the iron-clads was about to depart. Adams made another appeal to Russell. Russell replied that there was no legal evidence against M. Bravay's claim and that the government could not interfere.[5]

On September 5, 1863, Adams made his memorable reply, in which he said, "I trust I need not express how profound is my

[1] Diplomatic Correspondence, 1863: 316.
[2] See C. F. Adams, *Charles Francis Adams*, chapter 16.
[3] Adams, *Treaty of Washington:* 67, footnote.
[4] C. F. Adams, *Charles Francis Adams:* 340.
[5] Diplomatic Correspondence, 1863: 362.

regret at the conclusion to which her Majesty's government have arrived. . . . . It would be superfluous in me to point out to your lordship that this is war. No matter what may be the theory adopted of neutrality in a struggle, when this process is carried on in the manner indicated, from a territory and with the aid of the subjects of a third party, that third party to all intents and purposes ceases to be neutral." [1] On September 8, a short article appeared in the Morning Post announcing that the government had decided to detain the vessels. The government did so; and the bonds of the Confederacy fell fourteen points. In order to avoid another case like the "Alexandra," the government bought the Laird iron-clads for £220,000; the original contract price had been £187,500.[2] James Russell Lowell said later of this victory of Adams, "None of our generals in the field, not Grant himself, did us better or more trying service than he in his forlorn outpost of London."

Englishmen began to subdue their commercial fervor. The ship owners of Liverpool petitioned Parliament to pass an adequate foreign enlistment act. No one put the idea more pointedly in the House of Commons than did the head of the banking house of Baring Brothers on May 13, 1864: "Under the present construction of our municipal law there is no necessity that a belligerent should have a port or even a seashore. Provided she has money, or that money is supplied to her by a neutral, she may fit out vessels, and those vessels need not go to the country to which they are said to belong, but may go about the seas dealing destruction to British shipping and property." Succeeding events pointed the way. The House of Representatives passed a bill, July, 1866, designed to remove the prohibition against selling ships of war to foreign citizens or governments at peace with the United States. The unrest in Europe over the former Danish Duchies and finally the shadow of the Franco-Prussian War led Parliament, in 1870, to pass stringent modifications of the foreign enlistment act.

This change of conscience in Great Britain added to the

[1] Diplomatic Correspondence, 1863: 367.
[2] Adams, *Treaty of Washington:* 67, footnote.

strength of the requests by Adams for compensation for the damages committed by the cruisers. Great Britain refused consistently until 1868 to assume any responsibility. It needs be said that the United States befogged the issue by demanding reimbursement for damages incurred by the British proclamation of neutrality, which greatly encouraged the Confederates, for the cost of chasing the cruisers, and for loss incurred by the transfer of vessels to other flags. These constituted the so-called "indirect damages" or "national injuries."

On August 27, 1866, Seward sent to Adams one of the most important papers on this subject. A change of ministry had taken place. The Liberals had gone out and the Conservatives with Lord Derby at the head had come in. Lord Stanley took charge of the Foreign Office. Adams was to present "in a respectful and earnest manner" to Stanley a long list of claims of American citizens for depredations committed by the cruisers. Adams was to point out that, "While as yet the civil war was undeveloped, and the insurgents were without any organized military force or a treasury, and long before they pretended to have a flag, or to put either an armed ship or even a merchant vessel upon the sea, her Majesty's government, acting precipitately, as we have always complained, proclaimed the insurgents a belligerent power, and conceded to them the advantages and privileges of that character, and thus raised them in regard to the prosecution of an unlawful armed insurrection to an equality with the United States. This government has not denied that it was within the sovereign authority of Great Britain to assume this attitude; but, on the other hand, it insisted in the beginning, and has continually insisted, that the assumption of that attitude, unnecessarily and prematurely, would be an injurious proceeding for which Great Britain would immediately come under a full responsibility to justify it, or to render redress and indemnity." Adams should then mention the inadequacy of the laws of Great Britain to properly maintain her neutrality. While insisting upon the claims he could propose that if Great Britain had any counter claims the United States would be willing to have them considered, and thus remove at one time "by one comprehensive settlement, all existing causes of misunderstanding." [1]

On November 30, 1866, Lord Stanley replied to the communication. On the subject of liability incurred by the hasty recognition of the belligerency of the Confederates, he maintained that it was the President who had first recognized their belligerency by proclamation of a blockade. And he rested his conclusion upon the decision of the Supreme Court in the case of the "Hiawatha" and of the highest court in the District of Columbia in the case of the "Tropic Wind." Lincoln issued his proclamation of a blockade on April 19, 1861, and the Queen's proclamation of neutrality bore the date of May 13, 1861. On this point Lord Stanley held "no reference to arbitration is possible." On the score of the damages inflicted by the escaped cruisers, he refused to admit liability. But he expressed that her Majesty's advisers were "fully alive to the inconvenience which arises from the existence of unsettled claims of this character between two powerful and friendly governments. . . . . they will not be disinclined to adopt the principle of arbitration, provided that a fitting arbitrator can be found, and that an agreement can be come to as to the points to which arbitration shall apply." [2]

Seward refused to yield on the indirect claims. Another year passed with no result apparent but an increase in the ill will between the two countries. Irishmen, who had become naturalized Americans, went back to foment trouble among their countrymen, which caused disputes about the rights under naturalization. The North Atlantic fisheries reverted to an unsettled state after the abrogation in 1866 by the United States of the reciprocity treaty of 1854. Possibilities of hostility existed in the unsettled boundary relating to the island of San Juan. On January 13, 1868, Seward proposed again the arbitration of all claims. Shortly afterward, Adams resigned as minister and was succeeded by Reverdy Johnson of Maryland.

[1] Diplomatic Correspondence, 1866: 177.
[2] Ibid., 1867: 184.

Both Johnson and Seward became eager to achieve a settlement of the disputes with Great Britain during their tenure of office. Several agreements were signed, not one was ratified; among them was one on claims, January 14, 1869, the so-called Johnson-Clarendon Convention. The "Alabama" claims were not expressly mentioned. All claims should be submitted to a board of four. Should a claim fail to obtain a majority vote, the commissioners could agree upon an umpire; and if they failed to agree, the umpire should be chosen by lot.[1] This haphazard method would hardly permit a careful consideration of a man's qualifications to pass upon a difference nor would it secure harmony in the various decisions on points in dispute.

When the convention reached the Senate, Sumner opposed it because it contained "not one word of regret," because it provided for the settlement of private claims only, and because Great Britain assumed no responsibility for conceding belligerency to the Confederacy, nor for building and equipping the cruisers. The private claims he estimated at about $15,000,000. But the years of war and costly sacrifice which England had added by her acts could not be estimated. He mentioned $110,000,000 for the national loss of the merchant marine, due to the transfer of vessels to British ownership; but that was, he contended, one of the smallest items.[2] The Senate rejected the convention by a vote of 1 to 44. Of course, the strained relations between President Johnson and Congress must be taken as one of the reasons for the decisiveness of the vote.

When Grant became President, Hamilton Fish succeeded Seward as Secretary of State and John Lothrop Motley succeeded Reverdy Johnson as minister to England. Because Motley assumed to present the views of the chairman of the Senate committee on foreign relations, Sumner, especially on national claims, rather than those of the Secretary of State, Fish had to transfer the negotiations to Washington, and, on Grant's insistence, he had to recall Motley.

At this stage an unofficial and exceedingly helpful personage

[1] Diplomatic Correspondence, 1868: 401.
[2] Sumner, *Works*, XIII.: 53.

brought his influence to bear. John Rose was of Scotch birth, but he had made a fortune and a political reputation in Canada. He was a member of the ministry there and he was serving as British commissioner on the board created by the Treaty of 1863 to settle the outstanding Oregon claims. He had as such won the friendship of the counsellor for the United States, Caleb Cushing. The two talked over the "Alabama" claims and agreed to coöperate in bringing about a settlement. In June of 1869 Cushing at Washington wrote to Rose at Ottawa that he had seen Secretary Fish and arranged for a meeting. "I am not sanguine of the immediate conclusion of such a treaty as either you or I might desire. But I think the time has arrived to commence, ..."[1]

Rose came. At the dinner table with Fish on July 9, 1869, the first of a series of discussions took place, which resulted in the Treaty of Washington two years later. Fish thought that the time had not arrived for a settlement, that Sumner's speech on the indirect claims had led Americans to expect too much, and that the rejection of the Johnson-Clarendon Convention for the reasons given by Sumner had irritated the British. He felt that when the excitement should subside, if Great Britain would send some person of high rank to express some kind word of regret, a settlement could then be reached. And he outlined a scheme which was the one virtually carried out.[2] Rose left immediately for England to confer with public men there, with whom he had no doubt been in communcation previously.

Rose reported to Fish periodically on progress made with W. E. Forster, John Bright, and Gladstone. Frequent exchanges of notes took place between Fish and Edward Thornton, the British minister in Washington, but no common basis for an agreement could be reached. However, international events furnished their assistance. Early in July, 1870, the news spread that General Prim had offered the throne of Spain to Leopold of Hohenzollern-Sigmaringen; and on July 13, 1870, Bismarck transcribed the Ems telegram. France declared war on Prussia,

[1] C. F. Adams, *Treaty of Washington:* 123.
[2] J. C. Bancroft Davis, *Mr. Fish and the Alabama Claims:* 45.

July 19. On September 2 Napoleon III surrendered at Sedan. Britain did not know when it might become necessary to intervene. The need for having her differences with the United States settled became greater. Fish saw his opportunity and inserted in the President's annual message, December 5, 1870, a regret that no conclusion had been reached with Britain and a recommendation that Congress authorize the appointment of a commission to take proof of the amount and the ownership of claims and that Congress would authorize their payment, so that the government would have the ownership and the responsible control of all claims against Great Britain.

On January 9, 1871, Rose arrived in Washington on a confidential mission. He dined with Fish on the evening of the same day. Their conversation lasted until about three o'clock the next morning. The Assistant Secretary of State, J. C. Bancroft Davis, was the only other person present, and he preserved a memorandum of the leading points.

Rose stated that he had been authorized unofficially to ascertain what could be done to settle all pending questions by a joint commission modelled upon that which negotiated the Treaty of Ghent; and he dwelt upon the urgency of an immediate settlement. Fish replied that before he agreed to such a commission he wanted some assurance of its success and asked if Britain was ready to admit liability for the "Alabama" claims. The British government would not admit such liability, said Rose; but he gave it as his judgment that Britain would be willing to submit the claims to arbitration. With his usual candor Fish explained that it would be useless to negotiate a treaty which did not admit such liability, that the almost unanimous vote of the Senate against the Johnson-Clarendon Convention revealed the opinion of that body on the claims, and that if Great Britain should accept liability for the acts of the "Alabama," the United States might be willing to submit the matter of liability for the acts of the other cruisers to arbitration. Rose argued long and forcibly against this view, submitting that if the two nations met in commission, such a body would not break up without reaching an agreement, that the Confederates who had fitted out the "Alabama" were now in the full enjoyment of their rights as American citizens, and that, therefore, the question was a domestic one. Fish recognized that the latter argument might be a good one if Great Britain had not recognized the belligerency of the South. He would not ask that England should humiliate herself by acknowledging that her laws were deficient, but she might well feel that her local officers had been negligent, and that thereby the government had become liable. Rose mentioned, then, that the British government could not take the initiative on the "Alabama" claims, that it would propose a commission to settle the San Juan boundary, the fisheries, and other Canadian questions. To this proposal the United States might accede on condition that the claims were also to be considered. Fish consented.[1]

Two days later, January 11, 1871, Rose submitted a memorandum, covering the points in the conversation, urging the need of a settlement before the approaching fishing season, and before the time of the Parliament should be taken up with Russia and the Black Sea question, with the relations of Prussia to Luxemburg, and with the problems growing out of the Franco-Prussian War. "Supposing, then," said Rose, "that an attempt was made to have Sir Edward Thornton authorized by cable, now, to propose such a commission with reference to all other subjects—omitting the "Alabama"—and that the United States were to say they would only agree, provided the Commissioners were authorized to deal with the "Alabama" and all other subjects as well as with a view to a comprehensive settlement;—might not the English Commissioners come out at once, ..."[2]

The negotiations having reached this stage, Fish thought it best to lay Rose's proposals before Sumner, chairman of the Senate committee on foreign relations. Sumner deliberated for two days and then replied, January 17, 1871, that he approved the idea that all sources of irritation between the United States and England should be removed forever. As a preliminary step he advocated the withdrawal of the British flag from

[1] Davis, *Mr. Fish and the Alabama Claims:* 59.
[2] Moore, *International Arbitrations*, I: 523.

the western hemisphere, "including provinces and islands."[1] Fish realized that to incorporate Sumner's demands in the negotiation meant no treaty and that, if he wanted a treaty, he would have to work without Sumner's coöperation. On that same day he began conferring with senators of both parties, outlining his plan of a treaty, and obtaining support for his proposition.

After feeling the pulse of the Senate for a week, Fish invited John Rose and J. C. Bancroft Davis to his house for dinner. Davis kept a memorandum of the conversation. Fish approved of a previous suggestion made by Rose that a joint commission should meet in Washington to arrange a treaty but not to adjudicate the amounts or the validity of claims. The adjudication should be performed by arbitral tribunals. He had decided, after consultation, that it would be unwise to specify the "Alabama" claims as differentiated from those against the other cruisers, because such action might arouse opposition in the Senate. Fish would not, therefore, insist upon the admission of liability by Great Britain but upon a general statement that concessions should be made. Rose suggested that such a statement could be inserted in the protocol; to which Fish assented. Fish handed to Rose the memorandum of Sumner, which Rose read and returned. Fish said that if the British commissioners should come on the basis indicated that the United States government would spare no effort to secure a favorable result, "even if it involved a conflict with the Chairman of the Committee on Foreign Relations in the Senate." Rose replied that he would communicate by cable with his government the result of the interview.[2]

Rose cabled. Earl Granville assented, even to the extent of expressing regret for the escape of the "Alabama" and its depredations; but he insisted that the points of law involved should be submitted to arbitration. Having prepared the way for the formal negotiations, Rose willingly stepped to one side. On January 26, 1871, Sir Edward Thornton handed to Secretary Fish a note proposing the appointment of a joint high commission to treat on the fisheries and on all questions affecting the

[1] Moore, *International Arbitrations*, I.: 525.
[2] Ibid., I.: 529.

relations of the United States with British North America. Fish accepted on January 30, with the provision that the claims arising out of the acts committed by the "Alabama" and the other Confederate cruisers should be included. Thornton approved the addition of these claims, February 1, and asked that all claims, British and American, arising out of the acts committed in the Civil War should be included. Fish agreed, February 3, 1871.[1] Officially, these four short notes, written within a week's time, brought to a successful conclusion the efforts of twenty months of brilliant secret diplomacy.

President Grant appointed the Secretary of State to head the American commissioners; the others were Samuel Nelson of the Supreme Court, R. C. Schenck, minister to Great Britain, E. R. Hoar of Massachusetts, and George H. Williams of Oregon. For Great Britain appeared Earl de Grey and Ripon, a member of Gladstone's cabinet, Sir Stafford Northcote, member of Parliament, Sir Edward Thornton, minister to the United States, Montague Bernard, professor of international law at Oxford, and Sir John A. Macdonald, premier of Canada. They met in Washington, February 27, 1871, and exchanged copies of their full powers, which were found satisfactory.[2] The British commissioners gracefully proposed that Secretary Fish should act as chairman; but Fish felt that this would entail unnecessary formality and expressed the desire that no president be named. The commission held thirty-seven long sittings, February 27 to May 6, 1871.

As concluded, the treaty consisted of a preamble and forty-three articles. The first subject taken up consisted of the claims on account of the acts of the "Alabama" and the other cruisers; and articles one to eleven of the treaty were devoted to it. These claims were to be referred to a tribunal to consist of five arbitrators, one to be designated by each of the following, the President of the United States, the Queen of Great Britain, the King of Italy, the President of Switzerland, and the Emperor of

[1] Moore, *International Arbitrations*, I.: 532, and Foreign Relations, 1871: 496.

[2] Foreign Relations, 1871: 495 for protocol.

Brazil. These arbitrators should meet at Geneva and a majority might render an award. Cases and counter cases for the parties were provided for, as well as written and oral arguments. The British commissioners expressed on the part of their government, in a friendly spirit a regret "for the escape, under whatever circumstances, of the 'Alabama' and other vessels from British ports, and for the depredations committed by those vessels."

The American commissioners were very anxious to define the term, neutral duty, for the guidance of the future tribunal. The debate on this subject occupied the time for six sessions. The British had been instructed to revise the rules of maritime neutrality; but, they contended, this was for future guidance alone. The Americans insisted that these rules should be made to apply to the "Alabama" and the other escaped cruisers. And they won their point; although the British inserted the statement that the three rules of due diligence were not international law at the time the cruisers escaped, but out of a desire to strengthen friendly relations Great Britain would consent to the application of the rules in the coming arbitration. These rules were:

"A neutral Government is bound—First, to use due diligence to prevent the fitting out, arming, or equipping, within its jurisdiction, of any vessel which it has reasonable ground to believe is intended to cruise or to carry on war against a Power with which it is at peace; and also to use like diligence to prevent the departure from its jurisdiction of any vessel intended to cruise or carry on war as above, such vessel having been specially adapted, in whole or in part, within such jurisdiction, to warlike use."

Fish had used in the first draft "to use active diligence to prevent the construction, fitting out," etc. The British objected and tried to insert the phrase, "reasonable care." Finally, they adopted Earl de Grey's suggestion of "due diligence."[1] The

[1] Commenting on this phrase in 1909, A. Pearce Higgins stated that it has become celebrated by its obscurity. The Second Hague Conference, made the following modification of the rule, "A neutral Government is bound to employ the means at its disposal to prevent the fitting out or arming of any vessel," etc. (Convention XIII, article 8). And "A neutral

British objected to the term "construction." Justice Nelson explained that the American courts had held that "construction" was covered by the term "fitting out." The British thought the word too broad, and so it was omitted.

A neutral government is bound, "Secondly, not to permit or suffer either belligerent to make use of its ports or waters as the base of naval operations against the other, or for the purpose of renewal or augmentation of military supplies or arms, or the recruitment of men."

"Thirdly, to exercise due diligence in its own ports and waters, and, as to all persons within its jurisdiction, to prevent any violation of the foregoing obligations and duties."

The foregoing rules and the principles of international law not inconsistent therewith were to be applied to each vessel separately. The tribunal was given power to award a gross sum; if it was found that Great Britain had been negligent. The two parties agreed to abide by the award as a final settlement.

Before taking up the remainder of the treaty, it will be well to see how the "Alabama" claims were settled. Great Britain appointed as her arbitrator Sir Alexander Cockburn, Lord Chief Justice of England; the United States, Charles Francis Adams; the King of Italy, Count Frederick Sclopis; the President of Switzerland, M. Jacques Staempfli; and the Emperor of Brazil, Viscount d'Itajuba. The agent for the United States was J. C. Bancroft Davis, and the agent for Great Britain, Lord Tenterden. As counsel for the United States appeared William M. Evarts, Caleb Cushing, and Morrison R. Waite. Sir Roundell Palmer appeared alone as British counsel, but Montague Bernard and Mr. Cohen sat at the table with him. The tribunal met on December 15, 1871, at the Hotel de Ville in Geneva. On the motion of Adams, seconded by Cockburn, Count Sclopis of Italy was chosen president.

The cases for the United States and Great Britain were then delivered by their respective agents. The tribunal directed that the counter cases and additional documents be delivered to the

Power is bound to exercise such vigilance as the means at its disposal permit to prevent any violation. . . . (Convention XIII, article 25).

secretary on or before April 15, 1872. On the following day, the tribunal adjourned to meet again on June 15.

The authorship of the American case is justly attributed to J. C. Bancroft Davis, who had the assistance of the members of the American counsel and of President Woolsey of Yale. The case reviewed in an able manner the beginnings of the Civil War, the relations of the British to the Southerners, the proclamation of neutrality, the duties of Great Britain as a neutral in the light of the three rules of due diligence and of the principles of international law. The case presented the facts in the building and equipping of the cruisers, of the "Alexandra" and the decisions by the courts, of the attitude of Lord Palmerston, Earl Russell, and of the local officers in Nassau, Trinidad, Gibraltar, Capetown, Singapore, and Melbourne. The favoritism granted Confederate vessels and the discrimination against Union vessels were portrayed. The case pointed out wherein Great Britain had failed to perform her duties as a neutral. The case closed with the plea that the tribunal should award a sum in gross to the United States to cover:

1. The claims for direct losses growing out of the destruction of vessels and their cargoes by the insurgent cruisers.

2. The national expenditures in pursuit of those cruisers.

3. The loss of the transfer of the American commercial marine to the British flag.

4. The enhanced payments of insurance.

5. The prolongation of the war and the addition of a large sum to the cost of the war and the suppression of the rebellion.[1]

Interest was asked for at the rate of 7 per cent., the legal rate in New York, from July 1, 1863, as the most equitable day.

The British case conceived of neutrality as synonymous with "impartiality toward the belligerent powers."[2] It compared the British proclamation of neutrality and orders to enforce it with those of other powers. The Confederates had complained that United States vessels had been favored in British ports. And the United States vessels had obtained coal more frequently in

[1] Geneva Arbitration, I.: 185.
[2] Ibid., I.: 211.

the West India ports than had the Confederate vessels.[1] But the law had been laid down alike for both belligerents. Great Britain had used "unremitting care and vigilance." Even the "Alabama" had been ordered seized; and it was not for lack of due diligence that the vessel got away. "A vessel becomes a public ship of war by being armed and commissioned" was laid down as a principle of international law.[2] The "Alabama" had been armed and commissioned beyond British jurisdiction. This being so, when that ship appeared in British ports, it became the duty of Great Britain, as a neutral, to extend to her the privileges of a belligerent vessel.

The British foreign enlistment act of 1819 had been modelled upon the American neutrality law of 1818.[3] The government had applied that law in the case of the "Alexandra." And when it had lost in the courts for want of sufficient evidence and at a cost of £3700, the vessel had been seized again at Nassau, had undergone a trial, and been released at a further expense of £300. The "Florida" had been seized at Nassau, tried, and released for want of proof. The Laird iron-clads had been seized and the government had taken the extraordinary precaution of purchasing them for £220,000 in order to prevent them from passing into belligerent hands. Two vessels had been seized in Glasgow, held on mere suspicion until the end of the war, and then returned over to their owners. The officers of the government had given every attention to the complaints made by Consul Dudley and Minister Adams; but neither one had furnished evidence sufficient for the detention of the vessels.

The "Shenandoah" had been the "Sea King," a merchant vessel, British owned, and engaged in the New Zealand and China trade. On her last outward voyage from London with a cargo of coal, she had been transferred, November, 1864, at the Madeira Islands to the Confederate States. Her guns and equipment arrived from England in the steamer, "Laurel." After capturing and destroying a large number of American merchant-

[1] Geneva Arbitration, I.: 235.
[2] Ibid., I.: 237.
[3] Ibid., I.: 239.

men she put into the port of Melbourne for repairs. This accomplished, she put to sea, February 18, 1865. The British case admitted that several men had been clandestinely enlisted in the port and that her crew had thus been augmented; but the case relied on the fact that the commander had, before leaving, given his word in writing that no one had been enlisted since his arrival and that he had in no way violated the neutrality of the port.[1] The "Shenandoah" continued her depredations more than six months after the Civil War had closed. When she finally arrived in Liverpool, the British government seized her at the request of Adams and handed her over to the United States. The vigilance of the British government had been, in this case, defeated through artifice and concealment; but every action of the government proved that due diligence had been observed.

Shortly after the American case became known in London, expressions of apprehension on the indirect claims appeared in the British journals. The Times for January 2, 1872, urged that Britain should stand upon her rights, should not wait for the decision by the tribunal, but demur to claims for indirect damages. The Morning Advertiser for January 4, 1872, asked if these demands had been referred to arbitration. If they had not, the demands "must either be at once withdrawn, or we must withdraw from the treaty." If these demands had been referred, the jurisdiction of the court ought to be repudiated. In Parliament a cabinet crisis developed. It became difficult to sell United States bonds and American stocks. Disraeli in the opposition pointed out that the American case demanded of the country a tribute greater than could be exacted by conquest. Gladstone replied that there could be only one true and unambiguous meaning. Statements by the British commissioners revealed that there was no unanimity on whether the claims were or were not excluded. The American commissioners were unanimous that the indirect claims had not been excluded, and, inasmuch as the treaty stipulated that "all complaints and claims on the part of the United States" on account of the "Alabama" and the other vessels should be adjusted, these indirect claims

[1] Geneva Arbitration, I.: 405.

were therefore constructively included. Considerable discussion took place between the Foreign Office and the State Department. But the saviour of the situation was the American arbitrator, Charles Francis Adams. Before he sailed for Geneva Adams expressed the opinion to Fish that as a matter of public law a state was not liable in damages for injuries like those listed under the indirect claims. Fish suggested that he exchange opinions with Cockburn or some member of the British cabinet; thus giving the government assurance that the American and British arbitrators agreed on that point.[1]

Arriving in England, Adams learned that Sir Alexander Cockburn regarded the arbitration as dead. He saw several members of Gladstone's cabinet and proceeded to Geneva. There he found that the British agent had been instructed to obtain an adjournment of the tribunal for six months or to come home. Adams laid his plan before the American agent first; who saw the members of counsel on both sides while Adams consulted the other arbitrators. The result was that at the meeting of the tribunal on June 17, 1872, an agreement to exclude the indirect claims was in sight. On June 19, Count Sclopis declared that the members had arrived, individually and collectively, at the decision that upon principles of international law the indirect claims did not constitute a "good foundation for an award of compensation or computation of damages between nations, and should upon such principles be wholly excluded from the consideration of the tribunal in making its award, even if there were no disagreement between the two governments as to the competency of the tribunal to decide thereon."[2] The agents received, thereupon, instructions from their governments to proceed with the case.

The indirect claims being eliminated, only two points in the American case remained. 1. The claims for direct losses growing out of the destruction of vessels and their cargoes by the insurgent cruisers. 2. The national expenditures in the pursuit of those cruisers.

[1] Moore, *International Arbitrations*, I.: 643.
[2] Geneva Arbitration, II.: 578.

The counter cases with documents had been delivered by the agents to the secretary of the tribunal on April 15, 1872. On June 15 the printed arguments had been delivered. The counsel for neither party could thereafter present as a matter of right any further arguments or elucidations either orally or in writing. Article V of the treaty specified that the arbitrators alone could call for further arguments on any points indicated. The tribunal did call for such arguments on seven different points, 1, the meaning of due diligence; 2, the effect of a commission on a belligerent vessel entering a neutral port; 3, the amount of coal that a neutral may furnish a belligerent vessel; 4, the recruitment of men for the Shenandoah in Melbourne; 5, the effect of the entry of the Florida into the port of Mobile; 6, the question of interest and the rate; and 7, the amount of damages.[1]

As soon as Staempfli had received the cases and the counter cases of the parties, he secluded himself in an Alpine retreat to master their contents. And when the tribunal met on June 15, he appeared with abstracts of evidence and elaborately written opinions on the main questions involved. This gave him the advantage over Adams even, familiar as the latter was with the history of the claims; not to mention the advantage over Cockburn, who had been convinced the tribunal would break up in failure and who admitted that he had not yet begun to examine the cause. At the session of July 15 Staempfli submitted a program, proposing that the tribunal should consider the facts and the principles of law in the case of each cruiser in regular order. He mentioned that this order was the one he had pursued in the examination of the evidence and arguments and that he had reached conclusions on all points, though these were subject to modification. Cockburn protested and submitted that the principles of law should be agreed upon before considering the facts respecting the vessels.[2] Baron Itajuba observed that such a plan would consume much time in theoretical discussion. "We are here as judges," retorted Cockburn, "and as such must deliberate slowly." Count Sclopis replied, "It is not necessary

[1] Geneva Arbitration, III.: 385–638.
[2] Ibid., IV.: 27.

for Lord Cockburn to state that we are here as judges. We all have felt from the commencement and still feel a deep appreciation of our duties as such. I have presided for many years in the highest tribunal in my country. There the facts are universally discussed first, then the principles which govern them." [1]

The various questions involved and the decisions reached were well summarized in the award. This was read at the thirty-third conference on Saturday, September 14, 1872. For the first time the doors of the Salle des Conferences of the Hotel de Ville of Geneva were thrown open to the public. The secretary read the official copy of the award in English. Four arbitrators concurred in the award; Cockburn did not and handed in a bulky and contentious dissenting opinion,[2] which was not read. The archives were deposited with the council of state at Geneva. Thereupon, the president declared the labors of the arbitrators to be finished and the tribunal to be dissolved.

The award stated that the arbitrators had been governed by the three rules of due diligence and by the principles of international law not inconsistent therewith. The due diligence mentioned in the first and third of these rules ought to be exercised by neutral governments in exact proportion to the risks to which either of the belligerents might be exposed from a failure to fulfil the obligations of neutrality. The facts constituting the subject matter in this controversy arose out of such circumstances and were of such a nature as to call for all possible solicitude by the British government in the observance of the rights and duties involved in its proclamation of neutrality. The tribunal held that the commissioning of a vessel by a belligerent did not absolve the neutral in whose jurisdiction it had been constructed, equipped, and armed from responsibility for the acts of the vessel after it had been commissioned; nor could the consummation of a fraud by a belligerent become the means of establishing the innocence of the neutral.

The privilege of exterritoriality accorded the vessels of war of a

[1] Moore, *International Arbitrations*, I.: 648, and Geneva Arbitration, IV.: 26.

[2] Geneva Arbitration, IV.: 230–544.

belligerent in neutral ports by the law of nations was a privilege and not a right and proceeded solely from courtesy and mutual deference and could not be used by the neutral to protect acts done in violation of neutrality. The fact that the United States was in some instances unable to give Great Britain due notice that her neutrality was being violated served in no way to shield the latter.

In the case of the "Alabama" Great Britain failed to use due diligence in stopping her construction and in preventing the "Agrippina" from carrying the equipment and armament from England to Terceira. The orders for her seizure came so late that they could not be executed. After the vessel had escaped Great Britain failed to take proper measures for her pursuit and arrest. Moreover, the "Alabama" was permitted to coal freely in British colonial ports on several occasions with no effort being made to seize her. All of the five arbitrators agreed in this case that Great Britain had failed by omission to fulfil the duties prescribed in the first and third rules of due diligence. Cockburn did not agree with the reasons of the other four judges but he reached the same conclusion.

In permitting the construction of the "Florida," her escape from Liverpool, her release from Nassau, her enlistment of men, taking on supplies and armament with the aid of the British vessel "Prince Alfred" at Green Cay, Great Britain had been guilty of negligence. The "Florida" had thereafter been permitted to coal freely on various occasions at British ports. And the fact that the "Florida" had entered the Confederate port of Mobile did not "extinguish the responsibility previously to that time incurred by Great Britain." By a majority of four to one the tribunal decided that in the case of the "Florida," Great Britain had violated all three of the rules of due diligence.

In the case of the "Shenandoah" which had been engaged in the merchant trade and left London as a merchant vessel under her original name of "Sea King," under British registry and ownership, the tribunal agreed unanimously that Great Britain had observed due diligence; that Great Britain could in no way be charged with responsibility for her transformation into a Confederate war vessel off Madeira, nor for her career of destruction thereafter until she entered the harbor of Melbourne. But by a majority of three to two the tribunal held that, by permitting the augmentation of force through the enlistment of men at Melbourne, Great Britain had been negligent and would therefore be obliged to assume responsibility for the destruction wrought by the "Shenandoah" after she left Melbourne.

So far as the tenders were concerned, it was decided that they should follow the lot of their principals. The United States claimed that Great Britain was responsible for the destruction committed by eleven other vessels for want of due diligence, but the tribunal absolved Great Britain entirely in six and excluded five from consideration for lack of evidence.

The United States claimed indemnity for the cost of pursuing the cruisers. The tribunal held that these costs could not be distinguished from the general expenses of the war and that no allowance could be made. Another claim was based upon the prospective earnings of the merchantmen destroyed by the cruisers; but the tribunal was unanimously of the opinion that this constituted no ground for an award inasmuch as these earnings depended upon future and uncertain contingencies. On the claim of freight for the actual cargo, net freight only was allowed. Interest at a reasonable rate was recognized in principle, but the amount was not specified. The tribunal expressed itself in favor of an award in gross.

By a majority of four to one, the tribunal awarded $15,500,000 in gold as the indemnity to be paid by Great Britain to the United States in satisfaction of all claims referred to the tribunal.[1]

Public opinion in the United States received the announcement of the award with satisfaction. True, the indirect claims still furnished substance for party cavil. In Great Britain opinion appeared to be more divided. The disposition of the indirect claims was hailed as a victory and the sum awarded was

[1] Malloy, *Treaties*, I: 717.

looked upon as a price which Britain deserved to pay.[1] Considerable doubt arose in the minds of several Englishmen as to the construction of the three rules of due diligence, among these were Earl Granville, the head of the Foreign Office, Mr. Gladstone, Vernon Harcourt, and Roundell Palmer. The Institute of International Law noted that the rules were declaratory of the law of nations, at its session in Geneva, 1874, but in order to eliminate disputes on the interpretation that body adopted a redraft of the rules.[2] Bismarck expressed himself as averse to approving the three rules, as they stood in the treaty, for Germany and so did Count Beust for Austria. The result was that neither Great Britain nor the United States urged other powers to accede to the three rules of due diligence as a definition of the obligations of a neutral. Indeed, it may be said that the substance and the application of those rules did not become a part of international law until the Second Hague Conference, 1907, had completed its work.[3]

For the adjudication and disposition of the money received by the Geneva award the United States had to set up two courts. The first one found valid claims for only $9,316,120.25; so that a second court was created to dispose of the remainder. The first court consisted of five judges. It became their duty to examine all claims "directly resulting from damage caused" by the "Alabama," the "Florida," and the "Shenandoah" after she left Melbourne and to decide upon the validity of such claims in accordance with the "principles of law and the merits of the several cases." No claim could be allowed for damage covered by insurance, for unearned freights or prospective profits, nor to an insurance company unless it could show that its losses in respect to war risks exceeded the sum of its premiums. Claims made by persons not entitled to protection from the government at the time of the loss should not be allowed, nor the claims of persons who had failed to bear "true allegiance" to the United States during "the late rebellion." Interest at 4 per cent. could

[1] Moore, *International Arbitrations*, I.: 664.
[2] Ibid., I.: 674.
[3] Higgins, *Hague Peace Conferences;* 480.

be allowed. In its general provisions the statute kept within the lines of the award.[1] By a statute of March 3, 1873, Congress had merged the amount of the award with other funds to be used in redeeming the public debt of the United States. A special bond for $15,500,000 was accordingly written out with a pen.[2] The Secretary of the Treasury was therefore directed to pay the judgments of the court "out of any such money in the Treasury not otherwise appropriated."

Only one claim for national losses was presented, that by the Secretary of the Navy for pursuit of the cruisers; and it was disallowed. Claims for injuries to the person were rejected on the ground that the United States had not mentioned such claims in its diplomatic correspondence with Great Britain and that Congress had intended to limit the claims to the loss of property only. On the subject of "true allegiance" the court held it insufficient that claimant had not been guilty of treason as defined by the constitution or that he had received a pardon. Pretty much all persons domiciled in the United States were considered entitled to the "protection of the United States." This included foreigners employed in the merchant marine and in the whale fisheries; but the court held that the claims of British subjects so employed could not have been intended by the award to be included. On the claims "directly resulting" from the acts of the cruisers the court ruled out those based on a loss of catch due to being chased, those based on an average adjustment on a ransom bond, and those based on service rendered as cartel ships in taking crews of destroyed vessels to a place of safety.[3] In all the court disposed of 2,068 claims amounting to about $14,500,000. Of this amount the court allowed $9,316,125.25. The interest and profits on the sale of the bonds made the remainder of the fund amount to $10,089,004.96. On June 23, 1874, the remaining bonds in which the fund was invested were cancelled. Consequently, the fund did not grow further.

[1] 18 Statutes at Large, 245.
[2] Hackett, *Geneva Award Acts:* 178.
[3] See Davis' Report.

Five classes of claimants arose for participation in the remainder: 1, those who had had property destroyed by the inculpated cruisers, that is, the "Alabama," "Florida," and "Shenandoah;" 2, those who had had property destroyed by the exculpated cruisers, that is, those Confederate cruisers for which Britain had not been held responsible at Geneva; 3, those who had paid higher insurance premiums because the Confederate cruisers roamed the seas; 4, those who had underwritten risks on property destroyed by the inculpated cruisers and these wanted their claims considered apart from the premiums collected and on the same grounds as the insured; and 5, the claims of those who did not at all times during the war bear true allegiance to the United States.[1]

In response to the demands of the claimants various proposals were made in Congress. One was to return the remainder of the fund to Great Britain. Another proposed to revive the act of 1874. Still another would leave the matter with the Court of Claims. None of these plans met with favor. Finally, Congress passed the statute of June 5, 1882. It created a court with three judges which could render judgments for "claims directly resulting from damage done on the high seas by Confederate cruisers during the late rebellion." The damage done by the exculpated cruisers was therefore included. It could also render judgments for "claims for the payment of premiums for war risks, whether paid to corporations, agents, or individuals, after the sailing of any Confederate cruiser." Claims should accordingly be divided into two classes; and the judgments in favor of the first class should be paid first; and if there should not be sufficient money in the fund to satisfy judgments in favor of the second class, these should be paid proportionately.

Of the cases coming under the first class the court disposed of 1,602, with judgments in favor of 994 claimants to the aggregate amount of $3,346,016.32; all based on damages committed by the exculpated cruisers. The court disposed of 4,149 cases coming under the second class or war premium claims. Judgments were rendered in favor of 3,662 claimants to the aggregate

[1] Hackett, *Geneva Award Acts:* 87.

amount of $16,312,944.52. The judgments of the second class had of necessity to be prorated. The first court ruled out the claims of British subjects serving on the American merchantmen destroyed by the Confederate cruisers as not being covered expressly by the statute. These claims were now included.[1]

Articles XII to XVII of the Treaty of Washington provided for the settlement of claims of American citizens, other than the "Alabama" claims, and of British subjects growing out of the Civil War. Under the terms three commissioners were appointed, J. S. Fraser of Indiana by the United States, Russell Gurney by the Queen of Great Britain, and Count Louis Corti by the King of Italy. The treaty specified that they should sit in Washington. This they did until an amendment was obtained which permitted them to sit in Newport. They completed their labors on September 25, 1873. The American claims amounted to about $1,000,000. Twelve grew out of a raid on St. Albans, Vermont, October, 1864, made by Confederate soldiers who came as "peaceable individuals" by way of Canada. Four claims were for damages for the alleged unlawful detention of vessels laden with saltpeter at Calcutta in January, 1862. All of the American claims were dismissed.[2]

On behalf of British subjects 478 claims were presented. Of these 187 received favorable awards by the commission, amounting to $1,929,819. Several of the awards were based on claims for cotton destroyed by the American military forces; for property confiscated on the assumption that it belonged to Confederates; for vessels captured at the mouth of the Rio Grande while lying in neutral waters and condemned by the United States prize courts; for unlawful warning off of British vessels from ports not under effective blockade; and for the conscription of British subjects into the American army. In the case of the "Springbok" an allowance of $5,065 was made for the detention of the vessel but nothing for her cargo that had been condemned. Claims based on the cotton loan bonds of the Confederacy were disallowed, as were those based on property destroyed by the

[1] Cassidy *v.* United States, docket number 144.
[2] Report of Robert S. Hale, Foreign Relations, 1878, III.: 21.

military forces of the Confederacy, and likewise those based on the capture of the "Peterhoff." [1]

Articles XVIII to XXV and XXXII and XXXIII of the Treaty of Washington related to the North Atlantic fisheries. The British negotiators wanted the reciprocity treaty of 1854 revived, but the Americans refused. The agreement reached provided for the liberty of Americans to take fish of every kind except shell fish in common with British subjects on the coasts, shores, bays, and harbors of Quebec, Nova Scotia, New Brunswick, and Prince Edward's Island in addition to the fishing rights obtained by the Treaty of 1818. The rights of private property were to be respected; and the salmon and shad fisheries of the rivers were reserved for the British. A reciprocal provision was made for British subjects to fish in common with Americans within the three mile limit of the United States north of the thirty-ninth parallel, which would not include Delaware Bay. Fish and fish oil were to be admitted reciprocally free of duty. The British negotiators asserted that the privileges accorded American citizens were of greater value than those accorded British subjects. Consequently, a commission was created to evaluate the advantage enjoyed by Americans. That commission sat at Halifax in 1877 and awarded $5,500,000 in gold to be paid by the United States to Great Britain for the ten year period that the treaty was to be binding. The United States protested but paid the award. As a safeguard for the future Congress passed a joint resolution giving notice that this part of the treaty would be considered terminated on July 1, 1885. The final settlement of the fisheries dispute did not come until the Hague arbitration of 1910.

Articles XXVI to XXVIII opened the St. Lawrence north of the northern boundary of New York to American navigation. The navigation of the Yukon, Porcupine, and Stikine was declared free and open to British subjects and American citizens alike. Great Britain agreed to urge the government of Canada to secure to American citizens the same privileges on the Welland, St. Lawrence, and other canals as Canadians enjoy. The United

[1] Moore, *International Arbitrations*, I.: 688; IV.: 3838, 3928.

States agreed to urge upon the State governments to secure the same privileges for British subjects upon the various State canals as those enjoyed by Americans. The United States agreed that American citizens and British subjects should be treated alike in their use of the St. Clair Flats canal.[1] Article XXVIII provided for the opening of Lake Michigan to British subjects for a term of ten years after passage by Congress of the proper legislation. Congress did not and never has passed this legislation; consequently this article remains inoperative. Articles XXIX, XXX, and XXXIII provided for the reciprocal transit of goods in bond and for a slight modification of the coasting trade regulations. These articles terminated on July 1, 1885, on notice given by the United States.[2] Article XXXI specified that New Brunswick could levy no duty on lumber or timber cut on American territory "watered by the river St, John and its tributaries," when floated down that river and destined for the United States.

The remaining articles, except the one on exchange of ratifications, pertained to the settlement of the San Juan boundary dispute. This was submitted to the Emperor of Germany for arbitration. The United States was fortunate in choosing for its representative the eminent historian and statesman, George Bancroft. The British representative was Admiral James C. Prevost, who, like Bancroft, had personally participated in the history of the controversy. Emperor William decided on the Haro Channel which gave San Juan and numerous other islands to the United States.[3]

In the number of issues involved, issues big with danger, and in the number of questions of long standing dispute put to rest, the Treaty of Washington ranks easily as one of the most important in American history. The enunciation of the principles of international law relating to the obligations of neutral states made the treaty take rank as one of the first in the world's history. The treaty has in every war since 1871 influenced the

[1] Moore, *Digest*, I.: 635.
[2] See Harrison's message of February 2, 1893, Richardson, IX.: 335.
[3] Moore, *International Arbitrations*, I.: 229.

political affairs of every continent and island, indeed, of the sea itself.

Political principles, international as well as national, have an enduring aspect in so far as they correctly express the needs of the state. The outstanding characters who spoke the words of progress during these negotiations were Sir John Rose for Great Britain, Charles Francis Adams and Hamilton Fish for the United States. Grant and Gladstone might be included as the chiefs of their respective governments.

BIBLIOGRAPHY.

ADAMS, CHARLES FRANCIS.—*Charles Francis Adams*. New York, 1900.
ADAMS, CHARLES FRANCIS.—*The Treaty of Washington: Before and After, in Lee at Appomatox and other papers*. Boston, 1902.
BERNARD, MONTAGUE.—*The Neutrality of Great Britain during the American Civil War*. London, 1870.
BULLOCH, JAMES D.—*The Secret Service of the Confederate States in Europe*. 2 volumes. New York, 1884.
CUSHING, CALEB.—*The Treaty of Washington*. New York, 1873.
DAVIS, J. C. BANCROFT.—*Mr. Fish and the Alabama Claims*. Boston, 1893.
DAVIS, J. C. BANCROFT.—*Mr. Sumner, the Alabama Claims, and Their Settlement*. A letter to the New York Herald, Jan. 4, 1878.
Diplomatic Correspondence, 1862 to 1869. Washington.
Foreign Relations, 1870 to 1874. Washington.
HACKETT, FRANK W.—*The Geneva Award Acts*. Boston, 1882.
HAYNES, GEORGE H.—*Charles Sumner*. Philadelphia, 1909.
MACDONALD, SIR JOHN A.—*Memoirs*, (edited by Joseph Pope). 2 volumes. London, 1894.
NORTHCOTE, SIR STAFFORD.—*Life, Letters, and Diaries*. (Edited by Andrew Lang). 2 volumes. London, 1890.

CHAPTER XIV

THE TREATY OF PARIS, 1898

"Arbitration precedes war, to avoid its horrors; it does not come after the trial by battle to enable either party to escape its consequences."—FROM AMERICAN REPLY TO A PROPOSAL MADE BY THE SPANISH PEACE COMMISSION.

At the Congress of Verona, 1822, Austria, Russia, Prussia, and France bound themselves "mutually and in the most solemn manner, to use all their efforts to put an end to the system of representative governments in whatsoever country it may exist in Europe, and to prevent its being introduced in those countries where it is not yet known." That same congress commissioned France to reëstablish absolutism under Ferdinand in Spain. This the Duc d'Angouleme accomplished when he entered Madrid with a French army, May 23, 1823. Thereupon, Ferdinand argued that to put down rebellion in the former colonies of Spain in America would be an object as holy as that of replacing him on the throne. Report had it that if France would assist, Ferdinand would reward her with the cession of Mexico or Cuba.

The apprehensions of Canning concerning the openings for British trade in South and Central America were stirred. He notified France that the separation of the colonies from Spain had been decided by the course of events and expressed the conviction that France would make no attempt to bring any of those colonies under her jurisdiction.[1] On August 20, 1823, Canning wrote to the American minister, Richard Rush: "Is not the moment come when our governments might understand each other as to the Spanish American colonies? And if we can arrive at such an understanding, would it not be expedient for ourselves, and beneficial for all the world, that the principles of it should be clearly settled and plainly avowed?" He conceived of the question of the recognition of the independence of the for-

[1] Moore, *Digest*, VI.: 386.

mer Spanish colonies "to be one of time and circumstances." He disavowed any intent on the part of Great Britain to take possession of them. But he could not with indifference see them transferred to any other power. He wanted to know if Rush did not have power to negotiate and sign a convention on the subject. Coöperation between the United States and Great Britain he felt would ward off any meditated jurisdiction of European powers over the new world.[1]

The American Secretary of State was John Quincy Adams. In his instructions to the newly appointed minister to Madrid, Mr. Nelson, he had on April 28, 1823, expressed himself on the war between France and Spain. "Whatever may be the issue of this war . . . it may be taken for granted that the dominion of Spain upon the American continents, north and south, is irrevocably gone. But the islands of Cuba and Puerto Rico still remain nominally, and so far really, dependent upon her, that she yet possesses the power of transferring her dominion over them. . . Cuba, almost within sight of our shores, from a multitude of considerations has become an object of transcendent importance to the commercial and political interests of our Union. Its commanding position with reference to the Gulf of Mexico and the West Indian seas; the character of its population; its situation midway between our southern coast and the island of San Domingo; its safe and capacious harbor of the Havana fronting a long line of our shore destitute of the same advantage; the nature of its productions and of its wants, furnishing the supplies and needing the returns of a commerce immensely profitable and mutually beneficial,—give it an importance in the sum of our national interests with which that of no other foreign country can be compared, and little inferior to that which binds the different members of this Union together."

Adams feared an invasion of Cuba by France. And he commented on the refusal of Great Britain to join the Holy Alliance as foreboding an alliance between Great Britain and Spain against France. "As the price of her alliance, the two remaining

[1] Moore, *Digest*, VI.: 389.

islands of Spain in the West Indies present objects no longer of much possible value or benefit to Spain, but of such importance to Great Britain that it is impossible to suppose her indifferent to them."[1]

John Quincy Adams revealed thus an attitude of suspicion toward France and toward Great Britain. President Monroe asked Jefferson for an opinion on Canning's propositions. Jefferson replied, "The question presented . . . is the most momentous which has ever been offered to my contemplation since that of independence. That made us a nation, this sets our compass and points the course which we are to steer through the ocean of time opening on us. . . . . Our first and fundamental maxim should be, never to entangle ourselves in the broils of Europe; our second, never to suffer Europe to intermeddle with cis-Atlantic affairs."[2] Madison received a similar request for an opinion. In his reply he asked "What is the extent of Mr. Canning's disclaimer as to 'the remaining possessions of Spain in America?' Does it exclude future views of acquiring Porto Rico, etc., as well as Cuba? It leaves Great Britain free, as I undersand it, in relation to other quarters of the globe."[3]

It was this international situation with respect to Cuba, as it appeared to American statesmen, that inspired the Monroe Doctrine as announced in the message of December 2, 1823. True, Russia came in for her share of suspicion. She had given active support to the intervention in Spain. Her minister in Washington, Baron Tuyll, informed Secretary Adams that Russia had determined not to recognize any government recently formed in the New World. Adams feared that Russia planned the extension of her jurisdiction indefinitely southward from Alaska and that, under the circumstances, Spain could not and would not resist. On November 27, 1824, almost a year after the announcement of the Monroe Doctrine, he declared to Baron Tuyll: "that the United States of America, and their Government, could not see with indifference, the forcible interposition

[1] H. Ex. Doc. 121, 31 Cong., 1 sess., 6.
[2] Moore, *Digest*, VI.: 394.
[3] Ibid., VI.: 397.

of any European power, other than Spain, either to restore the dominion of Spain over her emancipated colonies in America, or to establish monarchical governments in those countries, or to transfer any of the possessions heretofore or yet subject to Spain in the American hemisphere, to any other European power." [1]

The vital interests of the United States in Cuba inspired the Monroe Doctrine. From that time on those interests have been permanent with slight changes in form only. From 1823 to the compromise of 1850, American policy toward Cuba was characterized by a desire to prevent the transfer of the island by Spain to any other power.

"Should you have reason to suspect" said Secretary Forsythe to Minister Vail at Madrid, July 15, 1840, "any design on the part of Spain to transfer voluntarily her title to the island, whether of ownership or possession, and whether permanent or temporary, to Great Britain, or any other power, you will distinctly state that the United States will prevent it, at all hazards, as they will any foreign military occupation whatsoever." [2]

During the decade from 1850 to 1860, American policy was characterized by efforts to annex Cuba. The incorporation of Texas and of California had appealed to the desire for expansion. Cuba appeared to be the next step . All the more so, because by the compromise of 1850, the already hemmed in slave states had been deprived of their natural right to grow. Polk offered Spain in 1849 one hundred million dollars for Cuba. Spain refused. Then appeared the Ostend manifesto, signed by Soulé, Buchanan, and Mason, declaring that if Spain should refuse one hundred and twenty million dollars, then, "by every law, human and divine, we shall be justified in wresting it from Spain if we possess the power;. . . . ." Besides the volatile spirit of Soulé two reasons prompted this action at Ostend. There existed an apprehension that Spain would emancipate the slaves on the island, which would render local conditions even more unstable

[1] Moore, *Digest*, VI.: 401.
[2] Ibid., VI.: 450.

and would have a disquieting effect upon the slaves in the southern states. Moreover, Americans had acquired an easy leadership in the trade of the island in spite of obnoxious restrictions. The import duty on flour was $10 a barrel; its market value in the United States was $4.50. This caused American flour to go to Spain to be reshipped in Spanish bottoms to Havana. Spain refused again to sell. And Secretary Marcy neutralized the threat of war contained in the manifesto. President Buchanan appealed to Congress in three successive annual messages for coöperation between the executive and legislative departments in the acquisition of Cuba, but Congress held back.

American policy toward Cuba during the years from 1860 to 1895 was marked by non-interference and by an approval of the promised liberal reforms in the island. American enterprize was absorbed in domestic problems. Cuba fought a ten years' war for independence between 1868 and 1878. President Grant favored at one time a recognition of the belligerency of the Cubans, but his move was deftly thwarted by Secretary Fish. Shortly afterward came the gradual abolition of slavery, the only important reform that Spain accomplished.

In 1895 an insurrection broke out in the island again. Tomas Estrada Palma set forth the causes clearly in a letter to Secretary Olney, December 7, 1895: "The causes of the insurrection of 1895 are substantially the same as those of the former revolution lasting from 1868 to 1878, and terminating only in the representation of the Spanish Government that Cuba would be granted such reforms as would remove the grounds of complaint on the part of the Cuban people. Unfortunately the hopes thus held out have never been realized. The representation which was to be given to the Cubans has proven absolutely without character; taxes have been levied anew on everything conceivable; the offices in the island have increased, but the officers are all Spaniards; the native Cubans have been left with no public duties whatsoever to perform except the payment of taxes to the government and blackmail to the officials, without privilege to move from place to place in the Island except on the permission of governmental authority.

"Spain has framed the laws so that natives have substantially been deprived of the rights of suffrage. The taxes levied have been almost entirely devoted to the support of the army and navy in Cuba, to pay interest on the debt that Spain has saddled on the Island, and to pay salaries of the vast number of Spanish office-holders, devoting only $746,000 for internal improvements out of the $26,000,000 collected by tax. No public schools are within the reach of the masses for their education. All the principal industries of the Island are hampered by excessive imposts. Her commerce with every country but Spain has been crippled in every possible manner, as can be seen by the frequent protests of shipowners and merchants.

"The Cubans have no security of person or property. The judiciary are instruments of the military authorities. Trial by military tribunals can be ordered at any time at the will of the Captain-General. There is, besides, no freedom of speech, press or religion." [1]

To this day these charges remain as one of the fairest indictments of Spanish rule in Cuba. The causes of the American Revolution in 1775 paled besides those of the Cuban revolution beginning in 1895.[2] The insurrection had been skilfully organized through numerous secret clubs or juntas, not unlike the committees of correspondence. Maximo Gomez commanded the forces; and they revealed small respect for the rules of civilized warfare. They plundered and robbed the loyalists and burned sugar mills and plantations. The revolt was financed largely by Cubans and their friends in the United States. Contributions came the more willingly because in 1894 Spain cancelled the reciprocity treaty respecting Cuba. During the two complete years that this agreement was effective, 1892 and 1893, American exports to the island had jumped from $11,297,198 in 1889 and $12,669,509 in 1890 to $17,662,411 in 1892 and $23,604,094 in 1893. In 1895, the exports fell to $12,533,260,

[1] Sen. Doc. 231, 56 Cong., 2 Sess., pt. 7.: 96.

[2] For various views of the causes of the Cuban insurrection see *N. Amer. Rev.* 161: 362 by Alvarez; *Rev. des deux mondes*, 139: 553 by Benoist; Le Fur, *La Guerre Hispano-Americaiue:* Merignhac, *L'Autonomie Cubaine et le Conflit Hispano-Amerieaine in Revuc du Droit Public*, 9: 237.

and in 1896 to $7,512,347.[1] Trade was again diverted to Spain and then sent to Cuba, consequently greatly curtailed.

The sinister General Weyler replaced the moderate Marshal Campos as Captain-General. Weyler prosecuted the campaign with creditable vigor; but the climate and the topography favored the reconcentrado policy. The insurgents depended upon the farmers for supplies. Consequently, Weyler ordered that all the inhabitants of the country should leave their homes within eight days and take up their abode in places assigned to them within the towns occupied by Spanish garrisons. All those who were found outside the Spanish lines after eight days would be treated as rebels irrespective of age or sex. Transportation of provisions from one garrisoned town to another was prohibited except under military permit. The object was to destroy the sources of supplies for the insurgents, to compel the neutral part of the population to take sides, and to make it easier to destroy opposition. This concentration policy fell within the scope of good usage in civilized warfare, provided the obligation of supplying the concentrados with food, clothing, medical care, shelter, and proper immunitv of person was fulfilled.

The result of Weyler's proclamation was that the able bodied men in the country joined the insurrection. Their wives, children, and the feeble men reported at the fortified towns. Weyler had made and decided to make no provision for the care of these dependents of the insurgents. He reasoned that harsh treatment of the wives and children would destroy the morale of the rebels and bring them more quickly to submission. The American press took up the cause of the suffering noncombatants and no doubt exaggerated the evils of the military system. Eventually between seven and eight hundred American citizens were included in these camps. Leaving alone the question of the legality of concentration as executed, the measure turned out to be highly inexpedient. It was impossible to take the means of livelihood away from the native Cuban, vegetables and fruits

[1] U. S. Tariff Commission, Reciprocity and Commercial Treaties: 182, Washington, 1919.

could be gathered overnight. The insurrectionist sources of supplies had not been destroyed. The insurrection had grown greatly. The misery of the wives, children, and dependents of the insurgents, which would have been great enough in their shacks in the country and largely unobserved, had been concentrated and accentuated in the camps under Weyler's orders so that newspapermen could appeal to public opinion in America and in the world at large.

As American impatience with Spanish irresponsibility in Cuba rose the Spaniards began to suspect that the United States assisted the insurgents and thus prolonged the internal strife of the island. The Minister of State pointed out to Secretary Olney, May 22, 1896, proper means by which the United States could contribute to the pacification of Cuba. The United States could prosecute with more vigor "the unlawful expeditions of some of its citizens to Cuba" and provide more effective means of curtailing "the powerful assistance which the rebellion finds in the territory of the great American Republic." [1] President Cleveland had recognized not the independence or the belligerency of the Cubans but their insurgency on June 12, 1895—a new move in international relations, although the Supreme Court found later that such action had been in contemplation by Congress while passing the neutrality law of 1818.[2] The purpose was to announce to American citizens that an insurrection existed in Cuba, that it was temporarily beyond the control of Spain, that intercourse with the insurgents was open, but that the United States would enforce the neutrality laws.[3] With respect to the Cubans the United States did not step beyond this recognition of insurgency until after the Treaty of Paris. There grew in the early part of McKinley's administration a sentiment in favor of the recognition of belligerency and a few insisted on the recognition of independence and intervention. These few were composed of owners of plantations, sugar

[1] Spanish Diplomatic Correspondence: 8.
[2] The Three Friends, 166 U. S. 1.
[3] See G. G. Wilson on *Insurgency* in Am. Jour. of Int. Law, I.: 46. Int. Law Situations, Naval War College, 1901: 108; 1902: 57; 1904: 26; 1907: 127; 1912: 9.

mills, railroads, and mines, with an estimated value of $50,000,000.

The chief distinction between the belligerency and the insurgency of the Cubans for American interests was that under belligerency Spain would immediately acquire the right of visiting and searching American merchant vessels on the high seas. Under the recognition of insurgency the United States was left free to enforce its own neutral obligations toward Spain or toward the insurgents. The distinguished Spanish jurist, Marquis de Olivart, criticized severely the laxness of the American government.[1] He collected a list of seventy-one filibustering expeditions, necessarily incomplete, to Cuba fitted out in the United States. Of these, twenty-seven landed successfully in Cuba. Of those which failed the United States stopped thirty-three, Spain, five; storms, four; and the British colonial authorities, two. The most famous of the vessels engaged, "The Three Friends," made eight voyages and "The Dauntless" made twelve. The insurgents followed closely the plans of the Confederates in Great Britain during the Civil War. The merchant vessel would leave port with clearance papers for Santa Martha, Kingston, San Salvador, or some other Gulf port. A short distance out at sea the vessel would be met by a tug or lighter loaded with guns, ammunition, supplies, and Cubans returning from exile to join their compatriots. These would then be transferred to the vessel, which would at times go directly to Pinar del Rio or Camaguey or to some port on the Cuban shore under the control of the insurgents; but more frequently the insurgents would send out boats to meet the vessel either on the high seas or in some British or Mexican port, take the cargo and the returning patriots, and thus allow the vessel to proceed to its destination and return to New York with a cargo of fruit.

It was consequently difficult to collect evidence sufficient for conviction under the neutrality act. At times the judge in his charge to the jury was groping for a definition of a military expedition, as did Judge Wales in U. S. v. Pena [2] and Judge

[1] Revue de droit international public, V.: 358, 499.
[2] 69 Fed. Rep. 983.

Brawley in the "Laurada."[1] In the case of United States v. Hart et al.,[2] decided by the circuit court in April, 1896, several personages were involved. Hart chartered vessels frequently for the Cuban service. Four times he was tried for violation of the neutrality act and convicted only once. In this case the "Bermuda" left New York on February 24, 1896, for Jamaica with sixty unarmed men on board. Three other vessels left at the same time having on board men, arms, and equipment. Before the transshipment to the "Bermuda" could take place at sea a revenue cutter arrested several of the passengers, all of them leading Cuban agents. Among them were Calixto Garcia, Hart, and Buena Brabanzon. Judge Brown instructed the jury that there were five essential attributes of a military expedition, soldiers, officers, arms, organization under a definite command, and a hostile purpose of attack or defense. The jury failed to find that Hart's expedition had all of these attributes, with the result that the "Bermuda" made two expeditions in rapid succession.

Two of the cases reached the Supreme Court. The "Horsa" was a Danish steamer that left Philadelphia, November 9, 1895, for Jamaica. Passing Cape May she turned northward as far as Barnegat. There at night, beyond the marine league, a steam lighter from New York met her and transferred to her several cases, marked merchandise, and about forty passengers, mostly Cubans. On the voyage the merchandise turned out to be arms, ammunition, and a Maxim gun. The passengers received military drill. The expedition was successful. On returning to Philadelphia, the captain, Wiborg, and the two mates, Petersen and Johansen, were arrested. The jury decided that they had engaged in a military expedition under the neutrality law; and the court sentenced them accordingly. They appealed to the Supreme Court on a writ of error. Chief Justice Fuller delivered the opinion which held that the act of drilling was immaterial, that when they had organized to go to Cuba to make war on Spain and had provided themselves with the means, they had

[1] 70 Fed. Rep. 972; 75 Fed. Rep. 267.
[2] 74 Fed. Rep. 725.

then engaged in a military expedition. The question arose whether Wiborg and his associates were responsible, whether they knew when they left Philadelphia that they were engaging in a military enterprise. The opinion held Wiborg responsible, but the cases of the mates were remanded to the district court for a rehearing.[1] Undaunted by this strict interpretation of the neutrality law, Hart organized and carried out a successful expedition in August of the same year, was brought into court, convicted, and sentenced to pay a fine of $500 and to serve two years in prison.[2]

The other case to reach the Supreme Court was the "Three Friends." [3] The collector of customs seized the vessel in the St. John's River, Florida, on the complaint that she had arms and munitions on board intended for the Cubans. A suit for condemnation of the vessel was duly entered in the district court. Judge Locke released the vessel on the ground that the libel failed to show any intent that she was to be employed "in the service of a foreign prince, or state, or of a colony, district or people with whom the United States are at peace, or of any body politic recognized by or known to the United States as a body politic." Chief Justice Fuller delivered the opinion holding that the recognition of the insurgents as belligerents was not necessary and that the recognition of insurgency by the President was ample to bring into effect the neutrality law. In conclusion it may be said that lax as the enforcement of the American neutrality law may have appeared to Spaniards, yet the Spanish government did not and could not charge the United States with failure to observe the due diligence clauses of the Treaty of Washington. Nevertheless, filibustering influenced profoundly public opinion in Spain; and when the Spanish military campaign failed to bring results in Cuba, the government in Madrid shifted the responsibility from itself to that in Washington.

The case of the "Competitor" brought out clearly the disputes on the treaty rights of Americans. This schooner left Key West

[1] Wiborg, *v.* U. S. 163 U. S. 632.
[2] 78 Fed. Rep. 868; 84 Fed. Rep. 619, 799.
[3] 166 U. S. 1. See also 78 Fed. Rep. 175; 89 Fed. Rep. 207.

for Port Lemon, Florida, with twenty-four passengers. When off Cape Sable, the passengers took charge by force, received twenty-five others on board together with arms and ammunition. The schooner reached the Cuban shore at Point Berracos, April 25, 1896, and landed her passengers and material. Shortly afterward she was sighted and captured by the Spanish armed launch, "Mensajora." The master, Laborde, and the mate, Gildea, tried to escape by swimming ashore. They were taken together with three others to Havana. Laborde claimed American citizenship by birth, having been born in New Orleans of Cuban parents. Gildea claimed to have been born in Liverpool and was therefore a British subject. They appeared before a summary court-martial charged with rebellion and piracy. They pleaded innocence on the ground that the passengers had taken possession of the vessel by force off Cape Sable. Inasmuch as all American seamen, whether citizens or not, are entitled to protection, Consul General Williams called attention to the terms of the Treaty of 1795 and the protocol of 1877, the latter of which stated: "No citizen of the United States residing in Spain, her adjacent islands, or her ultramarine possessions, charged with acts of sedition, treason or conspiracy against the institutions, the public security, the integrity of the territory or against the Supreme Government, or any other crime whatsoever, shall be subject to trial by any exceptional tribunal, but exclusively by the ordinary jurisdiction, except in the case of being captured with arms in hand." [1] This protocol bore the signature of Señor Collantes, the Spanish Minister of State, and the signature as well as the earmarks of the draftsmanship of Caleb Cushing, American Minister to Madrid.

The judge-advocate argued that all foreigners were subject to the laws and courts of Spain for crimes committed within Spanish territory, that the protocol was merely an expression of private opinion and constituted no addition or complement of any preexisting treaty, and that, even if the protocol were binding it applied to resident American citizens, which meant that such persons must be registered with the Cuban authorities and with

[1] Malloy, *Treaties*, II.: 1669.

their consulate. These persons were not. Furthermore, the provision did not apply to those arrested with arms in hand.[1] The court-martial pronounced the death sentence upon all those captured except one.

Heated debates on the protection of citizens abroad took place in the United States Senate. Newspapers carried accounts of the long since forgotten "Virginius," which had been captured outside the marine league of Cuba in 1873, taken into Havana, and a large number of passengers and crew tried for piracy by a summary court-martial, which had completed its labors in one day. The result had been that fifty-three American citizens and British subjects were summarily shot. And the protocol of 1877 had been drafted as an interpretation of Articles VII and XX of the Treaty of 1795 in order to prevent such occurences in the future. And now the public of Havana and Madrid demanded that the prisoners from the "Competitor" be likewise shot.

Fortunately, the Department of State had been able to communicate with Madrid; and the Spanish government telegraphed the Captain-General of Cuba that all action should be suspended until the record of the court-martial could be reviewed. The death sentence had been pronounced on May 8, 1896. The case was under consideration at Madrid until November, 1897, when all of the prisoners were released. Writing in 1902, the Marquis de Olivart recognized that the protocol was binding, that at least the master and the mate captured in the water were unarmed, that they were not pirates, and that the suspension of the death sentence by Minister Canovas postponed for two years the opening of hostilities with the United States.[2]

Señor Canovas was assassinated in August, 1897. General Azcanaga succeeded him and lasted a month. Señor Sagasta assumed then the leadership. He recalled General Weyler and sent General Blanco with instructions to abandon the concentration policy. Sagasta revealed a commendable desire to grant reforms in Cuba provided the insurgents would yield, but these declared for independence. The United States expressed its

[1] Sen. Doc. 79, 54 Cong., 2 Sess., 212.
[2] Revue Générale de Droit International Public, IX.: 200.

sympathy with the reform proposals but confessed apprehension about further futile experiments by Spain in Cuba.

McKinley appealed to Congress, May, 1897, for $50,000 as a relief fund and for transporting American citizens to the United States. Congress voted the amount promptly. On Christmas Eve the President appealed to the American people for voluntary contributions. The authorities at Havana had been consulted and they agreed to admit all articles for charity duty free. This move brought home to the Americans concretely the suffering in Cuba.

In January of 1898 the supporters of the old regime in Cuba engaged in riots and revolt. The offices of the three newspapers advocating autonomy in Havana were attacked by mobs. Consul-General Fitzhugh Lee became alarmed for the safety of American life and property and asked for the presence of American naval vessels in the harbor. In response, the "Maine" was ordered to Havana, January 24. The Spanish officials received her with formal courtesy and promised to reciprocate by sending a Spanish war vessel to New York.

Another unfortunate incident occurred, which destroyed American confidence in Spanish diplomatic conduct; and this at a very critical time. The Spanish minister in Washington, Dupuy de Lome, wrote a letter in December, 1897, to a Spanish agent in Cuba in which he cast reflections on the President. Some Cubans intercepted the letter; and on February 8, 1898, the New York Journal published it. McKinley was spoken of as "weak and a bidder for the admiration of the crowd, besides being a would be politician who tries to leave a door open behind himself while keeping on good terms with the jingoes of his party." He went on, "It would be very advantageous to take up, even if only for effect, the question of commercial relations, and to have a man of some prominence sent hither in order that I may make use of him here to carry on a propaganda among the junta and to try to win over the refugees." [1] Dupuy de Lome admitted the authorship and resigned immediately.

Hostile sentiment increased in both countries. Minister Wood-

[1] Foreign Relations, 1898: 1007.

ford reported, February 12, 1898, from Madrid, "Spanish feeling grows more bitter against the United States each day." The Spanish government urged upon him that it had done all within its power, that the President should issue a new proclamation of neutrality, "prevent filibustering expeditions, and break up the New York junta at once." [1] In Congress the pacific element tried on February 14 to prevent an open rupture by proposing and securing the passage of a resolution providing for the publication of the consular correspondence relating to concentration and autonomy in Cuba. The situation on February 14 had the import of war.

On the next day the "Maine" was blown up in Havana harbor with a loss of 260 men. The Spanish officials expressed regret and sympathy and extended every courtesy. On a point of law General Blanco maintained that the "Maine" had lost its exterritoriality when it became a wreck and that the Spanish authorities alone had the right to investigate the disaster. But the home government waived this contention and permitted the United States board of inquiry to proceed. The board found that the forcing upward of the keel and the bottom plating thirty feet above their normal position could have been produced only by the explosion of a mine under the bottom of the ship. But no evidence was obtained fixing responsibility on any person or persons.[2] Nor has such evidence been found to the present day.

Secretary Sherman wrote to Minister Woodford that a grave responsibility appeared to rest upon the Spanish government. The "Maine" could have been excluded from Havana but she had entered with the express consent of Spain. Spain had control of the harbor and upon her rested the responsibility of protecting life and property there and especially the public vessel and the sailors of a friendly power. The United States made no demand for reparation, but left that matter to Spain's voluntary action. Woodford was instructed to notify Spain, March 20, 1898, that April 15 was none too early for the accomplishment of

[1] Foreign Relations, 1898: 1011.
[2] Ibid., 1898: 1037.

an honorable peace in Cuba. The Spanish officials temporized. On March 27 the demands of the United States were made specific: 1. Armistice until October 1st. In the meantime negotiations for peace between Spain and the insurgents through the friendly offices of the President. 2. Immediate revocation of the reconcentrado order. The needy were to be relieved with provisions from the United States. And 3, which was inserted as desirable, if terms of peace were not settled by October 1 the President should be the final arbiter between Spain and the insurgents.[1]

Spain realized the seriousness of the situation. Three days later General Blanco revoked the concentration orders with instructions for relief.[2] Spain proposed an arbitration of the "Maine" affair. She conceded a willingness to accept an armistice if the insurgents would ask for it; but General Blanco was to determine the terms and the duration.[3] Woodford expressed himself as unable to believe that Spain would refuse on a mere question of punctilio. The Pope sensed the gravity of the situation and offered his services as mediator. The holy father acted with the best of motives and his offer was so accepted in Spain and in Europe but not so by the American press, which assumed that this furnished evidence that Spain was searching for support. On April 6, 1898, the diplomatic representatives of Germany, Austria, France, Great Britain, Italy, and Russia called on President McKinley and presented an appeal for peace. Two days later the representatives of the same countries in Madrid called on the Minister of State and presented the same appeal with a recommendation that Spain comply with the demands of the United States. Spain yielded and General Blanco issued a proclamation temporarily suspending hostilities in Cuba,[4] April 9, 1898. Spain had reluctantly conceded substantially every demand of the United States; but it was too late to arrest the hostile momentum in both countries and to re-establish mutual confidence.

[1] Foreign Relations, 1898: 711.
[2] Ibid., 1898: 725.
[3] Ibid., 1898: 726.
[4] Ibid., 1898: 750.

In his message of April 11, the President reviewed the Cuban situation. He mentioned four grounds for intervention, humanity, protection to American life and property, to safeguard commerce, and to suppress an international nuisance which compelled the United States to maintain a semi-war footing. He summarized the negotiations and closed with a request to Congress to clothe him with full power to terminate the hostilities in Cuba and to secure the establishment of a stable government there, "capable of maintaining order and observing its international obligations." In turn the Cubans refused to accept the proffered armistice. The Spanish council of ministers denounced the President's message as an open interference in the domestic affairs of Spain. Congress authorized intervention by a joint resolution on April 19; the President signed it on the next day; and Spain considered that act as a declaration of war. The United States declared war on April 26, with a retroactive clause to April 21, 1898.[1]

The subsequent military operations will receive no description here. Dewey's victory in Manila Bay, the victory of Sampson and Schley at Santiago, the campaign of Shafter in Cuba, and the impending campaign of Miles in Porto Rico convinced Spain by July 18, 1898, that the time had arrived for negotiating an armistice.[2] Due to telegraphic and other delays the French ambassador in Washington could not present this request on behalf of Spain to the Department of State until July 26. The United States delivered on July 30 the terms not of an armistice but of a preliminary peace. First, Spain should evacuate Cuba and relinquish all sovereignty over the island. Second, the President would not for the time being ask for a pecuniary indemnity. But to compensate for the losses of the United States and to satisfy the claims of Americans the President required the cession to the United States of Porto Rico and the remaining Spanish islands in the West Indies and also one of the Ladrones to be selected by the United States. Third, on similar grounds the United States would occupy and hold "the city, bay, and harbor of Manila

[1] Foreign Relations, 1898: 772.
[2] Spanish Diplomatic Correspondence and Documents, 1896–1900: 200.

pending the conclusion of a treaty of peace which shall determine the control, disposition, and government of the Philippines."[1] The original draft had the word "possession" instead of "disposition." The substitution was made at the request of Ambassador Jules Cambon.

Spain thought the terms severe and made an effort to save her colonies by yielding Cuba alone. The United States replied by embodying the terms in a protocol which Spain might sign or reject. The terms of evacuation of the colonies by Spain were made more exact and more stringent. The protocol specified also that each party should appoint not more than five commissioners to negotiate a peace in Paris. And it stipulated that as soon as the protocol was signed hostilites were to be suspended, and notice to that effect was to be given as soon as possible to the military and naval commanders.[2] This protocol served then as an armistice and a preliminary peace settlement. The act of signing took place on August 12, 1898.

A dispute arose as to when the armistice had gone into effect. Spain contended that it became effective immediately upon signing. The United States maintained that it became so on notification to the commanders. The American command in the Philippines received the notice on August 16. On August 13 Manila had been bombarded and on the next day that city had surrendered. These acts accomplished the end agreed upon in the third article of the protocol, "That the United States will occupy and hold the city, bay, and harbor of Manila pending the conclusion of a treaty . . ." Differences arose also over the meaning of "evacuation" of Cuba; whether it meant military evacuation or civil evacuation as well. Finally, the United States fixed the date arbitrarily for both to take place on December 1, which was extended, on the application of Spain, to January 1, 1899, when the island was delivered to the American officers.

The peace commissioners met in the hall of the ministry of foreign affairs in Paris on October 1, 1899. President McKinley

[1] Foreign Relations, 1898: 821.
[2] Ibid., 1898: 824.

had appointed the Secretary of State, William R. Day; the chairman of the Senate committee on foreign relations, Cushman K. Davis; the ranking Democratic member of that committee, George Gray; another Republican member of the same committee, William P. Frye; and the editor of the New York Tribune, Whitelaw Reid. Premier Sagasta had named Don Eugenio Montero Rios, President of the Senate; Don Buenaventura de Abarzuza, Senator and former Minister of the Colonies; Don José de Garnica, Deputy in the Cortes and Associate Justice of the Supreme Court; Don Wenceslao Ramirez de Villa-Urrutia, Minister to Belgium; and General Rafeal Cerero. The secretaries were Professor John Bassett Moore and Don Emilio de Ojeda.

At this first session the Spanish commissioners presented a demand for a return to the status quo in the Philippines of August 12, the date of the signing of the protocol.[1] The Americans replied at the next session, October 3, that in the demand for the status quo questions of fact and of law were involved which fell outside the scope of the negotiations for a treaty of peace and, consequently, should be settled through diplomatic channels.[2] The Americans then proposed Articles I and II of the treaty. I. "Spain relinquishes all claim of sovereignty over and title to Cuba." II. "Spain cedes to the United States the island of Porto Rico and other islands now under Spanish sovereignty in the West Indies, and the island of Guam in the Marianas or Ladrones."

At the third meeting, in accordance with instructions, the secretaries reported a rule that if a proposition were presented and rejected each side should have the right to file a brief memorandum of reasons for or against the proposition. This was adopted. The significance lay in the fact that if the negotiations should fail, the minutes would show upon which party the cause therefore rested. The Spaniards proceeded to reserve the rights of Spain to take up again the question of the status quo as of August 12 in the Philippines. They agreed to relinquish sovereignty

[1] Treaty of Paris, Protocol: 15.
[2] Ibid., 21.

over Cuba and to transfer it to the United States. But they proposed also to relinquish and to transfer to the United States all the obligations of Cuba incurred in a constitutional manner. This meant charges for the military, civil, and ecclesiastical services in the island, including pensions.[1]

In their reply the Americans stood squarely on the provision of the protocol of August 12, that "Spain will relinquish all claim of sovereignty over and title to Cuba." Spain proposed to yoke with this relinquishment of sovereignty a mass of indebtedness which the United States could not admit. The Spanish commissioners argued firmly that these debts belonged to sovereignty, that all of the South and Central American states had assumed similar obligations when they achieved their independence and that Napoleon had respected this principle. Spain placed her sovereignty over Cuba at the disposition of the United States "in the condition which she now holds it, and therefore, with the rights and charges at present constituting it." [2]

In the succeeding sessions each side failed in its efforts to convince the other. The American commissioners recognized the strength of the Spanish contention and telegraphed home, October 25, whether they might offer the good offices of the United States with the Cuban people to accept such indebtedness as had been incurred for existing public improvements of a pacific character.[3] Secretary Hay replied that no part of the Cuban debt would be assumed and that the United States would not consent to use its good offices with the Cubans for such a purpose.[4] This resulted in a repetition and enlargement of argument. The Spanish commissioners said they dared not return to Spain with an assumption of the Cuban debt unless some compensation were offered in some other point. The American Ambassador in Paris, General Porter, suggested that the United States might be willing to make concessions in the Philippines.[5]

At the next session, October 26, the Spanish commissioners

[1] Treaty of Paris, Protocol: 27.
[2] Ibid., 43.
[3] Foreign Relations, 1898: 931.
[4] Ibid., 1898: 932.
[5] Spanish Dip. Correspondence and Documents, 1896–1900: 299.

agreed to waive tentatively their demands relating to the Cuban debt and asked the Americans for the terms on the Philippines. Not until October 31 did the Americans present these terms. They had cabled to Secretary Hay, who instructed them to claim the entire Philippine archipelago by conquest, but the disposition, control, and government were subjects for negotiation. He was aware of the distressed financial condition of Spain and whatever consideration the United States might show must come from a sense of generosity and benevolence.[1] The Americans asked accordingly for all of the Philippines and expressed a willingness to assume the indebtedness of Spain incurred for public works and improvements of a pacific character.[2] The Spaniards asked for an adjournment in order to examine the proposal.

The Spaniards gave their reply on November 4. They rejected the proposal to cede the Philippines on the ground that it was not within the stipulation of the protocol of August 12, which stated: "The United States shall occupy and hold the city, the bay and the harbor of Manila pending the conclusion of a treaty of peace which shall determine the control, the disposition, and the government of the Philippine Islands." This meant a temporary and provisional occupation of one port in the islands. The protocol contained no suggestion of a cession of the sovereignty over the entire archipelago. The temporary character of this occupation was supported by documents from the French Foreign Office based upon the statements of President McKinley. Furthermore, the United States had made compliance with the protocol unduly harsh by allowing General Merritt to bombard Manila and compel its surrender and he had not yet returned the arms delivered. As a counter proposal the Spaniards stated that in accordance with the protocol the treaty should embody the immediate delivery of Manila to Spain, the release of the garrison, the return to Spain of all funds and public property taken, and the indemnification of Spain for all damages incurred, including those wrought by the

[1] Foreign Relations, 1898: 937.
[2] Treaty of Paris, Protocol: 107.

insurgents who would have been held in check had the garrison been free.[1]

In their reply on November 9 the Americans made clear that they based their claim to the Philippines not on the right to hold Manila but on the fact that the protocol included the Philippines with Porto Rico and one island in the Ladrones in the scope of the indemnity. How could this indemnity be fulfilled if the Spanish government in the islands should remain untouched? The protocol stated also that the "control, disposition and government of the Philippines" should be included in the peace negotiations. Ambassador Porter had gone to the French Foreign Office to ascertain the character of the documents mentioned by the Spanish negotiators. The Minister for Foreign Affairs had stated that the documents referred to contained "simply a brief resumê of the general features of the preliminary peace negotiations," and that the Foreign Office had made no attempt to interpret the protocol. The Americans stated that the United States might limit its demand to a pecuniary indemnity covering the enormous cost of the war, but the demand actually was for Porto Rico, Guam, and the Philippines. And what was Spain asked to give up in the Philippines? A country constantly in rebellion, one which she would have to rule by force of arms.[2] Both parties inserted in the record memorandums of the reasons for the respective positions taken.

The Spaniards refused to yield. So firmly were they convinced of the correctness of their position that they proposed to leave the questions of the Cuban debt and of the temporary American occupation of Manila to arbitration. This move had a tactical advantage as well in that the settlement would be postponed, the popular desire among Americans for peace would become stronger; and Spain could not possibly be the greater loser on either point.[3] Despite the fact that the Americans had been victorious on sea and land, the Spaniards held a certain strategic advantage. If negotiations should be broken off the

[1] Treaty of Paris, Protocol: 109.
[2] Ibid., 128.
[3] Ibid., 195.

war would have to be resumed. Virtually all of the Spanish possessions had been captured. The renewal of war meant the invasion of Spain. Both Wellington and Napoleon had found inherent difficulties in such a venture; and they had fought near their bases. What might such a campaign mean for the United States with a base 3000 miles away? Such a campaign involved the invasion of Europe, a deviation from traditional American policy; it had possibilities of European complications. To American public opinion the object of the war had already been more than realized; consequently popular support for a campaign in Spain might not be forthcoming.

The Americans pointed out that arbitration preceded war, to avoid its horrors; it did not come after the appeal to trial by battle. The Americans presented their final concessions. If Spain would cede the Philippines the United States would pay $20,000,000. They announced that it was "the policy of the United States to maintain in the Philippines an open door to the world's commerce." For a term of years Spanish ships and merchandise would be admitted into Philippine ports on the same terms as those from America. They proposed also a mutual relinquishment of all claims for indemnity, national and individual. They expressed the hope that they might receive from the Spanish commissioners on or before November 28, 1898, "a definite and final acceptance of the proposals." The last clause gave a peremptory character to the proposal, although hardly that of an ultimatum.[1]

On November 28 the Spaniards gave their reply as authorized by their government. They acknowledged that Spain had exhausted all diplomatic arguments in defense of her rights and even of equitable compromise. But their government would not assume the responsibility of reopening the war with all its horrors. Spain accepted, therefore, the terms of the United States.[2]

At the session on November 30, the seventeenth in order, the Americans presented a draft of the treaty. Various minor points

[1] Treaty of Paris, Protocol: 198.
[2] Ibid., 211.

remained in dispute. The Spaniards asked for commercial concessions in Cuba and Porto Rico similar to those obtained in the Philippines. The Americans tempered their refusal with the suggestion that such an arrangement might be made in a separate commercial treaty. The Spaniards asked that each nation should return at its own expense the prisoners it had taken. This was a one-sided proposal, for Spain had taken few prisoners to the peninsula from Cuba or the Philippines, and she held no Americans; while the United States had taken more than 35,000 prisoners. The Americans accepted the proposal with the condition that the prisoners should be returned to the nearest port of their home country. The Spaniards asked for the return of war material in Cuba and Porto Rico. The Americans replied that this subject fell outside their instructions, there being special military commissions for the purpose. The same reply was given to a request for the war material in the Philippines. The Spaniards maintained that the cession of the archipelago included only fixed material and that portable material should be either purchased or returned to Spain. The Americans yielded and defined what portable material should include.[1]

At the conference on December 6 the Americans expressed a desire to take up the revival of former treaties. The Spaniards replied that such an article might be relevant but it was usually the last one in a treaty of peace. The commissioners took up the subject of nationality, contracts for public works, contracts for mail and cable service, and matters pertaining to religion, the "Maine," pension for the Duke of Veragua, consuls, jurisdiction of courts, copyrights and patents, Strong Island in the Carolines, and claims.

Three of these subjects were omitted from the treaty. The Duke of Veragua was held to be a descendant of Christopher Columbus. Spain had paid him a pension of $7,400, chargeable partly on the treasury of Porto Rico and partly on that of Manila. The Americans rejected the request that the United States should pay this pension in the future.[2] The Spaniards brought

[1] Treaty of Paris, Protocol: 227.
[2] Ibid., 244.

up the subject of the "Maine." They pleaded earnestly that the investigation of the disaster be turned over to an international commission of experts to determine whether Spain had been responsible even were it through negligence. And they referred to President McKinley's characterization of the disaster as "suspicious" in his annual message of December 5, 1898. They wanted a decision which would quiet the passions of the two peoples on the point. The Americans declined to enter upon a discussion "in obedience to well established precedents and practice in the history of their country." [1] The Americans offered one million dollars for Strong Island in the Carolines. The Spaniards replied that the subject fell outside the scope of the treaty and that Spain had no intention of disposing of one of the Carolines.[2] As a matter of fact Spain sold the entire group two months later to Germany for about five million dollars. Nothing was said about the revival of treaties existing before the war. And by the Commercial Treaty of 1902, Article XXIX, all treaties prior to the Treaty of Paris were expressly annulled except the Treaty of 1834 for the settlement of claims between the two countries.[3]

By Article I of the treaty, Spain relinquished all claims of sovereignty over Cuba. The United States assumed all obligations for the protection of life and property during its military occupation of the island so far as could be proved under international law.

By Article II Spain ceded Porto Rico and her other islands in the West Indies and the island of Guam in the Ladrones or Marianas to the United States.

By Article III Spain ceded the Philippine archipelago for which the United States agreed to pay $20,000,000. The boundaries by degrees latitude and longitude were drawn. It so happened that the Sulu Islands lay outside these lines. These had been under the recognized jurisdiction of Spain and the United States took possession of them. Spain protested; but on Novem-

[1] Treaty of Paris, Protocol: 262.
[2] Ibid., 252.
[3] Malloy, *Treaties*, II.: 1710.

ber 7, 1900, Spain agreed to accept as compensation for her claim $100,000.[1]

By Article IV the United States agreed to admit for a term of ten years from the exchange of ratifications Spanish ships and merchandise. Nothing was said about the policy of the "open door" in the text of the treaty, but the policy was expressly mentioned in the protocol.[2] The concession to Spanish ships and merchandise was observed. But the open door in the Philippines constituted a reversal of American commercial policy, which had as its fundamental concept that the domestic market should be hedged in by protective tariffs and exclusive navigation laws. Could it be that McKinley and John Hay conceived of the Philippines as a part of the Far East and apprehended that the United States had more to lose than to gain by mercantile barriers? Whatever may have been their view the United States closed the open door by a statute, approved April 30, 1906, which was to become effective April 11, 1909. That statute restricted all trade between the United States and the islands to American vessels.[3] And by the Philippine tariff act of 1909 Congress exempted from import and export duties American and Philippine products passing between the two regions by direct shipment.[4]

By Article V the United States agreed to send back to Spain the soldiers taken as prisoners of war during the capture of Manila and to restore the arms to the soldiers. Spain agreed to evacuate the Philippines and Guam at a time to be later determined. Guns of all kinds including field artillery, military supplies, and uncaptured war vessels were to remain the property of Spain. Heavy ordnance and coast defenses should remain in place for six months, and the United States might buy them if a satisfactory agreement could be reached.

Article VI provided for a reciprocal release of prisoners of war and transportation of them at the captor's expense to their respective home ports.

[1] Malloy, *Treaties*, II.: 1696.
[2] Treaty of Paris, Protocol: 218.
[3] Statutes at Large, 34, pt. 1.: 154.
[4] Ibid., 36, pt. 1: 173, 174.

Article VII provided for the mutual relinquishment of all claims for indemnity, national and individual. The following clause was inserted by the American commissioners, "The United States will adjudicate and settle the claims of its citizens against Spain relinquished in this article." This might be considered domestic legislation, for it concerned the United States and its citizens alone. Nevertheless, it was wise to insert this provision in the supreme law of the land, for it gave the claimants something to which they could point definitely in urging Congress to act. A similar provision in the Convention of 1800 with France would have made more smooth the path of the spoliation claims. As it was Congress took two years in which to act. The statute of March 2, 1901, authorized a treaty claims commission of five members. This commission drew up a set of eleven stringent rules and in accordance therewith claims of American citizens to the extent of $60,000,000 were adjudicated.[1]

Article VIII provided that in the ceded territories Spain should relinquish her title to all immovable property in the public domain, such as buildings, wharves, public highways. But this relinquishment could in no way affect the property rights of provinces, municipalities, ecclesiastical or civil bodies, or of private individuals.

Three interesting cases arose in the Philippines under this article. During the revolutions of 1896 and 1898, the Dominicans, Augustinians, Recolletos, and Franciscans, commonly called the friars, had been driven from their parishes. Some had been killed, others had gone to China or returned to Spain, and a remnant had taken refuge in Manila. Out of 1,124 in 1896 only 472 remained when the Americans took possession. These friars had Christianized the Filipinos. And Spain found it expedient to place a large share of the civil administration in their hands. No recruits were taken from the natives. The friars were exempt, except for heinous crimes, from trial in the civil courts. They had immense sums of money to lend. They owned one-third of the realty within Manila and over 400,000

[1] Sen. Doc. 25, 25th Cong., 2nd Session.

acres of the most fertile agricultural land in the islands. Their tenants had to pay exactions of rents and dues more onerous than those of feudal days. Taft saw, in his investigations, that it was these exactions that made the friars hated, that the opposition to them was political and not religious. With the authority of Congress and the aid of the Papacy he was able to purchase the lands and to provide for their sale on long term and easy payments.[1] This action removed a cause of friction and enabled the friars to resume more effectively their functions as spiritual guides of the people.

The Manila Railway Company was a British corporation which had constructed a line to Dagupan. Spain had guaranteed in the franchise a return of 8 percent. on the investment and she made the payments regularly. After the Treaty of Paris this company presented its claim for the guaranteed amount to the United States on the ground that the obligation had been transferred with the sovereignty. The matter was referred to the Attorney General who ruled that the United States would observe the franchise rights of the company, but the contract made by Spain was partly for her own benefit and as such could not become obligatory upon the new sovereignty.[2] The company received afterwards an equitable compensation through congressional action.

The Eastern Extension Australasia and China Telegraph Company was another British corporation which owned the cable between Manila and Hong Kong. Spain had agreed to guarantee a fixed rate in return for exclusive rights to be accorded her. Early in his occupation of Manila Bay Dewey had ordered the cable cut. The British ambassador, Sir Julian Pauncefote, brought a representation in behalf of the company for the subsidy and for the cost of splicing the cable. The matter was referred to the Attorney General who could give no opinion because he did not have the terms of the contract. Later, Charles E. Magoon, the law officer for the bureau of insular affairs, found that this company was making more than the

[1] Reports of the Phillippine Commission, 1900–1903: 39, 466.
[2] 23 Op. 181.

percentage stipulated and that if the United States were substituted for Spain in the contract the company would by its terms have to make a considerable refund. He advised that the question of subsidy be treated as though the company had made an original application for the construction of a quasi public improvement.[1]

In Cuba at least two cases arose under Article VIII. Another British corporation, the Cuba Submarine Telegraph Company, presented a request through the British government that the United States protect it and assume the obligations of Spain. The Attorney General refused to allow the claim on the ground that the United States was not the successor of Spain in Cuba, but was merely arranging for the succession of the government of Cuba.[2] So strictly did the United States construe its temporary occupation that it refused to grant any title to property, any franchises or concessions of any kind.[3]

The Countess of Buena Vista and Don Gustava Duplessis brought a joint claim for the emoluments of the office of sheriff of Havana. This office had been hereditary in the family of the countess since 1728, when it had been bought at public auction. In order to raise money to satisfy a debt she sold in 1895 a one half interest in the office to Duplessis. On August 8, 1900, the claimants petitioned the Secretary of War for relief, pleading that they had been deprived of their property in contravention of Article VIII of the Treaty of Paris. Magoon wrote the opinion which Secretary Root approved and which the Supreme Court sustained.[4] The claim for indemnity rested upon the terms of the contract with Spain; and the contract was a personal contract of the Spanish state. The obligations did not pass with the transfer of sovereignty and the United States refused to assume them. Whether or not the municipality of Havana became liable was a subject which the Cuban courts might properly determine.[5]

[1] Magoon's Reports, 529; Moore, *Digest of Int. Law*, I: 408.
[2] 22 Op. 384.
[3] See Foraker Resolution in Army Appropriation Act of March 3, 1899.
[4] 209 U. S. 45. For an opposing view see Percy Bordwell's article in Am. Journal of Int. Law, II.: 119.
[5] Magoon's Reports, 194.

In Porto Rico Señor Guillermo Alvarez y Sanches presented a claim for $30,000 for having been deprived of his office of notary, which he had purchased in 1896. General Brooke had offered to renew the appointment if Guillermo would take the oath of allegiance. This he refused to do, preferring to base his claim on a property right. Magoon decided against him on the ground that the office had been cancelled as a military measure and therefore came under the mutual relinquishment of damages in Article VII.[1] This decision was upheld by the Court of Claims.[2]

By Article IX Spanish subjects who had been born in the peninsula were given one year in which to make a declaration that they reserved their Spanish allegiance; otherwise they would be held to have renounced it and to have adopted the nationality of the territory. The rights of Spanish subjects would be the same as those of other foreigners. The civil rights and political status of the natives should be determined by Congress.

Article X provided for the free exercise of religion in the ceded territories.

Under Article XI Spanish subjects residing in the ceded territories should be subject to the jurisdiction of the local courts and have the right to appear before those courts.

Article XII provided that in judicial proceedings pending at the time of the exchange of ratifications in the ceded territories the judgment should in civil and criminal cases be executed by the competent authority. There should be no appeal if it were not permitted by Spanish law. Criminal actions against citizens in the ceded territories pending in the supreme court of Spain should be disposed of by the court and the judgment should be executed by the competent authority of the place in which the case arose.

Under Article XIII the rights of property secured by copyrights and patents by Spaniards in the ceded territories should continue to be respected. Spanish scientific, literary, and artis-

[1] Magoon's Reports, 454.
[2] 42 Court of Claims, 458.

tic works should be admitted free of duty to the ceded territories for ten years, unless they were subversive of public order.

Article XIV authorized Spain to establish consular officers in the ceded territories.

By Article XV each party agreed to accord to the merchant vessels of the other party the same treatment that it accorded its own merchant vessels, except those engaged in the coast-wise trade.

The United States agreed by Article XVI to recommend to the future government of Cuba to accept for itself the obligations assumed by the United States for Cuba in the treaty.

The final article provided that the ratifications should be exchanged at Washington within six months.[1]

The treaty was signed at Paris on December 10, 1898. The President ratified the treaty on the same day. The ratifications were exchanged on April 11, 1899; and the treaty was proclaimed on the same day.

A voluminous debate took place in the Senate and in the House on the question of imperialism, on whether the Philippines should be incorporated in the American domain or set free as had been provided in the Platt amendment for Cuba. A faction in the Philippines aided materially in settling this question by carrying on an insurrection. On March 2, 1899, Congress voted the $20,000,000 to be paid to Spain; and on May 1 the payment was made. On June 3 the Duke de Arcos was received in Washington as the minister of Spain.

The United States took formal possession of Cuba on January 1, 1899. The Cuban army was disbanded during the following months, the soldiers receiving $2,600,000 from the United States. Delegates to a constitutional convention were elected on September 15, 1900. Except for the definition of the relations with the United States the convention completed its labors and adopted the constitution on February 21, 1901. The Platt amendment to the army appropriation bill became law on March 2, 1901. General Wood communicated the terms of the amendment to the Cuban convention. The members felt that the terms impaired

[1] Malloy, *Treaties*, etc., II.: 1690.

the sovereignty and independence of Cuba. The convention authorized a committee to confer with President McKinley. He explained that he could not change a law. The committee returned, made its report, and the convention adopted the Platt amendment with reservations. These proved to be unsatisfactory to the United States. So on June 12, 1901, the convention ratified the Platt amendment verbatim as a part of the constitution by a vote of sixteen to eleven.

This amendment contained eight articles. 1. Cuba would never make a treaty with any foreign power that might impair her independence. 2. No debt would be contracted that could not be met by the ordinary revenues of the island. 3. The United States might intervene for the preservation of Cuban independence and the maintenance of a government adequate for the protection of life, liberty, and property, and for discharging its obligations under the Treaty of Paris. It was under this article that the United States intervened in September, 1906. 4. All acts of the United States in Cuba during the military occupation were validated. 5. Cuba would carry out the plans of sanitation for the cities of the island. 6. The Isles of Pines should be left to future adjustment by treaty. Such a treaty was negotiated in 1902, giving the Isle of Pines to Cuba; but the American Senate refused to ratify it. The Supreme Court decided in Pearey v. Stranahan, April, 1907, that this island was not American territory and that the customs duties imposed by Cuba must be paid. 7. To enable the United States to maintain the independence of Cuba, to protect the Cuban people, and to provide for its own defense Cuba would sell or lease to the United States land necessary for coaling and naval stations at points to be agreed upon. Two stations were agreed upon, Guantanamo and Bahia Honda; but the latter was receded, 1911, in exchange for an enlargement of Guantanamo. 8. Cuba would embody the foregoing provisions in a treaty with the United States. Cuba did so in 1903.[1] On May 20, 1902, the constitution was promulgated and the Americans transferred the government of the island to the Cuban authorities.

[1] Malloy, *Treaties*, I.: 362.

BIBLIOGRAPHY

Benton, E. J.—*International Law and Diplomacy of the Spanish American War.* Baltimore, 1908.
Chadwick, F. E.—*The Relations of the United States and Spain, Diplomacy.* New York, 1909.
Foreign Relations.—1898. Washington, 1901.
Latane, John Holladay.—*America as a World Power,* 1897–1907. New York, 1907.
Moore, J. B.—*The Treaty of Peace, a Chapter in the American Spanish War.* Published by Charles C. Haskell & Son. Norwich, Conn., 1899.
Reid, Whitelaw.—*Problems of Expansion.* New York, 1900.
Spanish Diplomatic Correspondence and Documents, 1896–1900. Translation. Washington, 1905.
Treaty of Paris, 1898. *President's Message and Papers,* Washington, 1899.

CHAPTER XV

THE PANAMA CANAL TREATIES

"Appearances to the mind are of four kinds. Things either are what they appear to be; or they neither are nor appear to be; or they are and do not appear to be; or they are not, and yet appear to be. Rightly to aim in all these cases is the wise man's task."—EPICTETUS.

Since the time of Balboa the need for a canal across the isthmus of Panama has been apparent. Cortez emphasized this necessity in his letters to Charles V. That monarch revealed considerable interest and ordered an exploration of the Chagres River at Colon. The opening of the silver mines of Peru made the building of a road between Panama on the Pacific and Nombre de Dios on the Atlantic imperative. This trade route became the richest in the world. Gold, silver, pearls, and ornaments from the region of the Incas; wool, indigo, dyewoods, mahogany, cocoa, and tobacco from various sections of Spanish-America crossed this route. The law required the products of present Argentina to be carried westward through the mountain passes to the Pacific, thence north to Panama, across the isthmus where they were loaded on vessels for Cadiz. Even cargoes of Philippine products reached Spain by way of Panama.

Gradually the King of Spain granted numerous exclusive franchises, with the result that all along the route the products paid toll to those who held exclusive privileges from the crown. In the reign of Philip II some persons asked permission to explore the river Atrato, which might, they thought, connect the Gulf of Darien with the Pacific. So encrusted with vested privileges had the Panama route become that Philip II forbade under penalty of death all attempts to go up that river.

In 1550 the Portuguese navigator Antonio Galvao published a book demonstrating the feasibility of cutting a canal at either Tehuantepac, Nicaragua, Panama, or Darien. In the following year the Spanish historian F. L. de Gomara made a futile appeal for action to Philip II. In 1695 William Patterson organized the Darien Company which ended in disaster three years later. By 1771 the Spanish government had changed its policy and ordered surveys, but internal disturbances prevented action. Alexander von Humboldt examined the isthmus in 1808 and pronounced in favor of the Nicaragua route. The successful revolt of the Spanish American colonies and the consequent opening of their ports to the trade of the world increased the interest in a canal. A Dutch corporation under the patronage of the King of the Netherlands obtained a concession, 1830, to build a canal in Nicaragua. But a strongly worded protest on the basis of the Monroe Doctrine from President Jackson and the revolution in Belgium prevented the execution of the plan.

An international congress met in Panama, 1826. The American delegate arrived too late; but he carried significant instructions from Henry Clay, the Secretary of State. Should the canal be cut, "the benefits of it should not," wrote Clay, "be exclusively appropriated to any one nation, but should be extended to all parts of the globe upon the payment of just compensation or reasonable tolls.[1] DeWitt Clinton played with the idea of a canal but accomplished nothing. The United States Senate passed a resolution, 1835, in favor of constructing a canal at Nicaragua. President Jackson sent Charles Biddle to negotiate a treaty. But Biddle decided in favor of the Panama route and negotiated accordingly, with the result that his work was repudiated.

Then followed the colonization of Texas, Oregon, and California. The settlement of the Oregon boundary in 1846 gave the United States a Pacific coast line. The annexation of Texas, the war with Mexico, the acquisition of California, and the discovery of gold made a Panama route necessary. In 1848 Aspinwall, Stephens, and others obtained from the government of New Granada the right of way for a railroad at Panama. This famous road was opened to traffic in 1855. In August, 1849, Cornelius Vanderbilt, Joseph L. White, and others organized The American Atlantic and Pacific Ship Canal Company and

[1] Moore, *Digest of International Law,* III.: 2.

obtained a concession from Nicaragua. The company sent Colonel Childs to make a survey, which he performed with accuracy.

It is from this period that the diplomatic negotiations begin. The negotiations divide themselves into three parts. Those with Great Britain have the Clayton-Bulwer and the Hay-Pauncefote Treaties as centers; those with Colombia have the Treaty of 1846 and the proposed Hay-Herran Treaty; and those with Panama have the Hay-Bunau-Varilla Treaty as a center. These centers will be described in their proper order.

Why did the United States enter into the Clayton-Bulwer Treaty? Because by 1849 Great Britain controlled the entire Atlantic seaboard of Central America and Tigre Island in the Gulf of Fonseca on the Pacific side. The acquisition of this control had been gradual. In 1838 the Central American Republic had broken up into four states. A London bank had loaned considerable money on the defunct republic's bonds. The British consul general, Frederick Chatfield, apportioned arbitrarily the debt and proceeded to enforce payment. He allowed Salvador twenty-four hours. Salvador rejected the terms; and Chatfield ordered a blockade of her coast. Neither could Honduras comply; so he ordered the occupation of the Atlantic ports of Omoa and Truxillo on Honduras Bay and on the Pacific side he ordered the seizure of Tigre Island which commanded the Gulf of Fonseca and the western terminus of the proposed canal.[1] In Costa Rica the party in power agreed that the state should become a British protectorate. Whereupon, Costa Rica revived an obsolete claim to the part of Nicaragua lying south of the San Juan River. At the same time Chatfield ordered the seizure of San Juan or Greytown in Nicaragua. Chatfield had previously espoused the cause of the King of the Mosquito Indians and agreed that he should be protected in his territory from the Rome River on the north to the San Juan River on the south with Bluefields as the British commercial center. In Belize, or British Honduras, the English woodcutters had received protection from their government for more

[1] Sen. Ex. Doc., 43, 32 Cong., 2nd Sess., 5, 46.

than a century, although a colonial government was not established there until 1862.

President Polk appointed, 1848, the first American diplomatic agent to the Central American states, Elijah Hise. He received instructions to collect information on the British encroachments, to refrain from acquiescing in their pretensions, and to negotiate treaties of amity and commerce with those states that could be regarded as independent.[1] He soon became convinced that the British had in mind obtaining control over all the possible canal routes. Mindful that Trist's instructions to obtain a canal route had been frustrated in the Treaty of Guadalupe Hidalgo, Hise proceeded to negotiate for a canal concession across Nicaragua and included a guarantee of Nicaraguan independence.[2] But President Taylor's administration represented a reaction to the aggressive expansionist policies of Polk. E. G. Squier received the appointment to replace Hise; and the Hise treaty was never submitted to the Senate.

Secretary Clayton instructed Squier to negotiate a new treaty with Nicaragua which should assure equal right of transit for the commerce of all nations through the canal. He was "not to involve the country in any entangling alliances, or any unnecessary controversy." The United States could not permit another nation to possess a monopoly of such a canal. However, Nicaragua should be left free to enter into treaty relations with other powers and foreign capital might be used in financing the project. The instructions mentioned that an American company had been formed to dig the canal. Squier could render it friendly assistance but he was not to implicate the government in any scheme of speculation.[3]

Squier obtained for Vanderbilt's company, August, 1849, the right to construct a canal from any point on the Gulf coast to any point on the Pacific and the exclusive right to navigate by steam all Nicaraguan lakes and rivers.[4] Squier inserted in the treaty that the United States would guarantee the neutrality of

[1] House Ex Doc. 75, 31 Cong., 1 Sess., 92.
[2] Ibid., 110.
[3] Ibid., 117.
[4] Ibid., 173.

the canal and the independence of Nicaragua.[1] At every step Squier met British intrigue and thought he met more than there actually was.

Squier hurried into Honduras and signed a treaty, September 28, 1849. Honduras agreed to cede Tigre Island to the United States for eighteen months and parts of the shore of the Gulf of Fonseca for a naval station and fortifications.[2] On October 16, a British squadron appeared in defense of Tigre Island. Squier notified Chatfield that the British were occupying soil belonging to the Unitd States and requested them to leave.[3] Chatfield refused. Squier gave Chatfield six days in which to evacuate Tigre Island or the United States would consider the occupation an unfriendly and violent aggression. The British admiral yielded possession in December, 1849; and the island remained under the American flag until after the conclusion of the Clayton-Bulwer Treaty when it was restored to Honduras.[4]

Squier had brought the Whig administration into a dilemma. The Whigs could not support the Squier treaties nor his action toward the British, for they did not want war with Great Britain. Neither could they repudiate Squier, for they might incur the charge of yielding unduly to British bullying.

Secretary Clayton approached the problem open-mindedly. He directed the American minister in London, George Bancroft, to ascertain upon what grounds Great Britain held Greytown and maintained the Mosquito Protectorate. If the Foreign Office revealed a desire to substantiate the British claims he should point out the inexpediency of British control over the San Juan River as a possible interoceanic highway. He could assure the Foreign Office that the United States did not aspire to such an exclusive control of a canal for itself; nor would it approve of such a claim by any other power.[5] Lord Palmerston replied that Great Britain had no intention of occupying or colonizing Central America. The occupation of Greytown was temporary.

[1] British Blue Book on Central American Affairs, 1856, 18.
[2] Sen. Ex. Doc. 75, 31 Cong., 2 Sess., 10.
[3] Ibid., 16.
[4] Sen. Ex. Doc. 43, 31 Cong., 2 Sess., 76.
[5] House Ex. Doc., 75, 31 Cong., 1 Sess., 230.

He indicated that the British were opposed to turning the port over to Nicaragua and he would mention no time of withdrawal.[1] Bancroft was soon afterward recalled.

Clayton instructed the newly appointed minister to France, W. C. Rives, to stop at London and interview Palmerston on the canal and Mosquito questions. Rives did so. Palmerston held the opinion that Nicaragua had gone beyond her power in granting a concession to the Vanderbilt company. He denied that Greytown had been occupied for the purpose of controlling a canal. And he expressed a willingness on the part of Great Britain to join the United States in opening a canal by way of the San Juan River. The Mosquito Indians should be recognized as an independent nation.[2]

On reading Rives' report Clayton concluded to enlist the coöperation of Great Britain in building a canal open on equal terms to the commerce of all nations and, at the same time, to check British jurisdiction in Central America as much as possible. He communicated to Crampton, the British minister, his readiness to negotiate a treaty. Palmerston appointed as special envoy for the purpose one of the most astute and ingratiating of British diplomats, Sir Henry Lytton Bulwer. He had achieved fame with Lord Byron in Greece. He had served with distinction as a diplomat in Brussels, Paris, Constantinople, and Madrid. Palmerston had pronounced his Treaty of 1838 with the Porte a masterpiece.

Bulwer knew how to arouse the latent forces in Washington in favor of his mission. The popular demand for a treaty on a canal grew daily more urgent. Clayton held confidential the Hise and Squier drafts of treaties; but he did not know how soon members of Congress might obtain information of them through other channels. Indeed, the Senate had already asked the President for the correspondence relating to the proposed canal. Rather than deliver the Hise and Squier drafts Clayton became eager to submit an agreement with Great Britain. Aided by these two pressures upon the Secretary of State, Bulwer forced

[1] House Ex. Doc., 75, 31 Cong., 1 Sess., 235.
[2] Sen. Ex. Doc., 27, 23 Cong., 2 Sess., 20.

the canal question to the front, and within a month he had the project of a treaty agreed upon.[1] He had carefully excluded all points that might pertain to British influence in British Honduras or the Mosquito region.

Clayton's colleagues in the cabinet expressed apprehension on the omission of the Mosquito question and a fear that Great Britain might thereby dominate the canal. Moreover, the news of the seizure of Tigre Island by the British reached Congress and inflamed public opinion to such an extent that delay became necessary. Bulwer asked Palmerston to disavow the seizure or take the risk of having Squier's treaty with Honduras submitted to the Senate, which might mean war. Palmerston's qualified disavowal reached Washington only by March, 1850. By that time Clayton had submitted the Squier treaty to the Senate. The Democrats clamored for the correspondence. Clayton held back. Meanwhile, he obtained Bulwer's consent to two important changes in the project. First, in Article I both parties agreed to refrain from using any alliance, connection, or influence that either might possess with any state or government through whose territory the canal might pass for the purpose of obtaining any exclusive rights or advantages. Second, in Article VIII the treaty was made to apply to all possible isthmian routes. Clayton and Bulwer signed the treaty on April 19, 1850. The Senate advised ratification by a vote of forty-two to eleven on May 22, 1850.

The treaty had nine articles. Both parties declared that neither would obtain for itself any exclusive control over the proposed canal. In case of war between the United States and Great Britain neither would resort to a blockade of the canal or detain or capture each other's vessels in the canal. Both parties agreed to join their efforts in maintaining the neutrality and protection of the canal. The canal should be open to the commerce of all nations on equal terms. In order to conserve time they determined to give their support to such persons as might first offer to commence operations with adequate capital and the consent of the local authorities. The treaty

[1] British Blue Book on Central American Affairs, 1856, 38.

applied to all communications whether by canal or railway across any part of the isthmus. Ratifications were to be exchanged in Washington within six months.[1] They were exchanged on July 4, 1850. On the next day President Taylor proclaimed the treaty.

Too much was expected of this agreement. The turbulent conditions in Central America convinced the Foreign Office that Great Britain should continue in possession of Greytown, in the protection of the Mosquito Indians, and in the support of Costa Rica. Webster succeeded Clayton as Secretary of State and asked that Great Britain should turn Greytown over to Nicaragua. An American vessel, the "Prometheus," refused to pay the port dues at Greytown. The British fired upon her and compelled her to do so. A large number of American adventurers collected in that port for transportation across the isthmus on their way to the California gold fields. These rebelled against all restraint, especially British rule. Accordingly, Great Britain and the United States looked with suspicion at the attitude and acts of each other; and both used the treaty as a basis for accusing the other of bad faith. Coöperation in promoting an isthmian canal became impossible.

In Washington a movement got under way in favor of abrogating the treaty. This might have been accomplished. But Clayton, then a senator, defended the treaty. "The abrogation of the treaty restores," said Clayton, "the British protectorate with renewed vigor; and, unless immediately after it shall be annulled we shall be prepared to attack her in Central America, she will reassert her title so effectually that in one year the whole isthmus will be under her influence." [2]

Secretaries Marcy and Cass adopted Clayton's view. As a result Great Britain agreed to negotiate treaties with the Central American states in compliance with the American construction of the Clayton-Bulwer Treaty. In the treaty with Guatamala, 1859, the boundaries of British Honduras were determined.[3]

[1] Malloy, *Treaties*, I.: 659.
[2] Congressional Globe, 1855–56, appendix, 441.
[3] Sen. Ex. Doc., 194, 47 Cong., 1 Sess., 251.

In the treaty with Honduras, the same year, that state received the Bay Islands and its share of the Mosquito protectorate.[1] With Nicaragua Great Britain agreed to withdraw her protectorate from the Mosquito Indians and to yield all claims to Greytown with the understanding that it should be a free port.[2] After these treaties had been communicated to the Department of State President Buchanan announced in his message, December, 1860, that the negotiations had resulted "in a final settlement entirely satisfactory to this government."

The Civil War did not promote mutual confidence between the United States and Great Britain. Nor did Louis Napoleon's plans for an empire in Mexico encourage the United States to invite other powers to accede to the Clayton-Bulwer Treaty. In his special message to Congress, March 8, 1880, President Hayes gave concise expression to American opinion on a canal: "An interoceanic canal across the American Isthmus will essentially change the geographical relations between the Atlantic and Pacific coasts of the United States and between the United States and the rest of the world. It will be the great ocean thoroughfare between our Atlantic and our Pacific shores, and virtually a part of the coast line of the United States. . . . . . The policy of this country is an American canal under American control."

Hayes' Secretary of State, James G. Blaine, sought to apply the principle of rebus sic stantibus to the Clayton-Bulwer Treaty. Said Blaine in an instruction to James Russell Lowell, November 19, 1881: "This convention was made more than thirty years ago under exceptional and extraordinary conditions which have long since ceased to exist,—conditions which at best were temporary in their nature, and which can never be reproduced." The remarkable development of the United States on the Pacific coast had brought new responsibilities. Furthermore, France had become a sponsor for and patron of a canal at Panama. Blaine requested Lowell, therefore, to present for the consideration of the Foreign Office that the prohibition on the United States to

[1] Sen. Ex. Doc., 194, 47 Cong., 1 Sess., 308.
[2] Ibid., 151, 315.

fortify the canal should be cancelled and that the United States should be free to acquire naval bases on the isthmus.[1] Lord Granville replied that the British government relied with confidence upon the execution of all the engagements entered into in the Clayton-Bulwer Treaty.[2]

Frelinghuysen succeeded Blaine as Secretary of State in December, 1882. He contended that the primary objects of the Treaty of 1850 were the construction of a canal and the release by Great Britain of her settlements in Central America. Neither had been accomplished, due to the attitude of Great Britain. Hence, he held the treaty to be voidable at the pleasure of the United States. The Foreign Office denied stoutly this proposition. The real reason for the attitude of the United States was that American sentiment in favor of a canal under exclusively American control had become insistent.

The events of 1898 reinforced this conviction. The voyage of the "Oregon" from San Francisco around the Horn to join the Atlantic fleet covered 13,400 miles; whereas the voyage would have covered only 4,600 miles through the canal. The acquisition of the Philippines and the absorption of the republic of Hawaii led President McKinley to urge action in his annual message for 1898. The Senate adopted a resolution requesting McKinley to obtain a modification or the abrogation of the Clayton-Bulwer Treaty. Fortunately, John Hay occupied the position of Secretary of State. He promptly and quietly negotiated with Lord Pauncefote a treaty providing for the construction, operation, and regulation of a canal by the United States alone. But the principles of neutralization in the treaty of 1850 still held. There could be neither fortifications nor a blockade. The President sent this treaty to the Senate, February 5, 1900.

The Senate proceeded to amend the treaty by providing for the cancellation of the Clayton-Bulwer Treaty, by giving the United States the right to defend the canal, and by refusing to

[1] Foreign Relations, 1881, 554.
[2] Ibid., 563.

permit other powers to adhere to the convention.[1] The Foreign Office did not approve of this method of negotiating a treaty and therefore rejected it. However, Lord Lansdowne suggested the negotiation of a new treaty, which Hay and Pauncefote completed November 18, 1901.

The first article abrogated the Clayton-Bulwer Treaty. The second gave the United States the complete right to construct and, subject to the treaty, to regulate and operate the canal. The third article contained substantially the rules of neutralization and free navigation of the Suez Canal, copied from the Treaty of October 28, 1888. There were six of these rules. The first rule stated: "The canal shall be free and open to the vessels of commerce and of war of all nations observing these rules, on terms of entire equality, so that there shall be no discrimination against any such nation, or its citizens or subjects, in respect of the conditions or charges of traffic or otherwise. Such conditions and charges of traffic shall be just and equitable."

In legislating on the subject of tolls Congress assumed that "all nations" meant all except the United States and enacted a law, 1912, granting exemption from tolls to American vessels engaged in the coastwise trade. The British government feared further discriminating legislation and asked that the coastwise vessels be included in the computation of a reasonable rate. The Foreign Office conceded that the United States might remit or refund the amount of the tolls on coastwise vessels as a subsidy. On March 5, 1914, President Wilson urged Congress to repeal the exemption granted to coastwise vessels. Congress did so, June 15, 1914.

The second rule stipulated that the canal should neither be blockaded nor any act of war or hostility be committed within it. The United States should be at "liberty to maintain such military police along the canal as may be necessary to protect it against lawlessness and disorder." The treaty contained no statement giving the United States the right to fortify the canal. Great Britain could give no such right. Nor was there any statement forbidding fortification. The canal has been fortified. The

[1] Sen. Doc. 456, 63 Cong., 2 Sess., 9.

right to do so is based on Lord Lansdowne's note[1] of August 3, 1901, expressing acquiescence, and on Articles III and XXIII of the Hay-Bunau-Varilla Treaty. Panama granted thereby to the United States the same right as "if it were the sovereign of the territory. . . and grants expressly the right to establish fortifications for the safety or protection of the canal." [2]

The third rule regulated in general terms the passage through the canal of vessels of war and prizes. The fourth specified that barring accidental hindrance to transit no belligerent could there embark or disembark troops or munitions of war. The fifth rule applied all of the six rules to the marine league at either end of the canal and specified that no belligerent vessel should remain in those waters more than twenty-four hours at one time, except when in distress, and that twenty-four hours should elapse between the departure of war vessels of opposing belligerents. According to the sixth rule the canal, the buildings, and the machinery necessary for operation should in time of war be immune from attack or injury by belligerents.

By Article IV the parties agreed that no change of territorial sovereignty should affect the principles of neutralization of the obligations of the contracting parties. The last article provided for an exchange of ratifications within six months.[3]

The Senate advised ratification by a vote of 72 to 6 on December 16, 1901. The President ratified on December 26; the ratifications were exchanged on February 21; and President Roosevelt proclaimed the treaty on Washington's birthday, 1902. The more than half century of sparring between the United States and Great Britain over Central American and isthmian canal affairs ended in triumph for American diplomacy.

The United States had before it the task of deciding upon a route and of obtaining the right of way. Americans favored generally the Nicaragua route. That route had received the approval of Alexander von Humboldt, of the King of the Nether-

[1] Sen. Doc. 456, 63 Cong., 2 Sess., 52.
[2] See Am. Journal of Int. Law, V.: 298 (R. Olney), 615 (E. Wambaugh), and 620 (C. Kennedy).
[3] Malloy, *Treaties*, I.: 782.

lands in 1828, of Louis Napoleon while a prisoner at Ham, of Colonel Childs in his accurate survey of 1850, and of a group of New York business men headed by Commodore Vanderbilt. The Vanderbilt company operated a line of steamers on the San Juan River and Lake Nicaragua together with a stage coach line on to the Pacific for the benefit of the California gold seekers. In 1872 President Grant sent an able commission to make surveys of the various isthmian routes. The report favored Nicaragua. A group of New York business men obtained from Nicaragua the exclusive right to build a canal, April 24, 1887.[1] Warner Miller became president of the construction company which spent during three years more than $5,000,000 in dredging the harbor of Greytown and in building two miles of a canal. The stringency leading up to the panic of 1893 compelled this company as well as the French company at Panama to go into the hands of a receiver. Senators Sherman and Morgan favored governmental aid at Nicaragua, but Congress did not act. In 1898 the Grace-Eyre-Cragin syndicate was formed with such men as W. R. Grace, J. A. McCall, Warner Miller, J. J. Astor, George Westinghouse, D. O. Mills, Levi P. Morton, and G. T. Bliss as directors. These movements and men kept interest alive in the Nicaragua route.

The Treaty of 1846 with New Granada had for an object a canal as well as a railway by the Panama route. The Clayton-Bulwer Treaty included Panama as one of the possible routes. Lucien N. P. Wyse obtained a charter from Colombia for a canal company and he induced Ferdinand de Lesseps, the builder of the Suez canal, to serve as president. Between 1881 and 1889 the French company spent $260,000,000 without having half completed the project. Rumors of scandal compelled a parliamentary investigation which uncovered sufficient fraud and corruption so that the company could raise no more money and went into bankruptcy. Several interested Frenchmen organized the New Panama Canal Company to keep alive the franchises of the old company, to take over the administration of the Panama Railroad, and to salvage the equipment. With the

[1] Senate Report No. 1, 57 Cong., 1 Sess., 479.

revival of American interest in a canal during the Spanish American war this company became anxious to sell its rights to the United States.

Congress created in 1899 the isthmian canal commission with Admiral Walker as chairman to examine all practicable routes. For physical reasons the report favored the Panama route with a lock canal. But Colombia had granted an exclusive concession to the French company which held at least until 1904. Colombia was therefore not free to grant the necessary rights to the United States, except upon condition that an agreement be reached with the New Panama Canal Company. That company had refused to sell its franchise but would allow the United States to become an owner of a part of its stock. The commission considered such an agreement impracticable.

The Nicaragua route would require the construction of an artificial harbor at each end; the Panama route had the good harbors of Colon and Panama. The estimated cost for a lock canal at Nicaragua was $200,540,000 as against $156,378,258 for Panama. The time required for a vessel to pass through the 170 miles at Nicaragua would be 33 hours as compared with 12 hours to pass through the 40 miles at Panama. But the distance from New York to San Francisco would be 377 miles shorter by way of Nicaragua. The estimate of cost of maintenance at Nicaragua was the greater. But in order to place the canal "under the control, management and ownership of the United States" the commission recommended the Nicaragua route.[1]

The report caused the New Panama Canal Company to express its willingness to sell and it obtained permission from Colombia to do so.[2] The price on its franchise, property, and unfinished work dwindled from $109,141,500 in 1901 to $40,000,000 in January of 1902. Admiral Walker asked for and obtained from M. Hutin of the canal company copies of the approval of the proposed transaction by the minister of Colombia,

[1] Sen. Doc. 54, 57 Cong., 1 Sess., Pt. 1: 263
[2] Foreign Relations, 1903, 139.

Martinez-Silva.[1] Thereupon, the canal commission issued a supplementary report, reversing its previous conclusion and recommending the Panama route.

Since May 15, 1897, the Department of State had been receiving communications from ministers of Colombia favoring the Panama route and even laying claim to the territory through which the Nicaragua canal would have to pass.[2] On March 31, 1902, Minister Concha wrote to Secretary Hay: "Colombia has no lust of unjust gain through the construction of the canal in her territory, and a final convention on this subject will not be hampered by pecuniary considerations."[3] He enclosed a memorandum of points to be considered in drawing up a treaty.

Two weeks later Concha submitted a draft of a treaty. Colombia authorized thereby the Panama Canal Company to "transfer to the United States its rights, privileges, properties, and concessions, as well as the Panama Railroad and all of the shares or part of the shares of that company," with the exception of the public lands situated outside of the canal zone. The United States should have the exclusive right to build and operate the canal and for that purpose should receive a strip, ten kilometers wide, across the isthmus for a term of ninety-nine years. The provision in the Treaty of 1846 that the United States should guarantee the neutrality of the isthmus for purposes of transit was inserted. The United States should recognize the sovereignty of Colombia within the canal zone. The Hay-Paunceforte Treaty received recognition. Should it happen that Colombia could not effectively protect the canal with her armed forces the United States should then furnish the adequate force. As compensation the United States should pay an annuity of $250,000 for the railroad, a cash payment of $7,000,000 for the zone and, fourteen years after the exchange of ratifications, a reasonable annuity for the use of the canal route.[4]

[1] Sen. Doc., 474, 63 Cong., 2 Sess., 384.
[2] Ibid., 250, 493.
[3] Ibid., 552.
[4] Ibid., 556.

Secretary Hay acknowledged the receipt of this draft, April 21, 1902: "I am directed by the President to inform you that I shall be ready to sign with you the proposed convention as soon as—First, the Congress of the United States shall have authorized the President to enter into such an arrangement; and—Second. As soon as the law officers of the Government shall have decided upon the question of the title which the New Panama Canal Company is able to give of all the properties and rights claimed by it and pertaining to a canal across the Isthmus and covered by the pending proposal." [1]

The recommendation of the isthmian canal commission won gradually the support of President Roosevelt and the leaders of both houses of Congress. The House of Representatives passed the Hepburn bill favoring Nicaragua. But the Senate substituted a bill drafted by John C. Spooner, authorizing the President to buy the franchises, property, and unfinished work of the New Panama Canal Company for not more than $40,000,000 and to obtain from Colombia the perpetual control of a strip of land not less than six miles wide. The United States should have the right to make and enforce police and health regulations and to establish courts on the canal zone and in the ports at each end. And should the President be unable to secure a satisfactory title from the French canal company or the specified right and control of the strip from Colombia "within a reasonable time and upon reasonable terms," he should then negotiate treaties with Costa Rica and Nicaragua for the territory necessary to construct a Nicaragua canal.[2] President Roosevelt signed the measure with alacrity on June 28, 1902.

In accordance with his agreement Secretary Hay proposed the changes in the Concha draft made necessary by the Spooner act. One change related to the phrase "in perpetuity." Concha pointed out that this would mean an alienation of the canal zone and would require an amendment to the Colombian constitution. He proposed to lease the zone "for the term of one hundred years, renewable at the option of the United

[1] Sen. Doc., 474, 63 Cong., 2 Sess., 565.
[2] 32 Stat. 481.

States. . ." Hay yielded, although he made the term more definite, thus: "for the term of one hundred years, renewable at the sole and absolute option of the United States for periods of similar duration so long as the United States may desire." [1]

Concha came forward with three proposed changes in his own draft. First, that the property of the Panama Canal Company lying outside the canal zone should not be transferred in the sale to the United States but should revert to Colombia. Second, that the canal company must obtain a prior release from Colombia before it could sell and transfer its rights and property to the United States. Third, that Colombia should have additional indemnity.[2] Hay expressed surprise at the fresh basis of pecuniary indemnity. In connection with the first and second points he could not believe that Colombia meant to hamper the United States in the construction of the canal. It had been ascertained by the Attorney General that the canal company was in possession of valuable property in the ports of Colon and Panama outside the canal zone, consisting of terminal facilities and means of transportation requisite and essential to the construction of a canal.[3] The Spooner act conceived of this property as being covered by the $40,000,000 to be paid to the New Panama Canal Company, which owned six-sevenths of the shares in the Panama Railway Company.

In his reply Concha pleaded lack of instructions and continued to do so until October 26, 1902. He then acknowledged that he had received instructions, and stated that in his opinion these had been vitiated by the action of the United States naval officers during a recent insurrection in the department of Panama. This action, Concha held, constituted a new interpretation of Article 35 of the Treaty of 1846, which article had been included in the proposed treaty.

During this insurrection Rear Admiral Casey had ordered the landing of marines to insure that no interruption to traffic

[1] Sen. Doc. 474, 63 Cong., 2 Sess., 261.
[2] Ibid., 258.
[3] Ibid., 261.

on the Panama Railroad occurred. He had complied with a duty well established by the United States through practice in execution of Article 35 of the Treaty of 1846.[1]

This article forms by itself a distinctive international agreement. Under its terms "the government of New Granada guarantees to the government of the United States that the right of way or transit across the Isthmus of Panama upon any modes of communication that now exist, or that may be hereafter constructed, shall be free and open to the Government and citizens of the United States." In return "The United States guarantees positively and efficaciously, to New Granada. . . . .the perfect neutrality of the before mentioned Isthmus, with the view that the free transit from the one to the other sea may not be interrupted or embarrassed." And "in consequence, the United States also guarantee, in the same manner, the rights of sovereignty and property which New Granada has and possesses over the said territory."[2]

Secretary Hay refused to admit that any question concerning the interpretation of this article existed. The United States had thereby obligated itself to protect New Granada, later Colombia, against foreign invasion, not against domestic insurrection or its consequences.[3] Hay was not the first Secretary of State to so interpret the treaty. Colombia had asked for American troops to put down an insurrection in Panama in 1865. Secretary Seward replied that the request had been submitted to the Attorney General whose opinion held that "The purpose of the stipulation was to guarantee the Isthmus against seizure or invasion by a foreign power only."[4] Secretary Fish expressed the same view to the Colombian minister May 27, 1871.[5] And for the protection of transit across the isthmus the United States had at the request of the local authorities at Panama landed troops in 1856, 1860, 1861, 1873, and 1901; at the request of Colombia in 1862; and at the request

[1] Sen. Doc. 143, 58 Cong., 2 Sess., 2.
[2] Malloy, *Treaties*, I.: 312.
[3] Sen. Doc., 474, 63 Cong., 2 Sess., 256, 260.
[4] Ibid., 476.
[5] Ibid., 502.

of the United States consul in 1865, 1885, and September, 1902.[1]

The Concha correspondence continued to express apprehension for Colombia's sovereignty. He feared the courts specified in the Spooner act could not be provided for in the treaty. But the main point at issue was money and more money. Hay offered $10,000,000 in cash and $10,000 annual rental or $7,000,000 in cash and $100,000 annual rental. Concha refused to accept either alternative.[2] But he did mention that the franchise of the New Panama Canal Company would soon expire, that by the terms of the contract the company could not transfer its rights to a third party, and that at the expiration of the contract the rights of the company would be restored to Colombia. He stated: "The time during which the companies are to have the usufruct of those properties being thus limited, it is clear that if the properties have any considerable value that value belongs to Colombia, and there is no reason or motive for paying the value over to the companies or for Colombia to cede the properties gratuitously."[3]

This sentence furnishes the keynote to the policy adopted by the Colombian government toward the canal. Had not the United States committed itself to the Panama route? True, the Spooner act contained a possible alternative. But were not the leaders of Congress determined and the young President and his able Secretary of State impatient to begin operations at Panama? Why should the New Panama Canal Company be paid for the port and terminal facilities and other rights in Colon and Panama? Said Concha: "Colombia has already exercised an act of exceptional liberality in extending, in favor of the canal company, the time limit for the construction of the work which has had the sole effect of allowing to the company the possibility of recovering a part of its capital which, without this

[1] Sen. Doc., 143, 58 Cong., 2 Sess., 4, 5, 7, 12, 25, 44, 52, 176.
[2] Sen. Doc., 474, 63 Cong., 2 Sess., 268.
[3] Ibid., 265. Official translation slightly changed. The original follows: "limitado como esta el tiempo por el cual las Companias han de usufructuar esas propiedades, es claro que si estas tienen un gran precio, el pertenece a Colombia, y no hay razon o motivo para que se le pague a las Companias, o para que su dueno las ceda gratuitamente."

extension of time, would have passed months ago to Colombia."[1] Why should not Colombia wait until the expiration of the franchise of the canal company, October, 1904, and reap for itself at least the $40,000,000 which the Spooner act provided should be paid to the canal company for its franchise and property rights?

Colombia recalled Minister Concha and left the legation in the care of the chargé d'affaires, Tomas Herran. The question of compensation continued in suspense. Hay increased the cash offer from $7,000,000 to $10,000,000 and the annual rental from $10,000 to $100,000. Herran asked for $10,000,000 in cash and an annuity of $600,000 and the right to reach an agreement with the canal company before that company could transfer its rights to the United States.[2] Finally, Secretary Hay wrote to Herran, January 22, 1903: "I am commanded by the President to say to you that the reasonable time that the statute accords for the conclusion of negotiations with Colombia for the excavation of a canal on the Isthmus has expired, and he has authorized me to sign with you the treaty of which I had the honor to give you a draft, with the modification that the sum of $100,000, fixed therein as the annual payment, be increased to $250,000. I am not authorized to consider or discuss any other change." [3] Hay and Herran affixed their signatures on the evening of the same day.

Essentially, the treaty contained the provisions of the Concha draft. Colombia approved the sale of the canal company's rights and properties to the United States, including those in the ports and terminals of Colon and Panama. The United States had increased the compensation. The United States expressly recognized the sovereignty of Colombia over the canal zone. Colombia could establish courts in the zone for the hearing of cases affecting her citizens. The United States could do so for the hearing of cases affecting its citizens. Both parties agreed to establish a joint tribunal to decide cases between the citizens of the United States and those of Colombia and cases affecting foreigners.[4] After a rather long and sharp debate the United

[1] Sen. Doc. 474, 63 Cong., 2 Sess., 266.
[2] Ibid., 399.
[3] Freehoff, America and the Canal Title, 71.
[4] Sen. Doc. 474, 63 Cong., 2 Sess., 278.

States Senate advised the ratification of the treaty, March 17, 1903.

The constitution of Colombia required President Marroquin to give forty days notice of a call for a special session of Congress. He made no move until May 7, when he set June 20 for Congress to convene. When Congress did meet he gave his opinion of the treaty in these words: "My Government is faced with this dilemma: We must either allow our sovereign rights to suffer and renounce certain pecuniary advantages to which, according to the opinion of many, we have a right, or we must rigorously stand up for our sovereign rights and claim peremptorily the pecuniary indemnification to which we have a right to consider ourselves entitled. In the first case—that is, should we consent to the curtailment of our sovereignty and not aspire to the full indemnity, should the canal be opened through Panama, the just wishes of the inhabitants of that department and of all Colombians will be satisfied; but the Government lays itself open to being charged in the future with not having duly defended our sovereignty and with having sacrificed the interests of the nation. In the second case, should the canal not be opened through Panama it will be laid to the charge of the Government that it did not allow Colombia to benefit by the undertaking which is regarded as the foundation of our future greatness. . . . . Happily for me, the immense responsibility of coming to a decision falls to Congress." [1] He closed the part of the address relating to the canal with these words: "It has been our indisputable diplomatic triumph that the Senate and Government of the United States should declare, notwithstanding every effort to the contrary, the superiority of the Colombian route."

At no time did Marroquin or any of his ministers advocate before Congress the acceptance of the treaty. Marroquin did notify M. Mancini, the local agent of the canal company that the treaty would probably not be ratified, because of the inadequate compensation; but if the canal company would advance $10,000,000, the ratification could then be secured.[2] At the

[1] Sen. Doc. 474, 63 Cong., 2 Sess., 407.
[2] Foreign Relations, 1903,: 150.

same time, Dr. Rico, Minister of Foreign Affairs, conducted a lengthy dispute with A. M. Beaupré, the American minister in Bogota, over the right of the United States to acquire the franchise and property of the canal company without the consent of Colombia.

Secretary Hay replied that Colombia had given her approval when she authorized the signing of the Hay-Herran Treaty and that she had given her approval in various other ways. First, her minister, Dr. Martinez-Silva, had officially assured the United States, March 27, 1901, that Colombia would authorize the canal company to transfer its concessions. Second, Martinez-Silva had written M. Hutin, president of the canal company, April 29, 1901, requesting a statement of the general terms on which the company proposed to transfer its property to the United States. Hutin furnished the statement, May 1, 1901, and thereupon took up negotiations with Admiral Walker. Hutin notified Martinez-Silva of the progress of these negotiations on May 6, 1901. On the next day Martinez-Silva wrote Hutin, approving his action and stating that the following words had been used in a memorandum submitted to the Department of State, "no condition is formulated relative to the sale of the private rights and interests of the company." Third, Secretary Hay noted that Colombia had been the second largest shareholder in the canal company and that her consul general in Paris had been especially accredited to attend a meeting of the shareholders, December 21, 1901, and had voted the shares of Colombia in favor of the sale. Furthermore, at a meeting of the board of directors of the company, Paris, December 23, 1901, Samper, the Colombian representative, had voted in favor of the sale. Hay concluded that separate and apart from the Hay-Herran Treaty Colombia had given her consent fully and freely to the acquisition of the property of the canal company by the United States. "It is not necessary here," said Hay, "to consider the questions of good faith toward the canal company which would be raised by new exactions of that company at this time." [1]

[1] Foreign Relations, 1903: 136.

By July 15, 1903, nothing had been accomplished. On that day the Senate referred the treaty to a special committee, which should report on or before July 31. On July 21, Beaupré reported to the Department of State that he had "certain, but private, information" that Senator Uricoechea of the special committee had called on Baron Grünau, the German chargé d' affaires, to inquire what attitude the German government would take if failure to ratify the Hay-Herran Treaty should cause trouble with the United States. Baron Grünau had replied that he had no instructions, that he was of the opinion that Germany desired at that moment to remain on friendly terms with the United States, and that he would submit the matter to Berlin. Desirous as Germany at that time was to expand territorially and commercially, Colombia had good reason to approach her; but it is not known that Germany in any way urged Colombia to refuse to ratify the treaty. Shortly afterward a member of the lower house called on the British minister in Bogota to inquire what the British attitude would be. The British minister replied that his government had considered the question thoroughly and that it felt satisfied with the arrangements in the Hay-Pauncefote Treaty.[1]

The special committee of the Senate made its report on August 4, 1903, and recommended various amendments. 1. Before the canal company could transfer its rights to the United States the company should be obliged to obtain permission from Colombia. 2. The idea of tenancy on the zone by the United States should be made more specific so as to exclude any conception of ownership. 3. Any reference to the application of United States law in the zone should be suppressed. 4. Additional indemnity to Colombia received mention but the committee left the amount indefinite. 5. The committee insisted that the guaranty in the Treaty of 1846 should apply to the zone and to the whole department of Panama.[2]

On August 12, 1903, the treaty came up for debate in the Senate, the only debate that the treaty received. Senators

[1] Foreign Relations, 1903, 166.
[2] Ibid., 172.

Caro and Arango taunted the government with cowardice for not daring to assume responsibility for the treaty. Senator Ospina felt that the constitution should be first amended so as to enable the government to lease the zone and to allow the United States to establish tribunals there. Senator Rodriguez expressed his friendly disposition toward the United States, but he would, as privately agreed upon, vote against the treaty. At the close of the debate the vote was taken. Every senator present voted against the ratification of the treaty. The few senators who had previously announced their support of the treaty remained absent. This held notably true of Obaldia of Panama. He had grown so disappointed with the course of events at Bogota that he declared openly his department would revolt and declare its independence.[1]

A joint committee of the two houses was appointed to draft a law authorizing the President to negotiate a treaty concerning a canal or a contract with a private company. This committee reported a bill, September 4, 1903, which provided that any treaty negotiated should include a payment to Colombia of $20,000,000 in cash and of an annuity of $400,000 and a payment of $10,000,000 by the canal company before Colombia would give her permission for the transfer of the company's rights. The police and sanitary measures on the canal zone should be completely under Colombia's jurisdiction.[2]

This bill was referred to a Senate committee which made its report on October 14, 1903. The report concluded that the Hay-Herran Treaty had ceased to exist because of its rejection by the Senate and because the time for the exchange of ratifications, September 22, had expired. The report advised that no action be taken for another year, for by that time the franchise of the New Panama Canal Company would expire. To quote from the report, "By the 31st of October of next year—that is to say, when the next Congress shall have met in ordinary session—the extension will have expired and every privilege with it. In that case 'the Republic will become the possessor and owner

[1] Foreign Relations, 1903, 180, 184.
[2] Ibid., 191, 199.

without any need of a previous judicial decision and without any indemnity, of the canal itself and of the adjuncts that belong to it, according to the contracts of 1878 and 1890.' When that time arrives, the Republic, without any impediment, will be able to contract, and will be in more clear, more definite, and more advantageous possession both legally and materially." The committee considered a six year extension of the franchise, granted in 1900, of questionable validity.[1] Neither house acted on the bill or on the report. Congress adjourned October 31, 1903.

Throughout, the Colombian press took the attitude that a powerful nation was seeking for selfish motives to take advantage of a weaker one. "El Correo Nacional" on May 11, 1903, carried a long article by Senator Perez y Sota in which he prophesied the rejection of the treaty and concluded: "The insult, however, which Herran has cast upon the Colombian name will never be wiped out. The gallows would be a small punishment for criminals of this class." Dr. Nova Zerda, a prominent Bogota lawyer, published a statement that under the Hay-Herran Treaty the United States would reap during the first hundred years a net profit from the canal of $1,186,537,377. An Englishman, J. T. Ford, consulting engineer to the Colombian government, published a reply with the conclusion that if Colombia should attempt to build the canal herself she would suffer a deficit annually of $1,540,187.[2] Probably the only Colombian to write a defense of the treaty in the newspapers was Enrique Cortez. In response he was accused of being in the service of the Colossus of the North; and Ford was accused of wanting to obtain payment of the claims of companies in which he was interested.[3] The press advocated with apparent unanimity that the United States was abundantly able and would gladly in the end pay a much larger sum than that stipulated. And if the United States refused, some other country would avail itself of the golden opportunity.

[1] Foreign Relations, 1903, 213.
[2] Ibid., 170.
[3] Ibid., 192.

With regard to affairs in the department of Panama, President Marroquin appointed Obaldia to the governorship, because Obaldia as the most popular man in Panama supported General Reyes for the presidency in the coming elections. Marroquin had settled on Reyes as his successor. The Senate entertained a resolution in which the appointment was considered "as a menace to the safety of the Republic." [1] But the Minister of Foreign Relations replied that in case of insurrection in Panama the United States would be bound by the Treaty of 1846 "to support the Government." [2]

In the department of Panama despondency reigned. Had not haggling and intrigue at Bogota robbed the Panamans of the canal route which belonged to them by nature? They were willing that Bogota should reap the heavy initial payment and the annuities. But to have the prospect of one of the world's great commercial arteries pass from them with all that this prospect meant in growth of real estate values, increased trade, better sanitation, and closer contact with intellectual centers was enough to arouse revolution. The situation intensified the recollection of the unsatisfactory relations with Colombia in the past. How Panama had declared her independence from Spain in 1821 and upon promises from New Granada had allied herself with that state; and the promises remained unfulfilled. How in 1830 Panama had resolved to ask for annexation to Great Britain but had been dissuaded by the aged patriot, Simon Bolivar. How in 1840 she had dissolved all connection with Colombia and had established her own constitution. How again upon representations from Bogota in 1842 she united with New Granada only to find all promises fallacious. Revolution and oppression continued to succeed each other through the century until the refusal at Bogota to ratify the Hay-Herran Treaty appeared to shatter all bonds of union.[3]

The Panama patriots had organized and were maintaining a junta in New York with M. Lindo and Dr. Amador at the head.

[1] Foreign Relations, 1903, 193.
[2] Ibid., 1903, 214.
[3] Sen. Doc., 474, 63 Cong., 2 Sess., 518.

They articulated well with W. N. Cromwell, counsel for the New Panama Canal Company, and with Philippe Bunau-Varilla, an ubiquitous Frenchman, who had served as chief engineer on the isthmus for the original Panama Canal Company. Bunau-Varilla gathered snatches of information in Paris, Panama, New York, and Washington and wove these together so that he could estimate accurately how, in case of a revolt at Panama, the officials of the Panama railroad would act, what Colombia would do, and what action the United States would take. How he was able to watch and to assist in the coördination of the various forces Bunau-Varilla has told in his book, "Panama, the Creation, Destruction, and Resurrection."

In 1885 Bunau-Varilla had witnessed an insurrection in Panama. The rebels captured the terminal cities and they burned Colon to the ground under the eyes of Commander Kane of the United States war vessel "Galena." Rear Admiral Jouett ordered a court of inquiry to investigate Kane's action. Jouett landed troops for the protection of communications and forbade the Colombian troops from Buenaventura to disembark. Bunau-Varilla assumed that the United States would take similar action under similar circumstances again. It became his purpose to promote a revolution strong enough to establish independence.[1]

Dr. Amador had come from Panama with the notion that Secretary Hay would extend open arms to receive him, would gladly negotiate a treaty, and advance liberal funds. Amador could then settle down as the minister of Panama in Washington and watch the American navy protect his countrymen. Instead, he found that the doors to the office of the Secretary of State would not open for him. No one would lend him or his cause money. And the chances for an independent Panama appeared hopeless.

Bunau-Varilla found Amador ready to grasp any straw of hope. Buanu-Varilla submitted to him a program of military operations, a draft of a declaration of independence, an outline of a constitution, and a flag designed by Mme. Bunau-Varilla. He knew well that all of these projects would be modified but he

[1] Bunau-Varilla, Panama, etc., 285.

knew also that the people of Central America were quicker at modifying than at creating. A secret code for telegraphic communication was arranged. Bunau-Varilla announced boldly that as the best qualified man he would assume for himself the post of minister for the new republic in Washington. Finally, he agreed to lend $100,000 from his own private funds to the cause of Panama.[1] He gave Amador until November 3, 1903, to accomplish the independence of Panama. Dr. Amador sailed from New York on October 20, 1903, and landed at Colon seven days later.

On October 22 Bunau-Varilla read in the New York Evening Post that the cruisers "Marblehead" and "Mohican" had departed from San Francisco for a cruise in southern waters. On October 25 he read in the New York Sun that the cruiser "Dixie" had sailed from Philadelphia under sealed orders, carrying with her 400 marines. On October 26 he read with joy a news dispatch that General Tovar with his troops, who had expected to leave Barranquilla for Panama shortly, might not do so until early in November. On October 28 the New York Times published that the "Dixie" had arrived at Guantanamo and in case of revolution in Panama would be sent to Colon. Another news dispatch informed him that the cruiser "Nashville" lay at Kingston, five hundred miles from Colon. His friends asked "What is going to happen in Panama?" He told them to wait for November 3.

Bunau-Varilla went to Washington and called on his friend, Francis B. Loomis, first assistant secretary of state. He reviewed the revolt in Panama of April, 1885, the destruction of Colon, and the part taken by Commander Kane. "Tomorrow," he concluded, "a similar disaster will be imputed to President Roosevelt for not having taken the slightest preventive measure. He will not have sent even a little cruiser." On the next day, October 30, Loomis assured him: "The situation is really fraught with peril for the town of Colon. It would be deplorable if the catastrophe of 1885 were to be renewed today. If you have any news please communicate it to me." [2]

[1] Bunau-Varilla, Panama, 320–326.
[2] Ibid., 330.

Bunau-Varilla had no news. But on the way to New York he stepped off at Baltimore and cabled Amador that in two and one-half days a United States war vessel would appear in Colon.[1] The New York Times confirmed his prediction the next morning, "Kingston, Jamaica, October 31. The American cruiser 'Nashville' left this morning with sealed orders. Her destination is believed to be Colombia." The "Nashville" reached Colon on the evening of November 2.

On the morning of November 3 General Tovar arrived quietly in the same port with about 500 Colombian soldiers. He and his staff took the train for Panama, leaving the troops to come later under the command of Colonel Torres. At 11 o'clock General Huertas, the trusted agent of Amador, met General Tovar at the station in Panama and extended every courtesy. General Tovar asked to be conducted to the fortifications. Huertas expostulated that they stood in full dress uniform, that it was hot, that the hour for the siesta had arrived, and that after they had rested and gotten into their fatigue uniforms he would be glad in the cool of the day to conduct them through the fortifications.

Toward the middle of the afternoon General Tovar realized that his troops had not arrived at the appointed hour and suspected a plot. He ordered that the local troops be mustered, placed at his disposal, and that he and his staff be conducted to the batteries on the sea wall. General Huertas assented readily. Heeding an urgent "Do it now" from Amador, he ordered out the troops with rifles loaded. When Tovar and his staff approached the troops leveled their rifles at them. General Huertas placed his own commanding officer and staff under arrest and marched them off to police headquarters. In order not to place Governor Obaldia between his honor and his duty, he, too, was placed under formal arrest.

The insurgents expected the three Colombian gunboats in the harbor to join them. The "Bogota," Martinez commanding, sent word that if the generals were not released by 10 o'clock that evening, he would bombard the city. He did fire three shells, one of which killed a Chinese coolie, the only bloodshed of the

[1] Bunau-Varilla, Panama, 331.

revolution. The "Bogota" steamed away and the other two gunboats hoisted the Panama flag.

At Colon Colonel Torres had camped with the troops in the street. The superintendent of the railroad had refused to provide a special train for them unless the governor of Panama should so order. The telephone and telegraph to Panama failed to work. On November 4 Torres received the news that General Tovar and staff had been imprisoned. He immediately threatened to seize the railroad and to kill every American in Colon. The railway officials appealed to Commander Hubbard of the "Nashville" for protection under the Treaty of 1846; and he landed promptly fifty men and directed the railway superintendent to refuse transportation to the troops of either party. Thereupon, Colonel Torres decided not to march to Colon or to remain and subdue the insurgents but to await offers that would make it worth while for him to leave. The Panamans offered $8000 in gold if he would go. He accepted. On November 5, 1903, he, his men, and their wives embarked on the English steamer "Orinoco." [1] General Tovar and his staff were offered their freedom on condition they would leave the country. They accepted gladly.

The municipal council of Panama met on November 4, 1903, discussed the trend of events, adopted a declaration of independence, and placed an executive board of three in charge of the temporary government. The provisional government notified the American vice consul-general, Felix Ehrman, of their action, and he reported to the Secretary of State. On November 6, Hay sent a message authorizing Ehrman, if he felt satisfied that a de facto government had been established, to enter into relations with it. Hay had announced his intention to Colombia to do so the day before. On November 13, 1903, President Roosevelt received Bunau-Varilla as the minister of Panama, and by that act Panama became a member of the society of nations. Before the end of the month France, China, Austria-Hungary, and Germany had recognized her independence; and before the end of the year Denmark, Russia, Sweden and Norway, Belgium, Nicaragua,

[1] Foreign Relations, 1903, 268, 269.

Peru, Cuba, Great Britain, Italy, Japan, Costa Rica, and Switzerland had likewise done so.[1]

Colombia sent her most distinguished citizen, General Rafael Reyes, to conciliate Panama; but Panama would not permit him to land. In accordance with instructions Reyes proceeded to the United States and arrived in Washington, November 28, 1903. He pleaded that in refusing to ratify the Hay-Herran Treaty the Colombian Congress had exercised a constitutional right similar to that of the American Senate. Second, that the United States had been premature in its recognition of Panama. Third, that the American cruiser had, as reputable American newspapers stated, come to the isthmus for the express purpose of assisting the handful of revolutionists. Fourth, that after November 18, 1903, the United States had refused Colombia the right to land troops in Panama for the purpose of reëstablishing order. Fifth, that by the Treaty of 1846 the United States had bound itself to guarantee the perfect neutrality of the isthmus which held in the case of domestic insurrection as well as foreign invasion. Sixth, that the United States would not have recognized Panama had not that state afforded the best route for a canal. And seventh, that by the Treaty of 1846 each party had agreed that in case of injury, the suffering party should not authorize acts of reprisal or declare war until that party had laid before the other a statement of grievances, which Reyes was now doing. He closed his appeal with the request that all claims connected with the events in Panama should be submitted to the Hague tribunal for arbitration.[2]

Secretary Hay replied that the independence of Panama was an accomplished fact, recognized by the governments of seventeen powers, which could leave no doubt as to the public opinion of the world on the propriety of recognizing Panama. The materials in "reputable American newspapers" could hardly furnish an adequate source for diplomatic argument much less for grave accusations. Hay denied the charge that the American government or any responsible member of it had held inter-

[1] Foreign Relations, 231, 689; Buanau-Varilla, Panama, 349.
[2] Sen. Doc. 474, 63 Cong., 2 Sess., 481.

course official or unofficial with the agents of revolution in Colombia. The United States took the same precaution in November, 1903, to safeguard the transit route under the Treaty of 1846 that it did in 1902 and 1901 and on numerous previous occasions. Colombia understood perfectly what the interpretation of the treaty and the practice of the United States had been. Hay noted that this guaranty of neutrality necessarily followed the isthmus, hence Panama had succeeded to the protection. He recognized that the interests of the United States had been at stake, that Panama stood for those interests and that Colombia opposed them. "Compelled to choose between these two alternatives, the government of the United States, in no wise responsible for the situation that had arisen, did not hesitate. It recognized the independence of the Republic of Panama, and upon its judgment and action in the emergency the powers of the world have set the seal of their approval." The question of the recognition of a new state was one of policy, purely political, one which nations with the most advanced ideas of international arbitration had not proposed to deal with by that process, for the question did not fall within the domain of judicial decision. But if there should be questions of a legal nature between Colombia and Panama, such as delimitation of boundaries, apportionment of pecuniary liabilities, and the government of Colombia should so desire, the United States would gladly exercise its good offices in bringing such questions to the attention of Panama.[1]

During the early part of Reyes' administration as President, 1905 and 1906, a revolutionary movement in favor of joining Panama developed in the rich provinces of Cauca on the Atlantic, Bolivar on the Pacific, and Antioquia between. This danger led Reyes to urge a definite settlement of questions relating to the use of the canal with the United States and of outstanding questions with Panama.[2] The Minister for Foreign Affairs announced that Colombia waived the demands for money indemnity and arbitration.[3]

[1] Sen. Doc. 474, 63 Cong., 2 Sess., 491.
[2] Ibid., 112, 121, 122.
[3] Ibid., 129.

On his trip to South America in 1906 Secretary Root met at Cartagena, September 24, the Minister of Foreign Affairs, Vasquez Cobo. Cobo proposed that a new treaty be negotiated to replace that of 1846. By this treaty Colombia should have the free use of the canal for her public vessels, troops, and war material even in time of war with another country. Colombian products should be admitted to the canal zone on the same terms as American products. Her mails should enjoy the same right of free passage through the canal as American mails. Colombian products passing over the isthmian railway should pay only a small duty; whereas her seasalt conveyed from one coast to the other should pay freight only. Root assented to these propositions with the understanding that Great Britain be asked whether she had any objections under the Hay-Pauncefote Treaty. Cobo then asked for a preferential tariff in the United States on Colombian sugar and molasses. Root felt that this point would be rejected by the Senate and might endanger the whole treaty. Cobo asked that the United States interpose its good offices between Colombia and Panama in the negotiation of a treaty by which Panama should assume her proportion of Colombia's foreign debt as it stood on November 3, 1903, and by which Panama should accord special customs privileges to Colombian products. Moreover, Panama should respect the boundary to be fixed in the treaty. Root assented. These tripartite treaties were to be negotiated in Washington.[1]

The subsequent negotiations were conducted by Cortes for Colombia, who attempted to saddle on Panama claims for the seizure and sale of the Panama railway and canal works, the expenses in the arbitration of the boundary with Costa Rica, a share of the interior debt as well as her proportional share of the foreign debt. Secretary Root conferred with Obaldia, the Panama representative, and obtained from Colombia a reduction of her claims to $3,000,000; the payment of which the United States agreed to guarantee. Panama agreed to give up all claim to the shares of Colombia in the New Panama Canal Company.

[1] Sen. Doc. 474, 63 Cong., 2 Sess., 129, 131.

The United States stipulated with Panama that the annual payments of $250,000 should begin in 1908 instead of 1913 as provided by the Hay-Bunau-Varilla Treaty; and Panama agreed to assign ten of these annual payments, 1908 to 1917, to Colombia. Both parties agreed that neither would admit to its nationality any part of the territory of the other which might break away by force. Cortes and Obaldia agreed, with Root's mediation, upon the boundary except for the region of Jurado which should be submitted to arbitration.[1]

The treaty between the United States and Colombia contained substantially the items agreed upon in the conference between Root and Cobo in Cartagena in September, 1906, with the addition that ships using the canal might in distress seek refuge in Colombian ports and enjoy exemption from anchorage and tonnage dues.[2] The treaty between the United States and Panama contained various agreements relating to boundaries of the canal zone, the water supply of the city of Panama, the arbitration of disputes, and to navigation and commerce. All three of the treaties contained the provision that they should become operative only upon the simultaneous exchange of ratifications in Washington.[3] The treaties bore the same date, January 9, 1909.

Panama ratified her treaty with Colombia on January 30 and the treaty with the United States on January 31, 1909. The United States Senate approved the treaty with Colombia on February 24 and the treaty with Panama on March 3, 1909. In Colombia President Reyes summoned Congress to meet on February 22, 1909. Congress met and the opponents of the administration charged Reyes with strangling the freedom of speech and of the press. They refused to allow the region of Jurado to remain a subject for arbitration and they asked for an election of a new Congress to pass upon the treaties. The people of Bogota indulged in anti-Reyes riots and wrecked Cobo's house, with the result that Reyes declared a state of siege. Under the circum-

[1] Sen 474. Doc. 63 Cong., 2 Sess., 320.
[2] Ibid., 318.
[3] Ibid., 315.

stances Reyes could do and did nothing to obtain the ratification of the treaties.[1]

Undaunted by various vicissitudes at home and in Washington Colombia renewed her requests for an arbitration treaty during 1910 and 1911.[2] Secretary Knox refused to permit the arbitration of the political acts of the United States and suggested that Colombia might remove all existing disputes by ratifying the dormant tripartite treaties. Colombia refused. Knox proposed that Colombia grant an option on the Atrato route and receive a consideration of $10,000,000 from the United States. Colombia would not listen and decided to wait for the terms which the Wilson administration might concede.[3]

The Colombian minister renewed the request for arbitration as soon as Bryan had been installed as Secretary of State.[4] In reply Bryan asked for a postponement of the question of arbitration in the hope that direct negotiations might accomplish the desired result. On September 29, 1913, he instructed the American minister at Bogota, Thaddeus Thomson, to offer $20,000,000 in full settlement of all claims that Colombia might have upon the United States and upon Panama.[5]

In return, Thomson forwarded to Bryan a draft of a treaty drawn by Dr. Francisco Urrutia, Minister of Foreign Affairs, by which the United States conceded to Colombia all of the rights granted by Root in his conference with Cobo in Cartagena, September 24, 1906. By the Urrutia draft Colombia assumed no obligations whatsoever. Moreover, the United States should pay an indemnity of $50,000,000 and express regrets for whatever had occurred on the isthmus in 1903. Thomson expressed a personal plea for acceptance of the word "regrets." [6] Colombia claimed the completely free use of the canal for her war vessels, troops, and munitions and for her coastwise trade. The boundary with Panama should be fixed at the seventy-ninth longitude and the

[1] Sen. Doc. 474, 63 Cong., 2 Sess., 221.
[2] Foreign Relations, 1913, 284.
[3] Ibid., 288, 297.
[4] Ibid., 309.
[5] Ibid., 321.
[6] Ibid., 324.

United States agreed to use its good offices for the establishment of diplomatic relations and the adjustment of pecuniary questions between Panama and Colombia.

Three significant changes appeared in the final draft. The boundary with Panama was left as provided in the tripartite treaties with the stipulation that Colombia should have the region of Jurado. The amount of the indemnity was reduced to $25,000,000, "gold, United States money." And the expression of regret was made to read, "The Government of the United States of America, wishing to put at rest all controversies and differences with the Republic of Colombia arising out of the events from which the present situation on the Isthmus of Panama resulted, expresses, in its own name and in the name of the people of the United States, sincere regret that anything should have accurred to interrupt or to mar the relations of cordial friendship that had so long subsisted between the two nations." [1] The document carried the date of April 6, 1914. President Wilson submitted it to the Senate on June 16, 1914. That body took no action during the succeeding six years.

Why should the United States pay $25,000,000? Had any right of Colombia under international law been violated? John Hay, Elihu Root, and Philander C. Knox maintained that no such right had been affected in the least. Nowhere in the diplomatic correspondence available do the representatives of Colombia show that such a right had been infringed upon. William Jennings Bryan did not specify such a legal right. He did mention that Colombia had suffered losses. It may have been that the Wilson administration felt that although the attitude of the Roosevelt administration had been strictly and legally correct a moral advantage might be gained by handing over $25,000,000 as a present to Colombia in order to pacify her.

But why should the United States express "sincere regret?" Could the United States under the principles of international law or under a reasonable interpretation of the Treaty of 1846 have acted otherwise than it did? Or could the United States under

[1] Sen. Ex. Doc. H., 63 Cong., 2 Sess., 2.

a high conception of international morality and the progress of civilization have acted otherwise than it did?

After the negotiations had been lying fallow for seven years, President Harding recommended to the Senate, March 9, 1921, a favorable consideration of the treaty with revisions. The revisions made in the committee on foreign relations struck out Article I, which provided for the expression of sincere regret by the government and people of the United States. The right of Colombia to use the canal for the transportation of troops, materials and ships of war, without paying any charges to the United States was made to apply only when Colombia remained at peace. As originally drafted this right applied "even in case of war between Colombia and another country," which would have made the United States an ally of Colombia. With these two revisions and a few minor ones the Senate advised, April 20, 1921, the ratification of the treaty. The United States thereby seized the opportunity of giving Colombia $25,000,000 in order to remove all distrust and to bring about friendly relations between Colombia and Panama.

In order to complete this chapter a digest of the Hay-Bunau-Varilla Treaty should be included. Bunau-Varilla had been received as the minister of Panama by President Roosevelt on November 13, 1903. Two days later Secretary Hay sent him a draft of a treaty corresponding almost identically with the Hay-Herran Treaty. To make certain of obtaining the prompt approval by the Senate Bunau-Varilla deemed it wise to make some additional concessions to the United States and to obtain adequate protection for Panama. He recast the document. At a luncheon on November 18, 1903, Hay discussed the merits of the two drafts with the most influential Republican senators. That afternoon Hay asked Bunau-Varilla to call at his house at six o'clock. Bunau-Varilla complied. "I have requested you," said Hay, "to be so good as to keep this appointment in order to sign, if it is agreeable to Your Excellency, the Treaty which will permit the construction of the interoceanic canal."

"I am at the orders of Your Excellency," replied Bunau-Varilla, "to sign either of the two projects which, in Your

Excellency's judgment, appears best adapted to the realization of that grand work."

"The one that appears best adapted to that end," said Hay, "not only to myself, but also to the Senators, who will have to defend it in the Senate, is the one Your Excellency has prepared."[1]

Hay made one change in the terminology of Article II. The phrase "leases in perpetuity" yielded to the phrase "grants to the United States in perpetuity the use, occupation and control."

The treaty contained twenty-six articles. The preamble stated that the treaty had for its purpose to carry into effect the provisions of the Spooner act, June 29, 1902. By Article I the United States guaranteed the independence of Panama.

By Article II Panama granted in perpetuity "the use, occupation and control of a zone" ten miles wide, including three miles out to sea at either end; and likewise any other lands and waters outside of the zone which might "be necessary and convenient for the construction, maintenance, operation, sanitation and protection" of the canal. Four small islands in the bay of Panama were added. But this grant should not include any part of the cities of Panama and Colon.

By Article III Panama granted all the rights, power, and authority within the zone "which the United States would possess and exercise if it were the sovereign of the territory."

By Article IV Panama granted in perpetuity the use of her "rivers, streams, lakes, and other bodies of water" for the construction, maintenance, operation, sanitation and protection of the canal.

By Article V Panama granted in perpetuity a monopoly of all ocean to ocean rail and canal routes across her territory.

Article VI preserved the private property rights within the canal zone; but these might be expropriated by the United States on payment of just compensation to be fixed by the joint commission created by Article XV.

Article VII authorized the United States to acquire by the right of eminent domain lands, buildings, and water rights,

[1] Bunau-Varilla, Panama, etc., 376.

including disposition of sewage and distribution of water, in Colon, Panama, and territory adjacent for the maintenance, protection, and sanitation of the canal. And the United States could collect water and sewerage rates sufficient to pay interest and the amortization of the principal of the cost within fifty years, after which time the sewer and water works should revert to those cities. Article VII provided further that if in the judgment of the United States the cities of Colon and Panama did not comply with the sanitary ordinances and the republic of Panama should not be able to maintain order the United States might enforce the ordinances in the cities mentioned and maintain order in the republic.

By Article VIII Panama relinquished all claim on the property of the Panama railroad and French canal companies.

By Article IX Panama agreed that Colon and Panama should be free ports for all time and the United States agreed that no duties should be collected except the tolls and charges for the use of the canal.

By Article X Panama agreed to impose no taxes in the canal zone nor any taxes on the works or personnel connected with the canal although these might be located in Panama.

By Article XI the official dispatches of Panama should be carried over the telephone and telegraph lines on the zone at the same rates as those paid by the United States. By Article XII Panama permitted the free ingress and egress of workmen and their families connected with the canal. Article XIII permitted the free importation into Panama of all materials for building, maintaining, and protecting the canal.

Upon the exchange of ratifications, Article XIV provided that the United States should pay Panama $10,000,000 and beginning nine years thereafter, which turned out to be 1913, $250,000 annually.

Article XVI specified that an extradition convention should be negotiated.

By Article XVII vessels bound to or from the canal, when in distress, might seek refuge in any port of Panama without paying anchorage or tonnage dues.

Article XVIII recognized the Hay-Paunceforte Treaty.

Article XIX gave Panama the free use at all times of the canal for transporting her vessels, troops, and munitions of war.

By Article XX Panama agreed to cancel or modify in accordance with the present treaty any existing treaty which might impose conflicting obligations.

By Article XXI Panama gave her pledge that all the concessions granted to the United States stood free from any anterior debt or lien of any kind.

By Article XXII Panama renounced all participation in the future earnings of the canal to which she might be entitled by the Wyse contract, owned by the New Panama Canal Company, or by the concessions to the Panama Railroad Company.

By Article XXIII Panama permitted the United States to fortify the canal.

By Article XXIV Panama agreed that no change in her government, laws, or treaties, or even her absorption in another state should affect the rights granted to the United States.

By Article XXV Panama agreed to lease or sell coaling stations necessary for the protection of the canal to the United States.

Article XXVI provided for the exchange of ratifications in Washington at the earliest date possible.[1]

John Hay and Philippe Bunau-Varilla signed the treaty on November 18, 1903, two years to a day after the signing of the Hay-Paunceforte Treaty. The Senate advised ratification on February 23, 1904. President Roosevelt ratified on February 25. On the next day the ratifications were exchanged and the treaty proclaimed.

On August 15, 1914, the canal was opened to commercial traffic. And today the prospects are that in order to accommodate future intercourse the canal will have to be enlarged or another canal will need to be constructed.

[1] Malloy, *Treaties*, II.: 1349.

BIBLIOGRAPHY

AMADOR, MANUEL.—*The New Republic of Panama*, Independent, Nov. 26, 1903, volume 5: 2782.

ARIAS, HARMODIO.—*The Panama Canal, a Study in International Law and Diplomacy*. London, 1911.

BENNETT, IRA ELBERT.—*History of the Panama Canal*. Washington, 1915.

BUNAU-VARILLA, PHILIPPE.—*Panama, The Creation, Destruction, and Resurrection*. London, 1913. *La Question de Panama*, Nouvelle Revue, April 15, 1904; volume 27: 433.

CHAMBERLAIN, LEANDER T.—*A Chapter of National Dishonor*. New York, 1912.

Colombia, Ministerio de Relaciones Exteriores. Documentos Diplomaticos sobre el Canal y la Rebelion del Istmo de Panama. Bogota, 1904.

EDER, PHANOR J.—*The United States and the Panama Canal*. Outlook, Oct. 21, 1911; volume 99: 433.

FREEHOFF JOSEPH C.—*America and the Canal Title. New York, 1916.*

House Document, 680, 62 Congress, 2nd Session. Washington, 1912.

JOHNSON, EMORY R.—*Four Centuries of the Panama Canal*. New York, 1917.

JOHNSON, WILLIS FLETCHER.—*America's Foreign Relations*. 2 volumes, New York, 1916.

KNOX, P. C.—*Summary of Negotiations with Colombia, 1911 to 1913*. Foreign Relations, 1913, 297. Washington, 1920.

MEYER, H. H. B.—*List of references on the Panama Canal*. Washington, 1919.

OPPENHEIM, L. F. L.—*The Panama Canal Conflict between Great Britain and the United States*. London, 1913.

REYES, RAFAEL.—*The Two Americas*. New York, 1914.

ROOSEVELT, THEODORE.—*An Autobiography*. New York, 1913.
How the United States acquired the right to dig the Panama Canal, Outlook, Oct. 7, 1911, volume 99: 314.
The Panama Blackmail Treaty, Metropolitan, Feb. 1915, volume 41: 8, 69.
Message of December 7, 1903, Foreign Relations, 1903, XXXII.
Message of January 4, 1904, Foreign Relations, 1903, 260.

ROOT, ELIHU.—*The Ethics of the Panama Question*. Address before the Union League Club, Chicago, Feb. 22, 1904.

Senate Document 143, 58 Congress, 2nd Session. Washington, 1905.

Senate Document 191, 62 Congress, 2nd Session. Washington, 1912.

Senate Document, 456, 63 Congress, 2nd Session. Washington, 1914.

Senate Document 474, 63 Congress, 2nd Session. Washington, 1914.

SULLIVAN, G. H. AND CROMWELL, W. N.—*Compilation of Executive Documents and Diplomatic Correspondence relative to a Trans-Isthmian Canal*. New York, 1903.

THAYER, W. R.—*The Life of John Hay*. 2 volumes. Boston, 1915.

TRAVIS, IRA D.—*The History of the Clayton-Bulwer Treaty*, Ann Arbor, 1900.

United States, Isthmian Canal Commission, Report, 1899–1901. Washington, 1904.

WILLIAMS, MARY W.—*Anglo-American Isthmian Diplomacy*. London, 1916.

INDEX